Compelling Stories for English Language Learners

Also Available from Bloomsbury

Teaching English to Young Learners, edited by Janice Bland
Using Literature in English Language Education, edited by Janice Bland
Children's Literature and Learner Empowerment, Janice Bland
Children's Literature in Second Language Education, edited by Janice Bland and Christiane Lütge
Learning Words from Reading, Megumi Hamada
Using Graphic Novels in the English Language Arts Classroom, William Boerman-Cornell and Jung Kim
Taking Literature and Language Learning Online, edited by Sandra Stadler-Heer and Amos Paran

Compelling Stories for English Language Learners

Creativity, Interculturality and Critical Literacy

JANICE BLAND

BLOOMSBURY ACADEMIC
LONDON • NEW YORK • OXFORD • NEW DELHI • SYDNEY

BLOOMSBURY ACADEMIC
Bloomsbury Publishing Plc
50 Bedford Square, London, WC1B 3DP, UK
1385 Broadway, New York, NY 10018, USA
29 Earlsfort Terrace, Dublin 2, Ireland

BLOOMSBURY, BLOOMSBURY ACADEMIC and the Diana logo are
trademarks of Bloomsbury Publishing Plc

First published in Great Britain 2023

Copyright © Janice Bland, 2023

Janice Bland has asserted her right under the Copyright,
Designs and Patents Act, 1988, to be identified as Author of this work.

For legal purposes the Acknowledgements on p. xv constitute an
extension of this copyright page.

Cover design by Holly Capper
Cover image © hellokisdottir/iStock

All rights reserved. No part of this publication may be reproduced or transmitted
in any form or by any means, electronic or mechanical, including photocopying,
recording, or any information storage or retrieval system, without prior
permission in writing from the publishers.

Bloomsbury Publishing Plc does not have any control over, or responsibility for,
any third-party websites referred to or in this book. All internet addresses given
in this book were correct at the time of going to press. The author and publisher
regret any inconvenience caused if addresses have changed or sites have
ceased to exist, but can accept no responsibility for any such changes.

A catalogue record for this book is available from the British Library.

A catalog record for this book is available from the Library of Congress.

ISBN: HB: 978-1-3501-8998-0
PB: 978-1-3502-0285-6
ePDF: 978-1-3501-8999-7
eBook: 978-1-3501-9000-9

Typeset by Integra Software Services Pvt. Ltd.

To find out more about our authors and books visit www.bloomsbury.com
and sign up for our newsletters.

CONTENTS

List of Figures vii
List of Tables xi
Foreword, Kathy G. Short xii
Acknowledgements xv

Introductory Remarks 1

PART ONE The Place of Children's Literature with English Language Learners 5

1. A Literary Apprenticeship: Engagement with Story 7
2. Interculturality: Engagement with Diversity 29
3. Literature with English Language Learners: Activating Language and Response 51

PART TWO Visual Literacy and Interculturality 73

4. Early Steps in Literature Learning with Picturebooks 75
5. Refugee Stories as Visual Narrative 101
6. The Grandeur of Graphic Novels 127

PART THREE Participation in Literature and Creativity 149

7. Responding to Literature with Creative Writing 151
8. Experiential Learning with Plays and Drama 179
9. The Versatility of Verse Novels 201

PART FOUR In-Depth Learning and Critical Literacy 225

10 Encountering Global Issues in the Storyworld 227
11 Speculative Fiction for Deep Reading 257

PART FIVE Glossary of Key Terms 281

Glossary of Key Terms 282
Bibliography 320
References 324
Index 345

FIGURES

0.1 English subject pedagogy 3
1.1 Deep reading framework 26
2.1 Syndrome of group-focused enmity 40
2.2 Three-panel comics for character-based, character-implied and characterless stories 45
2.3 Geometric figures in Heider and Simmel's animated film 46
3.1 Formulaic sequences: Different terms and types 59
3.2 Story Tree: Story potential as the roots of language growth 61
3.3 Nasreddin Hodja and the magic pot, illus. Elisabeth Lottermoser 65
4.1 Cover of *Malala's Magic Pencil* by Malala Yousafzai, artwork by Kerascoët 80
4.2 Functional literacy mind map (Norwegian student teachers) 83
4.3 Walled City of Lahore. From *King for a Day* by Rukhsana Khan, illus. Christiane Krömer 84
4.4 The blanched corals. From *The Brilliant Deep* by Kate Messner, illus. Matt Forsythe 92
4.5 Word Cloud of feelings 96
4.6 How do they feel? (A ten-year-old's interpretation relating to Anthony Browne's *Zoo*) 97

4.7 Reflective review with tigers, based on *My Activity Record* in Ellis and Ibrahim (2015) 98

5.1 Cover of *Wherever I Go*, by Mary Wagley Copp, illus. Munir D. Mohammed 106

5.2 Do you think you could live in a place where there is no water? from *My Name Is Not Refugee* by Kate Milner 109

5.3 Leaf alone. Extracted from *Leaf* by Sandra Dieckmann 110

5.4 Annotations – Abia's thoughts on leaving the camp 111

5.5 Cover of *A Story Like the Wind*, by Gill Lewis, illus. Jo Weaver 118

5.6 *Illegal* (2017: 10), by Eoin Colfer and Andrew Donkin, illus. Giovanni Rigano 123

5.7 *Illegal* (2017: 52), by Eoin Colfer and Andrew Donkin, illus. Giovanni Rigano 124

6.1 Cover of *The Life of Frederick Douglass*, by David F. Walker, illus. by Damon Smyth 131

6.2 Literacy forbidden for slaves (2018: 36). From *The Life of Frederick Douglass*, by David F. Walker, illus. by Damon Smyth 134

6.3 Douglass the orator (2018: 86). From *The Life of Frederick Douglass*, by David F. Walker, illus. by Damon Smyth 137

6.4 Hugo fixing a mechanical mouse (Selznick 2007: 158–9). From *The Invention of Hugo Cabret* by Brian Selznick 144

6.5 The significance of story (Selznick 2007: 178–9). From *The Invention of Hugo Cabret* by Brian Selznick 146

- 7.1 The unicorn at the lake, illus. Elisabeth Lottermoser 155
- 7.2 Lila shape poem, based on *The Firework-Maker's Daughter* 164
- 7.3 At the mouth of the volcano grotto 165
- 7.4 Dr Kalmenius – Wanted poster 166
- 7.5 Crime board 167
- 7.6 Comic strip based on *Clockwork* 168
- 7.7 Oliver Woodman's letter. From *The Journey of Oliver K. Woodman* by Darcy Pattison, illus. Joe Cepeda 169
- 7.8 Red crayon's letter. Excerpt from *The Day the Crayons Quit* by Drew Daywalt, illus. Oliver Jeffers 171
- 7.9 Harry Potter and the Hungarian Horntail 174
- 7.10 Fantastic Beast – The Nayseer 175
- 7.11 And it gobbled them up. Excerpt from *Mouse Bird Snake Wolf* by David Almond, illus. Dave McKean 177
- 8.1 Preparation for intrapersonal role-play (student teachers' design) 193
- 8.2 Role-on-the-wall – Harry Potter 195
- 8.3 Role-on-the-wall – Delphi 196
- 8.4 Role-on-the-wall – Albus 197
- 8.5 Role-on-the-wall – Scorpius 198
- 9.1 Iceberg task template 217
- 9.2 Cultural X-ray template 222
- 10.1 Identities impacted by culture 229
- 10.2 When I walk into a room I hear whispers. From *I Go Quiet* by David Ouimet 231

10.3 Screen grab from *The Inter-Relationship of Mental Health States: Language Matters* by Stan Kutcher 233

10.4 Cultural X-ray, fifth grade student 234

10.5 Astronauts don't wear dresses. From *Morris Micklewhite and the Tangerine Dress* by Christine Baldacchino, illus. Isabelle Malenfant 236

10.6 Paperback cover of *The Sleeper and the Spindle*, by Neil Gaiman, illus. Chris Riddell 238

10.7 She was sitting up in the bed. Pages 54–55 from *The Sleeper and the Spindle*, by Neil Gaiman, illus. Chris Riddell 239

10.8 *There are choices*, she thought. Page 67 from *The Sleeper and the Spindle*, by Neil Gaiman, illus. Chris Riddell 240

10.9 Awakening Sleeping Beauty. Screen grab from Walt Disney's *Sleeping Beauty* 242

10.10 ME. Page 1 from *Planet Omar. Accidental Trouble Magnet* by Zanib Mian, illus. Nasaya Mafaridik 251

10.11 The Black Mambas. Page 71 from *Climate Rebels* by Ben Lerwill 253

10.12 Sacks of mobile phones in Agbogbloshie, Ghana. Image created by Fairphone 255

11.1 Cover of *Animal Farm, The Graphic Novel* by George Orwell, illus. by Odyr 260

11.2 Page 166 from *Animal Farm, The Graphic Novel* by George Orwell, illus. by Odyr 268

11.3 Excerpt from *Animal Farm* 1950 comic strip 270

11.4 Iceberg task – Haymitch Abernathy 276

TABLES

1.1 Teaching Language Arts and Teaching Language – Differences according to Thornbury 8
1.2 Differentiating Subject-specific and Educational Goals of English Language Education 10
8.1 A Pedagogic Contract for Drama 181

FOREWORD
Story as Life-Changing Learning

Kathy G. Short, University of Arizona, USA

In the current global context, strategies for teaching English as a language have become a frequent topic of academic writing and research by scholars from many parts of the world. This book sets itself apart from much of this work in several significant ways. The first is that the ideas are based in story as a way of thinking and knowing that goes far beyond books or reading materials, providing a context for why story matters for language learners. The second is Bland's focus on deep knowing and engaging language learners in enquiries around ideas and knowledge in which they are deeply invested – a contrast to the vocabulary lessons and comprehension exercises that skim the surface and dominate many books about English language learning. The third is that the book is framed within a critical lens that recognizes English is often viewed as a colonizing language that acts as a predator to eliminate other languages but can instead become a tool for multilingualism and social transformation.

We live storied lives, with stories filling every part of our everyday activities to the point that we often overlook their significance. Stories are not just a book or a multimodal text – they are the way our minds make sense of our lives and world (Short 2012). Stories allow us to move from the chaotic 'stuff' of daily life into understanding by constructing a story about those experiences to work out their significance. Story is thus a mode of knowing and one of the primary acts of mind in creating meaning and reflecting on our experiences. Our world views are a web of interconnected stories in our minds so that the stories we tell and how we tell those stories reveal what we believe.

Story thus lies at the heart of who we are as human beings and who we might become. Literature is one of the ways in which we shape and tell those stories, not as a 'cute' book or an instructional lesson, but as meaning making. Children's books are often used to teach something in language learning, reduced to a lesson on vocabulary or a grammatical structure, but these books are, first and foremost, literature. Literature is written not to teach something, but to illuminate what it means to be human and to make accessible the most fundamental experiences of life – love, hope, loneliness, despair, fear and belonging. Literature is the imaginative shaping of experience and thought into the forms and structures of written language and visual images. Young people read literature to experience life and their experiences inside the world of a story that challenge them to think in new ways about their lives and world.

Because this book is based in story as an act of mind, Bland invites us into a broader semiotic definition of text as a chunk of meaning that has unity and can be shared with others. This understanding of text allows for connections to many kinds of texts that tell stories, such as film, songs, plays, poetry and graphic novels. Although Bland highlights literature for youth, this definition supports engagements with many forms of multimodal texts and book formats, providing readers with multiple ways both to build understanding of the issues under discussion and to encourage their own language learning.

Since story is rooted in life and what it means to be human, the interactions around those stories need to be rooted in life as well. By emphasizing deep reading, Bland challenges educators to go beyond literal comprehension questions to engage readers thoughtfully and critically with the personal and societal issues raised by those texts. She challenges the assumption that since the language is new for the reader, engagements should remain at the level of comprehension, on answering questions or doing exercises to get at basic facts explicitly stated within the text. Instead, she argues that deep engagement with these books around global and societal issues that matter in students' lives invites readers to invest in their learning. They struggle to make sense of the language and meaning as they read because they care about the issues, not because their focus is on learning the language. Their focus moves from school learning to life learning.

Another important aspect of deep reading is the use of multiple texts to provide many points of connection and build experience. Instead of pre-teaching vocabulary or background knowledge, Bland shows how educators can engage readers in multiple texts to develop knowledge and perspective. Rosenblatt (1978) points out that a focus on background knowledge assumes that there is a 'correct' interpretation of a text that students must reach and has been pre-determined by teachers. Instead, she argues that reading *is* experience and so intertextual connections across a range of texts facilitate readers building knowledge and experience because they are invested in the issues. The teacher plays an essential role in gathering text sets that support readers and open the possibilities for connection, instead of forcing readers to go in a particular direction.

Bland provides examples throughout this book of enacting a deep reading framework that includes interactions with multiple types of texts related to the focus book to support the construction of meaning. This strategy is reflective of out-of-school experiences in which readers gradually build their knowledge and language through multiple experiences with an idea or concept.

This book is also based in the recognition that language learning is not neutral. Freire (1970) reminds us that teaching is always a political act, based in ideologies about learning and learners. Bland notes that the teaching of English can be seen as an act of linguistic imperialism that eliminates or devalues other languages. She proposes a perspective of multilingualism to appropriate English for purposes that are significant for learners, while also maintaining local languages. Paris (2012) argues that a culturally sustaining pedagogy must also emphasize the need for social action, transformation and systemic change, a perspective reflected in the critical literacy and interculturality lens that Bland weaves throughout the examples in this book.

Compelling stories provide a means for critiquing and re-imagining our world, which, in turn, is the basis for taking action that actually makes a difference in the world. The goal is that students not only gain fluency in a language to use as a tool for their own purposes, but they also develop the power to direct and change their lives and communities through language.

References

Freire, P. (1970), *Pedagogy of the oppressed*, Herder.
Paris, D. (2012), Culturally sustaining pedagogy: A needed change in stance, terminology, and practice, *Educational Researcher*, 41(3), 93–7.
Rosenblatt, L. (1978), *The reader, the text, and the poem*, Southern Illinois Press.
Short, K. (2012), Story as world making. *Language Arts*, 90 (1), 9–17.

ACKNOWLEDGEMENTS

My sincere thanks go to Kathy Short for her generous foreword. Thanks and appreciation also to the anonymous readers organized by Bloomsbury Academic for their constructive comments and helpful suggestions. I am indebted to Graphic Service Centre, Nord University, for their design of Figures 0.1, 1.3, 3.2, 4.2 and 9.1 – I am sure my ideas were sometimes challenging to visualize. An earlier version of the second part of Chapter 8 appeared as Bland, J. (2018), 'Playscript and Screenplay: Creativity with J. K. Rowling's Wizarding World', in J. Bland (ed.), *Using Literature in English Language Education. Challenging Reading for 8–18 Year Olds*, 41–61, Bloomsbury. An earlier version of the second part of Chapter 11 was published as Bland, J. (2020), 'Sharing Critical Perspectives in ELT with The Hunger Games', *Education and Society*, 38(1): 39–55.

Introductory Remarks

In this book I argue for the value of compelling stories in school settings for English language education with elementary and secondary school cohorts. The book focuses on deep reading as a central means to inspire the intensity of in-depth learning, when students become invested in their learning and engage, for example, with innovative ideas, knowledge of the outside world, ideology and social justice.

This book explores issues related to the use of story in classroom settings and how children's literature can augment language learning with learning of related educational goals. The focus is on creative work around literature, interculturality and critical literacy, encouraging dynamic dialogic interactions within an active community of readers, many or all of whom may be reading in English as an additional or second language (L2), and taking part in dialogue chains both orally and in writing, embracing different perspectives and learning about different cultural contexts through story. The examples of literary texts have been chosen for their suitability for English language education at different school levels, offering children and adolescents experience of a variety of stories and meanings from around the world. I have chosen to focus on recent narratives in different formats: picturebooks, graphic novels, plays, oral storytelling, narrative poems, short films, verse novels and young adult novels. The wide range of genres examined here includes dystopia, refugee stories, fantasy, postmodern fairy tales, biography, realistic fiction and historical fiction.

Teachers are becoming ever more mindful of the multilingual and multicultural nature of mainstream classrooms across the world – where English is the vehicle of teaching, but many or all students have a home language other than English. This book is hopefully useful in first language (L1) classrooms too; however, there is an urgent need to prepare for emergent bilinguals throughout education and teacher education. My own context is responsibility for pre-service and in-service teacher education for

English teachers preparing for different school grades where the language of schooling is Norwegian or German.

In this volume, I have tried to avoid using pigeonholing acronyms such as EFL (English as a foreign language), EAL or ESL (English as an additional or second language) for there are now many crossovers. Language learners often have a range of linguistic resources and frequently fail to fit any of these categorizations precisely. The status of English in some European countries is in transition (Brevik and Rindal 2020). Moreover, the construct of EFL is problematic, as the concept of foreignness suggests that English is owned by some and is foreign to others, whereas the English language has long escaped any national ownership or dependence on national boundaries. Adrian Holliday (2015: 23) supports 'moves to do away with old boundaries of English use such as ESL, EFL, EAL, ELF and EIL', and Bertoldi and Bortoluzzi (2019: 16–17) consider that *foreign* is

> a term that evokes borders, barriers and otherness. Potentially, for children (especially very young children), there are no 'foreign' languages, but only ways to grow and linguistically develop while 'languaging' to explore the world. English, for some children, is an L3 or L4 because they live in a plurilingual household where they can switch from one linguistic code into another naturally and easily.

Compelling Stories for English Language Learners – Creativity, Interculturality and Critical Literacy discusses the field of English language education, including the slightly narrower concept of English language teaching. As this book refers to English education in school settings, the term *English subject pedagogy* is often used to underscore the wide educational remit, embracing aspects of applied linguistics, literary studies, cultural studies, education studies and teaching methodology (see Figure 0.1). The term 'language didactics', well known in teacher education in Europe, is generally avoided in international discourse (and also here) due to the historical negative connotations of 'didactic' in English-speaking countries. Recognition that the field of subject pedagogy is central to teacher education is steadily growing (Niemi 2016: 29).

Learning language through literature sits well alongside a focus on content-based teaching in English language education and the acquisition of interculturality, multiple literacies and creative writing. The imaginative scope of children's and young adult literature can broaden students' understanding of humanity and open a doorway to new perspectives and interculturality – in the case of English through the many literatures in English from nations throughout the world. The habit of literature creates a path to lifelong learning, and this needs to begin as early as possible. The concept of childhood is culturally determined as well as biological, and there is no clear boundary between childhood and adulthood. For the purposes of this book, I refer almost exclusively to literary texts and compelling story

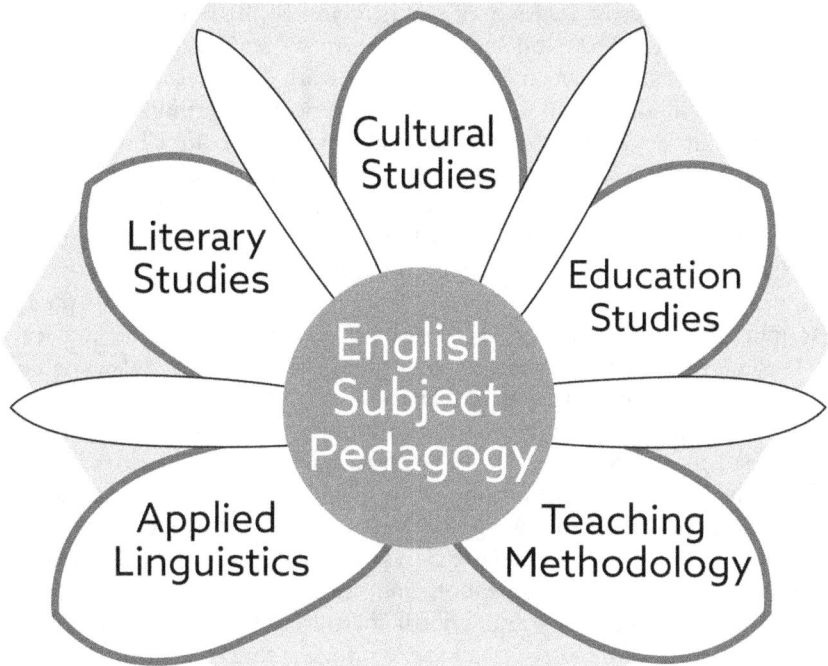

FIGURE 0.1 *English subject pedagogy.*

addressed to children and adolescents, and neither to simplified texts nor to literature addressed to adults. There are many important reasons for this that are discussed throughout the chapters, not least that readers respond best to narratives that are age-appropriately as well as most carefully crafted.

English language learning now often spans as many as ten or twelve years of schooling, so the content and educational affordances of the language-learning space in the school programme are more important than ever before. In elementary and secondary school settings, the educational goals of language teaching are likely to be a central component in the curriculum. English language education, its methods and content can play a fundamental role in helping school students (and their teachers) derive critically aware advantage from the diversity of the world, but also from the often-diverse world of the classroom. Language teachers and teacher educators are crucial in this endeavour, as Alastair Pennycook (2016: 30) maintains: 'As ELT professionals, we are never just teaching something called English but rather involved in economic and social change, cultural renewal, people's dreams and desires.' A positive attitude towards diversity is a key factor in mitigating against intolerance, as Michael Roth (2019: 6) states: 'The alternative to learning, to experimenting with other points of view and new domains of inquiry, is parochialism.' Education thrives when we 'cultivate inquiry on the basis of a variety of points of view' (2019: 6). This is true for all educational contexts and subjects, elementary and secondary school as well as colleges and universities, the context Roth discusses.

With this book I aim to provide theoretical underpinnings, applied thinking and evidence-informed practice for how compelling story in school settings can help attain pleasure in story and pleasure in language. The book offers teachers and student teachers an understanding of the wide and eclectic field of children's literature, and explores opportunities for discovering other points of view in English language education. Above all, learner autonomy can grow. For, as Frank Smith (2012: 190) puts it: 'By joining the club of readers, even as beginners, individuals can learn to become readers and writers. [...] Reading is the club of clubs, the only possibility for many experiences of learning'.

Although the chapters are part of a whole, they can also stand alone or be read in a different order. In the final part of the book, the glossary of key terms provides definitions of over 250 terms as they are used in the discussions in the following chapters, terms that belong to the broad field of English subject pedagogy and its cognate academic disciplines (see Figure 0.1), teacher education and children's literature scholarship. Creativity, interculturality and critical literacy are the recurring themes, while the matter of inclusivity and social justice is threaded throughout and as a strong influence on many of the book choices.

PART ONE

The Place of Children's Literature with English Language Learners

CHAPTER ONE

A Literary Apprenticeship: Engagement with Story

This chapter questions the purpose of a literary apprenticeship for English language learners, and how this might lead to in-depth learning. In this book, the term 'literary apprenticeship' refers to creating a doorway to reading that will remain open over several school grades and years, so avoiding the loss of interest in reading print books that often occurs once children are functionally literate. A literary apprenticeship supports deep reading of compelling texts, engaging with characters and interculturality, engaging with language and creativity, and engaging with motivating topics and critical literacy.

English Language Learning: Subject-specific Goals and Educational Goals

Many stakeholders in the global business of English language learning are not very familiar with the goals of language teaching in school settings with children and adolescents. Nonetheless, applied linguists who publish internationally on second language acquisition tend to be influential on teacher education courses for language teachers, and their writings may dominate the university reading lists. The majority of applied linguists in English-speaking countries (such as BANA countries; see Chapter 2) work with adults in tertiary education or private language schools, preparing adult language learners linguistically to be able to follow undergraduate courses in English. They often have little or no experience of English teaching in school settings with children and adolescents. This is problematic, as Penny Ur points out (2020: 518), for 'the bulk of English teaching activity is in state schools in non-English-speaking countries world-wide'. Helping school students progress through their long years of language learning is a very different matter to teaching English language in tertiary education. In many school settings, there is a content-based emphasis with English increasingly becoming the vehicle of instruction.

An example of what may cause confusion can be found on Scott Thornbury's for the most part excellent blog *An A-Z of ELT* (English language teaching). This includes a table (see Table 1.1) that lists major differences between teaching language arts, where students are fluent speakers of English, probably with English as their first language (L1), and teaching English language learners. In his representation of major differences, Thornbury refers to *children* learning language arts (on the left) and *adults* learning language (on the right), as the second bullet point in each list clarifies.

According to Thornbury, a focus on interpretation, expression and creativity, with literacy development and higher-level thinking skills, is a target that belongs only to teaching language arts with L1 speakers and not to language teaching with L2 speakers, those learning English as a second or additional language. This is not the case for English in many or possibly most school settings. In my current context, for example, the Norwegian curriculum for the school subject of English requires 'reflecting on, interpreting and critically assessing different types of texts in English' (Utdanningsdirektoratet 2020: 3), and educational goals of language

TABLE 1.1 Teaching Language Arts and Teaching Language – Differences according to Thornbury. Excerpted from Thornbury, S. (2017), L is for language arts, *An A-Z of ELT. Scott Thornbury's blog*

Teaching (English) language arts	Teaching (English) language
• L1 speakers	• L2 speakers
• Usually children, young learners	• Often adults
• Fluent from start	• Lacking fluency
• Relatively large vocabulary in place	• Reduced vocabulary
• Focus on style	• Focus on meaning
• Focus on interpretation, appreciation	• Focus on comprehension
• Focus on expression, creativity	• Focus on communication, intelligibility
• Associated with literacy development	• Associated with communicative competence
• Prioritizes literary texts	• Prioritizes functional texts
• Targets development of higher-level thinking skills & problem-solving	• Targets development of communication strategies and text-attack skills
• Prescriptive grammar	• Descriptive, pedagogical grammar

education are as important as the subject-specific ones. However, language assessment in many countries tends to focus on what is easier to assess, namely subject-specific goals; this seems to be most often the case when assessment is centralized. When national tests fail to fully reflect a well-developed curriculum, teachers need strong arguments for reforms to the testing climate.

In some countries, assessment is increasingly conducted digitally. This has problematic consequences, as Støle, Mangen and Schwippert (2020: 10) write: 'Frequent high-stakes digital assessment among children (e.g. annual national testing) may lead teachers and educators to infer that reading instruction is best done digitally.' It is important not to entirely supplant book reading with digital reading because complex cognitive growth in both L1 and L2 is best achieved through print reading, for digital reading habits often lean towards quick skimming or scanning for key information. The strong implications of the study conducted by Støle et al. with ten-year-olds in Norway indicate that 'in order to ensure comprehension development, children still need time to read enjoyable long-form texts to consolidate reading, develop vocabulary, automaticity and fluency, and thereby comprehension. If this does not happen in the home, it is even more urgent that schools encourage book reading' (2020: 10). The Pisa report *21st-Century Readers: Developing Literacy Skills in a Digital World* delivers findings on print versus digital reading on a wide scale: 'Reading fiction texts more frequently was positively associated with reading performance in 55 countries and economies after accounting for students' and schools' socio-economic profiles. Reading digital texts more frequently, however, shows a negative association with reading performance after accounting for students' and schools' socio-economic profiles' (OECD 2021: 120).

Throughout this book I try to illustrate the value particularly of the educational goals of language learning using compelling stories. In Table 1.2, I have listed common subject-specific *and* educational goals of learning English in school settings.

Age-appropriate and well-selected, relevant literary texts can be a potent way of promoting interculturality, multiple literacy, metacognition, empathy, learner autonomy, critical thinking and creative problem solving, engagement in cross-curricular topics and global issues in the language-learning classroom, as well as focusing on language. Within the classroom, teachers should discuss the point of educational learning goals with their students, for it is crucial that students themselves do not see language learning as the acquisition of isolated sub-skills – grammar and vocabulary – alone. Sissil Heggernes, for example, found in her doctoral study on intercultural competence that when the learning goals do not match students' handed-down expectations 'that learning English consisted of learning grammar and vocabulary' (2022: 176), the learning outcomes may be affected.

TABLE 1.2 Differentiating Subject-specific and Educational Goals of English Language Education

Subject-specific goals of English language learning	Educational goals of English language learning
• Developing oral and aural communication skills • Developing reading skills and writing English-language text • Developing language awareness • Developing English-language pragmatic skills • Developing language learning strategies • Developing academic writing in English	• Interculturality and diversity competence • Multiple literacy • Critical thinking and creative problem solving • Engagement in cross-curricular topics and global issues • Developing empathy • Developing creativity • Developing metacognition and learner autonomy

Curricula vary in the different countries of course; however, there is often a certain freedom in the choice of coursebooks and other texts to be used for language teaching in state-funded schools. Indeed, it is better this way, as teachers best know their contexts and their students' needs (Duncan and Paran 2018), as well as assessment needs. Even so, partly due to lack of knowledge of suitable literary texts (Bland 2019), before the learners are sufficiently advanced linguistically as well as sufficiently mature to manage and enjoy literary texts that are culturally marked (by some) as classics of the adult canon, a coursebook is very often exclusively used. Over-reliance on coursebooks and digital texts can and often does stifle curiosity about physical books, closing the door to pleasure in reading long before students reach the stage when they could enjoy a work of the traditional canon.

Some Uses of Narrative in English Language Education

This book is about deep reading of different text formats and genres. Deep reading has a cooperative emphasis on transacting with peers and dialogically participating in the literary text, experiencing empathy, sharing critical perspectives and responding creatively. It is not the only possible reading approach; there are a number of approaches to exploiting narrative in language education, including intensive reading, with reading comprehension activities, and extensive reading.

Intensive Reading

Coursebooks for English language learners often include a variety of short texts – including nonfictional texts, poems and lyrics, short stories or brief excerpts from novels – with a focus on making use of these for language development. Learners might be invited to answer true or false statements, fill gaps in a summary, answer multiple-choice reading comprehension questions or scan the text to match headings to paragraphs. Sometimes known as intensive reading, this somewhat mechanistic approach does not include critical thinking and other educational goals, and rather sees 'literacy as functional, reading in the ELT classroom as informational, and facilitated through reading comprehension questions' (Hunt 2018: xi). The role of a literary text is then frequently reduced to a decoding exercise, to check whether the students' language skills allow them to master at least the surface level of meaning in the extract. Fenner (2012: 381) declares: 'Very often textbook tasks, for instance related to literature, are only concerned with who the characters are, what the setting is and what happens in the story.' This encourages reading to extract information, or the efferent reading stance (Rosenblatt 1982). Louise Rosenblatt, however, affirms that the aesthetic reading stance – transacting creatively with the literary text – 'is the kind of reading most neglected in our schools' (1982: 271). Aesthetic reading calls for investment through affective as well as cognitive involvement in the text. Stephen Krashen has called for *compelling* comprehensible input (Krashen and Bland 2014), but this cannot be supplied by brief, disconnected extracts from longer works.

Extensive Reading and Extensive Listening

The goal of extensive reading is pleasurable language acquisition and does not claim to focus on the aesthetic value of literature. Important principles of extensive reading, based on Robin Day and Julian Bamford (2002), are that the reading material for L2 students is easy; with the choice of a wide range of topics, the learners choose their books themselves and read extensively; the reading – for pleasure and information – is its own reward; and the teacher must be a role model as reader. Extensive reading is also individual and silent and is therefore an approach that is in contrast to deep reading – but could be a highly profitable addition. According to Ralph Peterson and Maryann Eeds (2007: 12), in extensive reading 'we do not take a critical stance. It is lived meaning and not intellectual responding that is valued foremost. We might share what we have read with others, but we do not wrestle with meaning, reading between and behind the lines.'

Graded readers are simplified texts that are often recommended for extensive reading, a method that can support the development of leaner autonomy as well as second language acquisition, provided the learners have library access to a broad range of texts of their choice for individual reading and according to their interests (Grabe 2009, Krashen 2004 and 2013). Extensive reading of children's literature can strongly contribute to second language acquisition too (Kreft and Viebrock 2014, Thompson and McIlnay 2019), and this would be an excellent addition to students' literacy development if sufficient books were available.

Day and Bamford argue (2002: 137), 'all but advanced learners probably require texts written or adapted with the linguistic and knowledge constraints of language learners in mind'. However, there are very good reasons to prefer texts in multimodal formats such as picturebooks and graphic novels to monomodal, simplified graded readers. Very often it is the cultural content as much as the language that confuses culturally and linguistically diverse students, and illustrations can be a wonderful introduction to cultural content. Graphic novels bridge the wordy world of the past with the visual present. In this way, the pictures assist learners in understanding the verbal text by communicating much of the meaning so that learners can manage brief, well-written original text. Most importantly, a well-designed multimodal text has the added artistic value of a first-rate illustrator. An award-winning graphic novel, for example, may stay on the bookshelf for a lifetime. A graded reader cannot match this longevity.

Extensive listening through ample exposure in different media is becoming ever more important in contributing to out-of-school English learning. Opportunities for out-of-school English have recently been greatly augmented through services offering online streaming with a choice of languages and subtitles, through audio books (Isozaki 2014 and 2018, Padberg-Schmitt 2020) and through collaborative video gaming (Brevik 2016, Sundqvist and Sylvén 2014). James Paul Gee (2018: 10) asserts that a well-designed video game is 'entirely consistent with recent research in the learning sciences [...and] gives players interesting and challenging problems to solve, varied opportunities to learn, and instruction and mentoring as needed'.

Extensive reading and extensive listening can contribute considerably to fluency in the second language as well as vocabulary acquisition. School students learning English may have relatively wide-ranging access to the language through out-of-school interests and social media landscapes, through the use of video games, online streaming services and platforms such as YouTube. However, context-sensitive pragmatic skills and academic skills, including accurate control over form, are much more likely to be refined through in-school learning than in out-of-school media and web-based affinity spaces. Yet it is highly important that the motivational power and passion of such spaces – which is often connected to narrative – is recognized and to some extent replicated in the design and content of classroom language teaching. On the increasingly important contribution of video games to language skills, Gee (2018: 10) writes, 'Let me be clear, though: This is not a plea for educators to use video games in school. Rather, it is a plea for educators to consider what the world of video games gets right and to recognize just how much high-quality teaching and learning is going on outside school.'

I have found in my teacher education courses, and through my students' teaching practice, that hugely popular book series like *Harry Potter* (see Bland 2013) and *The Hunger Games* (see Chapter 11) can offer opportunities for connecting young people's passion with the learning goals of language education. Jerrim, Lopez-Agudo and Marcenaro-Gutierrez have found evidence for an advantageous 'fiction effect' (2020: 530) on young people's (aged 10–11 and 13–14) academic progress at school, but they only found a strong association when the children read fiction, as opposed to comics, newspapers or magazines. The challenging task for language teachers is to find books that school students at different levels and with dissimilar interests will be motivated by and fascinated to read cover to cover.

Graded Readers

Graded readers are popular as language teaching materials in many countries where there is little opportunity for out-of-school English. Graded readers are less suitable for school settings with children and adolescents, however, as transnational publishers tend to standardize their readers to be acceptable to a conservative international market. To this end, many publishers of graded readers give their authors strict guidelines to avoid topics that would actually be relevant and interesting for adolescent readers and critical reflection. The acronym PARSNIP refers to an approach often adhered to by transnational publishers of language-learning materials (Gray 2002: 159). The PARSNIP principle means the following topics are taboo in the published graded reader: Politics, Alcohol, Religion, Sex, Narcotics, -isms and Pork. In contrast, Linda Christensen (2009: 8) has explored the importance of students' engaging with and caring about what they read and write: 'Teaching students to write with power and passion means immersing them in challenging concepts, getting them fired up about the content so that they care about their writing, and then letting them argue with their classmates as they imagine solutions.'

Deep Reading

Reading narrative text deeply is about actively participating in and contributing to story, which is central to human meaning-making (Boyd 2009, Carroll 2018, Gottschall 2012 and Oatley 2017). Cognitive scientist Benjamin Bergen (2012: 16) has collected evidence for a suite of physiological reactions to language we hear or read, a very close connection between the perception of language and imagining ourselves engaging in the actions: 'While we listen to or read sentences, we simulate seeing the scenes and performing the actions that are described.' We connect sense to words, concepts and ideas through mentally and bodily simulating the experience, and so we grasp understanding. This is supported by Maria Nikolajeva (2014: 10) in connection to literature, who writes: 'Our engagement with fiction is not transcendental; it is firmly anchored in the body.'

However, Brian Tomlinson (2011: 363) found in his studies of second language readers that reading text with understanding is more difficult in the L2, because 'the ability to generate mental imagery seemed to be inhibited by the cognitive exhaustion of decoding each word in the text'. Yet embodied simulation processes are not optional for understanding, emerging only after a sentence has been carefully decoded. Meaning-making, according to Bergen's (2012), embodied simulation hypothesis, does not focus first on linguistic meanings and only second on multisensory, embodied understandings. These go hand in hand, or not at all. So, as Gee (2001: 716) states: 'Reading instruction must be rooted in the connections of texts to engagement in and simulations of actions, activities, and interactions – to real and imagined material and social worlds.'

This has important consequences. Language learners, especially those who have not had the chance to listen to and dive deeply into stories in English outside of school, need gradual and consistent help to engage and fully participate in sharing stories in the language class – starting in the elementary school. A literary apprenticeship means an early start with stories, for example teachers reading regularly to the children from picturebooks. When a picturebook is engagingly shared with a young audience, the physically present pictures support comprehension 'providing an anchor over a prolonged period of exploration', as David Perkins writes (1994: 83). Naomi Baron (2015: xiv) reminds us of the 'physical side of reading: holding books in your hands, navigating with your fingers through pages, browsing through shelves of volumes and stumbling upon one you had forgotten about'. Sensory anchoring of language and meaning is supported when students can touch and smell the books they read. Physical books tend to have a higher impact due to the richer palette of multisensory response, particularly younger students should be encouraged to use their senses to experience stories and language deeply.

In this way the literary apprenticeship begins with listening, imagining and understanding. Alexander Eitel and Katherina Scheiter (2015: 166) call pictures a 'mental scaffold' that helps readers generate inferences. While learners think and listen, the pictures scaffold the creative embodied simulation processes and the building of mental representations that are required for inference-rich comprehension. Gradually the teacher helps the students talk around the verbal text and pictures, supporting them in constructing dynamic mental representations of story scenes and their own interpretations – which will also differ according to their life experiences. Teachers help bring the story-simulation alive while students contribute to the narrative with their real-life experience. The storyworld and mental model of others can illuminate interaction in the real world, so that 'cognitive engagement with fiction is a two-way process: life-to-text and text-to-life' (Nikolajeva 2014: 25).

This literary apprenticeship continues in the lower-secondary or middle school, sharing chapter books, graphic novels and acting out plays, for instance, so that by the upper secondary school, the students are experienced readers of different formats. Gee (2001: 715) has suggested we store our individual experience rather like 'value-laden, perspective-taking movies in the mind', and these cannot be ideology free. Therefore, learning in dialogue with the teacher and peers and interacting with different perspectives in the text are all central for literacy and should be prioritized by the teacher and students as the most promising pathway to new horizons. In this way, students gain the perspective of others' experience, both from within the classroom and from within the text, so also gaining outside perspectives and alternative ways of seeing. Bem Le Hunte and Jan Golembiewski (2014: 73) declare:

> one of the great evolutionary advantages of being human is that we don't need to actually live through an event to gain the perspective of someone else's experience. We can identify a potentially disastrous or beneficial event because we can recognise these through story, mythology, recount and other narrative structures describing comparable situations.

Literature scholar Brian Boyd (2009: 176) emphasizes the prosocial nature of narrative, which can spread 'prosocial values, the likeliest to appeal to both tellers and listeners. It develops our capacity to see from different perspectives, and this capacity in turn both arises from and aids the evolution of cooperation and the growth of human mental flexibility.' The reader trains perspective-taking, the ability to comprehend others' feelings and attitudes, and this comprehension is dynamic, creative and embodied. Applied psychology research supports these findings. Using books from the *Harry Potter* series in three different studies, Vezzali et al. (2015: 117) found that 'encouraging book reading and incorporating it in school curricula may not only increase the students' literacy levels, but also enhance their prosocial attitudes and behaviors'. A remarkable example of this is the thriving fan activism community organized as the nonprofit *Fandom Forward* (formerly *The Harry Potter Alliance*).

An important aim of deep reading is to overcome the scruples identified by Claire Kramsch (1993: 200), that language learners 'do not generally view themselves as "constructing" meaning as they read: they believe they "find" the meaning enclosed in the text'. In language teaching contexts, even more than in L1 education, there still seems to be a dominant belief among teachers and their students that there are absolute meanings in texts that must be taught. Amos Paran and Catherine Wallace (2016: 447) call this the default position, which 'continues to be that of the text as "container" of meaning and of the reader as a "comprehender" who extracts meaning from texts'. However, already with picturebooks there will be different valid responses. For reading to lead towards in-depth learning, it is crucial for language learners to become dynamic and confident participants in, and recreators of, literary texts, rather than comprehenders of literature and receivers of half-understood wisdom provided by others (such as the teacher, the author, or published notes on the text).

Media Multitasking

There have been many studies involving behavioural and cognitive research, as well as massive anecdotal evidence from educators worldwide, that point to the splintered attention spans of the young. Nicholas Carr (2020: 138) considers that, due to the influence of browsing online, our reading style is changing: 'What is different, and troubling, is that skimming is becoming our dominant mode of reading. Once a means to an end, a way to identify information for deeper study, scanning is becoming an end in itself – our preferred way of gathering and making sense of information of all sorts.' Such a state of affairs has important consequences for education at all levels, and certainly for how – and if at all – a literary apprenticeship for all students in our classrooms can be achieved.

The adverse effects caused by media multitasking include higher distractibility and interference in task performance, with students becoming used to 'simultaneously navigating multiple streams and multitudinous fragments of disconnected information' as Ellen Rose reports (2012: 93), with consequent difficulties re-engaging after interruption. According to Michael Waterston, this has led to multitaskers incidentally 'cultivating the habit of being drawn to distractions rather than improving their ability to return to their original goal' (2011: 81). Smartphones, particularly, act as an attention magnet, with their promise of swift diversion and reward, emotional investment and satisfaction through social media such as Instagram, Snapchat, TikTok and Facebook. As smartphones distract and interrupt activities, it seems they can impair, in a long-lasting way through neural adaptation, students' ability to focus: 'Because learning requires strong mental focus and exertion, students are especially susceptible to the brain-depleting effects of smartphones' (Carr 2020: 231).

The plasticity of the human brain is said to account for our astonishing adaptability and flexibility as a species, as the brain's synaptic connections respond and coevolve with our environment and experience. Consequently, it also appears, as Katherine Hayles suggests, that young people 'growing up in media-rich environments literally have brains wired differently from those of people who did not come to maturity under that condition' (2007: 192). Hayles differentiates a cognitive style characterized by deep attention and the ability to focus on a single object for a prolonged period, from that characterized by hyper attention. This latter style is not considered to be a new development in our species, as hyper attention suggests a hyper awareness of the environment, fast reactions and alertness to potential danger, so a quick-thinking mode that, for example, street children growing up on urban streets around the world have had no choice but to develop for their very survival.

However, Rose (2012: 100) sees the current widespread increase of the hyper attentive cognitive style as a danger for the effectiveness of our students' learning through reading, when their 'reading practices are fragmentary, extremely distractible, and increasingly disinclined to follow a single narrative thread to its distant conclusion'. Hyper attention as opposed to deep attention is undoubtedly increasing among school and college students, a style 'characterized by switching focus rapidly among different tasks, preferring multiple information streams, seeking a high level of stimulation, and having a low tolerance for boredom' (Hayles 2007: 187). Besides, as Baron (2015: 163) observes, 'While video games may enhance speed of mental processing, they do little for cognitive depth.' This has urgent consequences for educators, not least that many of our school students – quite possibly the majority – have difficulty focusing on their reading due to their 'continuous partial attention' (Rose 2010).

A number of tech experts, high-position ex-employees of all major social media platforms in the remarkable Netflix documentary *The Social Dilemma* (2020, directed by Jeff Orlowski), have outlined the alarming impact of social networking – and recommend that children should not be given smartphones. If their warning is taken seriously, this will allow elementary-aged children at least to have the chance to develop deep attention and interest in reading before the distracting influence of smartphones takes over. For this reason, among others, beginning a literary apprenticeship with picturebooks (Chapter 4 in this book) is imperative.

Due to the rapid tempo of visual stimuli through screen-based media use in recent decades, our processing of visual cues has become swifter. In consequence, our students generally have less pleasure watching older, canonical films: 'In the 1960s it was common wisdom in the movie industry that an audience needed something like twenty seconds to recognize an image; today that figure is more like two or three seconds' (Hayles 2007: 191). In order to make the best use of students' visual processing style and superior visual attention, our offer of literary texts must include excellent multimodal texts – picturebooks, graphic novels, illustrated chapter books and short films – that even hyper attentive students will find intriguing and compelling. Such texts will support our students in developing deep attention over time, for all sustained narratives demand prolonged focus. This includes nonfiction, for increasingly informational literature is also narrative in nature (von Merveldt 2018), and in this book examples of biography and autobiography are included in Chapters 4, 5, 6 and 9. The aim is to support the neural circuits that are 'used for reading and thinking deeply, with sustained concentration [...and so preventing their] weakening or eroding' (Carr 2020: 141).

The concept of literacy has become more complex with the hugely influential role of screen-based media in addition to print media. We have therefore come to understand literacy as plural – multiple literacies that interact and interlace and are socially and culturally embedded, 'reflecting not one standard literacy but diverse literacies' (UNESCO 2017b: 60).

Multiple Literacies

Psycholinguist Frank Smith, in connecting reading to its original meaning of 'interpretation', highlights the natural human activity of endeavouring to make sense: 'We read the weather, the state of the tides, people's feelings and intentions, stock market trends, animal tracks, maps, signals, signs, symbols, hands, tea leaves, the law, music, mathematics, minds, body language, between the lines, and [...] we read faces' (2012: 2). In this sense the nature of reading is dynamic and active and extends far further than reading written text.

While literary narratives in the written word have long coexisted with the older modalities of oral and pictorial storytelling, the combinations of linguistic, visual, aural, spatial and gestural semiotic modes in global communications via the internet means that students' literacy practices are now principally multimodal. Margaret Meek identified this trend three decades ago: 'What once reached students as textbooks now comes in a range of symbolic presentations, including complex diagrams, mappings, charts, tables [...]. Our teaching will have to begin with the understanding that the complexities of literacy are linked to the patterns of social practice and social meanings. From now on there will be multiple literacies' (1993: 96). The educational approach of multiple literacy stresses the importance of connecting literacy practices in school to students' life experiences outside of school. It will be helpful to first distinguish certain literacies that are relevant for a literary apprenticeship.

Functional Literacy

A functionally literate person feels confident in the knowhow to engage in every-day activities in which literacy is required for effective functioning in a community, for example reading a local council leaflet, a recipe or a train timetable, or filling in a form to join a library. This type of reading requires the efferent reading stance, reading for information, and is very important for emergent bilinguals. However, Rosenblatt's standpoint on the aesthetic stance (1982: 271) is also highly significant for English language learners: 'Contrary to the general tendency to think of the efferent, the "literal", as primary, the child's earliest language behaviour seems closest to a primarily aesthetic approach to experience.' For already before school, children enjoy nursery rhymes, counting-out chants, skipping and clapping songs, which prepare them both for literacy and the pleasure of story.

Visual Literacy

In the current media-driven environment, it is no longer sufficient to be able to read and understand written text. Visual literacy is the ability to derive meaning from and interpret information presented in images, storyboards, charts, graphs and tables, paintings, picturebooks and so forth. Visual literacy includes map reading skills and how to create slideshows, short films, poster presentations, collages and the like that effectively communicate content multimodally.

The majority of literary formats discussed in this book are multimodal – picturebooks, graphic novels, illustrated chapter books and films – with the aim to exercise and extend visual literacy and its connections to creativity, interculturality, media literacy and critical literacy. This is vital for a literary apprenticeship with young English language learners, for images are powerful allies for students' engagement with the story while, at the same time, images can transcend communication barriers and provide opportunities for inclusive participation.

Literary Literacy

Frank Serafini (2005: 59) expresses the importance of beginning a literary apprenticeship early: 'Recognizing and understanding symbols is an important part of being a reader. If readers are not allowed to experience and discuss symbolic representations while in elementary school, they will have difficulty analysing the symbols represented in the poetry and novels they will encounter in secondary education.' Since the cultural turn in the last decades of the twentieth century, the understanding of literature has been re-conceptualized to become broader, pluralistic and fluid, with the consequence that understanding literature as literature has also changed. We see this development strongly in children's literature scholarship, which, though notoriously difficult to define, is usually understood to encompass the study of a wide variety of texts, some of which, like the graphic novel and verse novel, are still relatively new and exciting for young people particularly. Literary literacy refers to participating in the aesthetic nature of a literary text, being able to read between the lines and beyond the lines and interpreting metaphorical messages.

Children's literature is as manifold as literature aimed at adults and embraces a range of formats. Marek Oziewicz (2018: 29) has defined format as 'the vehicle of the story's delivery, independent of content and type of narrative, which are described by the term genre'. Genre as a term is then defined more narrowly by Oziewicz (2018: 30) as primarily '*the type of story content* the reader will experience – historical fiction, fantasy, romance, and so on – rather than [...] *how* that story will be delivered. And the *how* is exactly what the format is all about' (emphasis in original). Literary literacy includes learning to recognize some conventions of literary genres, and the tools of literary craftmanship such as imagery and rhetorical devices, characterization and settings.

Information Literacy

Information literacy is a crucial skill in order to take intelligent advantage of the information age. It refers to the reflective searching for and locating of information, usually on the internet, critical evaluation of the information source and context, as well as effective use made of the information that has been discovered. Neil Gaiman (2013: np) suggests that too much information brings new problems, and guidance for adolescents – for example through the support of qualified school librarians – is insufficient in most countries: 'The challenge becomes, not finding that scarce plant growing in the desert, but finding a specific plant growing in a jungle. We are going to need help navigating that information to find the thing we actually need.'

Covid-19 has highlighted the dangers of an infodemic (OECD 2021: 5), which can take hold when the information flood dramatically increases due to an urgent global topic. Executive functioning skills, including task monitoring and the ability to tune out distractions, to distinguish relevant and reliable information and focus attention only on this, are the important skills that constitute information literacy. In this way, information literacy is a research competence that is central for all academic work. It is a counter measure against ubiquitous misinformation on the web, but also a first defence against misleading *dis*information or fake news.

Social media platforms are potentially empowering as they enable wide participation in public discourse. However, the spread of intentional disinformation, as well as infodemics, can make it harder for readers to discover the truth, and can therefore influence elections and the processes of democracy. Information literacy is a crucial strategy to uncover deliberately misleading content and algorithm-led one-dimensionality, or misinformation that spreads rapidly in echo chambers, cancelling out diversity of opinion. Echo chambers, according to Andreas Schleicher (2021: 3), are 'virtual bubbles [that] homogenise opinions and polarise our societies; and they can have a significant – and adverse – impact on democratic processes'.

Channels of communication such as social media, video games, movies, images on the web, advertisements, news reports, fiction and nonfiction, and also school coursebooks, use visual and rhetorical means to demonstrate and persuade, and the most commonly used language is English. Therefore, information literacy should be a central educational goal in the English class. A study on information literacy in Germany shows the importance of education for information and media literacy. Over 4,000 internet users over the age of 18 took part in the survey, and while the results evidence mediocre to poor information literacy competence amongst test participants on average, it was found that with a higher level of formal schooling, the information literacy results are correspondingly higher (Meßmer, Sängerlaub and Schulz 2021). Nikola von Merveldt (2018: 233) investigates nonfiction picturebooks and finds 'they play an important role in building information literacy'. The knowhow of information literacy is further developed by a literary apprenticeship that is participatory, and contributes to learner autonomy, critical thinking and engaging in cross-curricular topic research and global issues.

Media Literacy

Media literacy means the ability to recognize that the world is represented in certain ways through the media that gives power, dignity and consequence to some and withholds it from others. Media literacy generally focuses on mass media, including newspapers that are online or print, magazines, radio, television, movies, theatre and websites. Media literacy involves learning to uncover the ideology of media that select and shape representations and therefore play a role in constructing views of reality. Plays and films, for example, are frequently characterized by androcentrism or ethnocentrism – see Chapters 8 on *Harry Potter and the Cursed Child* and Chapter 11 on *The Hunger Games* films. The film critic David Thomson considers media literacy as an important aspect of participation in society, urging the public to 'think of the agencies – from individuals and businesses to governments and ideologies – that would prefer us not to attend with too much critical concentration, but let the passing spectacle swim by without challenge. This is where watching cannot rest with mere sight. It waits to be converted into aesthetic judgement, moral discrimination, and a more intricate participation in society' (2015: 18).

Critical Literacy

According to Kathy Short (2011: 52), the notion of critical literacy 'presses for an awareness of how, why, and in whose interests a particular text might work and an understanding of reading positions and practices for questioning and critiquing texts as well as oneself'. Thus, critical literacy helps unlock our agency and autonomy as reader: we become a critically aware participant in the text, attempting to gain a distance from accustomed frames of reference. Literacy, according to Meek (1993: 95), 'is never neutral; it can always be used by some against others'. This position on the bias of texts is strongly supported by other voices, such as Vasquez, Janks and Comber (2019: 306): 'Texts are socially constructed from particular perspectives; they are never neutral. All texts are created from a particular perspective with the intention of conveying particular messages.'

Critical literacy sometimes leads to reading against the text in order to discover how certain worldviews have been, often unconsciously, imported into a text. Perry Nodelman and Mavis Reimer (2003: 156) consider that as 'writers assume that their own ideology is universal truth, texts always act as a subtle kind of propaganda and tend to manipulate unwary readers into an unconscious acceptance of their values'. With this in mind, it is important to encourage students to read against the text in order for them to discover any absences and misrepresentations in their reading. This applies to literature written in earlier times, where the absences are usually a predictable lack of agentic characters other than White men and boys, as well as to very recent literary texts.

Far from searching for an author's intention, known as the intentional fallacy, see also 'death of the author' in the words of Roland Barthes (1989), we can encourage students to search for what they find in the text that the author quite possibly did not intend, such as ethnocentrism, androcentrism, homophobia, ableism, anthropocentrism, even speciesism – the list grows ever longer as we come to understand how much ideology is hidden in plain sight. In contemporary texts, the absences are often so very familiar that they are more difficult to uncover, and of course there will also be ideological assumptions in the present text that readers are invited to examine. Aidan Chambers (2011: 160) suggests including texts that are written from different perspectives: 'Children need to hear alternative versions of the same story in fiction, and, later, to be aware that different newspapers may present conflicting accounts of "the truth", as do different historians and different scientists.' Similarly, student teachers are encouraged to attend to different voices and perspectives in their studies, and consider them critically.

Critical reflection in the classroom encourages an attitude of approaching problems in a thoughtful way, helping students shape their own thinking and evaluating, voice their thoughts in words and express them in writing with creativity, coherence and conviction. Significantly, Donald Lazere (1987: 3) has claimed there is a strong case to be made that the study of literature 'is the single academic discipline that can come closest to encompassing the full range of mental traits currently considered to comprise critical thinking'.

Theory of Mind

Literary texts do not offer solutions; they offer detailed representations of characters, their situations and their problems. It is the readers who may creatively consider solutions to the problems. Keith Oatley writes

(2017: 268), 'Children can move effortlessly between play and absorption in a story, as if both are forms of the same activity.' Indeed, it seems they are, for according to Boyd (2009) the human need for story is an adaptation of the human need for play. Thus, through literature, readers practice the 'psychological process of making mental models of others that is the same in fiction as in the interactions of real life' (Oatley 2017: 265). Similarly, Le Hunte and Golembiewski (2014: 74) argue: 'The very fact that Theory of Mind can be applied to real people as well as fictional people means that on a profound level, fiction provides an equally "real" milieu for the human brain to develop emotionally and express its full humanity.'

Oziewicz (2015: 6) has referred to reading as cognitive training, 'fiction as a kind of exercise program for Theory of Mind: the cognitive program built into the human mind'. This being so, fiction is clearly extremely important for attaining educational goals, particularly metacognition, empathy and critical thinking. Theory of mind (ToM) is a key psychological process and develops continuously throughout childhood and adolescence, gradually leading to the understanding that others have thoughts, ideas, feelings and beliefs that can be very different from one's own.

According to Virginia Slaughter (2015: 171), ToM can be influenced and further developed: 'One environmental variable that is crucial for theory of mind development is the regular exposure to language and conversations about mental states.' Oatley argues (2017: 264) that we need fiction to further develop ToM, empathy and understanding of others: 'Knowing others' minds is central to human life. But because what goes on in these minds is not immediately visible, we make inferences. We are good at inferring social truths but, because the social world is complex, we are not that good.' David Kidd, Martino Ongis and Emanuele Castano (2016: 43) also propose that the psychological consequences of 'reading fiction can be an exercise in advanced ToM that prompts readers to represent and engage with characters' nuanced mental states'. Their experimental studies indicate that engagement with literary texts that include complex characterization, with 'relative greater emphasis on the inner lives of characters, rather than plot development, [...] is what leads us to expect reading literary fiction to evoke ToM processes' (2016: 44). An argument in this book is that literary texts, when read deeply, with dialogue on literary characters' motivations, feelings and intentions, exercise this faculty powerfully by challenging the reader again and again to perspective-taking (see Chapter 2 on the significance of characterization and protagonism).

Proposing a Deep Reading Framework

Maryanne Wolf and Mirit Barzillai (2009: 32) define deep reading as 'the array of sophisticated processes that propel comprehension and that include inferential and deductive reasoning, analogical skills, critical analysis, reflection, and insight. The expert reader needs milliseconds to execute these processes; the young brain needs years to develop them.' Deep reading means transaction with the literary text, alone or in dialogic participation in the text with fellow students, sharing response and critical perspectives. As an alternative to relying solely on the one-size-fits-all solution of coursebook-driven language teaching, which will be explored in Chapter 2, carefully selected literary texts for children and young adults provide material written with young people in mind that is characterized by compelling and motivating story, appealing characters and important educational opportunities. A successful literary text is often accompanied by transmedia stories and reimaginings such as movies, audio books, graphic novels, fanfiction and images on the web, all of which provide more comprehension support through retellings, the all-important multisensory experience and opportunities for students' own creativity. The emotional resonances of story allow the cultural, literary and language input to become more memorable, while at the same time the reader learns to walk around in others' shoes – the reader constructs a mental representation of what the protagonist lives through.

With the objective of deep reading, it is best to shift the focus from *working with literature*, to the communicative process of reception, embracing *literature working on the reader*, and how the reader responds. Reading can contribute to a dynamic and multifaceted repertoire of knowledge and can support students in discovering new 'horizons of possibility, allowing them to question, interpret, connect, and explore' (Langer 1997: 607). Demands are now increasingly heard, as expressed by Leland, Lewison and Harste (2013: vii), for 'a new educational mantra that shifts the focus from raising test scores to raising readers'. Unlocking the agency of readers by including multiple perspectives in literacy education is not straightforward – it necessitates helping language learners to develop autonomy, involving the understanding of reading positions and the questioning of texts, as well as the avoidance on the part of the teacher of any kind of model response expectation. Deep reading of literary texts means the material is exploited in a reflective, contingent way and never in a prescriptive way.

To read a literary text, it is essential to create mental imagery while reading – the creative process of seeing, hearing, feeling and acting out storyworld scenes in the mind. David Herman (2005: 570) defines storyworlds as 'mentally and emotionally projected environments in which interpreters are called upon to live out complex blends of cognitive and imaginative response'. Deep reading of literature depends on content that encourages cognitive and emotional challenge, creativity and criticality, for example discovering when certain voices are privileged, and others are silenced. In addition to the practice of language skills, English language education could include many educational goals, including multiple literacy, interculturality and diversity competence, metacognition, learner autonomy, critical thinking and creative problem solving, empathy, creativity, as well as engaging in cross-curricular topics and global issues. Figure 1.1 illustrates a framework of four interweaving steps as a suggested guiding structure for the exploration of literary texts and their affordances for educational goals and their potential for differentiation through creative response without a focus on right or wrong answers. In each of the Chapters 4, 5, 6, 8, 9, 10 and 11, I have discussed one of the many literary texts introduced in this book in the light of the deep reading framework, as an exemplar of one possible pathway to deep reading.

In-Depth Learning

Deep reading of literature can promote engagement with text, including ethics, emotions, knowledge of the world, ideology and social justice issues (Bland 2018b, Nikolajeva 2014), and corresponds to the experiential approach to learning, which emphasizes the role of students' out-of-school experiences as well as classroom experience as important in their learning processes. Mary Breunig argues: 'It is agreed that critical theory continues to be excessively abstract and too far removed from the everyday life of schools' (2005: 110). In-depth learning is an approach that aims to reconnect school learning with the world beyond school. For in-depth learning it is important to consider how English language education can include the learner as an active and motivated participant, with agency. Michael Fullan, Mag Gardner and Max Drummy define in-depth learning, as 'learning that helps them [the students] make connections to the world, to think critically, work collaboratively, empathize with others, and, most of all, be ready to confront the huge challenges that the world is leaving their generation' (2019: 66). This suggests a link both to John Dewey's approach to education as a mechanism for social change and Paulo Freire's critical pedagogy approach, in which adults as well as children gain agency through reflecting on problems, developing critical consciousness and taking responsibility by working on possible solutions.

Connectedness is central to the notion of in-depth learning, and connecting across school subjects, learning through cross-curricular topics such global issues, interculturality and diversity competence, creates opportunities to expand subject knowledge and support the transfer of learning beyond school. Gavriel Salomon (2016: 155) accentuates connectedness and transfer of learning to new settings, 'knowledge needs to be constructed as a web of meaningful connections [...] Mastery of information can be demonstrated by its reproduction; mastery of knowledge is demonstrated by its novel application.' Connectedness may also be an ambition within the classroom, for in-depth learning creates an opening for teachers and students to work cooperatively across the generation gap, for example towards a more sustainable (and consequently more just) world. When children's literature offers representations of intergenerational solidarity, Deszcz-Tryhubczak

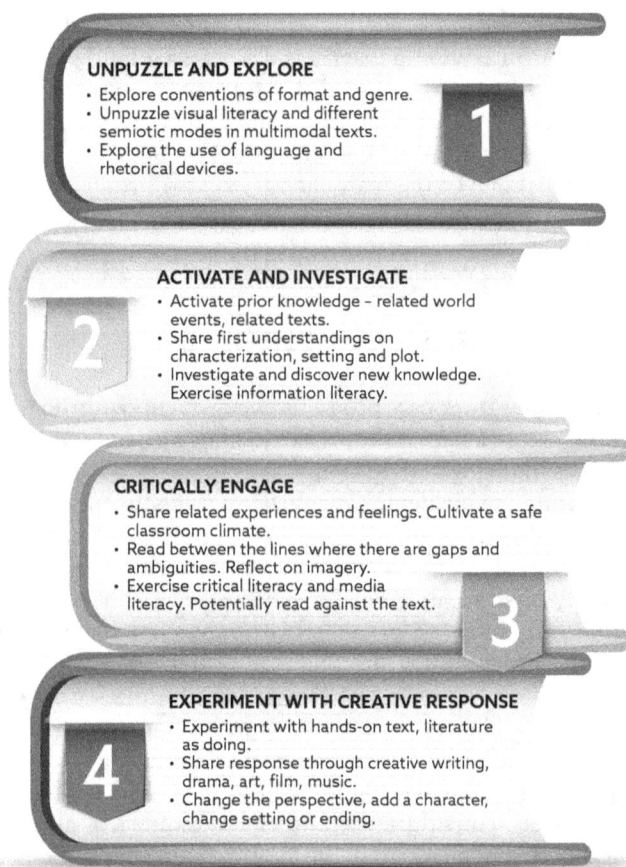

FIGURE 1.1 *Deep reading framework.*

and Jaques (2021: xii) argue, 'children's and adults' joint engagements with such texts may turn into collaborative cultural practices around reading that strengthen intergenerational bonds'. Fullan et al. underscore connectedness – connecting to others, connecting to the world and connecting to the purpose with passion (2019: 68).

There is a current worldwide interest in critical thinking and in-depth learning that may in part be a response to the ballooning of online environments, which amplify the impact of disinformation. Social media have been key in helping communications stay open during the Covid-19 pandemic; however, the echo chamber effect is a danger that has yet to be resolved. As Kramsch and Zhu write, 'such environments risk isolating them [people] in communities of like-minded peers, makes them vulnerable to electronic surveillance and makes them addicted to peer approbation and peer pressure' (2016: 45). Findings from the recent Pisa report (OECD

2021: 138) emphasizes: 'The more knowledge technology allows us to search and access, the more important it becomes to develop deep understanding and the capacity to navigate ambiguity, to triangulate viewpoints, and to make sense of content.'

In the third decade of the twenty-first century, we connect virtually more often than face-to-face, due to social media, to Covid-19, and increasingly for environmental reasons. But can learners amass embodied, multisensory experiences of language and of different issues required for in-depth learning entirely through online connectedness? Language acquisition depends to a large extent on wide exposure (Ellis 2017), and the internet is important for providing such opportunities. However, successful language learning also depends on students being able to learn in an enacted, whole-person way, for language learning and meaning making are embodied phenomena (Macedonia 2019), so that dynamic person-to-person encounters and motivation for genuine collaborative communication also seem to be essential.

In-depth learning increases when students recognize the relevance of their learning for life outside of school, and their own contributions become an important part of the fabric of the lesson so that they are keen to invest in their learning. The goal is for students to be empowered by having their out-of-school experiences made relevant in the classroom, and further empowered when their classroom learning helps them master fresh challenges by transferring new learning to different contexts outside of school. Working with compelling story, both the topic of students' deep reading and the ability of the storyworld to elicit an embodied and engaged response are crucial for in-depth learning. In Chapters 4 to 11, which focus on examples of children's literature, I have chosen texts for a literary apprenticeship that particularly afford learning in the area of global education – the environment, interculturality, human rights and diversity, both as reflected within the literary texts and in the diversity of different voices.

CHAPTER TWO

Interculturality: Engagement with Diversity

In this chapter, I discuss in more detail how reading literary texts can contribute to students' empathy and world knowledge, developing sensitivity to otherness as well as knowledge of self, encouraging students to relate to the outside world with critical curiosity, and to transfer insights to their own world. I propose that an important aim of literature for English language learning in school settings is discovering with the students how the literary text opens doors to the world and its diversity, including diversity in the local environment, allowing the avoidance of the often reductive and stereotyped, nation-oriented representations within language teaching coursebooks. To this end, I examine the following areas: the nature of materials most frequently used in the language classroom, our current understandings of the meaning of culture in the context of language teaching, interculturality and diversity competence and finally the affordances of literary texts in connection to diversity, multivoicedness and critical interculturality.

Materials for English Language Education

The terms 'coursebook' and 'textbook' are often used interchangeably. I will refer to the student books and workbooks published in a series to teach English over several years and school grades as a *coursebook*, and single volumes that gather content together on a particular academic subject – including handbooks on language teaching – as a *textbook*. Christopher Candlin has described the plethora of oversimplified and decontextualized textbooks on how to teach language as 'the welter of wall-to-wall predigested bite-sized manuals for language learning' (2014: xvi). Small wonder, then, when school coursebooks, if guided by decontextualized textbooks on language teaching, tend to be schematic and irrelevant to students' lived experiences outside of school.

Limitations of the Language Teaching Coursebook

The coursebook for language learners will typically offer informational texts, set in an attractive layout that may be richly accompanied by photos and other images to illustrate the topic, as well as activities designed to exercise the subject-specific goals of language learning, predominantly communication skills, focus on form, text comprehension and recreating text. The coursebook is usually marketed as a set, including supplements such as a workbook that students write in, a teacher's book, audio CDs, DVDs, practice tests for the students at each level as well as materials for the teachers with answer keys. Altogether, then, this is a very expensive commitment for any school, and coursebooks often *become* the curriculum rather than a contribution to curriculum observance. As coursebook series must be prepared years in advance of their introduction to the classroom, in-depth learning in the sense of connection to the students' world outside the classroom and a critical commitment to transformative learning is understandably difficult to integrate into the texts.

Yet, language teaching in school contexts consistently makes sole use – or very nearly sole use – of locally or internationally published coursebooks, at least in the elementary and lower-secondary or middle school (Fenner 2012: 371). Janez Skela (2014: 113) has examined some well-known English as a foreign language (EFL) coursebook series and revealed the absence of literature, despite 'the proven benefits of using literature in EFL'. It is debatable, however, whether literature, represented merely by brief excerpts, really belongs in coursebooks at all, as truncated excerpts mangle the dynamic force and opportunities of literature.

Keith Oatley and Maja Djikic (2014) report that research is now increasingly showing how the indirect communication and indirect influence of literary art encourages readers to think about themselves and others in new ways, with the result that literary texts are likely to be transformative. Unlike coursebooks, literary texts do not have to be fixed, but can have a life that continues long after their original publication, and that can transform the text itself, further adding to the transformative power of literary art – this is highlighted in this book through the notion of retellings in different formats, paratext such as reimaginings and fanfiction, and even fan activism.

Interculturality, according to UNESCO (2017a: 8), 'refers to the existence and equitable interaction of diverse cultures and the possibility of generating shared cultural expressions through dialogue and mutual respect'. However, it is an impediment for interculturality in language education when coursebooks try to teach about different national cultures, minoritized and marginalized groups, which means *didactic* in the sense of privileging fixed transmission over processes of dialogic transaction. Trying to teach culture tends to lead to essentialism – when we imagine that the essence of a cultural group is common to all members of that group at all times. The implication is then that the characteristics of all in the group are forever fixed, which is a clear contradiction to the current and now widely accepted understanding of culture as fluid. John Gray (2016: 100–3) emphasizes that when considering the suitability of materials for English language learners, the representation of the world must be considered critically. For this reason, the ideological aspect of coursebooks for language teaching – the representation of the world and its peoples – is an important topic to study in teacher education.

Gray has criticized the commercially motivated silencing or ongoing 'erasure of working-class characters, themes and concerns' in transnationally marketed coursebooks, as well as 'a relentlessly heteronormative view of human relations in which lesbian, gay, bisexual and transgender (LGBT) characters are rendered invisible' (2016: 103). This is partly because publishers of coursebook materials try hard to avoid offending different cultural groups, which would reduce their market; but this choice also radically reduces the range of subjects and representation of different identities in the books. This marketing strategy, which constricts the range of topics of graded readers as well, is known as the *PARSNIP* principle (avoiding Politics, Alcohol, Religion, Sex, Narcotics, -isms and Pork) and was discussed in Chapter 1 with reference to graded readers. This policy very much works against experiential approaches to learning, which require that students' experiences and identities, their real life going on outside of school, should be recognized as important in their learning processes.

Experiential education demands from the outset 'a commitment to the social, not just to the internal social order of the classroom and its participants, but to the location and positioning of the school as institution within the wider social formation which gives rise to it, and which so closely and strongly governs its practices' (Candlin 2014: xii). Students who are children and adolescents have their own cultural identities and are not just adults-in-waiting; they are the future doers and could already be agents of change. Yet, as Chris Kearney (2003: 8) forewarns: 'Both culturally and technologically, education seems to be becoming distanced from people's daily lives. The life stories reveal the wealth of experience to be explored, which could inform our teaching. The world is in the classroom. It can only be translated into new cultural webs if we enter into dialogues and explore people's lived experience.'

In student-led investigations in my own teacher education context, both in Germany and in Norway, student teachers have examined locally produced coursebooks for English. They have judged that in many coursebooks the verbal texts, and even more so the images, tend to stereotype or at least essentialize unfamiliar cultural features. Cecilie Brown and Jena Habegger-Conti conducted a study on the images of indigenous peoples in Norwegian coursebooks for English, and found the cumulative effect of the photos was to 'create "us"/"them" dichotomies between "whites" who are shown as active, complex and technologically advanced, and indigenous peoples who appear passive, primitive and simple' (2017: 26). They found English learners are all too often 'positioned to view indigenous people as belonging in the past' (2017: 28).

In a paper first presented as early as 1976, historian of art and culture Kenneth Coutts-Smith elaborated on Eurocentric 'colonial appropriation throughout the whole of world culture' (1991: 12). Coutts-Smith discussed in this respect the 'internally-colonized aboriginal peoples' (1991: 7), and our fascination with 'the element of strangeness itself, the element of *exoticism*' (1991: 12, emphasis in original). There seems to be a continuation of this fascination and othering in the coursebook industry, for minoritized cultural groups are most often typecast – for example, an Aboriginal Australian or a kilted Scot are far more likely to be stereotyped than a European Australian or English man or woman. Candlin (2014: xiii, emphasis in original) clarifies the importance of teaching intercultural competence:

> the foreignness of foreign language education is not merely a means by which exotica can be paraded, external to the lived experience and consciousness of teachers and pupils seen as voyeurs, but as a means and method through which, interculturally, learners as selves and persons may experience through their engagement with the Other [...] the nature of their membership of their own society, and may be enabled to hold its practices and beliefs up to critical observation and evaluation.

It is astonishing that it is relatively seldom considered whether those who author, illustrate and publish coursebooks, which are so ubiquitously used in schools, create culturally accurate and sensitive texts, illustrations and photos of the diverse ethnicities, different communities and cultural groups portrayed in the books (and also of those present in classrooms). This is all the more problematic in that for students, and no doubt also for many teachers, as Skela claims (2014: 122), 'the textbook represents an authoritative source of information whose truth value often goes unquestioned'. It is unrealistic to expect coursebooks to change in the short term; therefore, it is essential for the goal of interculturality as a transformative strategy that student teachers learn to read both visual and verbal representations critically, so that they can later bring these into an open classroom dialogue, thus hopefully diminishing their manipulative effect. This is an important aspect of visual literacy.

Children's Literature and Ideology

Children's literature is considered in this book as a vital supplement to the coursebook, although, depending on context and confidence of the teacher and their autonomy in the use of funds, it could also be a replacement. It is equally important to read authentic children's literature critically, of course, for the literature children read can exert 'massive cultural influence' (Hunt 2001: 2). An ideology close to that of the reader can be very difficult to recognize *as* ideology, and thus sneakily manipulative. Robyn McCallum and John Stephens (2011: 360) have noted that ideologies 'function most powerfully in books which reproduce beliefs and assumptions of which authors and readers are largely unaware', and Nodelman and Reimer assert, 'ideology works best by disappearing, so that people simply take their ideological assumptions for granted as the only, whole, and unquestionable truth' (2003: 80). It must be remembered, however, that not only are texts never neutral, but also our literacy practices: 'The ways we read text are never neutral' (Vasquez, Janks and Comber 2019: 307).

Children's literature scholarship, which has increasingly scrutinized ideological issues in children's literature in recent decades, has attempted to influence the publishing industry to more accurately reflect cultural and ethnic diversity (see, for example, Bhroin and Kennon 2012, Bishop 1990, Hollingdale 1988, Leland, Lewison and Harste 2013, Nodelman 1992, Reese 2000, Reynolds 2007, Stephens 1992 and Taxel 2003). In a critical article referring to the Norwegian arts scene, and with a particular focus on Nordic children's literature, Michell Mpike (2019: 64) writes: 'When minority children are absent, this communicates to both minority and majority children, that minority children are invisible or non-existent in society, that they do not belong and that they do not hold any value.' Mpike calls for a representation of the diversity of Nordic society in children's literature, a demand that is echoed almost worldwide in societies that feature diversity and othering.

Three decades ago, Rudine Sims Bishop (1990: ix) brought to light how minoritized children are regularly disadvantaged in their participation in storyworlds, as they lack mirrors of their own sociocultural identities: 'When children cannot find themselves reflected in the books they read, or when images they see are distorted, negative or laughable, they learn a powerful lesson about how they are devalued in the society of which they are a part.' It has taken twenty-first-century movements like #BlackLivesMatter, #OscarsSoWhite, We Need Diverse Books (https://diversebooks.org/) and Every Story Matters (https://www.everystorymatters.eu/), as well as horrific racist events such as the murder of George Floyd by a police officer in 2020, which ignited protests in the United States and internationally against police brutality towards persons of colour, for publishers and the film industry to begin to respond regarding diversity.

The #ownvoices movement, like the We Need Diverse Books movement, grew out of the world of children's literature and not that of literature for adults, which is unsurprising as children's literature scholars are very aware of the impact children's reading has on their sense of worth (which can in turn impact children's self-efficacy, willingness to communicate and language learning). The concept of #ownvoices is to support the publishing of books on ethnic minorities, the LGBTQ+ community and people with disabilities that have been written by authors and/or illustrated by artists from the same marginalized group. The educational significance for all school students is clear, for as Tschida, Ryan and Ticknor argue (2014: 29), books may be 'the only place where readers may meet people who are not like themselves, who offer alternative worldviews'. These issues are extremely important, and I have included examples of diverse minoritized perspectives and also #ownvoices throughout this book.

However, it should be remembered that children's literature is, in fact, written by adults who, across a cognitive gap, can only imaginatively convey the experience of children and adolescents. Thoughtful children's authors rise to the aesthetic challenge to fill gaps as far as possible, the gap between the child and the adult, for instance. Similarly, as Joel Taxel (2003) explains, dedicated non-insider authors can succeed through careful research combined with social responsibility and subjecting their work to critical scrutiny, in portraying different cultural groups accurately and sensitively. Committed non-insider authors can contribute as allies of the marginalized, for example in the case of refugee literature, where #ownvoices are very scarce. Imbalances should be further explored dialogically by students' deep reading of stories that challenge expectations, and by the addition of their own voices through creative writing and other kinds of creative response (see step 4: *Experiment with creative response* in the deep reading framework, Figure 1.1: 26).

Until more coursebooks, and more print and screen media generally, are developed that truly reflect the diversity of society, the subliminal ideology of materials used in classrooms must receive critical attention and be made visible – whether the materials were specifically published for language teaching or not. With the increased movement of people between countries – 'because of a shortage of labour in certain sectors, to be with their families, or as refugees to escape war, civil unrest, poverty or fear of persecution' (Simpson 2016: 178) – helping students develop an awareness of ideological issues in texts used in the classroom becomes ever more important in teacher education.

Culture as Plural and Fluid

English language education is a discipline with an international outlook, for many countries worldwide now strive to offer English at ever younger school grades. When a language-teaching coursebook is exclusively used, there is the difficulty that perspectives may be limited to those of BANA countries. Adrian Holliday (1994: 4) introduced the term BANA to refer to the dominance of Britain, Australasia and North America in the English language teaching industry. English coursebooks have traditionally relied on cultural input from BANA countries, including images of capital cities, BANA national customs and historical scenes, a choice that – at least until recently – was expected by language teachers and often supported by local curricular stipulations. This ignores the reality of English use throughout the world, including the *majority world*. Shahidul Alam (2008), a Bangladeshi social activist, coined the expression 'majority world' as a less disparaging term than 'developing world' or 'third world', and more accurate than Global South, to refer to nations in Asia, Africa, Latin America and the Middle East, which is where the majority of people live.

The Covid-19 pandemic as well as the climate crisis has shown once again how global threats have the most devastating impact on vulnerable social groups and peoples, and that consequently the building of empathy, trust and intercultural competence must become ever more central to education. Referring to the Covid health crisis, the need for international cooperation and trust is emphasized by the United Nations Development Programme (2020): 'We must rebuild trust and cooperation, within and among nations, and between people and their governments.' As English is understood as a lingua franca, English language education should become a strong support for the bridge building that is called for. However, English language teachers still widely believe they must teach selected elements of cultural information on BANA countries, while coursebooks too often concentrate their cultural references on these countries (unfortunately, this is still common in teacher education). As Michael Byram writes (2020: 170), 'In practice, textbook writers have made choices about culture on behalf of language teachers, but often with little or no understanding of what culture is.' This is hugely problematic for several reasons.

To begin with, significant cultural change will long have invalidated any purely information-focused teaching based on coursebooks, which take several years to compile and publish. Further, the concept of English-speaking countries has become permeable in current times, when, as Elisa Bertoldi and Maria Bortoluzzi (2019: 16) write, 'English is seen in its "plural" identity of language often directly experienced through media and social media even in countries where it is not the official language of communication.' If we restrict the texts we teach to those reflecting BANA countries because the concept of English-speaking countries is taken to mean specifically those countries, it can be difficult to avoid cultural imperialism. English touches everyone and is spoken just about everywhere, so why privilege forging intercultural communication with certain (more powerful) countries over others?

There has been much discussion of linguistic imperialism in English language teaching, while the need to balance the use of English languages and literatures with support for indigenous languages and literatures is a constant concern. However, Suresh Canagarajah (1999: 197) argues that for L2 English speakers in the majority world both appropriating English and maintaining their vernaculars will strongly support empowerment in the culturally hybrid world that confronts them: 'The maintenance of polyvocality with a clear awareness of their socio-ideological location empowers them to withstand the totalitarian tendencies – of local nationalist regimes and Western multinational agencies – enforced through uniformity of thought and communication.'

As Gustav Jahoda (2012: 300) emphasizes: 'It must be stressed that "culture" is not a thing, but a social construct vaguely referring to a vastly complex set of phenomena.' Byram (2020: 169) suggests as a definition that 'culture is the shared behaviours of a social group and the values, beliefs and knowledge which underpin them'. Cultural phenomena are complex and ever-changing, and broad generalizations in coursebooks can only lead to superficial caricatures that cannot support intercultural competence. Recognizing that culture is fluid and constantly shapeshifting, and on a micro-level also idiosyncratic, we now know that it is scarcely teachable without resorting to stereotypes. But essentializing is dangerous, as we already have the tendency to perceive members of outgroups as basically all the same while we see many distinctions in members of our own groups.

Culture, according to Linda Crawford and Peter McLaren (2003: 131), 'does not consist simply of isolated, bounded, and cohesive meaning systems, but rather reflects and is constitutive of a multiplicity of voices reflecting a whole array of conflicting and competing discourses'. Claudia Lenz and Peder Nustad (2019: 12) indicate that the significant change in our understanding of culture as plural and fluid is itself still in flux, yet our lived experience shows this to be so: 'There is a wide span between static and essentialist interpretations of culture on the one hand and dynamic and open interpretations on the other. [...] Every person is also a member of several different groups, which means that each and every one of us participates in various (sub)cultures.' Fred Dervin (2017b: 58) puts the concept of power and inequalities between groups at the centre of intercultural communication:

> Too often intercultural communication has been treated as a neutral transactional encounter, during which different groups face language barriers and cultural misunderstandings while interacting with each other. This view often ignores the fact that the 'intercultural' also encompasses and contributes to both unbalanced power relations between these groups based on gender difference, social class, religion, etc., and differential treatment based on origins, languages, skin colour of the people involved.

A Council of Europe publication, *Reference Framework of Competences for Democratic Culture*, attempts to bring some clarity to the prospect of opportunities for intercultural learning: 'If we all participate in multiple cultures, but we each participate in a unique constellation of cultures, then every interpersonal situation is potentially an intercultural situation' (2018b: 31). The document further defines intercultural dialogue:

> Intercultural situations, identified in this way, may involve people from different countries, people from different regional, linguistic, ethnic or faith groups, or people who differ from each other because of their lifestyle, gender, age or generation, social class, education, occupation,

level of religious observance, sexual orientation, and so on. From this perspective, 'intercultural dialogue' may be defined as an open exchange of views, on the basis of mutual understanding and respect, between individuals or groups who perceive themselves as having different cultural affiliations from each other.

(2018b: 31)

If our multiple cultural identities determine that communication itself is an intercultural process, then all communication can be explored interculturally. Instead of attempting to teach instances of culture, when culture is by nature transitory and ephemeral, we can enter many different storyworlds and exercise the taking on of new perspectives through literary reading. Gradually, according to Thein, Beach and Parks (2007: 55), students 'acquire the *capacity* itself to engage in and value perspective-taking through their literary experiences as a primary value for reading literature' (emphasis in original).

Interculturality and Diversity Competence

Fundamental to intercultural competence, according to Darla Deardorff (2006: 255), are 'attitudes of openness, respect (valuing all cultures), and curiosity and discovery (tolerating ambiguity)'. Deardorff also adds (2006: 258), 'Just as culture is ever changing, scholars' opinions on intercultural competence change with time.' Tolerance and the appreciation of diversity have become urgent twenty-first-century goals, leading to the building of confidence to communicate with different cultural groups with sensitivity and interculturality. The ethos of interculturality and social justice would seem to belong more than ever to teacher education, to prepare for the responsible role of teachers to educate for mutual respect.

On the multiplicity of voices in cultural settings, Dervin (2017c: 245) urges: 'It has become increasingly important to intersect culture and other identity markers (gender, social class, language, etc.).' Reflecting on the asymmetries between dominant and marginalized social groupings within a national group is central to interculturality. Already in many classrooms, children are from different backgrounds and equipped with unequal sociocultural, economic and academic resources. Candlin stresses the importance of interculturality at home as well as abroad: 'It would be paradoxical wouldn't it, if our learners became so familiar with the mores, histories, social practices and cultural artefacts and processes of those safely-distanced exotic societies that they ignored the immediate substance and potential for their foreign language education in their neighbourhoods and next-door streets?' (2014: xv). However, this is exactly what does happen in many schools and classrooms.

The German concept of *Bildung* goes beyond a narrow notion of education, to include personal growth and agency. Aase et al. (2007: 9) connect literature with enhancing chances for personal development and interculturality: 'A *Bildung*-perspective means to be able to accept and live with difference and controversy in society and to meet "the other" with respect. Experiences of literature from unfamiliar milieus and cultures provide possibilities for identification and understanding new ways of thinking.' David Selby and Graham Pike (2000: 142–143) discuss the inner dimension of global education as 'a voyage along two complementary learning pathways. While the journey outwards leads learners to discover and understand the world in which they live, the journey inwards heightens their understanding of themselves and of their potential.' Meanwhile, Lothar Bredella (2013: 434) expounds that 'literary texts produce different readings with different readers. A conversation about such different readings in the foreign language classroom can make learners aware of their prior knowledge, their expectations and the stereotypes they bring to the text. Thus they can become conscious of what guides them in the background, a critical insight essential for intercultural understanding.' A stirring literary portrayal of another's story can provide a kind of magical mirror, drawing students deeply into experiences of similarity and difference, which challenges their sense of self and heightens their awareness of their own situation, feelings and beliefs.

A literary apprenticeship is crucial for emotional investment in story characters to develop into in-depth learning processes including reflecting on stories, and sometimes challenging them. Students may then also reflect on popular stories; interestingly there is far more access to mirrors of young people's diverse identities in some recent popular viewing than in either language teaching coursebooks or canonical literature. For example, *Atypical* (Robia Rashid 2017) is a Netflix series in which the protagonist is an eighteen-year-old boy with autism spectrum disorder; *She-Ra and the Princesses of Power* (Noelle Stevenson 2018) is an animated series that features characters who are diverse in ethnicity, body shape and sexual orientation, and the majority of the most original characters are female; *Dragon Prince* (Aaron Ehasz and Justin Richmond 2018) includes agentic characters with disabilities, different ethnicities amongst the main characters, and diversity in the families represented, including same-sex parents; and the romantic comedy streaming series, *Heartstopper* (Euros Lyn 2022), based on Alice Oseman's young adult webcomic and graphic novel series (2018–2021), features appealing and well-portrayed adolescent characters with diverse genders and sexualities. My choice of literary texts for this book has been guided by the urgent need for inclusivity and authenticity, and an awareness of including #ownvoices.

Democratic Culture and Intercultural Dialogue

With their framework for democratic culture and intercultural dialogue, the Council of Europe puts forward a conceptual model of competences 'that need to be acquired by learners if they are to become effective engaged citizens and live peacefully together with others as equals in culturally diverse democratic societies' (2018b: 65). All of the following concepts included in this model are relevant for language teaching:

- *Values* – valuing human dignity, human rights, cultural diversity, justice and equality.

- *Attitudes* – openness to cultural otherness and to other world views and practices, respect, responsibility, self-efficacy and tolerance of ambiguity.

- *Skills* – learner autonomy skills, critical thinking, listening and observing skills, empathy, flexibility and adaptability, co-operation skills, linguistic, communicative and plurilingual skills, co-operation and conflict-resolution skills.

- *Knowledge and critical understanding* – critical understanding of the self, of language and communication, knowledge and critical understanding of the world, of human rights, culture and cultures, history, media, the environment and sustainability (adapted from Council of Europe 2018b: 38).

The model illustrates that interculturality and diversity competence are two sides of the same coin and are essential for a well-functioning democratic culture, as they guard against intolerance. Lenz and Nustad (2019: 2) maintain that 'intolerance can also be defined as undemocratic. The groupthink on which such attitudes are based undermines the inclusive and pluralist principles that are essential to a functioning democratic culture.' The tendency of any social ingroup to maintain unreflecting conformity and hegemony of perspectives leads to groupthink, and the submerging of individual autonomy, personal growth and critical evaluation of others' points of view. Groupthink creates one-dimensionality and bias, so leading to the exclusion of others who then feel they cannot belong. In order to overcome stereotyping and essentializing, critical understanding must be seen as an aspect of both intercultural learning and diversity competence.

Syndrome of Group-Focused Enmity

A decade-long research project led by Wilhelm Heitmeyer has compared prejudice and discrimination in eight selected European countries and published findings on the 'syndrome of group-focused enmity' (Zick, Küpper and Hövermann 2011). Six areas of prejudice were investigated: anti-immigrant attitudes, racism, anti-Semitism, anti-Muslim attitudes, sexism and homophobia (see Figure 2.1).

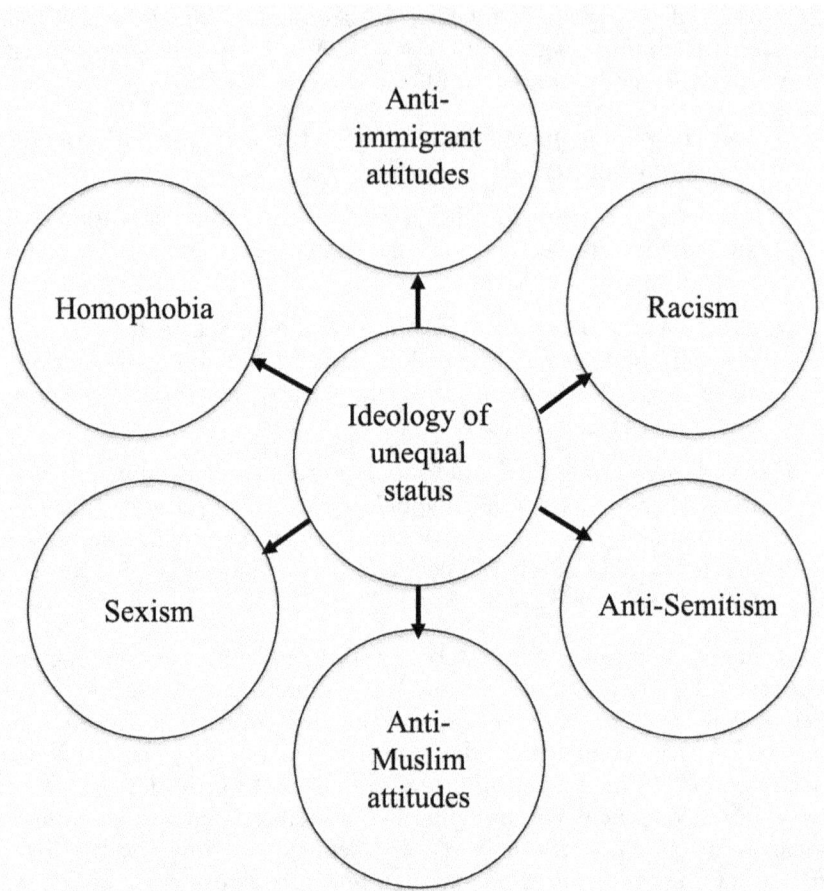

FIGURE 2.1 *Syndrome of group-focused enmity. Excerpted from* Intolerance, Prejudice and Discrimination. A European Report *(Zick, Küpper and Hövermann 2011: 39)*.

The researchers found that within Europe the prejudices are interconnected, 'that in all the countries all six prejudices are so closely related that they can be treated as a single dimension (group-focused enmity)' (Zick, Küpper and Hövermann 2011: 73). The common core of group-focused enmity was found to be based on an ideology of inequality – when outgroups, social groups with which individuals do not identify, are considered to be of lower status. The research findings revealed that 'anti-immigrant attitudes, anti-Semitism, anti-Muslim attitudes, sexism, homophobia and even racism are supported or at least tolerated in many sectors of the population' (2011: 159). Of the eight countries involved, the extent of group-focused enmity was smallest in the Netherlands. Significantly, the researchers found that in all eight countries higher manifestation of group-focused enmity was associated with lower levels of education: 'According to our findings, the main contextual conditions that make people susceptible to prejudiced opinions are a low level of education, low income in a low-income region and a culture where prejudices as a whole are more widespread (as is partly the case in eastern Europe)' (2011: 167).

The challenge, then, is to strengthen multiple literacy, critical thinking, bridge building and inclusion in school and in the classroom! Early measures are the most powerful for preventing prejudice, as we are often shaped by pervasive attitudes from our childhood environment. Dialogic, cooperative learning, community orientation, supporting *all* students' own voices and the reduction of isolationism can lead to a 'critically aware citizenry in the context of social interaction outside the school' (Candlin 2014: xii). The English language classroom is one of the areas where these core educational goals could be integrated into existing timetables.

The Affordances of Literary Texts for Engagement with Diversity

Entering different storyworlds, following different lives and discovering divergent histories can be an entrancing way to practise decentring and perspective-taking. This book makes the case for a study of literary texts for children and adolescents that, as Short (2011: 50) writes, 'expands children's life spaces through inquiries that take them outside the boundaries of their lives to other places, times, and ways of living'. Cultural groups are not homogenous, but characterized by a multiplicity of individual voices, as colourful as a rainbow but similarly intangible. Storyworlds can provide a meaningful glimpse into unfamiliar cultural contexts, drawing students in, surprising and fascinating them. The storyworld in children's literary texts provides a sheltered space in which complex and often controversial issues can be safely explored, and with picturebooks already in elementary school.

The Urgency of Global Education

Studying controversial topics through literary texts is a contribution to the requirements of global education which, according to Kip Cates (2013: 277), 'aims to promote students' knowledge and awareness of the world's peoples, countries, cultures and issues'. The urgency of global education is due to the interdependence between the world's peoples on many complex issues, including the environment. UNESCO (2013) states, 'at a fundamental level, biological and cultural diversities are closely interdependent. They have developed over time through mutual adaptation between humans and the environment, and therefore, rather than existing in separate and parallel realms, they interact with and affect one another in complex ways in a sort of co-evolutionary process.' Evolutionary literary critic Joseph Carroll (2018: 426) reclaims the argument that human culture is a part of nature for humans are a part of nature, and 'characteristics of human nature shape cultural practices', which suggests that interculturality should include an ecocentric perspective.

Jürgen Wehrmann (2019: 113) holds that the goal of global education should lead to a development in the concept of intercultural learning to 'a deep integration of linguistic, literary, cultural, and ecological learning'. Similarly, education for global citizenship includes, according to Oxfam (2015: 3), 'revealing the global as part of everyday local life, whether in a small village or a large city [and] understanding how we relate to the environment and to each other as human beings'. Gunther Dietz (2018: 15) refers to the increasing overlapping of diversity and intersectionality, including gender, race, class, sexuality and disability-related sources of difference, and compares cultural diversity to biodiversity: 'In this sense, cultural diversity is increasingly being employed and defined in relation to social and cultural variability in the same way as biodiversity is being used when referring to biological and ecological variations, habitats, and ecosystems.'

Deep reading of worthwhile narrative supports engagement through experiencing problems, vicariously, together with the protagonist, and real-world topics explored through story can be an excellent contribution to in-depth learning. Compelling story can offer an early beginning, for as Taxel maintains (2003: 159): 'Young children are strong and resilient and, with the guidance of caring and skillful teachers, are capable of handling complex and controversial issues when they are presented in a developmentally appropriate fashion.' Students' enthusiasm and engagement are the foundation for in-depth learning and empowered participation as citizens in the cultural, environmental and political spheres of life.

Dialogic Learning and the Principle of Multivoicedness

English is both a curriculum subject and a lingua franca. Consequently, English subject pedagogy is a field that is inherently characterized by diversity and dialogue. Multiple voices are necessary for effective dialogue, to introduce new perspectives in a dialogic process, each responding to and building on the other, while developing understandings of complex issues. Student groups from different ideological positions and backgrounds in a multicultural school can extend the range of voices and experiences in the classroom, for cross-curricular challenges such as environmental problems, interculturality, diversity and multiple literacy are best approached dialogically.

In addition, well-constructed narrative offers a built-in variety of differently modulated voices, which Bakhtin called heteroglossia. This is in contrast to many online exchanges, which incline to be uncritically cumulative rather than perspective-taking and dialogic, so that social media, though full of 'stories' (see *antinarrative*, Chapter 11), can have the tendency to close down all-important exploratory social interactions. The current mono-dimensionality and coarsening of public and political discourse is distressing, leading to 'a sense of a public discourse that is losing its power to explain and reconcile, or indeed to express anything beyond hatred and division' (Thompson 2016). In terms of education, it is essential to increase dialogue in order to actively listen to different voices and read about different ideas, expanding understandings and the potential for change.

Dialogic learning focuses on increasing awareness rather than knowledge accumulation – as knowledge will always be based on a limited selection of evidence. Byram, Gribkova and Starkey (2002: 24) recommend adding more voices and perspectives for intercultural competence by moving beyond the single text approach: 'Materials from different origins with different perspectives should be used together to enable learners to compare and to analyse the materials critically. It is more important that learners acquire skills of analysis than factual information.' The pedagogical concept of a *text ensemble* introduces a greater variety of voices than the extensive reading approach, for example. For relying only on extensive reading can entail the drawback, as Werner Delanoy points out (2018: 152), that 'people may read the same type of story again and again, and thus remain caught in a narrow understanding of themselves and others'. Though less advantageous for broad educational goals, the repetition associated with narrow reading can, however, have advantages for L2 acquisition (Chang and Millett 2017, Renandya, Krashen and Jacobs 2018).

Jessica Whitelaw's research into school practice (2017: 61) supports the inclusion of different viewpoints on a topic by combining a range of texts: 'Looking at issues across different texts helped students to develop an awareness that if stories are a way of knowing and understanding human phenomena, multiple forms of story have the potential to expand what can be accessed, known, and understood.' Maria José Botelho (2021: 122) concurs: 'Assembling a text collection around a similar cultural theme can provide multiple perspectives and nuanced cultural portrayals.' Howard Gardner (2006: 87) argues that 'multiple representations are grist for new ways of thinking about an entity, problem, or question: they catalyse creative questions and spawn creative solutions'. Helene Decke-Cornill proposes the *principle of multivoicedness* (2007: 255), and that using texts from different origins in a text ensemble will open up new perspectives and disrupt the dominant views, which are often male, White and from the West.

Thus, text ensembles and the principle of multivoicedness ensure that new voices and #ownvoices are heard that challenge traditional positions, help avoid the danger of a single story, as Chimamanda Ngozi Adichie (2009) has memorably set forth, and invite critical thinking. Rupert Wegerif (2013) describes *opening* dialogic space through reflective questioning, *widening* dialogic space by bringing in new voices and *deepening* dialogic space by exploring one's own framing assumptions:

> Referring to an ontological interpretation of dialogic is another way of saying that dialogic education is education *for* dialogue as well as *through* dialogue in which dialogue is not only treated as a means to an end but also treated as an end in itself.
>
> [...] I think it is useful pedagogically to be able to talk about 'opening dialogic space', through interrupting an activity with a reflective question, for example, or 'widening dialogic space' through bringing in new voices or 'deepening dialogic space' through reflection on assumptions.
>
> (2013: 33, emphasis in original)

Tschida, Ryan and Ticknor (2014: 31) emphasize: 'It is only by disrupting single stories with narratives told from other perspectives that we form a more nuanced picture of the people, issues, or ideas at hand.' Being able to make informed decisions is more important than ever, and education needs to support students' in developing information literacy and agency, and their perspective-taking. Over time – ideally beginning already in elementary school – this will become, as Thein, Beach and Parks state, 'a habit of mind that can help students acknowledge that other ways of understanding the world do exist and are worth considering or at least recognizing, even if they choose not to agree with those perspectives' (2007: 55).

The Significance of Characterization

Some decades ago, Noam Chomsky (1988: 159) surmised that 'it is quite possible – overwhelmingly probable, one might guess – that we will always learn more about human life and human personality from novels than from scientific psychology. The science-forming capacity is only one facet of our mental endowment. We use it where we can but are not restricted to it, fortunately.' With this, Chomsky seems to be observing that psychological dynamics and complex characters in a story drive the plot, rather than vice versa. Recent empirical evidence appears to confirm that narrative is indeed primarily character driven. Neuroscientist Steven Brown and his team have demonstrated that the mediation of characters and the psychology and experientiality of characters are central to storytelling (Brown et al. 2019). In their study, twenty participants were given the task of creating brief oral stories around three-panel comics, with twenty-four comics altogether in the set. These comics contained scenarios with characters, scenarios without visible characters but with an implied character presence and scenarios that did not include a human agent at all (see Figure 2.2).

Character-based

Character-implied

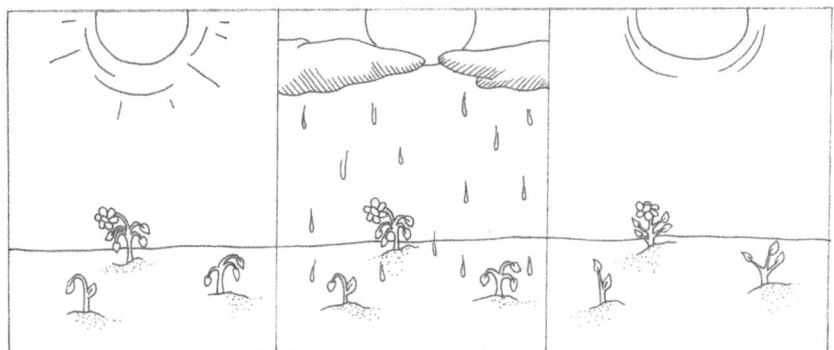
Characterless

FIGURE 2.2 *Three-panel comics for character-based, character-implied and characterless stories. Examples of wordless three-panel comics sequences used with permission of the project team, © 2019 Brown, Berry, Dawes, Hughes and Tu.*

The researchers found that the storytellers inserted two characters on average into each story with only implied characters. Surprisingly, they 'also observed a large amount of character insertion into the CL [characterless] stories, although roughly half of those insertions were of non-human characters' (2019: 335). The character-centred engagement in storytelling – a phenomenon the team names *protagonism* – was found to be more pronounced than predicted, with the insertion of both humans and non-humans as psychological vehicles and active protagonists, 'animate non-human beings (plants, animals) and inanimate objects can be inserted, animated, and personified for the critical purpose of serving as story protagonists' (2019: 336). Children, of course, instinctively animate inanimate objects, for example their soft toys and dolls, expressing a developmental tendency in humans that is clearly important for theory of mind.

The psychologists Fritz Heider and Marianne Simmel published (1944) their now-classic paper with the findings that subjects watching a two-minute animated film featuring geometric figures (a triangle, a smaller triangle, a small circle and a rectangle with an opening like a door – see Figure 2.3) almost unanimously interpret the triangles and circle as animate beings. The adult test subjects created their own stories around the geometric shapes,

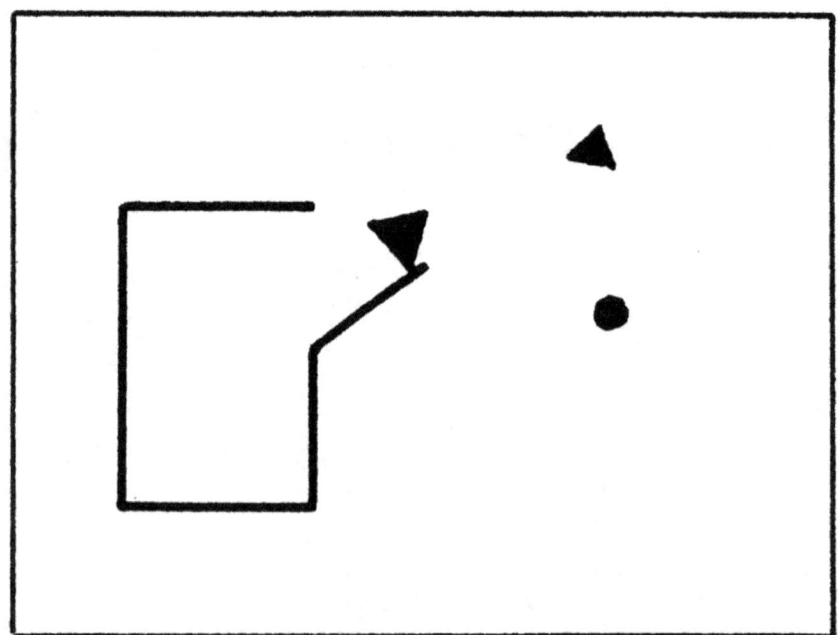

FIGURE 2.3 *Geometric figures in Heider and Simmel's animated film. Excerpted from 'An experimental study of apparent behavior' (Heider and Simmel 1944: 244).*

interpreting movements anthropomorphically as expressions of human emotions and motivations.

Character interaction and psychological dynamics are then central to story, and well-crafted literary texts can cause the reader to create mental representations of the unique individuality of characters (Bland 2022: 129–33). This is crucial, because humans develop relatively unbiased, non-stereotypical insights into the mental life, the beliefs, values, feelings and thoughts of others only if they are able to see others as unique individuals. Additionally, it is easier to recognize and learn about systemic prejudice and institutionalized discrimination in a storyworld than in the real world to which we belong. The findings in David Kidd and Emanuele Castano's experimental study (2013: 377) support the argument that the reading of polyvocal or multivoiced literary texts (but not popular fiction with flat characters or nonfiction) allows engaged readers access to the subjective experiences of complex characters, and in this respect even presents opportunities that real life cannot:

> Just as in real life, the worlds of literary fiction are replete with complicated individuals whose inner lives are rarely easily discerned but warrant exploration. The worlds of fiction, though, pose fewer risks than the real world, and they present opportunities to consider the experiences of others without facing the potentially threatening consequences of that engagement. More critically, whereas many of our mundane social experiences may be scripted by convention and informed by stereotypes, those presented in literary fiction often disrupt our expectations.

Characterization in high-quality literary texts can play an important role in helping overcome stereotyping, because complex literary characters appear as unique individuals. This disrupts essentializing, and what has been observed as 'an outgroup homogeneity effect and an ingroup heterogeneity effect: members of outgroups all appear the same while we perceive members of our own group to be quite distinct from one another' (Zick, Küpper and Hövermann 2011: 29).

It should be mentioned that children and adolescents might in some ways also be considered an outgroup, as power and privilege rest with adults, whether within families, schools or society. For example, the ideology of inequality comes into play when adults and educationalists think they must select the reading for school students from fragmented and truncated or simplified literature for adults rather than outstanding authentic literature specifically created for children and adolescents, although for young people the latter has a much better chance to become compelling comprehensible input (Krashen and Bland 2014). That literature is always a verbal construct is also an elitist adult perspective, as picturebooks and graphic novels popular with younger readers can also aesthetically evoke human experience in an imaginative virtual world, in a way that is distinctly literary. Twenty-first-century formats of children's literature relevant for language education with six- to sixteen-year-olds are frequently multimodal, not only image-mediated such as picturebooks and graphic novels, but also action-mediated with drama, and oral–aural in the case of oral storytelling and performance poetry. Thus, the concept of texts becomes ever more inclusive, and this should be reflected in language and literature teaching.

Carroll (2018: 431) argues that humans live in the imagination: 'Humans reflect on their own mental life, imagine other minds, and imagine themselves reflected in the minds of others.' This predisposition can provide the author with rich material for a narrative that revolves around characterization:

> Every individual human being has a unique identity that involves some particular configuration of personality traits, mental aptitudes, networks of family and social relationships, personal experiences, and ideas, beliefs, tastes, and attitudes. When some individual author sits down to compose a literary work, he or she has a virtually unlimited range of variables from which to select, and an unlimited range of possible ways in which to organize those variables.
>
> (Carroll 2017: np)

Thus, the wealth of opportunity for vicarious interaction with complex characters in storyworlds can be a strong contribution to overcoming essentializing, developing instead interculturality and engagement with diversity.

Critical Interculturality

Dietz (2018: 3) describes a view of critical interculturality 'as a transformative strategy to unveil, question, and change historically rooted inequalities within society [… and] these intercultural capacities are interpreted and/or acquired in terms of anti-discrimination, consciousness raising, and dealing with conflict'. Clearly, in this interpretation, the notion of interculturality has moved very far beyond a static concept of national cultures. Manuela Guilherme (2019: 2) also emphasizes the critical aspect of interculturality, 'in order to respond to current local/global demands for social and cognitive justice, the critical and the intercultural are inescapably intertwined'. Dervin's (2017a: 1) understanding of critical interculturality accentuates its polysemic nature and the aspect of power relations, 'a never-ending process of ideological struggle against solid identities, unfair power differentials, discrimination and hurtful (and often disguised) discourses of (banal) nationalism, ethnocentrism, racism and various forms of -ism'. Dervin calls for 'undertones and nuances, rather than generalizations when it comes to interculturality' (2017a: 17). He uses the term 'diverse diversities' to stress that we are all involved in diversity, 'the idea of diverse diversities is to counter the use of the word diversity in this very simple way that diversity is only the other' (2017a: 18), and to replace this othering with 'the idea that WE are all diverse' (Dervin 2010: 161, emphasis in original).

Individuals are diverse in so many ways – our plural identities, our adaptability and accommodation to different interlocutors and contexts, but also our tendency to wear figurative masks in certain situations, as Dervin suggests: 'Individual plurality is not always visible because, in any context of interaction, one needs to select an image of the self (and of the other) and use it' (2010: 169). Hua Zhu (2010: 189) emphasizes the hybrid, fluid and ongoing nature of social and cultural identities – interculturality, in consequence, 'is not only a dynamic process through which participants make aspects of their multiple and shifting identities relevant, but also a process of developing new social and cultural identities'. Jena Habegger-Conti (2021: 53) underscores the threshold situation of migrants and refugees: 'By nature of their national and cultural liminality, migrants and refugees emphasize the "inter" of intercultural, and the fluidity of culture and identity. By nature of their journeys, migrants and refugees also dismantle the over there/over here divide, as teachers and students around the world negotiate new multicultural realities in their classrooms.'

Discovering and unmasking aspects of one's own and others' individual identity is a central and recurring topic in literary texts. This theme is to a greater or lesser extent present in every literary text discussed in this book, as tension is created by the protagonist's need to discover facets of his or her own identity and also to unmask aspects of identity of other characters. This is why literary texts are so valuable for rehearsing interculturality and perspective-taking. For complex characters gradually reveal aspects of their identity to the engaged reader and we have the chance to empathize, whether the characters are purely fantasy or, in the case of biography, also exist or have existed in the real world. While reading and listening to story that is comprehensible and compelling, we generate mental imagery, and our vicarious ethical experience is embodied and tangible. Our actual lived contact with diversity will always be limited by the number of different local and global contexts we can visit, but we could learn vicariously and discover mutualities through a multitude of literary characters and storyworlds that can lead us 'towards an understanding of the nature of their [our] common condition' (Candlin 2014: xv).

The plurality of lifeworlds that can be introduced through story frequently, especially in the twenty-first century, include aspects that belong to global issues, such as racism, xenophobia, social class bias, sexism, homophobia, ableism, lookism, ageism, mental and physical health, and the environment. Deep reading and dialogue around the literary space of a storyworld is not only participatory but also an experienced-based interaction that can lead to in-depth learning. For this reason, it seems entirely reasonable to claim, as

Wehrmann does (2019: 114): 'Approaching literature and culture through longer texts like novels and plays or more complex text combinations can offer insights and experiences of global issues that natural or social sciences cannot.' Along the same lines, Nikolajeva (2021: 236) posits: 'Storytelling, as well as play, is the most effective way of generational knowledge and experience transmission, far more effective than straightforward instruction.'

The storyworld of selected texts for language education should mirror the diverse diversities in our classrooms, and value individual plurality, manifold cultural identities and marginalized narratives. Students' own cultural resources, including their linguistic resources, whether aligned to the dominant culture or not, become a part of the dialogic process and multivoicedness of the classroom. Particularly in the area of language education, Ronald Carter claims (2015: 316) that attention has shifted from sharing a literary text as an absolute canonical product to the communicative process of dialogic reception: 'Analysis has been extended to all texts as cultural products, with the notion of culture seen as increasingly dynamic and co-constructed interactively.'

The goals of intercultural education and culture of democracy demand we understand language learning as central to education and not simply as acquiring a useful commodity. This evidently necessitates, as David Valente and Sandie Mourão envision (2022: 2), 'a departure from a strictly linguistic way of being and doing in English language teaching.' Nonetheless, the aim cannot be to absolutely accomplish intercultural competence but rather to discover the process: 'Intercultural competence is not permanent, "for life", and its practice and learning never end' (Dervin 2010: 170). Narrative imagination is the ability to inhabit a strange world for a time and share in it cognitively and emotionally, and this is the 'promise of literature' according to Martha Nussbaum (1998: 111):

> It is for this reason that literature is so urgently important for the citizen, as an expansion of sympathies that real life cannot cultivate sufficiently. It is the political promise of literature that it can transport us, while remaining ourselves, into the life of another, revealing similarities but also profound differences between the life and thought of that other and myself and making them comprehensible, or at least nearly comprehensible.

CHAPTER THREE

Literature with English Language Learners: Activating Language and Response

Literature teaching with children and adolescents is increasingly seen as transaction, not transmission, and a highly communicative event. Even when readers are quietly enjoying a compelling book, they are involved in perspective-taking and dialoguing with the different stances of the various characters. Adults and adolescents take part in inner speech when they communicate with themselves – known as intrapersonal communication – sometimes also through private writing, such as diaries and reading logs. Small children speak their thoughts aloud, in private speech. Saville-Troike and Barto (2017: 122) recount how children's private speech can also take place in a second language, with a report on exchanges that demonstrate 'good evidence that even when they [small children speaking English as L2] were not interacting with others, they were not merely passively assimilating L2 input; they were using intrapersonal interaction in an active process of engagement with the input they heard, practicing to build up their competence'. We see that intrapersonal interaction can enrich language learning, and reading can be intrapersonal in addition to a community activity of booktalk, to use Aidan Chambers' term (2011), with meaning making as a form of shared contemplation. The idea that reading is a passive activity has now been thoroughly overthrown.

Fully Engaging with Language and Story

Nick Ellis and Diane Larsen-Freeman (2009: 91) emphasize the dynamic complexity of language, language use and language learning: 'Cognition, consciousness, experience, embodiment, brain, self, human interaction, society, culture, and history – in other words, phenomena at different levels of scale and time – are all inextricably intertwined in rich, complex, and dynamic ways in language, its use and its learning.' We now understand more about engagement with language – the affective, cognitive and sociocultural dimensions of language learning but also the physiological dimension – how language is experienced in an embodied way, and that we conjure mental representations or simulations, for example when reading a narrative: 'Simulation is the creation of mental experiences of perception and action in the absence of their external manifestation' (Bergen 2012: 15).

This depends, however, on the real-world experience of the reader and the perceptions they can activate: an older, experienced reader will have more real memories and memories of virtual experience (from life experience, viewing, listening, reading, etc.) than a younger reader. We must, therefore, take care that the stories we offer to children and adolescents are not solely accessible to an older, more experienced age group, as this would block younger readers from participating actively in the literary text, and building a mental representation of the storyworld. Bergen describes a creative and dynamic process: 'Meaning, according to the embodied simulation hypothesis, isn't just abstract mental symbols; it's a creative process, in which people construct virtual experiences – embodied simulations – in their mind's eye. […] It's not about activating the right symbol; it's about dynamically constructing the right mental experience of the scene' (2012: 16).

The Power of Language in Well-crafted Literary Texts

The relevance of high-quality and challenging input is certainly bound up with literature teaching for, as Susan Bassnett and Peter Grundy (1993: 7) contend, 'literature is a high point of language usage; arguably it marks the greatest skills a language user can demonstrate. Anyone who wants to acquire a profound knowledge of language that goes beyond the utilitarian will read literary texts in that language.' The Council of Europe (2018a: 15) identifies a synergy between literature, language subtlety, cultural context and imaginative possibilities:

> it is arguably literature that encapsulates language in its most subtle and intricate forms where nuances of meaning and ambiguity are more often found. Language has meaning not simply by reference to something outside itself, in a purely representational way, but through its occurrence in cultural contexts of human communities, which includes its potential to (re)-create in imagination new or existing communities. It is therefore unhelpful to see language narrowly as a disembodied, transparent tool that is bound by predetermined rules and structures.

Coursebooks and other especially written texts for language learners lack the poetic devices, emotional and musical intensity of literary texts – striking formulations that can be so helpful in making language patterns and lexical features, such as formulaic sequences, salient. Arresting language with the foregrounding devices of parallelisms (unexpected regularity) and deviation (unexpected eccentricity or irregularity) is for the reader more noticeable and emotional, can aid memorability and lead to slower, deeper reading.

Well-crafted literature typically features stylistic cohesion that is rich in meaningful lexical repetition, lexical chains and phonological patterns of rhythm and alliteration, with idiomatic multi-word units and the well balanced tricolon – the rhetorical rule of three. Creative writers craft their texts with stylistic features to convey meanings persuasively, engaging the reader by evoking an emotional response, resulting in thoughtful feelings (Ratner 2000). Rhetorical devices, such as alliteration, anaphora, cacophony, onomatopoeia, polysyndeton, and phonological and semantic repetition, can make the reading (and listening) more compelling.

Patrick Hogan (2014) describes powerful responses to art as *artefact emotions*, which seem to be inspired by a sublime blend of artistic, patterned cohesion with an inventive or astonishing schema-refreshing element. Hogan also refers to *outcome emotions*; these typically continue to influence the reader long after the end of a stirring narrative, as we see, for example, with many of the heartrending refugee stories in Chapter 5, and other moving stories throughout this book. Outcome emotions ensure that our response to story is empathetic, exercising conceptual and perceptual perspective-taking and helping to build theory of mind.

Phonological Recoding and Orthographic Decoding

For our teaching with compelling stories in school settings and heterogeneous classrooms, with students who are all or mostly English language learners and culturally and linguistically diverse, it is worthwhile to revisit the initial developments that take place when young children learn to read. Phonological recoding is the process that supports beginner readers' transformation of written words into their phonological representations – the mental representations of the sounds of words in spoken language. At this initial phase of learning to read in the language of schooling, the typical route is often called non-lexical (Coltheart 2005), and children sound out words with the aid of grapheme-phoneme correspondences.

During the process of reading acquisition, children soon build up a sight vocabulary store in their mental lexicon – their mental database of words and pronunciations – and are increasingly able to recognize orthographic word forms as wholes. This leads to the lexical route of orthographic decoding, which supports swifter and more efficient word recognition than grapheme-to-phoneme translation alone. Knoepke et al. (2014: 447) report: 'To become skillful readers, children have to acquire the ability to translate printed words letter by letter into phonemic representations (phonological recoding) and the ability to recognize the written word forms holistically (orthographical decoding).' It seems both lexical and non-lexical pathways into reading tend to co-exist, as the initial non-lexical path can still be activated when unfamiliar, infrequent words are encountered.

Studying elementary students in Germany, Knoepke et al. (2014: 465) report that already by the end of grade two with eight-year-old children learning to read in German (a language with high orthographic consistency), their 'orthographical decoding skills appeared to be more strongly predictive of sentence and text comprehension skills than phonological recoding skills'. Deacon et al. (2019: 57) highlight through their research that 'young children have powerful skill in learning spellings and meanings through their independent reading, with highly specific impacts of such learning on reading outcomes'. It appears the task demand or challenge is important, and that silent reading or reading aloud results in better orthographic learning and extracting of rule-based regularities than explicit teaching, which is less challenging because the students then do not need to predict from context.

When students are learning English as a second language, they may have largely developed beyond the phonological recoding stage in their L1, nonetheless initial shared reading in the English language classroom is supportive, also to help with pronunciations. Watching films with subtitles in English can additionally improve children's reading fluency, through repeated encounters with particular language strings during stretches of discourse. Furthermore, reading a book while simultaneously listening to the audiobook can support children and adolescent L2 readers in acquiring rich lexical representations and deep word knowledge, that is, all three elements of words: the meaning, the pronunciation and the orthography.

A literary apprenticeship in the elementary school can extend children's interest in patterns and text. Symbols and patterns are vital for children's search for meanings in the world about them, their daily lives, the stories they hear and the languages they learn. Interpreting symbols and pattern matching are integral to the pleasures of narrative, and a basic way that humans process meanings and acquire new information, as well as fundamental to language learning. And the reading habit brings invaluable additional benefits besides, such as intellectual, emotional, ethical and social development.

Language Learning as a Context-bound Phenomenon

Literary texts can provide comprehension support through a compelling, cohesive and often multimodal context. The importance of context in L2 acquisition with children and adolescents is increasingly highlighted by applied linguists. Referring to children younger than eight, Nicholas and Lightbown (2008: 28–9) suggest: 'differences between first and second language development may depend more on context than on abstract cognitive mechanisms.' Rather than an innate language-learning ability, it is increasingly recognized that it is a domain-general strong predisposition for social interaction and mirroring that enables and encourages language development in children. This naturalistic language learning comes about through the receptive usage of listening (and later reading) and productive usage of speaking (and later writing), ideally making optimal use of the kind of compelling context that stories can provide. While adolescent language learners are usually able to master explicit metacognitive strategies to support their language learning in the classroom and in the environment, younger children mostly make use of implicit learning mechanisms (Cook and Singleton 2014: 28, Murphy 2014: 5), potentially while watching films, listening to stories or playing games.

But if language-learning ability is not latent in the brain, not a hard-wired, instinctual capacity, but is a context-bound phenomenon, it follows that the language input and environment are key. This is a huge challenge in settings where there is little time for language learning, with classes just once or twice a week, and when – particularly for young learners – 'adequate exposure to the language is one of the essential conditions for successful language learning' (Rixon 2013: 29). Paradoxically, if children are implicit learners, but language acquisition is *not* innate, focus on form in language education – such as making multi-word chunks in literary texts salient through meaningful repetition, mirroring and recycling in stimulating and striking contexts – is crucial in instructed settings. Above all, the input must be learner-centred, such as stories, songs, games and so forth, so that children are motivated to understand, and will readily adopt high-frequency multi-word chunks in their own communications, using them according to Nick Ellis as 'phrasal teddy bears' (2012: 29).

However, high-quality, well-crafted input is key so that language learners can use their implicit mechanisms to acquire an inventory of grammatical categories and lexical patterns. The teacher therefore needs knowledge of and access to compelling literary texts to share with students, such as challenging picturebooks that are characterized by language artistry and skill and set in different cultural contexts. With the limited time available for teaching every input opportunity must be quality input! Ludovica Serratrice (2019: 35) argues: 'Quantity and quality input are strong predictors of children's early lexical skills, which in turn are closely related with emerging grammatical skills. Cultural practices like book reading, story-telling, and singing songs that are associated with larger vocabularies in monolingual children have also been found to be of importance in bilingual children.'

Language Learning as an Embodied Phenomenon

Neuroscientist Marco Iacoboni (2009: 91–2) examines embodied cognition: 'The fact that the major language area of the human brain is also a critical area for imitation *and contains mirror neurons* offers a new view of language and cognition in general. [...] The discovery of mirror neurons has strongly reinforced this hypothesis that cognition and language are embodied' (emphasis in original). In this way, Iacoboni argues that mirror neurons determine that our language experience is a social experience, for our embodied cognition ensures we accommodate to our conversation partners. Similarly, we bodily attune to our reading if the reading matter is compelling, for mirror neurons 'help us understand what we read by internally simulating the action we just read in the sentence' (2009: 94).

Iacoboni reasons that this is why we find it harder to speak alone, holding a monologue or speech, for example, even when we have plenty of time to prepare – much harder than to engage in conversation with a partner: 'Conversation is easier than monologue, and I believe the explanation is rooted in mirror neurons and imitation. During conversation, we imitate each other's expressions, even each other's syntactic constructions. [...] For instance, if one person engaged in a dialogue uses the word "sofa" rather than the word "couch," the other person engaged in the dialogue will do the same' (2009: 97–8). This insight reinforces that classrooms must aim for genuine exchanges and the community activity of booktalk in preference to demanding solo responses from students. This finding also helps explain why computer-mediated communication is more taxing and less stimulating than face-to-face exchanges, especially for less proficient speakers.

Considering that language learners imitate and mirror their conversation partners, language teachers have an important role, modelling the language the children are learning, modelling as motivated and successful learners themselves and modelling as motivated readers – also regularly reading aloud. Understanding that language use and language acquisition are embodied calls to mind the holistic or humanistic view of the learner. Geoff Hall (2015: 17) highlights this perspective: 'Humanistic views of the learner here replace laboratory-inherited ideas of "learning" (person vs. process). The emphasis moves from language as structures, lexis and phonology to language and meaning, language as discourse, which can support new ways of thinking, acting and being for the new language user.'

Usage-based Practices Supporting Pattern Recognition

Carmen Muñoz and Nina Spada (2019: 238) recommend motivating usage-based practices that are connected to story, 'activities such as interactive games, songs, reading aloud, and storytelling'. The patterned nature of most literary texts connects to concerns such as literacy (reading and writing skills) as well as oracy (listening and speaking skills). This supports discourse skills, while making language pleasurable and salient: 'The ability to understand, recall, and produce songs, rhymes, chants, and stories [...] are all examples of discourse skills' (Cameron 2003: 109). Psycholinguistically salient, curiosity-inviting language in literary texts will help the children notice the patterns. Language development can be accelerated by promoting adaptive-productive imitation of language patterns, for, as Larsen-Freeman (2011: 49) outlines: 'These patterns subsequently become part of learners' language resources, available for further use and modification.' Whereas formulaic sequences – fixed or semi-fixed expressions or multi-word chunks (see Figure 3.1) – raise awareness of underlying patterns (Wray 2002), many teachers focus on introducing single-word items removed from context, which Saskia Kersten (2015: 136–7) has called 'the noun problem', for meanings are fundamentally dependent on context.

The usage-based approach to language acquisition provides a valuable understanding of the role of context, formulaic language and usage in children and adolescents' language acquisition. This approach highlights the exemplar-based nature of language acquisition and how lexical and grammatical knowledge can *emerge* through engaging with extended input, 'with language, as with other cognitive realms, our experiences conspire to give us competence' (Ellis, O'Donnell and Römer 2013: 45). Kersten (2015: 135) voices the argument, 'usage-based approaches to L1 and L2 development hold that rules are abstracted solely from the input using general learning principles.' However, frequency and salience (which includes prominence of meaning and whether the feature – from a morpheme to a formulaic sequence – is easy to notice) are crucial. Repeated encounters with favourite picturebooks, chapter books and graphic novels with electrifying characters, and the exciting storyworlds of young adult fiction, which entice children and adolescents to revisit them again and again, are arguably the best way to gain the necessary salience and compelling input.

Usage frequency seems to be the ideal condition for input to become intake. Psycholinguistic research, according to Ellis et al. (2013: 30), 'provides the evidence of usage-based acquisition in its demonstrations that language processing is exquisitely sensitive to usage frequency at all levels of language representation'. Reiterations of meaningful language, for example in story retellings with the emphasis on meaning, lead to incidental language learning – perception and memory are affected by frequency of usage, helping language learners to tune into the system and notice patterns. Elementary school children have the advantage that their non-analytic processing mode can more easily, *with abundant input*, lead to the development of 'native-like grammatical intuitions' (Saville-Troike and Barto 2017: 89). Research studies by Kaminski (2016), Lugossy (2012) and Mourão (2016) have shown that if young learners' response is taken seriously in an approach that utilizes and values the multimodality of children's literature, then authentic communication emerges from the interaction between the learners, their books and their teacher.

Children's Literature as High-Quality Input

Well-crafted texts for children are characterized by gripping, aesthetic, challenging and above all vibrant and emotive language. As well as being more schema-related and linguistically appropriate for the target age group of young children or adolescents, multimodal literature for the young offers supportive visual iconicity through images, typographic experimentation and the auditory iconicity of onomatopoeia. In the case of young adult literature, there is often a paratext that includes blogs and multimodal reimaginings such as fanfiction on the web, helpfully supporting students' mental representations of the storyworld. While well-crafted children's literature is appropriate to the schemata of children, there must always be a challenge, a widening of horizons. There can be enriching intertextuality, and motivating, sometimes schema-refreshing allusions to the world of the child or young adult.

The optimal context that can challenge students to predict the meaning of new lexical items that they read or hear has been defined as *partly determining* (Krashen 1999: 12–14). The context of the language in a literary text includes the images in a multimodal text, the paratext (Genette 1997), which comprises the peritextual features of front and back covers, endpapers and endmatter in a nonfiction book, plus additionally sometimes masses of external material, such as reviews and fan websites. Pre-knowledge and world interest in the topic can also be included in the context. Too little helpful context will be insufficient to support the students' ability to predict meanings of words and formulaic sequences. Overdetermining context, on the other hand, reduces the demand to focus, notice and invest mental effort, all of which are important both for second language acquisition and for a literary apprenticeship generally. Gaps or indeterminacy, for example in postmodern literary texts and many multimodal texts, allow a creative response as contexts with tantalizing gaps remain partly determining. This might be compared to Stephen Krashen's concept of i + 1, which means challenging learners somewhat beyond their current level of language, or interlanguage, but not too far beyond.

We know that formulaic language is used extensively in the L1: 'corpus linguists have been able to show that language users make use of prefabricated language far more often than previously thought' (Kersten 2015: 130). However, English language learners, especially those with meagre L2 input, need support in perceiving, understanding and acquiring multi-word chunks or units. Used as single units in discourse, formulaic sequences facilitate fluency. Linguists use different names for these word strings, which include phrasal verbs, collocations and idioms (see Figure 3.1). The inclusion of

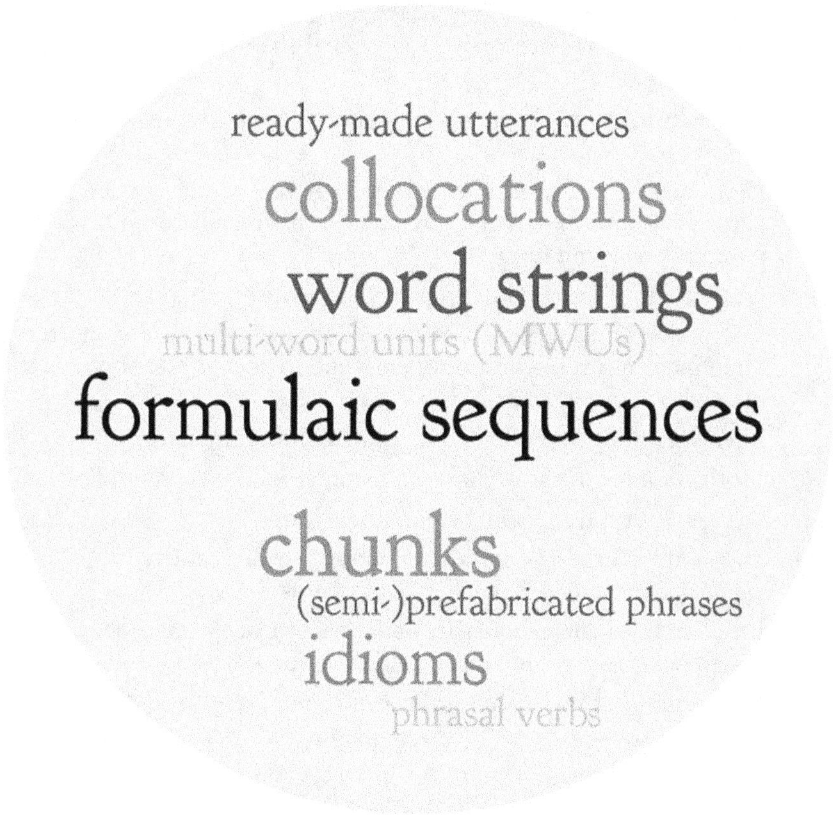

ready-made utterances
collocations
word strings
multi-word units (MWUs)
formulaic sequences

chunks
(semi-)prefabricated phrases
idioms
phrasal verbs

FIGURE 3.1 *Formulaic sequences: Different terms and types.*

accessible and appealing authentic stories – for example picturebooks, chapter books, young adult literature, verse novels, plays and graphic novels – rich in patterned language, with interest-igniting content, will strongly support the necessary recency, frequency and salience of language, as well as the surprise of novelty, that leads more readily to L2 acquisition.

Fifteen Reasons for Including Children's Literature in L2 Education

There are important reasons for including a focus on children's literature in language education (as well as language teacher education). These typically include providing:

1. High-quality language input, characterized by stylistic cohesion through marked lexical repetition, lexical chains, and the rhetorical rule of three.
2. Naturally idiomatic language and recurrence of multi-word chunks or formulaic sequences.
3. Phonological repetition, characteristically with strong sound patterning, such as dynamic rhythm, assonance, alliteration, onomatopoeia and refrains.
4. Opportunities for retellings – providing more essential reiteration.
5. Comprehension support through the cohesive context of compelling, often multimodal story that supports different cognitive styles, with pictures as a mental scaffold.
6. Interest-igniting and often challenging online paratext.
7. Motivation for dynamic and genuine interpersonal communication.
8. Occasion for intrapersonal communication.
9. Typographic experimentation and creative word choices, encouraging children's own creative writing.
10. Freedom from coursebook-driven language teaching and one-size-fits-all materials, potential for differentiation.
11. Opportunities for intercultural learning and perspective-taking when entering storyworlds and discovering different ways of living and being.
12. Encouragement of children's openness to difference, due to their 'weaker feelings of identity with people (other than close family or caregivers) who speak the same native language' (Saville-Troike and Barto 2017: 90).
13. Opportunities for connections across children's languages and their literacy development generally.
14. Children's own perspectives, noting that, as Peter Hunt (2018: xiii) writes: 'Even at its most abstract – and it can be very abstract – children's literature scholarship recognizes the essential presence of the child in the book, and equally recognizes the sophistication of even the apparently simplest text and the complexity of children's responses to texts.'
15. Last but not least, language teachers can also learn challenging new ideas and new language through children's literature.

Children's literature spans a wide spectrum from picturebooks for the very young to crossover literature that is enjoyed by adults as well as adolescents. While the motivation opportunities and extensive high-quality input of well-crafted young adult literature is well accepted for secondary school

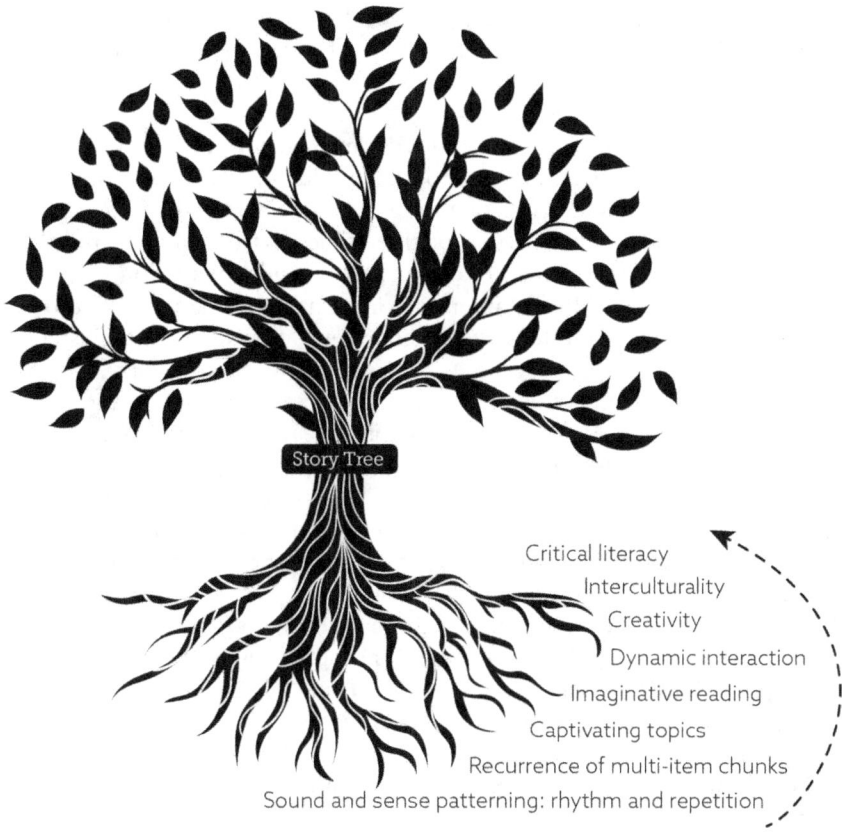

FIGURE 3.2 *Story Tree: Story potential as the roots of language growth.*

language learning, the opportunities for elementary language learners are less well known. Figure 3.2 provides an attempt to illustrate the strong foundational roots that compelling stories may offer for children's emerging language learning. The image of a Story Tree to symbolize language growth with its roots in stories seems apt. After all, stories are said to have begun the culture of humankind, and trees, owning the best carbon capture technology of all, may represent our best hopes for the future of humankind.

Repetition, Iteration but Not Duplication

Music is unthinkable without repetition, yet Philip Ball (2011: 124–5) highlights how, although 'music is *extraordinarily* repetitive [...] we never quite hear the same thing twice. It's clearly a different experience, for example, to hear a theme for the first time and then to find it returning some time later' (emphasis in original). Similarly for language, repetition can multiply meanings rather than duplicating and reducing them. Claire Kramsch (2009: 209) highlights the value of repetition as an educational device, and proposes:

> The same text, reread silently or aloud, can yield new meanings. The same utterance, repeated in various contexts, with different inflections, can index different emotions, evoke different associations. The same poem, memorised and performed two or three times in front of the same class, yields each time new pleasures of recognition and anticipation. The same story, told to three different interlocutors, can enable the storyteller to put different emphases on the same general theme depending on the listener.

The repetition of meaningful language patterns is essential for first and second language acquisition. At the same time, expressive reiterations of language can provide the reassurance of familiarity while accumulating layers of meaning. Teachers who are able to emphasize the language patterns in classroom interactions – repetitions and slight variations or fresh iterations of language in new contexts – can provide students with the opportunities for building associations around language, which we know is important for L2 acquisition. Choral speaking, readers theatre and drama are methods that include inbuilt reiterations of language that can lead to more depth of understanding (Winston 2022), as well as an implicit focus on form (Bland 2015b).

Literature, as well as music and language, relies on pattern. Literary repetition is, like music, a progressive recurrence of ideas and words, and not static. Michael Toolan (2008: 3, emphasis in original) considers repetition to be fundamental to literature:

> So *one* answer to the recurrent questions 'what makes literature literature?' and 'What is fundamental to the poetics of literature?' is, I believe, that literature exploits and privileges repetition – kinds of repetition, or repetitions with kinds of difference, but repetitions all the same. I think it is not difficult to characterize many literary schemes and tropes, for example, as forms of repetition: rhyme as partial phonic repetition, rhythm and metre as repetition of pulse or beat, assonance and alliteration as consonantal and vocalic repetition, and so on.

Renandya, Krashen and Jacobs (2018) report how extensive reading of compelling book series (usually out-of-school reading) strongly supports L2 acquisition. They argue this success is because popular series, often by the same author, tend to offer narrow reading with lexical repetition, and therefore can become 'a great source of comprehensible input and incidental vocabulary learning' (2018: 149). I suggest the repetition typical of book series that supports L2 acquisition is also likely to be related to genre characteristics in common and familiar-friendly characterization, which can further help students connect to and acquire new language, though potentially (depending on the series) offering fewer opportunities for deep reading or schema refreshment.

Oral storytelling also relies on repetition, using repetitive and additive language, repeated themes and often stock characters as techniques of remembering. Storytelling is an excellent way for language teachers to practise creative repetition, scaffolding and linguistic accommodation for their students, with the aid of creative teacher talk.

Creative Teacher Talk

The teacher can be a major source of language input, particularly with young learners, as Muñoz and Spada emphasize (2019: 246), 'the quality of input (e.g. teachers' language proficiency) is crucial at this very early age'. Thus, an important goal of language teacher education must be to help teachers master fluent language skills, as well as skills to cunningly scaffold language learners by using pattern-rich teacher talk that is modelled on child-directed speech, supporting children as seekers of meaningful patterns. Leo Selivan refers to 'teacher-led input flooding' (2018: 145) in his recommendation to language teachers to consider asking 'a lot of questions containing the same target pattern, in order to provide contextualized repetition'. This technique has the purpose to help students notice – that is to become consciously aware of – a linguistic feature such as a formulaic sequence or certain grammar pattern. Whereas Selivan's advice could be out of place for higher grades in secondary school if students can access abundant input in English and are gaining learner autonomy, it is essential guidance for most elementary L2 classes, and low-input contexts.

Creative teacher talk is a craft language teachers could gainfully practise, not only to help students enjoy oral stories, but also to help them to consciously register a target pattern or patterns in a story. Creative teacher talk is an important skill for teachers – for oral storytelling, picturebook read-alouds and classroom discourse generally. Creative teacher talk is interactive, highly repetitive and with chant-like routines and expressive prosodic features, including carefully modulated pitch, tempo, volume and rhythm to attract and hold attention and underline meanings. Depending on the topic, the teacher may make use of dramatic pauses and exuberant intonation. In addition, creative teacher talk is accompanied by the scaffolding of gestures and facial expressions, elaboration or reiteration of a point with slightly different words, a slower speech rate, additional contextual cues such as pictures, and realia – bringing physical objects into the classroom – as well as comprehension checks. The teacher extends and recasts children's incomplete responses, and maintains teacher-to-learner eye contact, shaping the talk to the audience of children or adolescents, for adolescents also enjoy listening to the teacher telling a story.

When the teacher shares a picturebook or tells a story, young children will offer many interjections in the language of schooling, or – if encouraged – sometimes in their home language if that differs from the language of schooling. Children will often quite naturally mirror the teacher's language if she recasts their interjections into English. Ideally teachers provide a running commentary in English as they demonstrate or supervise class activities. The children may echo their teacher's expressions quietly; they will also echo the words of the story. This murmured echoing, like young children's private speech, increases productive language usage in the very little time available and can help build up a repertoire of language patterns for imitation and adaptation (see also Annett Kaminski 2019).

Oral Storytelling

Saville-Troike and Barto (2017: 96) have documented certain personality traits that seem to be advantageous for successful L2 acquisition. The research is not entirely conclusive; however, the suggestion is that specific traits – imaginative, empathetic, tolerant of ambiguity, self-confident, risk-taking and adventuresome characteristics – correlate with more successful language learning. In their *Reference Framework of Competences for Democratic Culture*, the Council of Europe (2018a: 15) maintains that literature has a role to play beyond dialogue on specific issues, because literature addresses 'attitudes (such as tolerance of ambiguity and openness to cultural otherness) and skills (related to empathy, and flexibility and adaptability)'. Serafini (2005: 60) underlines the ability to tolerate ambiguity as a learner trait that enhances literary interpretation: 'I would suggest that those readers with a higher level of tolerance of ambiguity and uncertainty were more capable of making sense of meta-fictive elements.' These traits, which support language and literature learning as well as competences for democratic culture, are reinforced by a literary apprenticeship, engaging in story, responding to story and participating in a story event.

Oral storytelling makes use of the features of orality, including repetitive, additive and playful language (see also Chapter 7). Storytelling can make language features salient and offers the opportunity of pleasurable reiteration. Exercising oral storytelling in teacher education is a powerful means of supporting the craft of a language teacher. While oral storytelling is an ideal way for ongoing language teachers to practise creative teacher talk, unfortunately storytelling frequently plays next to no role in pre-service teacher education for language teachers (see Bland 2019).

Nasreddin Hodja stories offer a huge corpus of very short narratives that are suitable for oral storytelling. There are thousands of anecdotes told about the Hodja, which are usually funny, often wise and frequently with an educational twist. Nasreddin Hodja lived in the thirteenth century, probably in what is today Turkey, but these stories have become part of the folklore of very many nations throughout Asia as well as some European countries.

FIGURE 3.3 *Nasreddin Hodja and the magic pot.* Illustration © Elisabeth Lottermoser, used with permission of Contour Illustration & Grafik.

The story of Nasreddin Hodja and the magic pot is quite a typical one that I will retell as an example, for oral stories can best be retold in the teacher's own words, with repetition as necessary.

> Nasreddin Hodja decided one day to teach his rich neighbour a lesson. His neighbour happened to be the wealthiest man in the village, but also the meanest. For he never liked to share his good fortune and entertain his neighbours, despite having the most beautiful house, with a most spacious area for banquets and festivities. Nasreddin Hodja knocked one morning on his neighbour's door.
> 'My dear friend,' he said, 'please lend me your best cooking pot, for my entire family is dining with us today. I will need the biggest pot you have.'
> The neighbour tried to think of a thousand excuses for why he could not lend a pot to the Hodja. But in the end, he reluctantly agreed to lend

him the largest pot in his household, requiring its immediate return at daybreak the next day.

The Hodja was most punctual and returned the cooking pot first thing in the morning. 'What is this?', his neighbour exclaimed, 'there is a small pot inside my large one.'

'Oh yes,' replied the Hodja, 'the most wonderful event happened during the night. Your magical pot gave birth to this little child.'

The neighbour decided not to contradict the Hodja. He now had the nicest little pot inside his large one, and this had cost him nothing at all.

One week later, Nasreddin Hodja asked to borrow his neighbour's huge pot once again. This time his neighbour was happy to agree: 'Perhaps there will be another baby pot inside when he returns it,' he thought to himself.

However, the next day the Hodja returned to his neighbour without the pot, but with the gravest face. 'My dear friend,' he said, 'I have the saddest news. Your most illustrious pot has died, and I have buried her.'

'What nonsense,' the neighbour shouted, 'pots do not die. Return my pot at once!'

'Dear friend,' the Hodja responded, 'you know that your most splendid pot is capable of wonders. Recently she gave birth to a child, the finest little pot that you still have. But if a pot can give birth to a child, then sadly she must also die one day.'

This anecdote illustrates how oral storytelling can be used to focus on a chosen form, in this case the superlative. On hearing this story for the first time, lower secondary-school students are likely to concentrate more on the story of the tricky Hodja than on the language, they will need help in noticing the different instances of the superlative, fifteen in all, when the teacher retells the story. On the retelling, students could be invited to raise their hands each time they hear a superlative. When they have discovered all the superlatives, they can be invited to practise their own versions of the story (in groups of three, the Hodja, a neighbour and a narrator) choosing if possible some different superlatives for their retelling.

Working with student teachers, I encourage them to practise the storytelling role at home, perhaps in front of a mirror, to try out their creative teacher talk. Storytelling skills need practice, but this is also good training for imaginative, self-confident, risk-taking and adventuresome personality traits.

Ideology in Language Education, Agency and Canonical Issues

The fields of English language education and children's literature pedagogy are naturally immersed in ideology issues, as international discourse and texts from around the world are relevant for both. English in school settings is centrally situated both in education and in global issues, so that pedagogy and ideology are inextricably linked. Leland, Lewison and Harste (2013: 13) emphasize that trying to avoid all sensitive, potentially controversial and contentious issues in the classroom means taking sides: 'Because the books we as teachers choose to use or *decide not to use* is a pervasive and subtle form of censorship' (emphasis in original). Reading, which can be developed in the classroom as a community literacy event, cannot be entirely separated from the sociocultural context of the event, just as any text reflects the sociocultural context in which it was created. A literacy event in the classroom is social practice and process, and both ideology and sociocultural identities play important roles.

Ideology refers to socially acquired and shared thought and belief systems that underlie social practices and lived experience. These habits of thought, ideas and attitudes are often embedded in group interests and unexamined assumptions that are taken for granted. Alistair Pennycook (1999: 346) sees critical approaches to English language teaching 'rather as complex clusters of social, cultural, political, and pedagogical concerns' and 'located at the very heart of some of the most crucial educational, cultural, and political issues of our time'. In children's literature scholarship, ideology is a central concern. All texts, wherever and whenever they are produced, are pervaded by ideology, which, of course, will influence the reader, who may be young and very impressionable. Naturally, this also applies to coursebooks for language teaching and textbooks for whatever age group and topic. This includes the present book, for children's literature scholar John Stephens (2010b: 192) writes 'an ideology-free text is unthinkable'. He then goes on to reflect that 'many overtly interrogative texts also encourage audiences to think critically about the ideals they advocate because all ideologies are socially and historically contingent'.

In contrast to the quite widely held research interests into ideology in children's literature scholarship (see Chapter 2: 32–34), in English language teaching 'a widespread naturalized assumption in the field', according to Seyyed-Abdolhamid Mirhosseini (2018: 5), 'is that pedagogical traditions are based on no ideological beliefs'. Mirhosseini outlines 'how the mainstream ideology has continued to survive and reproduce itself through self-proclaimed non-ideological focus on professional and pedagogical purposes' (2018: 6). This can indeed often be observed in the practice of English teaching in schools and at university, even if it does not truly represent the theory of language teaching since Pennycook's observation more than two decades ago (1999: 346), 'I like to see critical approaches always in flux, always questioning, restively problematizing aware of the limits of their own knowing, and bringing into schemas of politicisation.'

A student's agency is strongly connected to ideology issues. Paulo Freire is the great twentieth-century educator who immediately comes to mind when considering the agency of students, his insistence on their empowering their imaginations, their learning to read both the word and the world as the way to be fully integrated in the struggle for critical agency and social justice. According to Freire (1985: 19), critical pedagogy begins already with young children, who 'should come full of spontaneity – with their feelings, with their questions, with their creativity, with their risk to create, getting their own words "into their own hands" in order to do beautiful things with them. The basis for critical reading in young children is their curiosity'. How students are positioned is determined to some extent by the imposition of ideology; for example, an individual's subject position is partly constructed at different times through family, peer groups, social class, ethnicity and gender expectations, but also through texts they read.

Questions on canonical literature in school and university are also connected to ideology. Who prescribes texts for English language education in school settings and at university? Are they too aligned with dominant cultural groups, with the West, potentially with 'dead White men'? As Mike Fleming writes (2007: 31), 'the canon is often accused by its critics of representing ethnocentric values which are antagonistic to diversity or of embodying absolute and ahistorical judgements which cannot be sustained.' From an educational perspective, students' engaged and agentic response to a compelling narrative on contemporary global issues is more valuable than apathy and rejection of a time-honoured canonical text that may only work well for readers who are both mature and proficient. Fleming (2007: 37) summarizes strong arguments against a traditional canon,

> 'specifically that it:
>
> - is insensitive to the diverse nature of contemporary societies;
> - underestimates the significance of pedagogy in the classroom;
> - ignores the challenge of engaging the interest of young people;
> - embodies an essentialist conception of literature that ignores the importance of context;
> - assumes that judgements of quality are straightforward and uncontested;
> - undervalues the professional judgements of teachers'.

This does not mean that quality and challenge do not play a role in the choice of reading. The texts I focus on in this book are aimed at children and young adults and have been published recently; they are texts that can support creativity, interculturality and critical literacy development at a stage when young people may be deeply immersed and experienced in virtual worlds but still lack understanding of the real world. For educational purposes, the notion of teaching literacy in a collaborative sense, rather than teaching literature in a knowledge-transmission sense, is centrally important: 'In teaching literacy, we are assuming a purpose or reason for reading; we are looking at reading as communication and at what readers will do with what they read – or what writers do with writing' (Paran and Wallace 2016: 442). Similarly, Jelena Bobkina and Svetlana Stefanova (2016: 679) in discussing critical literacy pedagogy, suggest 'the method implies teaching students to read texts in an active, reflective manner for a better understanding of power, inequality, and injustice in human relationships'.

In some countries, as Fleming writes (2007: 33, emphasis in original), 'publishers may have an influence on the *de facto* canon not just in their choice of core texts and how they market them but also in relation to the availability of auxiliary texts of criticism'. When teachers provide lacking background knowledge to their students – rather than encouraging students' own investigations – and trust publishers' auxiliary texts as the 'right' interpretation, they have unwittingly chosen a simplistic solution, blocking opportunities for dialogic, deep reading. In this way, what is often called canonical literature can be decidedly *less challenging* in the classroom than literature aimed at a younger audience.

In some English language education curricula, such as in Norway (Utdanningsdirektoratet 2020), children's literature, including picturebooks for younger grades and young adult literature for older grades, is included as part of the syllabus. No stipulations are made as to which literary texts should be used. This could be excellent for teacher autonomy in deciding the best for each class. Unfortunately, this can also lead to a *de facto* canon of weaker choices – for example books chosen previously may years later be the only books available due to limited school budgets and limited teacher time to prepare new lessons. Deep reading requires a teacher who can expertly select the right book for an entire class of differently sophisticated readers and language learners at just the right time. Teacher education should have a role to play in supporting such preparation and choices, but often does not fulfil this responsibility (Bland 2019). A balance of extensive reading (with the help of school or local libraries) and well-selected deep reading is probably more cost-effective than the expensive coursebooks and activity books that are purchased in many countries year in and year out. To this end, an understanding of the benefits of both extensive reading and deep reading should accompany all pedagogical and financial decisions on teaching English in language education.

While children need help noticing the language patterns in the stories the teacher brings into the classroom, teachers need assistance in discovering and selecting the materials that are most conducive to supporting children's and adolescents' language growth, their intercultural understanding and development towards multiple literacies. Second language learners may have concepts and interests well beyond their interlanguage, or current productive English-language skills, which creates a challenge for the teacher. Children's and adolescents' ideas and aspirations can be highly developed, so that teachers need the knowhow to bridge the gap between the cognitive level and the less developed linguistic skills of students by selecting the 'right' story. It is imperative that teachers are given the opportunity to learn, as Gail Ellis (2018: 84) expresses it, that 'real success depends on having the right story for the linguistic and cognitive ability and interests of the children in order to maximize their enjoyment, involvement and learning'. It is apparent that, to be able to make effective use of children's literature, teachers need in-depth guidance in extending their own literary competence, their own visual literacy, critical literacy and response to multimodal texts, in order to learn how to support, scaffold and recast students' responses to story.

Arizpe, Farrar and McAdam (2017: 377) argue that a key purpose of teacher education is to develop teacher knowledge: 'Knowing how picturebooks work and how to make multimodal meaning will lead to confident educators, mediators and other professionals who can critically select texts that develop "literacies" required for twenty-first-century life.' These literacies include not only functional literacy, but also digital literacy, information literacy, literary literacy, media literacy, visual literacy and critical literacy – competences that must be trained across the curriculum, as outlined in Chapter 1. Just as the literacy needs of our students are evolving, so are the many formats and genres of literary texts in English, and it is undoubtedly the English classroom that offers most opportunities for multiple literacy training due to the enormous diversity of English-language texts. Now, in the twenty-first century, we can be sure that the majority of readers of narrative texts in English are not native speakers of English. Then whose stories should we be reading about? Why should British and North American texts be prioritized over global literatures written in English? Children's literature appears in English, besides books published in indigenous languages, in very many countries around the world, including Nigeria and South Africa, Hawai'i, India, Singapore, Malaysia and Jamaica (see Stephens et al. 2018).

Scholars contend that the neglect of children's literature as an educational resource must now change, for, as Nikolajeva (2014: 227) claims, 'successful children's fiction challenges its audiences cognitively and affectively, stimulating attention, imagination, memory, inference-making, empathy and all other elements of mental processes'. Unfortunately, in most contexts children's literature plays an extremely limited or non-existent role in teacher education for language teachers. Equally, suitable literary texts tend to be little known by applied linguists, who are frequently the designers of courses in teacher education for language teachers.

The understanding of children's literary texts today strives to be global and inclusive, around themes such as cultural diversity, multilingualism, LGBTQ+ issues, the environment and social justice, featuring children with disabilities, in minoritized and refugee situations (Bland 2016, Leland, Lewison and Harste 2013, Oziewicz 2015). At the same time, a persistent belief remains in some contexts, partly due to institutional inaction in teacher education contexts and often in contradiction to the relevant school curriculum, that the learning of vocabulary and grammar is central to English learning rather than usage-based language development and a focus on multiple literacies. While traditionalists in teacher education may benefit from the stasis of tacit consensus, it should be remembered that tolerance of ambiguity, openness to cultural otherness, empathy, flexibility, adaptability and imagination are important attitudes for successful second language acquisition, that an early literary apprenticeship encourages such attitudes, that developing these attitudes is said to support competences for democratic culture (Council of Europe 2018a), and that a self-confident, adventuresome, engaged, autonomous and thoughtful teaching profession necessitates full support in these areas.

PART TWO
Visual Literacy and Interculturality

CHAPTER FOUR

Early Steps in Literature Learning with Picturebooks

The picturebook has over the last several decades developed into a highly sophisticated multimodal format. Yet, while challenging picturebooks are increasingly popular for all age groups (Ommundsen, Haaland and Kümmerling-Meibauer 2022), the picturebook can still be considered the quintessential children's literature format. Perry Nodelman (2010: 10) names the picturebook as 'the one kind of narrative invented specifically for children [which] might then represent the formal characteristics of children's literature in their most essential and characteristic form'. Connecting visual and verbal art, the picturebook offers many opportunities for cross-curricular teaching, however lack of experience of a wide range of texts, among teacher educators as well as teachers, undoubtedly impedes the move towards including the picturebook more widely for language and literature learning (Narančić Kovač 2016).

These days, the use of the internet and social media already among elementary students may offer a flood of attention-consuming content along with increasing opportunities for access to English. Constant access to online content that is both instant and fragmentary will, however, suppress the all-important slower processes of thinking through problems. This is also relevant for language learning. Curiosity is a vital attribute that is critical for learning as it serves to motivate children (and adults) to seek knowledge and understanding. Nicholas Carr describes (2020: 235) an 'ideal of knowledge as something self-created, something woven of the facts, ideas, and experiences gathered in the individual mind'. He warns this ideal continues to recede, which suggests all the more the need for in-depth learning with literary texts in the classroom. Moreover, books must be physically accessible for children – to leaf through in quiet moments, to treasure – only in this way can a book become a friend. This chapter proposes some thoughtful steps that could be taken with picturebooks, introducing exemplars with themes of social or environmental justice.

The Potential of the Picturebook

The picturebook format is extremely versatile. Picturebooks can be both fiction and nonfiction, traditional narratives or postmodern, as when the pictures and words tell somewhat different stories with resulting indeterminacy or ambiguity. The picturebook is essentially defined by the interaction or interanimation between the words and pictures as vital to the meaning-making process, and in many picturebooks there are complex opportunities for discovery and interpretation of meanings that are created by the combinations of pictures, verbal text, typographic creativity, layout and overall design. However, there are also wordless picturebooks, which tend to make clever narrative use of the interaction between the pictures and their layout on the spreads. As Evelyn Arizpe and Sadie Ryan (2018) show, the wordless picturebook invites participation to fill the enigmatic gaps, enticing co-authoring and inspiring creative writing.

As an artefact rich in meaning and potential dialogic spaces, picturebooks can offer excellent opportunities for multiple literacy learning and an early start to a literary apprenticeship. Increasingly scholars working in the area of picturebook scholarship and early language learning encourage teachers, as Sandie Mourão (2016: 39) suggests, 'to select picturebooks at the more complex end of the picture-word dynamic, so that learners are challenged to think and fill the gaps between the pictures and the words'.

Picturebooks can be deliberately indeterminate and even enticingly secretive. During booktalk the picturebook reveals its story and the students create an understanding of its secrets gradually, layer by layer, through the non-linear characteristic of reading pictures that may reveal something freshly meaningful to negotiate on each new reading. It is this roundabout negotiation of understanding that makes even a wordless picturebook extremely valuable for language learning and for encouraging thinking dispositions generally. A generative dialogic discourse will allow a progression to take place on many fronts between the readings: language development and cognitive development of the readers, and visual literacy of the teacher as well as the young learners.

The Role of the Teacher

Ingenious picturebooks can perplex teachers and children alike, stimulating teachers to ask open questions and avoid display questions, constructing booktalk and shared interpretation. Children's literature scholar and educationalist Lawrence Sipe (2008a: 143) accentuates the need for booktalk to be an exploration, not a test: 'Teachers should rarely ask questions to which they know the answer – these are really pseudo-questions, more suited to testing than to teaching. Open-ended questions that encourage inference and multiple possible answers are the key.' Open questions can kindle children's confidence in their own reading response as there are no ready-made answers of what is a right or wrong interpretation. Sipe advises teachers not to pre-prepare too many questions, 'an abundance of purpose-setting questions establishes one thing: that you as the teacher are in charge, and that you have a definite "agenda". In a way, this immediately cuts children off from the speculative, hypothesizing stance we want to encourage in order to promote their visual interpretive abilities' (2008a: 142). Peterson and Eeds (2007: 86–7) also argue for spontaneity and responsive teaching: 'Opportunities for literary teachable moments occur in every literature study group. Our task as aware critics and group leaders is to recognize these moments and seize the opportunity to build upon them – hence our stress on the use of responsive teaching rather than on a set strategy.'

Sipe (2008a: 143–4) has suggested that successful teachers have at least five roles to fulfil when reading with children, which I have adapted somewhat in the following for contexts with language learners. Teachers are *readers of the text*: they read the picturebook aloud, bringing it to life, interacting with the text, illustrations and students in making sense while implicitly or explicitly drawing attention to meaningful features. Teachers are *encouragers*: they give praise and support, recasting and expanding language, encouraging children to listen to each other, to respond and take risks. Teachers are *clarifiers*: they nudge students to share and articulate their ideas in some detail, so as to reach higher levels of pooled ideas and interpretation. Teachers are *fellow speculators*: they demonstrate tolerance of ambiguity by allowing uncertainty and asking genuine questions with different answers that may be equally plausible. Teachers are *extenders*: they take advantage of teaching opportunities as they arise spontaneously, making use of teachable moments to discuss a new idea, a new literary feature or help students notice new language.

Beyond the roles that Sipe outlined, experienced teachers supporting language learners develop several additional roles. Importantly, teachers are *language modellers*: they recognize and highlight the most useful and exciting grammatical and lexical features in the picturebook, bringing the new language into the classroom discourse when introducing the story, modelling the new language when asking questions and recasting answers, and reiterating the language in different contexts and in subsequent lessons. Teachers are also *teacher-actors*: they use a wide scaffolding repertoire to support understanding and creative teacher talk (see Chapter 3), which includes gesture, facial expressions, adapting prosodic features such as tempo, tone of voice, intonation, stress and rhythm, potentially also using realia and pictures to support meaning.

Picturebook Characters and Book Friends

Stories are mediated by the characters, and their emotions and experiences are the driving force, a phenomenon known as protagonism (Brown et al. 2019; see Chapter 2: 44–6). Picturebook characters, with their own bewitching, moving and enlightening stories, come alive for young learners, appealing simultaneously to the cognitive, affective and sociocultural dimensions of language learning. As artist Christiane Krömer (2014), illustrator of *King for a Day* (see pp. 84–5), writes, 'a good illustration can give flavor and sustenance to a story by visually depicting the human depth of its characters.' Wonderful characters in picturebooks support young readers in bonding with favourite books, which can help children defeat the reading blip – when many, around the age of twelve, reject reading for pleasure. A good variety of picturebooks (which are much cheaper to purchase than coursebooks) in schools and school libraries could vastly improve educational opportunities through story.

Unfortunately, the concept of a school library is not clearly defined, and varies from a wonderfully stocked, comfortable space to a single, uninviting bookcase in a corridor or cellar room – in Europe I have seen far more of the latter in schools. Children who do not have books at home live in book poverty in most countries worldwide, and lose the best opportunity – while they are young – to learn how to make book friends. Judith Graham (2005: 209) emphasizes the importance of an early literary experience: 'Picturebooks are almost invariably the first books that children encounter. This means that they shape aesthetic tastes, and introduce the principles and conventions of narrative. […] picturebooks are a vital part of artistic and literary culture, but they are also witty, entertaining and part of the child's world of play.'

The importance of character means that biography, autobiography and memoirs can also be excellent choices for language and literature learning. The multimodal biographies selected for this book focus on factuality over fictionality yet integrate information in a narrative, imaginative manner that strongly supports mental representation and empathy. In this chapter, picturebooks are introduced around the child world changers Louis Braille, Malala and Greta Thunberg, as well as coral reef hero Ken Nedimyer. Whether fictional or factual, well-told stories make us human, for, as Jonathan Gottschall puts it (2012), we are the *storytelling animal*.

Using the Deep Reading Framework with Malala Yousafzai and Kerascoët's *Malala's Magic Pencil*

Malala Yousafzai has written an inspiring story, based on her own childhood experiences, with delicate and beautiful illustrations by a husband-and-wife team who use the pseudonym Kerascoët. The following ideas are meant as suggestions (not directives!) for making use of the deep reading framework introduced in Chapter 1: 23–7, with *Malala's Magic Pencil* (Yousafzai 2017).

Unpuzzle and Explore

With 48 pages, *Malala's Magic Pencil* is rather longer than the typical 32-page picturebook, but otherwise is representative of the picturebook format. *Malala's Magic Pencil* has expressive front and back covers as well as meaningful endpapers that can be brought into the discussion. There is peritextual framing, with endmatter that includes a letter from Malala as the author, additional details of her life and a few family photos, indicating that this is a factual story. As children become less and less used to reading print books, it is important to point out the characteristics as well as pleasures of different story formats. It seems the printed book is becoming an unfamiliar object in many children's lives.

The genre is autobiography, and Malala tells her own story sensitively and gently, emphasizing the elements of hope, strength and resilience, and downplaying the violence she faced at the age of fifteen. Nonetheless, in order to discover wider meanings with the students, I would read this with children who are old enough to be interested in the global implications. When I shared the book with ten-year-old English language learners, even the reluctant readers were moved by the power and magic of Malala's story and were interested in learning more about her. In many language learning contexts, however, this picturebook may be more suitable, and is not too simplistic, for older groups.

The classroom exploration could begin by inviting students to interpret the golden designs that emerge from Malala's magic pencil on the picturebook cover; see Figure 4.1. The visually magical endpapers that frame the book are also worth spending time on. At first glance they seem to be covered in a pattern of white flowers over a shimmering gold background. If invited to look carefully, the students soon notice, however, that what appear as open blossoms are actually circular patterns of exercise books and pencils flowering across the pages. In this way, the symbolic pattern begins and ends the book thematically on a very important message for our times – the power of the pen and communication over fighting and violence. Kerascoët's exquisite watercolour-and-ink illustrations in pastel colours describe the settings of Malala's family and school life in northwest Pakistan in detail, while the gold ink designs that recreate Malala's childhood hopes and dreams immediately attract the students' attention.

Malala's Magic Pencil opens with 'Do you believe in magic?', and she explains how as a child she wished she had a magic pencil like that of a boy in a favourite TV show she watched with her brothers. She imagines: 'If I had

FIGURE 4.1 *Cover of* Malala's Magic Pencil. *Artwork by Kerascoët from* Malala's Magic Pencil *by Malala Yousafzai published by Puffin. Cover and interior illustrations by Kerascoët. Cover art © Salarzai Limited, 2017. Cover design by Sasha Illingworth. Cover copyright © Hachette Book Group and in Great Britain by Puffin Books 2017. Reprinted by permission of Penguin Books Limited.*

a magic pencil, I would use it to … put a lock on my door, so my brothers couldn't bother me' and '… stop time, so I could sleep an extra hour every morning'. Lots of ideas and golden illustrations of Malala's dreams follow. The dreamy nature of Malala's wishes are realized in gold ink drawings that enchantingly overlay the more realistic street settings depicting the cultural diversity of Pakistan, with characters wearing hijabs, salwar kameezes, burqas and occasionally Western-style dress. At this point students can be invited to think-pair-share in order to create their own special wishes. Some of these can then be shared in words as well as visually through drawing or using mime, each time introduced by the prompt – as a useful focus on form – *If I had a magic pencil, I would use it to…* .

As she grows older, Malala comes to recognize the inequality of opportunity around her, due to gender and sometimes due to poverty. Her father tells her, 'in our country not everyone sends their daughters to school', and soon Malala's magic-pencil wishes become the mighty dreams of an adolescent: 'if I had the magic pencil […] I would erase war, poverty and hunger. Then I would draw girls and boys together as equals.' Now, the think-pair-share activity could be repeated, with the suggestion of wishes connected to global issues and human rights. This can be developed into think-pair-square, when two pairs join in a group of four to share their ideas. While the global problems may currently seem insoluble, this activity may also encourage resilience, ambition and vision.

Activate and Investigate

Magic woven together with truth is quintessential storytelling. The tone of the picturebook darkens when Malala explains in brief words: 'But soon powerful and dangerous men declared that girls were forbidden from attending school. They walked the streets of our city now. They carried weapons.' Due to recent events, students can probably contribute some information on the Taliban, a fundamentalist Sunni Islamic military movement now in control in Afghanistan and influential in neighbouring Pakistan. The organization has been condemned internationally for its brutality, often directed towards civilian targets and fierce repression of women. Pakistan shares a long border with Afghanistan, and an armed group of local Pakistani Taliban caused terror in Malala's home city. The students sharing Malala's story do not need much detail, as the story is about overcoming violence through the power of words, not about the attack. Malala explains how she learned to speak out, inspired by her father, Ziauddin Yousafzai, who is an education activist. In his TED Talk recorded in 2014, Ziauddin refers to 'Talibanization. It means a complete negation of women's participation in all political, economical and social activities.'

Gracefully and with pictures as much as with words, *Malala's Magic Pencil* shows how Malala learned to use her voice for the right of education, writing a blog for BBC Urdu, composing speeches, using different platforms for her campaign and even sharing her experience internationally in English. Suddenly, the next picturebook page is stark black: 'My voice became so powerful that dangerous men tried to silence me.' On the opposite page, Malala stands at a window. We do not see her face, but we spot her hospital gown and bracelet. The combination of deep black on the verso and the sombre hospital scene on the recto is a hint that students can understand. Some may want to investigate the horrific attack and report back to the class: a Pakistani Taliban gunman made an assassination attempt on Malala in 2012 and shot her in the head when she was travelling home on the school bus. Mercifully Malala survived, and she tells how her fame now created a chorus of voices in a rising crescendo around the world. A double-page spread illustrates the protesting crowds and their placards with slogans supporting Malala's campaign, such as 'WE STAND WITH MALALA' and 'EDUCATION FOR ALL!'

The students could create a large classroom campaign poster, inspired by the picturebook. Different images can be included, for example a picture of Malala, of other children and of peace symbols. Norwegian eighth-grade students were very impressed by the shiny all-black page representing the attack on Malala. Similar black pages could also form a part of the collage, and students then create their own catchy slogans connected to human rights and social justice and write these on pieces of paper representing banners or placards which they stick onto the classroom poster. In demonstrations on global issues worldwide, slogans are very often written in English to attract maximum publicity. A classroom or school poster, however, could feature slogans in the different home languages of the students *and* in English, to emphasize the aspect of human rights for all. Some students might also investigate the gold medallion on the book cover: 'Winner of the Nobel Peace Prize', and what this represents. They will discover that Malala was, in 2014, the youngest ever recipient of the prize.

Critically Engage

Malala shows with her story and her writing campaign that young people can have a strong voice and can make a difference. She advocates for education, and particularly girls' education, across the world for she understands that education is powerful. As Martha Nussbaum writes (2004: 332):

> If there was a time when illiteracy was not a barrier to employment, that time has passed. The nature of the world economy is such that illiteracy condemns a woman (or man) to a small number of low-skilled types of employment. With limited employment opportunities, a woman is also limited in her options to leave a bad or abusive marriage. If a woman can get work outside the home, she can stand on her own.

Education is a human right

The majority of illiterate adults worldwide are women, for in many countries girls do not even have equal access to elementary education and basic, functional literacy. Students might create mind-map posters of the uses of literacy. This activity can begin with a brainstorming session on choosing the most important categories that radiate from the central notion of functional

EARLY STEPS IN LITERATURE LEARNING WITH PICTUREBOOKS

literacy. The first set of four or five relevant concepts that branch out from the key notion of literacy should be quite general.

A group of my student teachers (preparing to introduce *Malala's Magic Pencil* in the eighth grade in Norway) chose their literacy-related categories as: WORK, SOCIAL AND FAMILY LIFE, INFORMATION, INDEPENDENCE, PERSONAL GROWTH and PLEASURE (see Figure 4.2). Once a class has chosen the main categories, student groups create mind-map posters by first drawing these branching out from the central node of functional literacy, then debating on the subcategories that branch out further. The choice of subcategories will vary from group to group. A gallery walk following this activity will encourage students to reflect on the perspectives of the other groups. They can post sticky notes on their agreement, disagreement or on new ideas as they rotate from poster to poster.

Malala explains how she worked hard at school every day, aware that not all children could go to school. It is worth discussing the double-page spread showing Malala's classroom before Talibanization stopped the girls from attending school. The girls sit in rows at their desks, they wear school uniform, no books are visible but they appear curious, attentive, interested, respectful and alert. The atmosphere is dignified – just as Nussbaum has written (2004: 335): 'what is at stake in literacy is no mere skill but human dignity itself and the political and social conditions that make it possible for people to live with dignity.' In a final letter to the reader, Malala writes:

> Once, I wished for Sanju's magic pencil. Now I know that when you find your voice, every pencil can be magic.
>
> I hope that my story inspires you to find the magic in your own life and to always speak up for what you believe in. Magic is everywhere in the

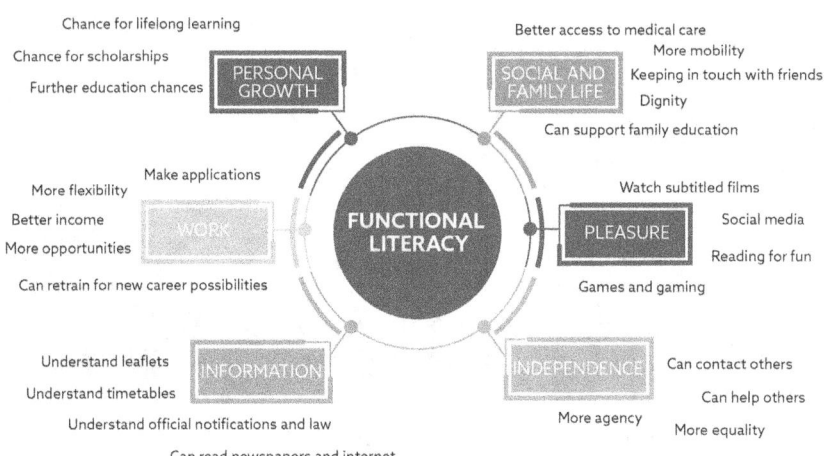

FIGURE 4.2 *Functional literacy mind map (Norwegian student teachers).*

world – in knowledge, beauty, love, peace. The magic is in you, in your words, in your voice.

(Yousafzai 2017)

A story can leave a stronger impression than a teacher's explanations (Heggernes 2022: 177). It is therefore important, wherever possible, to maintain the principle of multivoicedness by introducing a text ensemble. It is too easy to essentialize countries if we base our teaching on a single story. *Malala's Magic Pencil* is autobiographical, and has a symbolic focus on issues of literacy, agency and empowerment of women. Introducing an additional picturebook with a setting in Pakistan will help to avoid creating a single story around a multifaceted country, that is the fifth most populous in the world and with the second-largest Muslim population, after Indonesia.

Khan and Krömer's *King for a Day*

My suggestion for a partner picturebook set in Pakistan is *King for a Day* (2014), by Rukhsana Khan and illustrated by Christiane Krömer. *King for a Day* is about Basant, a spring festival of kites that is celebrated across South Asia. The story is set in Lahore, one of the largest and culturally richest cities in Pakistan. The beautiful collages in the picturebook include gorgeous Pakistani fabrics and different paper textures, portraying the colourful kites that soar and swirl against the skyline in the kite-flying competition, and present a vivid picture of the Walled City of Lahore (Figure 4.3). The story is quite short and

FIGURE 4.3 *Walled City of Lahore. From* King for a Day *by Rukhsana Khan © 2013, illustrations by Christiane Krömer © 2013. Permission arranged with Lee & Low Books Inc., New York, NY 10016. All rights reserved.*

easy to follow, around Malik, a wheelchair user who creates his own kite, then flies it from the rooftop with such skill and dexterity that he defeats all other kites to become the kite-flying festival king.

Bryant and Kulikov's *Six Dots: A Story of Young Louis Braille*

A further picturebook, this time a biography of a French child hero, would work well in the text ensemble. Louis Braille was only fifteen when he developed the revolutionary tactile code to enable the blind and visually impaired to read and write, a system still used to this day, and named braille after the inventor. There are several connections to Malala's story: the youthfulness, resourcefulness and bravery of young Louis, who became blind due to an accident at the age of three, his yearning for literacy and his understanding of the importance of communication. Olstrom (2011: unpaginated) cites Louis Braille's words on the situation of the blind in 1841:

> Access to communication in the widest sense is access to knowledge, and that is vitally important for us if we are not to go on being despised or patronized by condescending sighted people. We do not need pity, nor do we need to be reminded we are vulnerable. We must be treated as equals – and communication is the way this can be brought about.

Braille's words are a powerful argument against ableism. Jen Bryant's picturebook, illustrated by Boris Kulikov, is written in the first person as if Louis is telling his own story. The picturebook begins with colourful scenes of French village life in the early nineteenth century, but the first page after Louis loses his sight is stark black – and from then on Kulikov frequently uses a black background to illustrate how the child gradually learns to sense the world around him without sight, allowing the reader to get a feeling for his different perceptual experiences. After years of struggle and desperately wanting to read, Louis succeeds with his invention of braille: 'I worked until my back was stiff and my fingers ached. Often, I fell asleep a few minutes before morning.' The peritextual framing – with front- and endmatter giving more details on braille and Louis Braille's life as well as references and links to useful websites – indicates this is a nonfiction story despite the narrative technique of creating a first-person narrator (see also *The Life of Frederick Douglass: A Graphic Narrative of a Slave's Journey from Bondage to Freedom* in Chapter 6). The use of peritextual information to establish a book as nonfiction is common in children's books, 'to establish the information character of the book, confirm the factuality and accuracy of the information presented in what seems a fictional guise, and build authorial credibility' (von Merveldt 2018: 241).

Experiment with Creative Response

These three picturebooks revolve around children who are exceptionally brave and creative under very difficult circumstances – Malala and Louis Braille, as well as Malik, a wheelchair user who overcomes a bully and wins the day to become the Basant festival king. The settings are important in these stories, but particularly the inspiring determination and vision of the three characters (one of whom is fictive) are memorable. Students can be invited to create their own picturebook biography around a favourite character – perhaps a local hero or historical figure. Younger students might create an imagined autobiography of a story character about whom we know few details – such as the fairy godmother, the wicked wolf or Anansi. An autobiography is written in the first person, like the three picturebooks in this text ensemble. The children could write either in English or in their home language, which may or may not be the language of schooling, for if the follow-up interactions on the picturebooks are in English, the pictures, with help from the child author, should enable the teacher and other students to understand and enjoy the story.

If students can research online, the picturebook creation around child heroes past and present might be conducted in teams of three: the biographer who looks up some background details, the illustrator and the author. Apart from child heroes Louis Braille, Malala and Greta Thunberg, students might be interested in child world changers, artists and activists such as Pelé, Marley Dias, Helen Keller, Kelvin Doe, Anne Frank, Sophie Cruz, Melati and Isabel Wijsen, Claudette Colvin, Zuriel Oduwole, Anoyara Khatun, Xiuhtezcatl Martinez and Wolfgang Amadeus Mozart. The students could be encouraged to choose an epigraph or motto for their picturebook. *Malala's Magic Pencil* ends with Malala's catchphrase, the words she addressed to the United Nations in 2013: 'One child, one teacher, one book and one pen can change the world.'

Environmental Awareness – a Topic for Young Learners

Children are still very much involved in discovering the world – in particular the natural world – and their embeddedness in nature can be seen as an empowering source of strength. Greg Garrard (2012: 24) refers to 'the dualistic separation of humans from nature promoted by Western philosophy and culture', and that this is understood by many as the origin of the environmental crisis. John Stephens (2010a: 169) argues, 'humanity's anthropocentric assumptions privilege culture over nature, and this practice was exacerbated both in children's literature and its criticism by the domination of discourses around individual maturation that keep the human subject forever at the centre.' The concept of protagonism (Brown et al. 2019) shows how very much this is the case. However, the field of ecocriticism is now gaining ground in children's literature scholarship, as testified by the entry 'Ecocriticism' (Stephens 2010a: 168–9) in the *Routledge Companion to Children's Literature* (Rudd 2010). Furthermore, the International Research Society for Children's Literature's statement on the climate emergency (IRSCL 2022) proclaims, 'the IRSCL commits to advocating for climate justice, climate literacy, and climate activism; to highlight the invaluable voices of young people; and to support Indigenous, marginalized, and minority scholars, creators, and readers.'

It is now recognized that supporting and maintaining an eco-conscious attitude from the youngest age should be an educational priority. Richard Kerridge (2006: 532) elucidates: 'The threats that preoccupy environmentalists are not only to wildlife and wilderness but also to human health, food, and shelter, and they are global as well as local.' The widespread use of English as a lingua franca has empowered grassroots environmental movements like Extinction Rebellion to extend their influence transnationally, while technologies of mass communication help to create a new awareness – 'the global perspective that is fundamental to environmentalism: the sense of relationship between the most local things – some too small for the human eye – and the most large-scale' (Kerridge 2006: 533). Ecology and ethics, according to Hubert Zapf (2008: 847), 'share the assumption of an interconnection between *local and global* issues and are, therefore, transcultural and transnational in orientation' (emphasis in original).

Rather than introducing the world to our students as a mosaic of different nations, Karen Risager (2021: 131) argues 'for the position that the whole field of language teaching could gain from orienting itself more towards the real, diverse and interdependent world, already from beginners' level'. However, George Jacobs and Andrew Goatly (2000: 261) found in a study of seventeen international ELT coursebooks 'that environmental issues seemed to occur less often in coursebooks for lower proficiency students [which] might be attributed to materials writers believing that, at this level, students lack the language tools needed to interact on this topic'. This finding supports the argument for introducing this urgent topic through story, which children find compelling and motivating, while the images and teachers' scaffolding support can make good use of the students' zone of proximal development, maintaining a balance between challenge and their current level of skill. Jacobs and Goatly stress the need to connect students' learning with the world outside the classroom – in-depth learning – making the point that 'environmental issues certainly offer many opportunities for such connections, given that the effects of ecological problems are as close as the air we breathe' (2000: 262).

Zapf suggests that the recent ecological and ethical turn in literary and cultural studies inspires the combining of factual information with fictional creation: 'The need to "think globally" requires not only empirical information, but reflection and imagination, a capacity and readiness to think beyond oneself and one's own immediate interests and life-world' (2008: 850). The following environmental picturebooks offer a dignified representation of nature, which is seldom the case in coursebooks for young learners, and the natural world, both factual and imagined, is taken seriously. The picturebooks also comply with Lawrence Buell's (1995: 7–8) 'rough checklist' of ingredients that should be discoverable in a work that is environmentally oriented:

1. The nonhuman environment is present not merely as a framing device but as a presence that begins to suggest that human history is implicated in natural history.
2. The human interest is not understood to be the only legitimate interest.
3. Human accountability to the environment is part of the text's ethical orientation.
4. Some sense of the environment as a process rather than as a constant or a given is at least implicit in the text.

Environmental Picturebooks – Accessible for Younger Learners

A brief and moving introduction to the topic of the environment for younger learners can be provided with two animated short films by Greenpeace, each beautifully executed, and freely accessible online. The first, *Rang-tan: the story of dirty palm oil* (2018), narrated by Emma Thompson and only 90 seconds long, has already inspired thousands of young school children to create their own orang-utan videos against rainforest destruction, and post them on YouTube. The second, *There's a Monster in My Kitchen* (2020), two minutes long and narrated by Wagner Moura, is equally powerful and impressive, and tells the story of forest destruction due to industrially produced meat. The Greta Thunberg effect has shown convincingly that this topic is absolutely appropriate for young learners, and the following three picturebooks are conceptually well suited for elementary school students, with stories told primarily through the pictures.

Tucker and Pesico's *Greta and the Giants*

Most elementary school students will have already heard of Greta Thunberg. Greta initiated the Fridays for Future movement when a fifteen-year-old, which has inspired school students worldwide to take part in Friday climate strikes. Greta's highly effective environmental activism has resulted in her receiving three consecutive nominations for the Nobel Peace Prize.

Greta and the Giants (2019) by Zoë Tucker, and illustrated by Zoe Pesico, is not a nonfiction biographical account, although the endmatter provides information on Thunberg and advice on environmentally friendly action. This picturebook is an allegorical fairy tale about greedy giants who are destroying the forest, causing the animals to fear for their future. The protagonist, Greta, is tiny compared to the giants, who are described as 'huge, lumbering oafs and they were *always* busy'. The illustrations are true to the fairy tale genre, with dark forests and sociable animals, and a small but strong Greta standing up to a mighty adversary. Greta's placard campaign, though lonely at first, attracts more and more crowds (just like the real Greta's campaign) – followers of all different ethnicities protesting together with the forest animals. The giants are portrayed as foolish rather than evil, they finally promise 'to try harder' and begin to learn from the children. The hopeful ending, then, may be more fairy tale than realistic, but certainly the picturebook emphasizes how speaking out is important, as Greta's voice becomes a multitude of voices. This picturebook, and Greta's own story, show that young people can make change, by breaking rules when necessary to save the planet; moreover as educators, according to Hilary Janks (2020: 571), 'we have a responsibility to bring their ideas into the classroom so our students are able to read climate change critically and engage with the crisis that affects their futures'.

Barroux's *Where's the Elephant?*

This is a nearly wordless picturebook that combines the familiar game of hide-and-seek with an eloquent illustration of deforestation. In *Where's the Elephant?* (2015) by Barroux, the readers must search for the elephant, parrot and snake among brilliantly colourful trees on every double-page spread. This is challenging at first as there are so many potential hiding places for the three animals in the jungle scenes crowded with hundreds of trees. It is also challenging for young L2 students to explain in words where the animals are precisely, for instance: *the snake is hiding behind the yellow tree in the middle*; *the parrot is in the apple tree at the top of the page*.

While language is a struggle for English language learners, the meanings in the pictures are entirely comprehensible for elementary students. At first the trees disappear little by little as houses appear, then tall buildings, then streets filled with cars, so that the animals are ever easier to spot among the dwindling trees. Finally, there is only one tree left for the three animals, in a cage in a small zoo, crowded in by houses not trees. Despite the lack of verbal language in the book, there are many questions in the children's heads by the end. Groups of children could create their own drawings as a frieze, focusing on a specific animal and its disappearing habitat.

Lindstrom and Goade's *We Are Water Protectors*

The artwork in this book – with swirls of water on nearly every page that are both alive and life-giving – won the Caldecott Medal for the visual experience it creates. *We Are Water Protectors* (2020) by Carole Lindstrom, and illustrated by Michaela Goade, is allegorical, but inspired by a specific event. This was the international protest begun by the Standing Rock Sioux Tribe in 2016 against the construction of the Dakota Access Pipeline across tribal lands, and the resulting pollution of the environment. Information on the campaign, a glossary and an illustrator's note are provided in the endmatter, and both author and illustrator represent #ownvoices.

The text of *We Are Water Protectors* is beautifully simple, repetitive and poetic, emphasizing the interconnectedness of all life through the rhythm of the river and the pivotal role of water. Destruction takes the allegorical form of a huge black snake that will contaminate the water and destroy the land. In the Ojibwe culture, the women are the protectors of the water, and they take a stand with the refrain, repeated three times:

> We stand
> With our songs
> And our drums.
> We are still here.

In this picturebook there is also a double-page spread featuring a protest, with crowds of Native and non-native women, bearing their placards and banners: 'WE STAND!' 'WATER is LIFE', 'PROTECT the SACRED', 'ALL NATIONS'. The poetry of the pictures is echoed in the poetry of the language:

> We fight for those
> Who cannot fight for themselves:
> The winged ones,
> The crawling ones,
> The four-legged,
> The two-legged,
> The plants, trees, rivers, lakes,
> We are all related.
>
> (Lindstrom and Goade 2020)

This is a story of protest, but also one of strength and solidarity with the natural world, so that children can well understand the meanings.

Environmental Picturebooks – Beyond Elementary Level for Language Learners

The next two picturebooks are rather more difficult for English language learners due to their slightly more complex text and weightier lexical range. In many contexts with culturally and linguistically diverse students they would be ideal for lower secondary/middle school readers.

Morris and Mayhew's *Mrs Noah's Pockets*

This is a fantastical reimagining of the Noah's Ark story, an alternate version that suggests that rebellion is often necessary, and the encouragement that girls and women may be most capable to manage this. In *Mrs Noah's Pockets* (2017) by Jackie Morris, and illustrated by James Mayhew, the rain poured down, 'falling hard and fast, beating the earth, washing down tracks, making streams of pathways and rivers of roads'. Mr Noah, however, is not prepared to take all animals onto the ark, two of every kind, but decides this is a good opportunity 'to get rid of some of those more troublesome creatures' (Morris and Mayhew 2017). So, it is Mrs Noah who sets about saving all the others, by creating a magical cloak to hide them in her pockets. These turn out to be creatures of the imagination: dragons, centaurs, jackalopes, griffin, unicorns, phoenix, wolpertingers and more.

Once on the arc, Mrs Noah, a woman of colour, delights the children by reading to them of these wondrous creatures, something Mr Noah, a White man, does not comprehend. The book is hopeful that with nurturing care we can save creativity and the enchantment of nature – if we don't leave it up to the Mr Noahs, and other powerful White men. The book is also beautiful, with amazing colours for the seas, skies, and woods, with expressive textures and patterns created through collages of linocuts and paint, that almost camouflage the wild beasts (real and fantastical) that romp exuberantly across the pages, so that readers must look very carefully to discover them all.

Messner and Forsythe's *The Brilliant Deep*

Another picturebook that inspires the reader-viewer to empathetically imagine the existence of vulnerable creatures and environments is *The Brilliant Deep* (2018) by Kate Messner and illustrated by Matthew Forsythe. This picturebook is a biographical account of Ken Nedimyer, who discovered a way of painstakingly growing endangered corals, and founded the Coral Restoration Foundation. The endmatter provides more information, an explanation of coral reef vocabulary, and a list of organizations supporting coral reefs.

The coral reef comes alive in this story, which begins with 'It starts with one'. On the next spread we see how the magic begins in the dark waters of the ocean: 'One night, after a full moon, the corals begin to spawn – releasing first one, then millions of tiny lives – until the waters swirl like a snow globe.' There is a soft glow to the underwater scenes revealed at each page turn – the underwater life, and Ken's passion for the sea – wonderfully expressed both in pictures and words:

> The reefs of the Florida Keys teemed with life.
> They painted the ocean floor fire red and murky gold.
> How could the reefs grow so large?
> What made all the different colors and shapes?
> How could such tiny creatures build such elaborate homes of rock?
> (Messner and Forsythe 2018)

The double-page spread that shows Ken discovering the dying reef is all the more tragic in contrast to the life and beauty of the previous images. This spread is wordless, yet the silent and colourless corals seem to shout out to the viewer (see Figure 4.4).

Through patience, hard work and some luck, Ken and a team of volunteers develop a method to grow coral colonies, eager and hopeful to save the reefs. The story closes on another magical moonlit night: 'TONIGHT, the moon will be full and bright. The corals may spawn, and if one tiny life lands in just the right spot, another new colony will grow. And then another. And another. And another.' I find there is always a student who can guess the four words on the last spread, before I turn

FIGURE 4.4 *The blanched corals. From* The Brilliant Deep *by Kate Messner © 2018, illustrations by Matt Forsythe © 2018. Used with permission of Chronicle Books LLC, San Francisco.*

the page: 'It starts with one.' An eco-conscious attitude is supported by *The Brilliant Deep* and the previous picturebooks that focus on the interrelatedness between human and nonhuman nature. Ecocentrism is supported when the environment is portrayed as alive and dynamic and the protagonist's acceptance of accountability to the environment creates the ethical orientation of the text.

Good nonfiction, according to Kiefer and Wilson (2011: 291), 'is an art form, designed to give pleasure, and enlightenment, to arouse wonder, and to reveal our capacity for self awareness and understanding'. Nonfiction short films increasingly use the power of story too, such as the remarkable and accessible Global Goals films produced by the Project Everyone team. The films include the six-minute *The World's Largest Lesson Animation* (2020), written by Ken Robinson and introduced by Malala, and the three-minute film *A Call to Learning for Climate Education* (2020), which features adolescents around the world inspiring young fellow students to in-depth learning and environmental activism.

Exploring Anthony Browne's *Zoo*

Zoo (1992) by Anthony Browne is a picturebook classic that examines the relationship between humankind and animals, and highlights feelings that humans and many non-human animals seem to have in common. The short film *Three Seconds*, directed by Spencer Sharp, would be a good four-minute introduction to any environmental topic, including *Zoo*. Young learners are likely to get the message of the film, despite a fairly complex language level, for children can typically understand far more than they can themselves express in words. *Three Seconds* (which won first place for best short film, Film4Climate competition, 2016), conveys much of its meaning through the visuals, the music and the power of Prince Ea's voice, who performs his poem 'Man vs Earth' for the film. The title alludes to the mere three seconds humans have been on the Earth if the entire history of the world were compacted into twenty-four hours. Here is an excerpt, which is particularly relevant for *Zoo*:

> In the next 10 to 100 years,
> every beloved animal character
> in every children's book
> is predicted to go extinct.
> Lions? Gone.
> Rhinos? Gone.
> Tiger? Gorilla? Elephant? Polar bear?
> Gone. In three seconds.
>
> (Prince Ea 2015)

Reading Images

The visual level is demanding in Anthony Browne's *Zoo*, providing much to discuss that in some contexts will be more suitable for lower secondary language learners than for the usual target group of elementary students. The image of being caged and trapped is everywhere in the picturebook, beginning symbolically with a pet hamster in a cage on the title page. The book describes a family's visit to a zoo, and already on their way there the family is caged in by the traffic. Children tend to notice that a little snail is flying above the cars, which are at a standstill. Is this a comment on the slow progress of the vehicles? There is much detective work involved in reading this book, and as Sipe (2008b: 214) points out, 'success in discovering book secrets is extremely motivating for young learners, and supports their positive evaluation of themselves as responder to books.'

Zoo does not employ anthropomorphism, a standard trope of children's literature. In contrast, *Zoo* features zoomorphism, in that animal features are ascribed to the human characters, both in the pictures and in the use of language. This is unusual and therefore striking, and a challenge to children to interpret the meanings. The zoomorphism begins as an irate lorry driver stuck in the traffic jam appears to transform into an angry gorilla, growling 'GGRRRR!!' in his speech balloon.

As we follow a family of four through the zoo, the elder of two boys narrates the day. The male members of the family appear almost as entrapped by tedium as the animals: 'Me and my brother wanted to see the gorillas and monkeys, but we had to see all these boring animals first' (Browne 1992: unpaginated). Both boys buy a 'funny monkey hat' in the gift shop, and their behaviour becomes ever more monkeyish. Whereas the animals in captivity are realistically portrayed on the recto pages, for the most part torpid and all of them appearing despondent, the human visitors to the zoo on the verso pages seem to be gradually morphing into various animals.

The non-human great apes suffer in their enclosures, a thick black outline surrounds the recto images, emphasizing that the animals have no freedom. The orang-utan – beautifully drawn as all the animals are – is called a 'miserable thing' by the boy narrator because it will not show its face or move out of the corner. Browne combines the hyperrealism of his animals with surrealism in portraying the humans. Many of the human visitors observing the immobile orang-utan have animal features and thus appear less natural, even comical. This positions the humans, themselves great apes, as hyperseparated from nature, playing at being animals rather than accepting their close genetic relationship to the great apes in captivity. This could be a satirical comment on what ecofeminist Val Plumwood (2006: 123) identified as 'the western tradition of treating humans as superior and apart, outside of and hyperseparated from nature'. The class may wish to consider the interesting point that ecocritic Garrard makes (2012: 162), 'the startling conclusion must be that the species we most thoroughly anthropomorphise is our own'.

The animals communicate their anguish with their body language, which can be 'read' by the sensitive mother, but not by the rest of her family visiting the zoo. None of the animals in *Zoo* represent a 'demand' image; they do not seem to seek eye contact with the reader, strongly suggesting they have given up any expectations. Gunther Kress and Theo van Leeuwen (2021: 117) discuss the demand gaze in pictures and photos, when characters gaze directly into the viewer's eyes, as a way of establishing contact with the viewer and demanding a response. The extreme close-up of the gorilla's face on one of the last recto pages is one of the most moving images. The gorilla does not look into our eyes, but apparently seeks to establish eye contact with the distressed mother in the opposite image on the verso.

The emotional power of *Zoo* is due to the persuasive pictures, encouraging readers to bond with the silent animals, and achieve a critical distance to the squabbling and unthinking human visitors at the zoo, some of whom are allegorically depicted as more 'beastly' than the animals. A challenging exercise could be to discuss the meaning of words like brutal, beastly, feral, bitch, bearish, swine, bestial, wolfish and other terminology that sets humans way above animals. In one of the final pictures the role reversal is complete when the young narrator is trapped behind bars in his dream and he asks the reader, 'Do you think animals have dreams?'

Zoo with Ten-Year-Olds

A teacher in my in-service teacher development course in Norway 2019 selected Anthony Browne's *Zoo* for her three-week school project. In this course, the in-service teachers initially work on their role as both teacher and storyteller (Heathfield 2014). This includes reading the picturebook aloud at 'picture speed' (Hunt 2001) and allowing the children generous time to listen to the words and explore the pictures. While commenting on the pictures, the characters, the events and the children's interjections, the teacher-storyteller is modelling language, ideally employing creative teacher talk (see Chapter 3).

Teacher-storytellers attend not only to the children's linguistic needs but also to their emotional needs in studying and enjoying the pictures and the story. Pictures, like compelling verbal story, can cause emotions to be experienced bodily: 'A young child who smiles seeing a happy face in a picturebook, or starts moving at the sight of a fictional character running and jumping, who cries over a picture of a dead animal or shudders at the gaping jaws of a giant dinosaur is truly experiencing the emotions as if they were real' (Nikolajeva 2018: 115).

In her project, the Norwegian teacher was keen to discover whether a picturebook was a format that could challenge her ambitious ten-year-old students, a class of Norwegian speakers with some culturally and linguistically diverse students. The teacher decided to explore storytelling with *Zoo* to develop the students' visual, critical and emotional literacy, to help them consider what Gail Ellis (2018: 85) has called 'the emotional temperature of the images to capture atmosphere, to feel empathy by reading facial expressions, gestures and body language and thus to develop emotional literacy'.

Throughout the work with *Zoo*, the children were adept at reading the emotions of the humans and animals through their body language. The teacher supplied the class with a Feeling Wheel chart, and with this linguistic aid the children sought to identify the feelings of the members of the family, the man driving the truck in the traffic jam, the man at the ticket office, and ten different animals. The children adopted words from the Feeling Wheel, some created Word Clouds of feelings (the software is freely available) and they tried to recognize the feelings of the animals and the characters in the story (see Figures 4.5 and 4.6).

FIGURE 4.5 *Word Cloud of feelings.*

EARLY STEPS IN LITERATURE LEARNING WITH PICTUREBOOKS

How do you think the characters and animals in the story feel?

Mum	She feels sad
Dad	He feels powerful
Brother	He feels excited
Me	I feel happy
Man in the truck	He feels mad
Man at the ticket office	He feels mad
The elephant	It feels sad
The giraffe looking inside	It feels peaceful
The tiger	It feels sad
The rhino	It feels scared
The penguin standing alone	It feels alone
The polar bear	It feels foolish
The baboon in the middle	It feels angry
The orang-utan	It feels sad
The gorilla	It feels lonely
The birds in the sky	It feels happy

FIGURE 4.6 *How do they feel? (A ten-year-old's interpretation relating to Anthony Browne's* Zoo*).*

The children also found that the language of the picturebook connects the family of humans to certain animals, and they explored this by matching the verbs to animal pictures: ' "A traffic jam!" *roared* Dad.' (lion) ' "Daylight robbery!" Dad *snarled*.' (dog) ' "Why not?" *whined* Harry.' (dog) ' "You wouldn't say that if it was chasing after you," *snorted* Dad.' (bull) ' "What animal can you eat at the zoo?" asked Dad. "Don't know," I groaned. "A hot dog!" *howled* Dad.' (wolf) For long-term vocabulary retention, it is important that students develop associations around the new language through mental investment, by using and becoming involved with the language through output activities, as Chia-Ho Sun has shown (2017). To further their investment, the children were also given the creative-writing task of writing a diary entry about life at the zoo from the (often melancholy) perspective of one of the animals.

Collective reflection on the shared reading helps students shape their thinking, their thoughtful feelings, and voice their own reflections orally, or express them in drawing, writing or total physical response (TPR), for example individual students or small groups could follow commands: *act a sad orang-utan, act an excited boy, act an angry tiger, act happy birds* and so forth. The English teacher working with *Zoo* helped the ten-year-olds engage with the language and with their learning by giving them challenging, but achievable tasks. The students reviewed how well they had learned, as Gail Ellis and Nayr Ibrahim (2015) recommend, and documented this by colouring one, two or three tigers (see Figure 4.7).

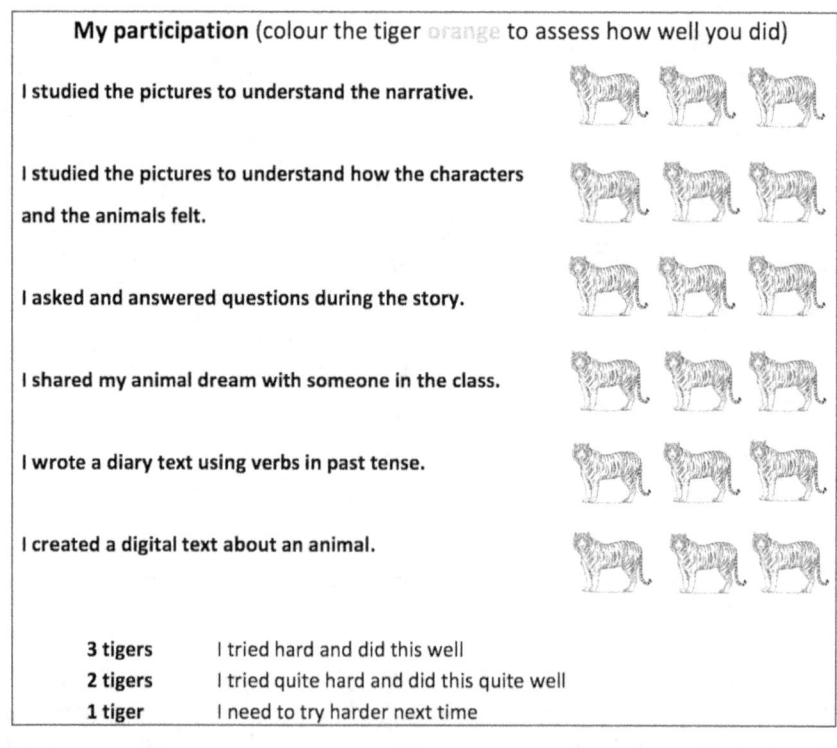

FIGURE 4.7 *Reflective review with tigers, based on* My Activity Record *in Ellis and Ibrahim (2015).*

According to Frank Serafini (2008: 9), 'picturebooks present possibilities and challenges for novice and experienced readers alike.' The discussion in this chapter has focused on nonfiction and fiction picturebooks on themes of social and environmental justice that can motivate students of different ages and abilities towards in-depth learning. The best contemporary picturebooks depict characters fully, with an emotional appeal that drives the story, portraying dreams and hopes that students can share, and conceptualized through pictures that add powerful layers of meaning to the words. Students' early experience with literature is of the utmost importance: literary picturebooks can initiate a challenging and simultaneously motivating literary apprenticeship.

CHAPTER FIVE

Refugee Stories as Visual Narrative

There are several compelling reasons why teachers may want to share literary texts with a refugee theme in the English language classroom. The difficult and dangerous situations of refugees and migrants have become an important topic of global relevance, with underlying causes that include war, human rights abuses, the climate crisis and destitution. There are huge numbers of forcibly displaced persons in the present day; by 2020 the figure was above 1 per cent of the world's population according to the UN Refugee Agency. Children all around the world are affected by the refugee crisis. Many families are internally displaced in their country of origin; families experience perils on the move and troubles in their host countries. School children in host countries are also touched by the problems of families on the move, and teachers need to plan for classrooms that become increasingly heterogeneous, with children who come from dissimilar cultural contexts, speak different languages from the language of schooling and may also be traumatized. Children's literature that promotes empathy and the understanding of suffering and the imperative to flee can help to rectify false media narratives and anti-immigrant rhetoric. As Michell Mpike (2019: 66) writes, 'Whatever learned prejudices that children pick up from the world around them can be countered by active choices from different sectors of society, including the media and the literary world.'

This topic is included in citizenship education studies and intercultural learning, and also belongs to English language education when the goal is in-depth learning. Karen Risager (2021: 124) describes the field: 'Citizenship education studies primarily sees the world as characterised by *a number of key problems* that (should) concern practically everybody, such as climate change, inequality and poverty. In this approach, intercultural learning is primarily seen as the development of the student into an engaged (national and global) citizen with some political awareness' (emphasis in original). Melina Porto and Michalinos Zembylas (2020: 357) argue 'that foreign language teaching can and should also explicitly aim to sensitise students about issues of human suffering and cultivate empathy, solidarity, hospitality and inclusion'.

Hospitality and inclusion are important aspects of citizenship education, which must be focused inward to preclude ingroups and outgroups in the classroom as much as outward to foster social justice responsibilities beyond the classroom. In the context of language teaching with university students, Porto and Zembylas call for pedagogies of discomfort, that is, to engage 'with "difficult" issues that promote critical intercultural citizenship values and habits of mind' (2020: 357) while being 'responsive to learners' emotional reactions in ways that other pedagogies may not be' (2020: 359). Such a pedagogy of discomfort can trouble students' emotional comfort zones, and therefore the notion of the classroom as a safe space must first be taken into consideration. This is imperative in school settings with children and adolescents, settings which are less frequently addressed by applied linguists.

Creating a Safe Classroom Climate

A classroom where all participants, including culturally and linguistically diverse students, feel safe and empowered to share their ideas and feelings requires an inclusive atmosphere for all. A safe classroom climate fosters mutual respect, promoting the sharing of personal experiences, honest self-exploration and diversity of voices, and supporting the affective, cognitive and metacognitive impact of learning. Holley and Steiner (2005: 60) found in their study that 'creating a safe classroom can contribute to increased student learning, or at least increased effort and commitment'. Classrooms that are characterized by respect for diversity, for others' voices and individual agency are likely to already have, within themselves, resources, and the potential for developing interculturality and empathy.

Juan Garibay suggests establishing ground rules that are helpful for a positive and inclusive classroom. Garibay's recommended rules for class discussions include (2015: 9):

- Respect the opinions of others in class discussions. When you disagree, make sure that you use arguments to criticize the idea, not the person.
- Avoid generalizations.
- This classroom is a safe space for disagreement. The goal of class discussion is not that everyone agree but that everyone in the class gain new insights and experiences.

- If you are nervous about speaking in class, remember that your perspective is valid and the class deserves to hear it.
- If a statement is made that offends you or you think might offend others, speak up and challenge it but always show respect for the person who made it.

In addition, it is helpful when students keep a journal so that they can write down thoughts and respond emotionally to what they are reading, especially if they have little time to respond during class. Some students may be more comfortable sharing journal responses first with the teacher, and then, with the teachers' support, potentially with the whole class.

Referring specifically to language education, Matthew Prior (2019: 521–2) writes as follows on perceptions of self-efficacy and fulfilment:

> Of interest are how positive personality factors and subjective feelings such as *gratitude, optimism, love, enjoyment, contentment, belonging, empathy, flow, spirituality, mindfulness, imagination, interpersonal skills, tolerance, responsibility*, and so forth contribute to perceptions of success, self-efficacy, and satisfaction. [...] The implications are obvious: to make language learning and teaching personally meaningful and enjoyable and to help learners (and teachers) become more resilient to various challenges.

While I have tried to select uplifting multimodal texts for this chapter, our emotions connected to refugee stories cannot always be positive. Well-crafted refugee stories involve the readers' and listeners' emotions dynamically, like our emotional lives in the real world. Several levels need to be taken into consideration:

- There may be students in the class who are themselves refugees or migrants and suffer from anxiety, frustration, pain or trauma.
- Majority students may feel conflicted or uneasy because they are upset by a new situation inside or outside of the classroom. They may have heard negative talk about migrants and refugees due to what the World Migration Report 2020 (McAuliffe and Khadria 2019: 7) describes as:

  > the understandable fear in communities that stems from the accelerated pace of change and rising uncertainty of our times. [...] we are increasingly witnessing the harnessing of social media as a means of division and polarization, not just on migration, but at certain times we have seen the deployment of online 'tribal tactics' by activists attempting to depict migration in a negative and misleading light.

- The teacher's feelings are very relevant too, and effort in this sensitive area may be particularly demanding and worrying: 'work in the area of emotion holds tremendous relevancy to classroom teaching and learning, and not only from the student perspective but also that of teachers' (Bigelow 2019: 516).

However, there is a benefit on all three levels of including refugee stories that strongly involve us emotionally: a heightened sensitivity towards fairness, in-depth learning due to better understanding of real-world events, as well as potentially an enhanced ability to cope. Deep reading involves encouraging the reader to contemplate these ethical issues while empathizing with a relatable protagonist.

Visual narratives are particularly potent as they help students to involve their senses in their learning – and of course the creator usually *wants* to involve and move the reader. This emotional response may help lead towards interconnected knowing. Indigenous scholar Polly Walker (2013: 303) suggests that interconnected knowing 'emphasizes the importance of the interrelationships of mind, body, emotion, and spirit, which many Indigenous scholars regard as integral in understanding human experience'. Feelings and emotions are very much part of our learning and knowing, and not separate from cognitive development. Carl Ratner (2000: 6) argues: 'Emotions are feelings that accompany thinking. They are the feeling side of thoughts; thought-filled feelings; thoughtful feelings. Emotions never exist alone, apart from thoughts. [...] We may be fascinated by intense feelings; however, we should not be deluded into thinking that they have an independent existence apart from cognition.'

Students, especially marginalized children, need to feel that they are valued through their stories. Mpike writes (2019: 59), 'being represented in the media or in the arts can give a child the feeling that they too can one day create stories and contribute to the richness of the cultural landscape. This also tells the child that they have a voice, that they can use it and that they will be listened to.' Stereotypical, oversimplified images in coursebooks are particularly damaging, as discussed in Chapter 2; 'this locks them [marginalized children] into a particular image, with little opportunity to be seen or show themselves as something else' (Mpike 2019: 64). While minority students need to see themselves in the books shared in the classroom, majority children should be provided with an enriching window into the lives of others. Dylman and Bjärta (2018) and Iacozza, Costa and Duñabeitia (2017) have moreover put forward evidence that suggests reading in L2 typically grants a certain affective distance. These are interesting findings, for it is significant if students can construct a space between any distressing personal experience and a story shared in the classroom, which could then be empowering instead of contributing to their anguish.

The next section deals with refugee literature that in many contexts could enrich English language education in the elementary school: *Wherever*

I Go (2019) by Mary Wagley Copp, illustrated by Munir D. Mohammed, *My Name Is Not Refugee* (2017) by Kate Milner, *Leaf* (2017) by Sandra Dieckmann, *The Suitcase* (2019) by Chris Naylor-Ballesteros and *The Day War Came* (2018) by Nicola Davies, illustrated by Rebecca Cobb. There are read-alouds of all these picturebooks on YouTube, some of them read by the authors themselves, so that introducing several books could be possible even when funds are severely limited, as they usually are. The publisher of *The Suitcase*, Nosy Crow, also provides helpful audio recordings of their picturebooks, which can be accessed by scanning the QR code on the verso of their picturebook covers.

Using the Deep Reading Framework with Copp and Mohammed's *Wherever I Go* and Text Ensemble

Mary Wagley Copp has created a refugee story, *Wherever I Go* (2019), that is uplifting while not eschewing realistic details of Shimelba refugee camp. The illustrator Munir D. Mohammed similarly manages to combine stunningly vibrant pictures of a resilient young refugee girl, Abia, and her love of games and make-believe, with grim details of the daily struggles of the camp. In the endmatter, the author writes that 'there is a Shimelba Camp in northern Ethiopia, [however] *Wherever I Go* is fictional and represents many children in many different camps' (Copp 2019: np). This wider, symbolic application is important because, since publication of this picturebook, the Shimelba Camp has been vandalized and destroyed by Eritrean government forces, which has led to the further displacement of the mostly Eritrean refugees. According to human rights and mental health researchers Peters, Golden, Eloul and Higson-Smith (2021), approximately 174,000 Eritrean refugees now live in Ethiopia.

In the following, I suggest a text ensemble with *Wherever I Go* and other refugee stories, using the deep reading framework (see Figure 1.1: 26).

Unpuzzle and Explore

Wherever I Go is a traditional picturebook with thirty-two pages. After the end papers of vivid royal blue, the title page follows and fifteen double-page spreads. The last spread (opening fifteen) contains a note from the author on refugees, with information on relevant websites and a list of children's books related to refugees and resettlement.

The story centres around Abia (see Figure 5.1), who refers to herself as Queen Abia, as she has faced the challenging environment of a refugee camp for seven years, longer than any of her friends, which means for most of

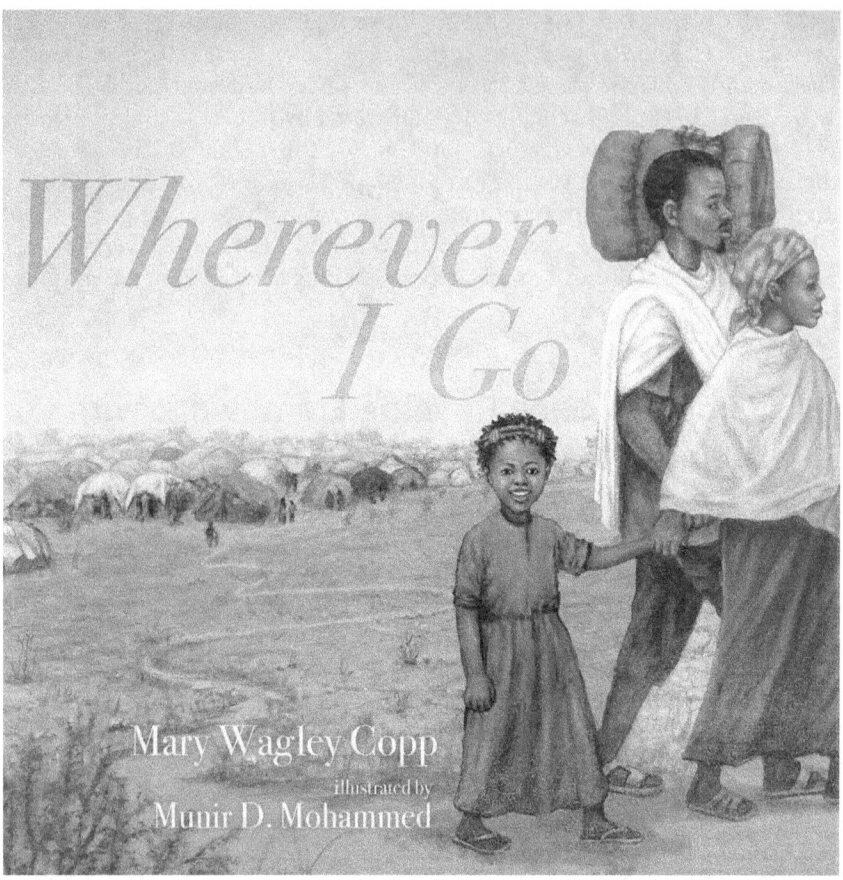

FIGURE 5.1 Cover of Wherever I Go From Wherever I Go by Mary Wagley Copp © 2019 with illustrations by Munir D. Mohammed © 2019. Reprinted with the permission of Atheneum Books for Young Readers, an imprint of Simon & Schuster Children's Publishing Division. All rights reserved.

her young life. Yet, the book is full of contrasts. On the first read-aloud by the teacher, the contrasts might be pointed out or elicited at each opening. The disparities are mostly to be found in the pictures, for example:

Abia, her group of friends and her family look:	Life in the refugee camp looks:	The night-time flight from their village home was:
bright, cheerful, imaginative, fun, royal, colourful, hopeful, helpful, active, noisy, warm, loving	crowded, endless, vast, dusty, shabby, prickly, poor, dull, nasty, exhausting, helpless, powerless	sudden, dark, frightening, hurried, dangerous, scary, unfamiliar, unknown, disorienting, haunting

Abia plays many roles as Queen of the Camp – the teacher might ask how many of her roles the children can remember after the first read-aloud. On a second reading, the students could chorus each queenly role, echoing the teacher, and adding gestures or sound effects each time (this may need some rehearsal). The queenly roles are:

Opening 1: I am Queen Abia

Opening 3: Queen of the Fields

Opening 4: Queen of Balance

Opening 5: strongest of all queens; noisy queen

Opening 6: Queen of the Hills

Opening 7: quiet queen

Opening 14: Wherever I go, I'll still be a queen.

The well-illustrated scenes of the different areas of the refugee camp provide an organic way to talk with students about how Abia does her chores, prepares food, sleeps and plays with her friends. The flight from Abia's wartorn homeland, the yelling men and their crackling gunfire, the fear of lions and hyenas on the way are intense and memorable instances of the dangers refugee families face. The illustrator uses warm earth colours and natural tones throughout (except for Abia's forever home in the last openings), but Abia wears a dress of deep blue. This helps the reader to focus their attention on her, and, far from being a story of an essentialized refugee, this becomes the story of an outstanding girl whose family and friends (and the reader) value and cherish.

Activate and Investigate

What do the children know about the circumstances of refugees and why they leave their home countries? Abia's mother has told her the story of their nighttime flight on foot from their village home. The pictures show how little time Abia's parents had to gather their possessions and baby Abia before they fled from the violent men. In pairs, the students might prepare a list of things they would take with them if they had to leave their home in a hurry, possibly never to return. How would they carry their belongings? The children could draw two or three objects in a suitcase that they would really want to take with them, and give each object a title or caption explaining why it is important.

The class could then discuss essential items to pack, such as a change of clothes, a change of shoes and clean underwear, a warm coat and blanket, toothpaste, a toothbrush, soap and a towel, plasters, a water bottle and some food, a mobile phone and charger, important addresses, some cash and photo ID, books and school certificates. Would they be able to carry all this?

What or who (people, pets, places, activities, occasions or things) would the students miss most if they never saw their home or homeland again?

The story of the refugee camp is told by Abia, who has a strong sense of self. Abia also has a powerful voice: 'When the hyenas howl, I howl right back'; and she can be gentle: 'I swaddle and sway and sing my baby cousin to sleep.' The lyrical text and vivid pictures express the resilience and courage of Abia and other refugee families who, though they lose all their possessions, gain inner strength. Abia's strength is also her anchor when she finds herself in her new, forever home. The students could list Abia's hardships at the refugee camp, such as carrying heavy water, standing in long queues for rice and oil, sleeping on a prickly mat, managing without running water, the pain of her family's past, their long wait for a forever home and uncertain future there: 'Forever homes are in strange and faraway lands,' Abia thinks. The students could also describe the games Abia plays to overcome boredom in the camp, and, after a little practice, act out the games in groups. Ideally, other refugee stories such as the picturebooks below could be introduced to create a text ensemble with *Wherever I Go*, helping children to investigate the refugee situation from different angles.

Kate Milner's *My Name Is Not Refugee*

Another picturebook that similarly shows the sorrows of the refugee situation by portraying how a mother gently explains everything to her son, as a way of protecting and shielding him, is *My Name Is Not Refugee* (2017) by Kate Milner. This is an interactive picturebook, with direct and meaningful questions to the reader that, together with the striking illustrations, immerse children in the story (see Figure 5.2). The name of Milner's book is an excellent reminder that displaced persons are far more than their circumstances, even though they are shaped by them.

Sandra Dieckmann's *Leaf*

This is a delightful tale of acceptance and assistance that would work very well in the elementary school. Whereas the picturebooks *Wherever I Go* and *My Name Is Not Refugee* focus on the tangible experience of the refugee situation, *Leaf* (2017), by Sandra Dieckmann, is an inventive and exquisitely illustrated fable about a climate crisis refugee. As such, the refugee (a polar bear) does not want to stay in the host country (the wild wood) but is desperate to get back to his Arctic home. The forest inhabitants call the outsider a creature or beast and name him Leaf because he collects leaves: 'Big leaves and small leaves, round leaves and colourful ones' (Dieckmann 2017). At first, Leaf is shunned and feared by the woodland animals. They do not know (and initially do not try to find out) that Leaf wants to use the leaves to make wings so that he can fly home to his family, from whom he has been separated due to rapidly melting sea ice in the Arctic (see Figure 5.3).

FIGURE 5.2 *Do you think you could live in a place where there is no water?* Extract from My Name Is Not Refugee *by Kate Milner* © *2017. Reprinted by permission of Barrington Stoke Ltd.*

The animals, led by the intelligent crows, eventually overcome their fears to listen to Leaf's story and find a way to help him return. The students should take note of the crows in *Leaf*, how many are there altogether? They will quickly discover that there is one more crow on each consecutive opening. Crows are birds that collaborate with each other, so that they symbolize teamwork; this is essential in the crows' eventual rescue action for Leaf. Crows also exemplify the Japanese proverb: 'All of us are smarter than one of us.' Students might consider the importance of teamwork in hosting and supporting refugees as well as fighting climate change.

FIGURE 5.3 *Leaf alone. Extracted from* Leaf *by Sandra Dieckmann* © *2017. Reprinted with the permission of Flying Eye Books, imprint of Nobrow Ltd.*

The students probably now have some idea of what being a refugee means. *Leaf* brings an environmental angle and new knowledge to the topic, for the climate crisis exacerbates the refugee situation, impacting humans as well as the animal world. Climate change worsens many humanitarian crises as peoples' homes become uninhabitable. The United Nations Refugee Agency (UNHCR) emphasizes this interconnectedness, explaining that protecting refugees must be supplemented 'by dedicated efforts to address root causes. While not in themselves causes of refugee movements, climate, environmental degradation and natural disasters increasingly interact with the drivers of refugee movements' (UNHCR 2018: 2).

Critically Engage

The title of *Wherever I Go* refers to the stories that Abia will take with her wherever she goes, even though her family must leave all their belongings behind when they leave the refugee camp. It is these stories of others that could enrich language classrooms. They could be stories of children in the classroom, elsewhere in the school, or in local neighbourhoods, and sometimes they will be stories of others that seem far away, like Abia. Students can reflect further on Abia's story, by annotating different double-page spreads in groups. Using Post-it notes – or writing on a larger sheet of paper the open picturebook rests on – they can write what they see in the pictures, ask questions or write Abia's thoughts in speech balloons (see example in Figure 5.4).

There are two journeys in *Wherever I Go*: the story of the journey on foot from Abia's village home to the refugee camp and the journey by plane to an unnamed host country. Both journeys convey emotions in the pictures. Studying the pictures carefully, the students could compare the emotions of the family. The flight from their village seems to be the more frightening, more urgent and more deadly of the two journeys. The plane flight, for Abia the first experience of flying, seems more hopeful, more mysterious, but also more separated from everything familiar, and more alone.

Chris Naylor-Ballesteros's *The Suitcase*

A heart-warming picturebook, *The Suitcase* (2019), by Chris Naylor-Ballesteros, would be excellent to share at this point. With charming colourful clarity for a young audience, *The Suitcase* illustrates the importance of packing memories in one's suitcase if one must move, and how these treasures might be shared with sceptics in a new host country, who may eventually become friends. Author-illustrator Naylor-Ballesteros explains (2019):

> I wanted to show that it might not always be easy to allow ourselves to accept someone or something unexpected, different and unknown that changes the status quo and makes us rethink and re-evaluate our place

FIGURE 5.4 *Annotations – Abia's thoughts on leaving the camp.*

and our relationships. I tried to show that we might make mistakes and disagree and get things wrong. [...] Even though we might mistrust or be wary of someone at first and are even unkind to them, if we acknowledge our mistakes and try to redeem our actions then perhaps things might just work out and friendship can blossom.

The characters in the picturebook *The Suitcase* are a red bird, an orange fox, a yellow rabbit and a strange turquoise animal that 'arrived one day, looking dusty, tired, sad and frightened' (Naylor-Ballesteros 2019). The direct speech in the picturebook is elegantly colour-coded to match each animal (red, orange, yellow and turquoise). This simple, but clever, device means that the narrating voice (in black) is kept to a succinct minimum, reporting clauses like 'he said' and 'she said' are not needed at all, and the animals entirely take over the story. Each animal expresses different feelings: the bird is inquisitive, the fox is suspicious, the rabbit is kind-hearted and the newcomer is sad and exhausted – in a dream we see the dangerous journey he has just completed. We do not discover the gender of the bird, the fox and the rabbit. Are the personified animals all 'he' by default? The story does not suggest this. The children could discuss whether they are male or female. Is the bossy fox a 'he' and the caring rabbit 'she'? This discussion could show how difficult it is to avoid stereotyping.

The animals are drawn in a very clear cartoony artistic style, with the focus on their facial expressions, thus increasing the opportunity for character interpretation with children. This technique is borrowed from comics and identified as amplification through simplification by Scott McCloud (1993): 'When we abstract an image through cartooning, we're not so much eliminating details as we are focusing on specific details. By stripping down an image to its essential "meaning," an artist can amplify that meaning' (30). The story is well suited for practising readers theatre in groups of five – the narrator and four animals – as the children can so easily spot who says what. *The Suitcase* is unique in showing how all of us can make mistakes, and how we can also make it right again through thoughtful actions. Creative problem solving is an important educational goal. After sharing this enchanting tale, students could think-pair-share how they would make amends if they had been unkind to a newcomer.

Davies and Cobb's *The Day War Came*

While *The Suitcase* uses teacups to symbolize acceptance and welcome, *The Day War Came* uses chairs. Nicola Davies's *The Day War Came* (2018), illustrated by Rebecca Cobb, is a poetic picturebook that could well belong to an elementary school text ensemble on this topic. Davies wrote the poem the book is based on 'in response to the government's decision not to allow lone refugee children a safe haven in the UK', and it was first published in *The Guardian*. The poem begins with an everyday family scene:

> The day war came there were flowers on the window sill
> and my father sang my baby brother back to sleep.
> My mother made my breakfast, kissed my nose
> and walked with me to school.
>
> (Davies 2016)

The unrhymed poem is moving and powerful, and the picturebook, which was published two years later, follows this poem exactly. While the words and pictures show how war takes everything, destroying school, home and even family, the details remain minimally sketched, again an example of amplification through simplification.

The little girl who narrates her story explains, 'I can't say the words that tell you about the blackened hole that had been my home.' There are many such gaps, which seem very realistic, for what child can easily speak of such things? The girl tries to journey to a place where she will be welcomed, but finds she is ignored:

> I walked and walked to try and drive war out of myself,
> to try and find a place it hadn't reached.
> But war was in the way that doors shut when I came down the street.
> It was in the way the people didn't smile, and turned away.
>
> (Davies 2016)

The girl is barred from school by the teacher, who tells her that 'there is no chair for you to sit on, you have to go away'. The school children, however, offer hope in the final pages of the story, and fill the silences and deficiencies of the adults by bringing chairs for the girl and other refugees so they can join school. After sharing this tale, students could be invited to draw a chair as a symbol of welcome to a new home, and draw and label an object on the chair that they believe would be a perfect gift for a refugee.

The class might discuss whether older students or adults could learn anything from these picturebooks. The class may be interested in learning a long and important word (that is not known to all adults): xenophobia, which refers to a fear and even hatred of strangers or otherness. The children could make an interesting display, around the central image: XeNOphobia (= **NO** to xenophobia).

Experiment with Creative Response

All of the picturebooks discussed so far include a journey, and *Wherever I Go* includes two journeys. In this last step of the deep reading framework, the teacher could make use of TPR to help the students get an idea of the terrifying journeying of refugees and migrants. In a large space, the teacher recites a story to the children that they act out in mime (without using words). Here is an example:

You are in bed, it is night-time and very dark. The sky is black and starless. Your parents are asleep – the whole village is asleep. You are quiet and trying to sleep too, but it is rather cold, and you are shivering. Listen to the wind whistling through the tall trees! Suddenly, you hear noisy trucks entering the village and angry shouting. Gunfire! You are terrified but you must be absolutely silent so that the dangerous men don't find you. Get up and quickly put on warm clothes, for you must leave your home at once. Listen! Your parents tell you to go far away, they will lead the men in another direction. Start walking now. You are frightened to go without your parents, but other children are running away too. Start walking silently! The journey will take days, weeks or maybe months. Everybody is shivering with cold. Keep walking onwards, even though you are tired, and your feet hurt. Everybody around you is tired too. Keep walking, but be careful, don't bump into anything or anyone. It is dark and you must not make a sound. Suddenly, very quietly, you stop. You think you can hear someone or something chasing you. Sit down on the ground and try to make yourself small so that you can't be seen in the dark. Listen carefully! You can hear your heart thumping. Shh! It seems all is silent again. Get up quietly, and go on walking, always listening out for the sounds of gunshot. You are so, so tired and it is very dark. You can hear the hyenas howling and perhaps the lions are out hunting. After many, many long hours you can't go any further. Sit down exactly where you are, and take a rest.

Garland's *Azzi In Between*, an In-Between Tale

Sarah Garland's *Azzi In Between* (2012) is an in-between tale, because it is neither clearly a graphic novel, nor clearly a picturebook; its suitability level is also somewhere in-between elementary school or secondary school, depending on context. *Azzi In Between* tells the tale of a family that must flee from an unspecified country in the Middle East. First Azzi's family is introduced – her father who is a doctor, her mother and grandmother – and we glimpse their colourful lives. Although their country is at war, the first pages describe a childhood recognizable by children nearly everywhere:

> In the mornings, Grandma still took Azzi to school.
> When she got home, her friends often came around.
>
> (Garland 2012: np)

However, details of the war, which comes ever closer to Azzi's house, can be seen in the powerful pictures. These show helicopter gunships darkening the sky and buildings on fire, rubble on the way to school, and grim rows of soldiers marching by, beyond their garden wall. *Azzi In Between* is shaped like a picturebook but tells the story through panels and captions like a graphic novel. Thus, the pages are divided into smaller picture panels, sometimes as many as nine per page, showing many vivid events and details of Azzi's story.

The gripping images relate the hardships Azzi and her family face when they become refugees, and are consequently an important support for sensory-anchored interaction in the classroom, helping readers engage deeply in the experience of the story. To make the most effective use of multimodal books in language education, teachers need to support children in responding to the eloquent images as well as the words.

Nikolajeva considers that the social knowledge that is to be inferred from fiction may be more complex and challenging than factual knowledge, and requires attention, imagination and memory. She writes in addition (2014: 40) that one of the purposes of fiction is to convey experience 'refracted through an individual consciousness'. Experimental research suggests that the brain responds to emotions in fiction exactly as if it were real life (Kidd and Castano 2013; see Chapter 2). Thus, the hardships of Azzi, who must leave nearly all her life behind her when she escapes the war, become very real to the young reader. With *Azzi In Between*, children experience the terrors, losses and devastation of family life even when refugees are kindly received and supported in a new home. In this way, refugee literature can move young learners towards flexibility of perspective, and rather than acquiring static (and in coursebooks often stereotyped) knowledge of other cultures, they have the opportunity to step outside of their own frame of reference.

A rhetorical approach to visual-verbal narrative reminds us not to neglect the aural and oral dimensions of poetic multimodal texts, 'the music-like characteristics of literature', as Patrick Hogan (2014: 524) puts it. The rhetorical approach means further that we pay particular attention to how a text creates its effect on the reader, the rich communicative modes of both pictures and verbal text need to be studied for their meaning-making. When we focus on the interrelationship between form and degrees of meaning, it can help students to fathom how, as Debra Myhill (2010: 176) states, 'ideas are shaped and shaded by the language in which we choose to express them'. *Azzi In Between* is characterized by verbal artistry, and it is important that children can hear it read aloud as well as see the silent print. Joy Alexander (2010: 219), in a study on the affordances of orality, emphasizes the importance of 'always relating sound to meaning, promoting the habit of attentiveness, and ultimately showing that careful listening to language is not only a basic part of English as a subject but essential to the full use of language as a human being'. The rhythmical repetition of *Azzi In Between* is an example of how meaning can be conveyed poetically. The refugee family's hardships on the long and arduous voyage to a new country can be heard in the rhythms:

> Up the waves and down the waves, through the days and through the nights, the little boat ploughed steadily across the ocean.
> When Azzi licked her dry lips, she tasted the salt sea spray.
> When she cuddled Bobo, his fur was stiff with salt seawater.
> (Garland 2012)

The language of well-written children's literature displays stylistic cohesion such as rhythmical parallelisms ('up the waves and down the waves, through the days and through the nights'), lexical chains (waves, boat, ocean, salt sea spray, seawater) and the phonological patterns of rhythm and alliteration. These rhetorical devices also provide a natural focus on form in English language education: through phonological and semantic repetition in a striking context the language becomes salient and thus noticeable. This is crucial for language education in input-limited classroom settings. When supported by shared classroom readings, striking language or exciting reiteration can result in interesting language and grammatical categories being acquired implicitly.

Language that is understood through the receptive skills of reading and listening may become a useful template for the future (Bland, 2015b: 161) and for the productive skills of speaking and writing. For example, the striking phrase 'the little boat ploughed steadily across the ocean' may well be retained in memory. Many years later, this can help the learner notice that the expression 'plough through' or 'plough across' is often used figuratively when the going is difficult, for example: she ploughed across the patch of deep snow, the refugees had to plough through much paperwork.

The next section deals with different formats of refugee literature that are suitable for enriching English language education in the secondary school. These are Lewis and Weaver's illustrated fable (2017) *A Story Like the Wind*, Warsan Shire's 'Home', a poem and cinepoetic film, Brian Bilston's 'Refugees', a poem and poetic picturebook, and the graphic novel *Illegal* (Colfer, Donkin and Rigano 2017).

Poetic Refugee Literature

Extremely brief formats and media, such as short films, short stories and poems, offer very condensed glimpses into another world. On the important matter of the refugee experience, many significant and urgent micro literary texts are being created which could be interspersed into teaching almost extemporaneously. Cumulatively, this could have a powerful effect.

Short Film of Toksvig's Poem 'What They Took with Them'

The film *What They Took with Them* (UNHCR 2016) is a recreation of a rhythmic poem by Jenifer Toksvig, which is based on the testimonies and stories of refugees from the Syrian Civil War. Cate Blanchett, Goodwill Ambassador for the UNHCR, leads the performance of this compelling poem, supported by fellow actors Keira Knightley, Juliet Stevenson, Peter Capaldi, Stanley Tucci, Chiwetel Ejiofor, Kit Harington, Douglas

Booth, Jesse Eisenberg and the writer, Neil Gaiman. The performers read aloud the objects and vital necessities refugees have reported they took with them on their flight. Some items are repeated many times, such as water and photos, and it is this repetition that creates the urgency and inescapable gunshot-like rhythm. In between, the rapid beat of the five-minute film occasionally comes to a standstill when an actor reads a first-hand anecdote, for example:

> One man only brought a cup. 'I'd have been ashamed to ask every day for a cup just to take a drink of water. People get tired of being asked for things all the time and eventually they will say no. Now, I have my own cup. It gives me independence, no matter where I go.'

Photographs by Brian Sokol from a UNHCR photography project, 'The Most Important Thing', are interspersed between images of the actors reading the poem and film scenes of refugees fleeing the fighting. The students might think-pair-share the difficulties of travelling long distances on foot with small children and babies. After watching the short film again, they could make a list of all the items and situations listed in the poem relating to fleeing with very young as well as elderly family members.

Gill Lewis and Jo Weaver's *A Story Like the Wind*

On the cover of this little book, we can read the words 'A small boat. A small hope. A dream of freedom' (see Figure 5.5). Gill Lewis's *A Story Like the Wind* (2017) is also a small book, with only eighty pages, but like the dream of freedom presented in the book, it is overflowing with the need for connection, compassion and kindness against a background of tragedy and danger. Gill Lewis's story perfectly pairs lyrical language with Jo Weaver's ethereal charcoal illustrations, which add to the magic, the light and dark, the effects of music, waves and wind, creating an exceptionally cohesive story.

At the outset of the tale, we learn that two adolescent brothers, a couple and their two small children, an old man and his little dog, as well as the protagonist Rami, a violinist who is not yet fourteen, are afloat on the night ocean in a flimsy vessel,

> which is not a boat. It is a toy, a plaything for beaches and swimming pools. Two layers of plastic and air are all that lie between its passengers and the bottom of the sea. A belt buckle or loose hairpin could tear it apart. A ride on this rubber dinghy is as expensive as a cabin on a cruise ship. A one way ticket, a thousand dollars each.
>
> (Lewis 2017: 15)

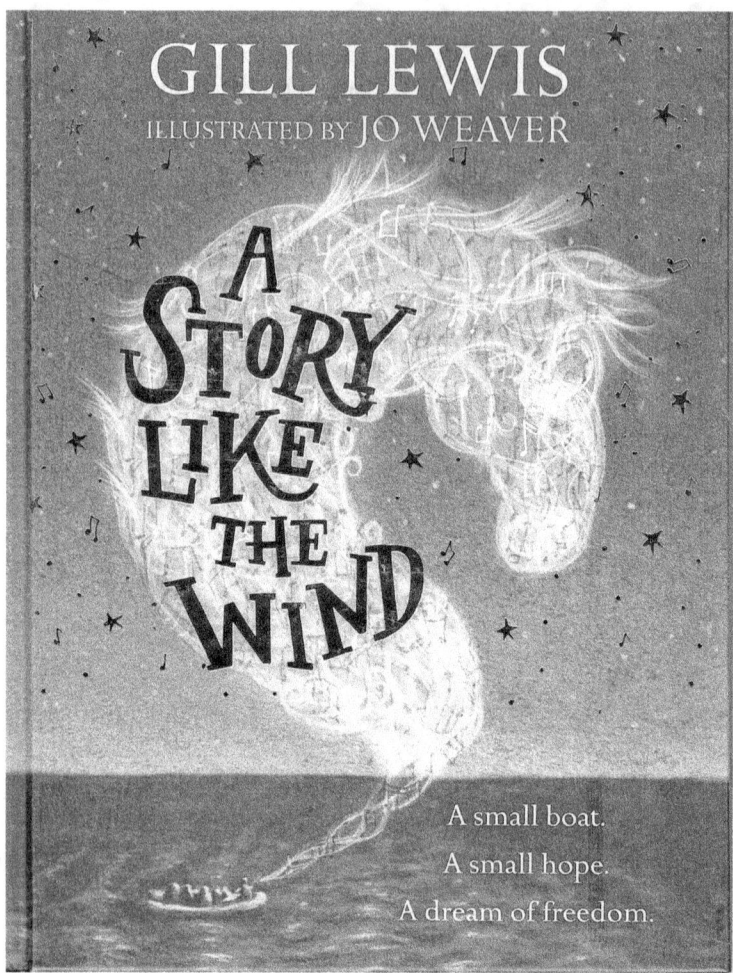

FIGURE 5.5 *Cover of* A Story Like the Wind. *Reproduced from* A Story Like the Wind *by Gill Lewis © 2017, illustrated by Jo Weaver © 2017, published by Oxford University Press.*

Somehow this story combines the tragedy of the refugee situation with many of the hopeful outlooks and emotions that Prior (2019: 521–2) mentions (see p. 103), such as *gratitude, optimism, love, belonging, empathy, spirituality, mindfulness, imagination, tolerance, responsibility*. This is due to the power of music and storytelling, for the fable interweaves the stories of the passengers, the ravages of war, but also reminiscences of their loved ones, with the fascinating story Rami tells, in words and through the music of his violin. The situation is dire, the refugees are adrift in the dark, they are barely clinging to life, but they ask Rami to play for them. He has managed to bring his violin with him, though everything else, including food, drink and warm clothes, had to be left behind when the soldiers came.

Rami's story within a story is an ancient Mongolian legend of the invention of the first *morin khuur*, or horse fiddle. This age-old tale tells of a white stallion that could run like the wind, and the love between the wild horse and a boy called Suke that led to the creation of the first fiddle. The entrancing music from this instrument united Suke's oppressed people, giving them agency to overcome persecution from a local tyrant, and obtain their freedom. In this way, Rami's story and his music in the terrible night becomes an allegory for the refugees about freedom from devastation and the hope for better things. The traditional Mongolian tale evokes a timelessness reminding us that throughout the ages people have had to struggle against tyranny, and have also been united through stories, music, love and hope.

The story, which has been endorsed by Amnesty International, ends with the ambiguous refrain:

> In a small boat
> With a small hope
> In a rising wind
> on a rising sea.

This powerful book is particularly suited to inspiring creative writing tasks. Groups could write the lyrics and melody to create their own song on the brotherhood and sisterhood of humanity. Another task can be to describe in brief words a fearful situation of terrifying loneliness, making use of typographic creativity and illustration. A further creative writing task could be to invent an ending to the refugee story, for the fate of the refugees at the end of *A Story Like the Wind* remains, like the wind, elusive and unknown.

Warsan Shire's 'Home'

A powerful narrative poem on the theme of the refugee journey is 'Home' by Warsan Shire (2015). The students could watch and listen to the cinepoetic short film on YouTube (Home 2017), with the poet reading her extremely moving poem. Here is an excerpt from 'Home':

> no one leaves home unless
> home is the mouth of a shark
> you only run for the border
> when you see the whole city running as well
> your neighbors running faster than you
> breath bloody in their throats
> the boy you went to school with
> who kissed you dizzy behind the old tin factory

is holding a gun bigger than his body
you only leave home
when home won't let you stay. (Shire 2015)

Secondary school students in groups could create a sequence of images as a storyboard of the poem, with captions under the different images. A cartoony style might help the students maintain some distance to the strong and tragic emotions of the poem ('you have to understand,/that no one puts their children in a boat/unless the water is safer than the land'). However, the teacher should take the age of the students into account as the poem alludes obliquely to the sexual violence that some refugees face before or during the journey.

Brian Bilston's 'Refugees'

A poem which brilliantly turns words of hate and negativity into generosity and positivity is 'Refugees' (2016) by Brian Bilston. This can be transformed into a multimodal text by inviting students to read the poem aloud – well-prepared reading aloud provides a motivating shared experience. In their research with secondary school students in language education, Sam Duncan and Amos Paran (2018: 257) found reading aloud to be 'an important pedagogical tool when used creatively and flexibly'. The students should have time to practise first, enjoying the element of surprise that is so special to this poem. Then one group of students reads the poem aloud, in the direction it is printed. The second group subsequently reads the poem aloud backwards, which completely reverses the meaning of the poem.

There is also a picturebook version of the poem, illustrated by José Sanabria (2019), with the poem printed and illustrated in both directions. The apparent use of newspaper cut-and-paste text for the title *REFUGEES* is reminiscent of newspaper coverage of the refugee crisis since 2016 (when the poem was first written in response to the refugee tragedies of that year) and the way some populist politicians have tried to make political capital of voters' fears in recent years. Sanabria is a Colombian illustrator based in Argentina. His style of magical realism seems to connect the real-world events the poem alludes to with fantasy and absurdity, perhaps in reference to the often-irrational nature of our fears of otherness.

If students want to try out their own kind of reverse poem, they should note that by splitting sentences using line breaks, as Bilston does, and by omitting punctuation, they can more easily restructure a poem into new and different sentences, with the aim of allowing the overall meaning of the poem to transform when read from bottom to top.

Refugees by Brian Bilston
They have no need of our help
So do not tell me

These haggard faces could belong to you or me
Should life have dealt a different hand
We need to see them for who they really are
Chancers and scroungers
Layabouts and loungers
With bombs up their sleeves
Cut-throats and thieves
They are not
Welcome here
We should make them
Go back to where they came from
They cannot
Share our food
Share our homes
Share our countries
Instead let us
Build a wall to keep them out
It is not okay to say
These are people just like us
A place should only belong to those who are born there
Do not be so stupid to think that
The world can be looked at another way

Now read from bottom to top!
(From *You Took the Last Bus Home*, copyright Bilston 2016, reproduced with kind permission of the author.)

The Tragedy of the Journey: Colfer, Donkin and Rigano's *Illegal*

Illegal, a fictional graphic novel by Eoin Colfer and Andrew Donkin (2017), illustrated by Giovanni Rigano, tells with sensitivity and compassion the story of the devastating risks that refugees and migrants undertake when journeying to reach Europe. The authors and illustrator outline the perils in an afterword:

> Every year, many thousands of men, women, and children risk their lives by trying to make the dangerous 300-mile sea crossing between Northern Africa and Italy. They pay large sums of money to smugglers who in return provide poorly prepared unseaworthy boats. The distances involved are formidable and the sea currents are unpredictable. The smuggling networks that run these operations make fortunes with no regard for human life. They send their victims out to sea in death traps.
> (Colfer, Donkin and Rigano 2017)

Illegal shows the dangers that unaccompanied children face, the orphaned brothers Kwame and Ebo, and their friend Razak whom they meet on a truck crossing the Sahara Desert. As a graphic novel, the epic and often fatal struggles are revealed in pictures that are difficult to forget, which makes this a harrowing tale, and an important one. The young migrants witness murder when paying passengers fall from an overcrowded truck and are left behind to die in the desert; they experience dehydration, sickness without medical care, and the brutality of smugglers who provide only death traps for the Mediterranean crossing.

Before reading this graphic novel with students, the beautiful book trailer could be watched and discussed (YouTube 2017 https://www.youtube.com/watch?v=pM5OLzlu7I4). The book trailer shows the wonderful artwork of Rigano, the inky blues of the sea voyage and the amazing facial expressions that tell so much of the story. How much can your students predict of the children's journey? It is likely they know little, even if they are older than Ebo and Kwame in *Illegal*, as the media reports of tragedies involving refugees and migrants who are trying to reach Europe are always brief, with very little follow-up.

At the beginning of the story, twelve-year-old Ebo is left alone as his brother Kwame has left the village to try to find their sister Sisi. Kwame left his brother a note:

Ebo –
I will go to Europe –
I will find Sisi –
I will send money for you to come later by helicopter –
this is mine to do –
Kwame (2017: 10)

The brothers Kwame and Ebo are from Ghana (2017: 61), and we perceive they are both literate in English, the official language of Ghana. However, they are orphans, and we see from some of the detailed panels that set the scene (see Figure 5.6) that they come from a small, impoverished village. It is most likely that they had no chance to attend education beyond elementary school; this would explain their very naïve notion of their likely reception and opportunities in Europe. Their lack of adult support clarifies why they risk their lives at the hands of nefarious men. The story is told through pictures, through dialogue and Ebo's thoughts. The background is scarcely touched upon in the graphic novel, but secondary school students may well notice the dangerously mistaken expectations of the brothers and their friends.

We jump back and forth through alternating time periods, so that a useful task in the classroom would be to create a chronological timeline of the full journey – that took nearly two years – with the geographic locations of each section. There is a helpful map on p. 124. We follow Ebo on his first

FIGURE 5.6 Illegal (2017: 10). *Extract from* Illegal *by Eoin Colfer and Andrew Donkin © 2017, illustrated by Giovanni Rigano © 2017, reproduced by permission of Hodder Children's Books, an imprint of Hachette Children's Group, Carmelite House, 50 Victoria Embankment, London, EC4Y 0DZ.*

trip after leaving his home village, balancing on the top of a bus all the way to the vast city of Agadez, where he is desperate to find Kwame. Agadez in Niger is a major transit city for West African migrants heading to Europe via Libya. Amazingly, the brothers find each other, and work for nearly half a year to save money to pay migrant smugglers to take them across the treacherous Sahara Desert (see Figure 5.7). The depiction of the brutal journey across the desert with the unscrupulous smugglers is terrifying, and some of the travellers do not survive.

FIGURE 5.7 Illegal (2017: 52). *Extract from* Illegal *by Eoin Colfer and Andrew Donkin* © *2017, illustrated by Giovanni Rigano* © *2017, reproduced by permission of Hodder Children's Books, an imprint of Hachette Children's Group, Carmelite House, 50 Victoria Embankment, London, EC4Y 0DZ.*

Important, full-page panels are ideal for the cooperative process of *reciprocal teaching*. With this method, groups of four discuss the panel with a specific role for each student: summarizers, clarifiers, predictors and questioners. Using Figure 5.7 as an example, the roles can be divided as follows:

- The *summarizers* describe the content of the panel orally – where, when and why does this take place? They suggest ideas for a title for this page.

- The *clarifiers* consider what is difficult, confusing or unfamiliar for the reader and attempt to clarify language, meanings, and content.
- The *predictors* look carefully at the picture to interpret the difficulties the people face and to predict what will happen next.
- The *questioners* investigate the meaning of migrant smugglers, migrants and refugees. What connections can be made to recent and current situations?

Once each student has briefly discussed and understood his role in the group of four, the groups disperse and all the summarizers, clarifiers, predictors and questioners meet, compare notes, potentially revise their findings and then report back to their home groups and then to the class.

Illegal does not show how the boys work for months in order to finance their journeying onwards to Tripoli in Libya, from where they mean to cross the Mediterranean to Italy. However, we see the terrible conditions of their stay in Tripoli, where they sleep in a drain and hide from the authorities as they have no papers, while trying to earn the money to pay people-smuggling gangs for the final, most deadly, journey. The voyage across the Mediterranean in an overloaded, patched-up rubber dinghy that soon leaks is an intense emotional experience for the reader. None of the boys can swim, and of course the criminal migrant smugglers did not provide life jackets. All of these are shocking but realistic details, emotionally drawn by Rigano, the master of facial expression and body language. A large, crowded vessel spots the children in the leaking rubber dinghy and the captain takes them on board, although his ship is also overloaded with refugees.

This is not the end of their ordeal, however. We have accompanied the determined, bright and musical young Ebo throughout the narrative, only to see him witness the drowning of his brother Kwame and Razak when a structure on the decrepit ship breaks apart, just as they are being rescued. This is realistic, and these stories must be heard. There is the consolation at the very end that Sisi discovers Ebo in the Italian refugee centre, but the students might not find this very convincing. Secondary school students are likely to know that Ebo's harrowing story is not yet over. Some EU countries forcibly return unaccompanied child migrants (currently Italy is not one of these). In other EU countries, once unaccompanied child migrants reach the age of eighteen, they lose their right to stay.

The students could choose to investigate some of the following questions relating to *Illegal* and, in small groups, prepare poster presentations that prompt openings for whole-class discussion, or with other groups during a gallery walk:

- How does *Illegal* show the worst and best of people?
- How many ways can you think of to interpret the title *Illegal*?

- Can you demonstrate that *Illegal*, though fiction, is rooted in nonfiction? You might like to refer to Helen's Story, the factual account at the end of *Illegal*.
- Do you consider that the lack of a refugee or migrant contributor to *Illegal* (#ownvoices) devalues the text?
- In what ways does Ebo seem to be a migrant rather than a refugee? How does this matter?
- How does the graphic novel format add meaning to the story?
- How might Ebo be disappointed with Europe?

Illegal, and all the previous texts introduced in this chapter, can help develop thoughtful feelings in the reader, an important educational addition to language competence. Thoughtful feelings involve cognition: 'feelings and thinking are two sides of the same coin' (Ratner 2000: 6). *Outcome* emotions are those that are longer lasting after having read or viewed compelling and moving stories (Hogan 2014). While persuasive and compelling stories such as those in this chapter support potentially long-lasting thoughtful feelings, experimental studies have also shown the beneficial effect of stories on ToM and our readiness to empathize (Kidd, Ongis and Castano 2016; Oatley 2017). Lastly, refugee stories also provide the value of bringing different experiences and perspectives into the classroom: 'Different, even contradictory perspectives must not only be tolerated, they must be nurtured. So long as there is open dialogue, they provide the best opportunities for improved understandings' (van Lier 1994: 342).

CHAPTER SIX

The Grandeur of Graphic Novels

The danger zone of losing the habit of literature, possibly for life, is at the beginning of adolescence, at around the age of twelve, according to a study conducted in Germany (Harmgarth 1999: 18). This reading blip is noticed by many educators, and may just be temporary, but if students are not given experiences of compelling stories while in school, that are suited to their developing passions as well as their developing language, the reading blip can become a permanent disinterest in reading.

Reading is an urgent matter both for lifelong learning opportunities and for democracy. The Pisa report (OECD 2021) *21st-Century Readers: Developing Literacy Skills in a Digital World* published findings on the literacy skills of fifteen-year-old school students in approximately seventy OECD countries. A crucial finding was that while the most proficient readers make optimal use of digital technology for reading for information, these strong readers are also those who enjoy reading a book on paper. The stronger the reader, the report indicates, the more likely they are to search for information on the internet by exploring a relevant source with focused attention, then create their own dynamic pathway by navigating to multiple sources in order to distinguish high-quality, credible information and to corroborate the information (OECD 2021: 52).

School has a vital role in enhancing enjoyment of reading, which is now on the decline in some countries. Enjoyment of reading among teachers as well as students is key, and according to OECD 2021 the most pronounced decline in reading enjoyment over the last decade is to be seen in Germany, Finland and Norway (2021: 79). Strong readers perform well whether reading in print or reading digitally. However, increasingly school students are not strong readers, and 'disinformation and fake news are jeopardising democracies that function poorly when citizens are not well informed or worse, misled. Disinformation is not unique to digital technologies but the Internet spreads and amplifies its impact' (OECD 2021: 20).

Graphic novels can bridge the pedagogic gap between the more visual and engaging multisensory educational culture of the elementary school and the often more abstract and verbal educational culture of lower secondary or middle school. In contrast to comic books, John Foster (2010: np) considers that graphic novels are 'likely to have a more sophisticated approach to artwork, subject, plot and characterisation. Additionally, graphic novels often deal with "bigger" topics [...] with some complexity.' In the twenty-first century, the graphic novel has metamorphosed from basically a longer comic to a multimodal format that incorporates pictures in a variety of ways that can be compelling fiction and nonfiction, and in addition ideal for deep reading. At the same time, many students will find the connection between comics and graphic novels an attractive trait, encouraging them to give them a try.

Conventions of Graphic Novels

There are certain distinctive elements that are often present in graphic narratives, and it is useful to consider how these conventions contribute to the characteristics of graphic storytelling. However, some award-winning books that are generally called graphic novels may hardly feature any typical conventions at all, for example the works of Brian Selznick.

Extensive use of direct speech in *speech balloons* and characters' inner speech in *thought balloons* deepens the reader's involvement with characters in the graphic novel storyworld. Thus, much of the language of graphic novels is dialogue, in which characters employ the rhythm and register of conversational language. This can be very supportive of second language acquisition as well as aiding character-centred engagement in storytelling, or protagonism (Brown et al. 2019). The *caption* is the (usually boxed) area of text that is narrated, not spoken in dialogue.

The *cinematic point of view* (Keating 2005: 440), or point-of-view shot (Bordwell and Thompson 2001: 433), refers to when we see what a character, usually the protagonist, is looking at, viewing a scene literally as if with their eyes. In Selznick's *The Invention of Hugo Cabret*, for example, we look through the clock face with Hugo at the old man in the toy booth, thus seeing this important character for the first time through Hugo's eyes (2007: 44–5). This is in effect a reinforcement of the *literary point of view* of verbal narratives, when we can share the perceptual as well as conceptual perspective of a protagonist, without literally seeing but rather imagining an image of what they see – a mental representation. The empathetic tie with a protagonist in multimodal texts can be very strong due to the combined literary point of view with the occasional use of cinematic point of view. The frequent *close-ups* of facial expressions also support the character-centred force of the graphic novel.

Each image in graphic novels is usually enclosed in a *panel*, and often surrounded by a *border*. The readers mentally construct the relationship between the frozen moments of each panel and close the gaps between the panels in their imagination. The sequence, size and shape of panels can affect the reading experience, for example by speeding up or slowing down the narrative. In *Animal Farm, The Graphic Novel* (Orwell and Odyr 2019), discussed in Chapter 11, there are no borders to the panels and the narrative seems to move forward fluidly and irrevocably. In *The Life of Frederick Douglass: A Graphic Narrative of a Slave's Journey from Bondage to Freedom* (Walker and Smyth 2018), discussed in this chapter, there is a certain rigidity to the panel shapes and borders, which highlights the way the slaves are entrapped and cut off from their humanity.

The space between panels is called the *gutter*. It is in these gaps that reader participation is required, which Scott McCloud (1993: 92) calls 'a silent dance of the seen and the unseen'. Vanderbeke (2006: 366) calls this space 'an integral part of the comic. In the classroom, this may offer itself for various tasks like telling what may have happened between temporally distant panels or adding one's own panels with additional dialogue in order to fill gaps.' A combination of panels and gutters with dialogue in speech balloons may seem simple elements, but they can combine in complex ways, forcing the reader to use their imagination, and occasioning participation and involvement.

A cartoony artistic style is common in comics and graphic novels. Scott McCloud (1993: 30) identifies this as 'amplification through simplification', meaning that the cartoon style is more abstract and therefore more universal, and potentially more focused and intense than realistic styles (see Chapter 5: 112). Other conventions that amplify meaning in stylized ways are *motion lines* and *sound effects*. Motion lines have become conventionalized to indicate the dynamic effects of movement, and a visualized soundtrack (sound effects such as *boom*! *crash*! *wham*!) creates dramatic energy and suspense through onomatopoeic sound play. The effect of the verbal text may also be enhanced through *typographic creativity*, the thickness of type and different fonts, for example, can contribute additional meaning through visual means: 'The idea that a picture can evoke an emotional or sensual response in the viewer is vital to the art of comics' (McCloud 1993: 121).

The Graphic Novel and Deep Reading

Although a graphic novel is a multimodal text in print medium, it can nonetheless connect the acquisition of literacies with the experience of digital natives, who, of course, are used to reading pictorial text alongside verbal text on screens. Moreover, graphic novels, once their complexities have been understood, can make reading a social event, just as comics do for younger children, which is appealing to highly networked digital natives. Graphic novels can make reading a pleasure, particularly for reluctant readers, who, increasingly (OECD 2021), are the larger proportion of adolescent readers in language education, as well as rather too many student teachers. Confident readers, on the other hand, may need to experience and discover the artistry of an excellent graphic novel, before being motivated to practise deep reading with this format. For it is still widely yet erroneously believed, as Aleixo and Norris (2010: 72) point out, that as adolescents deepen their literacy skills, 'sophistication in readers is demonstrated by reading words alone no longer accompanied by any images'.

Fortunately, the tendency to canonize only a narrow range of literature and the expectation of clearly defined, absolute meanings in literary texts is changing, and current language education curricula often include multimodal texts. However, teachers' attitudes towards perceived canonical texts are changing rather more slowly (Alfes et al. 2021). Multimodal texts can mentor the community of readers to engage with the text, in that they almost force a creative-literary response and deep reading. For graphic novels and picturebooks always feature gaps – the discrepancies from panel to panel or from spread to spread, as well as the interaction of pictures and words, which are re-assembled in the head of the reader. This allows not only an apprenticeship in how to read a literary text deeply, it also offers the maximum opportunities for talk around the text, or booktalk, defined as 'co-operative talk in which a community of readers makes discoveries far beyond anything they could have found on their own' (Chambers 2011: 164).

Not all comics and graphic novels are excellent, which is, of course, also true of novels, films and picturebooks. When selecting a graphic novel for deep reading in an educational context, the optimal use of the graphic novel format, the genre and the content should all be considered. For this chapter, I have chosen two graphic novels that have achieved great impact. The first is in the genre of biography: David Walker's *The Life of Frederick Douglass*, which undoubtedly deserves to reach audiences worldwide. The second is already a classic, a historical tale with fairy tale elements that has introduced exciting innovations to the graphic novel format: Brian Selznick's *The Invention of Hugo Cabret*.

Using the Deep Reading Framework with Walker and Smyth's *The Life of Frederick Douglass*

Unpuzzle and Explore

David Walker's graphic novel, illustrated by Damon Smyth and Marissa Louise (2018), *The Life of Frederick Douglass: A Graphic Narrative of a Slave's Journey from Bondage to Freedom*, tells a compelling story that is both historical and inspirational (see Figure 6.1, and Figure 1.1 for the Deep Reading Framework).

FIGURE 6.1 *Cover of* The Life of Frederick Douglass. *From* The Life of Frederick Douglass *by David F. Walker © 2018, illustrated by Damon Smyth © 2018. Reprinted by permission of Penguin Random House LLC.*

This is a nonfiction, biographical narrative that is replete with information on the historic personality of Frederick Douglass and the times he lived through – consequences of which reverberate well into the twenty-first century and the international Black Lives Matter movement. Beside the story of Douglass's life, there is a concise account of the institution of slavery in the United States, a brief explanation of the Civil War and a focus on the invention of photography when Douglass was a young man, which enabled a more truthful picture of African Americans than the stereotyped and dehumanizing paintings of the time. However, the story itself, narrated in Frederick Douglass's voice, and presenting scene after scene of his epic struggle, takes the reader to the heart of the matter, the inhumanity of slavery. First-person narrators are becoming more common in nonfiction, informational books. This can strengthen their impact, and even reach a profounder truth: 'Informational books thus go far beyond facts, readily available elsewhere, to awaken curiosity, inspire awe, and nurture community' (von Merveldt 2018: 232).

The graphic novel *The Life of Frederick Douglass* makes use of traditional graphic novel conventions: speech balloons and captions, full-page panels for pivotal moments and up to seven panels per page when the narrative hurries forward. The borders and gutters are uniform and unyielding, suggesting the lack of freedom that counterparts the topic. This rigidity is alleviated for the reader by the colour images, which downplay the brutality somewhat for the younger readership. The narrative makes excellent use of the pictorial, the gestural, the spatial as well as the verbal. David Walker uses Douglass's ideas and key words as expressed in his many speeches and three autobiographies to recreate the magnitude of his contribution and historical significance. In his introduction, Walker (2018: 2) explains his use of first-person narrative as a means to best express Douglass's overriding concern throughout his life, 'the reclamation of his humanity, and the humanity of all those held in the dehumanizing bondage of slavery'. The point of view is therefore that of Douglass, with occasional use of cinematic point of view when we see Douglass from behind as he gives a speech, and together we gaze on his audience.

The many close-ups of Douglass in different situations and at different times cause the circumstances of his life to play in the reader's mind like a documentary film, engaging the reader intellectually and emotionally, provoking thoughtful feelings. Students reading this graphic novel might like to consider in groups which scene moves them the most (and why), which is the most cinematic scene, and which is the most surprising one. As there is much to transport and amaze in the graphic novel – not least how much Douglass managed to achieve although without any means of obtaining formal schooling – there is potential for many different answers to these questions.

Activate and Investigate

Slavery has existed throughout world history in different forms. Slavery in the slave states of the United States before 1865 is often called chattel slavery, as slaves were legally property of their owners, who could buy, sell and bequeath slaves, split up families at any time, often tearing small children from their mothers, as happened to Frederick Douglass. Chattel slavery is now illegal throughout the world; however, related world events in the present day are the criminal industries of human trafficking, child labour, child soldiers and forced marriage. In pairs, students could create a timeline based on the information provided in the commentary 'A Brief History of Slavery in America' (2018: 12–15). They should leave space to fill in related events that followed the passing of the Thirteenth Amendment in 1865 and the outlawing of slavery in the United States. Some of these later events are covered in the story of Frederick Douglass, who lived circa 1817–1895. If time allows, perhaps as Content and Language Integrated Learning in the history class, it would be possible to continue the timeline of struggle and related world events to the present day, and the advent of the Black Lives Matter movement.

Reading and seeing a first-hand experience of slavery is heart-breaking, but it is also powerful and empowering, as we can only understand the present by trying to understand the past. The history of racism, the Black Lives Matter and Black Heroes Matter movements, taking the knee and the importance of representation of marginalized groups in stories are all interconnected. It is a privilege for school students to be able to come so close to a survivor of slavery as this graphic novel allows, for the huge majority of slaves were prevented from learning to read and write and thus had no chance at all to tell their stories. We read how Douglass discovered at a young age the importance of literacy as the key to agency, how he taught himself clandestinely, and also helped to teach others, despite punishments and violence. The dialogic, cooperative process of reciprocal teaching works very well at this stage. Groups of four students might gather around page 36 of the graphic novel (see Figure 6.2) each with a particular role:

> The *summarizers* describe the content of the panel orally – where, when, and why does this take place? They suggest ideas for a title for this page.
>
> The *clarifiers* consider what might be difficult, confusing, or unfamiliar for the reader and attempt to clarify language, meanings, and content.
>
> The *predictors* look carefully at the picture to interpret the different roles of the three characters and to predict what will happen next.
>
> The *questioners* investigate the meaning of chattel slavery and the significance of literacy. Can connections be made to current movements?

Frederick Douglass was one of the greatest abolitionists and civil rights pioneers of the nineteenth century, which is highlighted in the verbal text of the graphic novel. But for today's school students, the illustrations are of utmost importance to help them picture the time and the events that still cast a shadow across the twenty-first century. Douglass's life was momentous: 'The journey that I call my life has been one of suffering and

FIGURE 6.2 *Literacy forbidden for slaves (2018: 36). From* The Life of Frederick Douglass *by David F. Walker © 2018, illustrated by Damon Smyth © 2018. Reprinted by permission of Penguin Random House LLC.*

celebration. I have been kept in chains, and I have conferred with presidents' (Walker 2018: 6), yet the characterization of Douglass includes not only action and history, but also his self-doubts and a focus on his family, all of which humanizes him while shedding light on his life. An exercise in information literacy can be to ask students to find reliable information on the many leading figures of his day that Douglass met, which resulted in mutual influence, including Abraham Lincoln, John Brown, Harriet Tubman, Elizabeth Cady Stanton, Susan B. Anthony, Sojourner Truth and Ida B. Wells.

Critically Engage

Non-fictional accounts also select and interpret facts, of course. In picturebooks and graphic novels, as von Merveldt writes (2018: 232), 'this equally applies to the images: they do not merely represent or illustrate transparent data or facts; rather they render them visible or visualize them, which means they take on an active, interpretative role.' Readers might look critically at the images, to see how the situations and the atrocity of slavery are represented and interpreted. While very well researched, Douglass's story goes beyond known facts, and students could consider whether the narrative conveys a lesser or deeper truth in this way. The relationship between truth and art has been studied in-depth by author Salman Rushdie (2021: 26): 'The truth is not arrived at by purely mimetic means. An image can be captured by a camera or by a paintbrush. A painting of a starry night is no less truthful than a photograph of one; arguably, if the painter is Van Gogh, it's far more truthful, even though far less "realistic".'

Students might discuss the significance of #ownvoices in creating the biography of Frederick Douglass. This was undoubtedly important to the author, David Walker, and illustrator, Damon Smyth, who are both biracial: 'When they met at coffee shops for hours-long meetings to go over the graphic novel, they talked frequently about the likelihood that Douglass was biracial, as well (probably the son of one of his family's slave owners)' (Betancourt 2019).

The students could debate whether ignoring heroes of marginalized groups in the history curriculum constitutes epistemological racism. As long as a safe classroom climate has been established (see Chapter 5: 102–104), students might be willing to share their own experiences and feelings. Ryuko Kubota (2020: 722) refers to epistemological racism when she writes, 'White Euro-American values, beliefs, and worldviews, including individualism, meritocracy, progress, and so on, have dominated the rest of the world through colonialism, slavery, capitalism, and neocolonialism, negatively affecting nonwhite groups socially, culturally, economically, and psychologically.' It is a lifelong challenge to combat subtle epistemological racism, or unchallenged White privilege, and to promote instead resistance to all kinds of group-focused enmity, and to support each and every minoritized group in developing self-efficacy and their full potential. Kubota refers to the – for White people – often invisible ideology of epistemological racism when she claims it is a 'white Euro-American club of knowledge' (2020: 724) that maintains the existence of an unequal system and hierarchy.

As nonfiction and biography, *The Life of Frederick Douglass* depicts with graphic immediacy the cruelty of tearing children from their parents, the horrors of slavery in the slave states and the racist nightmare not only in the south of the United States. We also see Douglass crafting a new life, with the support of abolitionists and through his own determination, his achievements as an orator, his international travel and his influence on the

Civil War. In the interests of media literacy, students might like to consider how many major films, graphic novels and literary texts similarly and consistently uphold the point of view of a protagonist of colour. Writing on the UK, Karen Sands-O'Connor reports (2019, emphasis in original):

> While about a third of school-age children come from a minority ethnic background, the Centre for Literacy in Primary Education found that only 7% of children's books published in Britain in 2018 had a Black, Asian or minority ethnic character. [...] When characters of colour appear in children's books, they are rarely the protagonist with the agency to effect change. [...] Children's nonfiction, including history and science, either ignores contributions of people of colour to British society or pigeonholes particular ethnic groups into certain spaces only – such as the history of British slavery (and very specifically *not* the history of Afro-Caribbean uprisings against British slavery).

How does this affect students' sense of being welcomed into the world of books? Can books become a friend when the young reader feels misrepresented?

Experiment with Creative Response

Due to the many speech balloons and short stretches of text in captions, episodes from the graphic novel can be rehearsed in groups, with students acting out the parts and reading aloud, and potentially performing to the class. There are a number of episodes where Douglass holds a speech; in these scenes some students could practise playing unscripted roles, speaking freely (ad-libbing) as supportive or heckling members of the audience. In one episode, Harriet Tubman, legendary conductor on the Underground Railroad, brings eleven fugitive slaves to Douglass's home for shelter on their passage north. This scene could be extended, with the escapees telling of the lives they have run away from, their immediate needs, and their dreams for the future. At the beginning of *The Life of Frederick Douglass*, eighteen characters are briefly introduced, each with a picture. Students could role-play these persons in Douglass's life, and other students could interview them.

Group hot-seating is a useful drama convention for comparing understandings and readings of a literary text (see also Chapter 9: 209). Students play the role of different characters in the book, sitting at the front of the class. Other students ask questions, and the hot-seated students must answer in role. They may also talk to each other, always staying in role. After reading the beginning of the book, for example, five students could play young Douglass, his older self as the narrator of his story, his grandmother, his mother and Miss Lucretia Auld, while the class asks them questions.

Later, as an escaped slave, Frederick Douglass became a prominent public speaker, which strongly contributed to his influence and renown. The class could hold a public speaking competition, preparing short talks in pairs on any topic related to the matter of the book, and deliver their talk, perhaps as powerful speakers in the style of Frederick Douglass (see Figure 6.3). Students could write a short blog post on the topic of sending free-born African Americans and former slaves to establish a colony in Africa. This became Liberia, a colony designed to accommodate free-born people of colour and freed slaves, but also to circumvent slave rebellions. Douglass

FIGURE 6.3 *Douglass the Orator (2018: 86). From* The Life of Frederick Douglass *by David F. Walker* © *2018, illustrated by Damon Smyth* © *2018. Reprinted by permission of Penguin Random House LLC.*

condemns the policy of sending African Americans to Africa: 'We will not be cast aside... Placed on boats and shipped off like unwanted rubbish. We are human beings. As slaves, we built this nation, by force. We will not, as free men and women, be made to leave that which we have built' (2018: 86).

The students could be invited to write the lyrics of a song, perhaps in small groups, inspired, for example, by Bob Marley, or a poem inspired by Maya Angelou. In 2020, the estate of Bob Marley released an official animated video (accessible on YouTube) of one of his best-known songs, 'Redemption Song', with Marley accompanying his singing on acoustic guitar. 'Redemption Song' includes the haunting lines: 'Emancipate yourselves from mental slavery/None but ourselves can free our minds.' A video of Maya Angelou reciting her poem 'On the Pulse of Morning', at the inauguration of President Bill Clinton in 1993, may also be accessed on YouTube, courtesy of the Clinton Presidential Library. According to Lupton (1998: 17), Angelou's 'theatrical rendering of "On the Pulse of the Morning" is, in a sense, a return to African American oral tradition, when slaves like Frederick Douglass stood on platforms in abolitionist meeting halls [...]. The ode also echoes the rhetorical grace of the African American sermon, as practiced and modified by Martin Luther King Jr., Malcom X, Jesse Jackson.' Angelou's poem includes the memorable lines:

> History, despite its wrenching pain
> Cannot be unlived, but if faced
> With courage, need not be lived again.

Students might write about local or international injustices and sing, rap or render their own songs or poems in a vivid oral tradition.

Redressing the Balance – Films and Documentaries Directed by #ownvoices

In order to deepen understanding of the weight of *The Life of Frederick Douglass* for twenty-first-century concerns, many #ownvoices films and documentaries produced in the 2010s can be recommended that feature historical and present-day takes on African American and British African-Caribbean experience, and the systemic racism that continues until the present day. Recent informative and compelling narratives could be watched and discussed together, for example as an after-school film club. The following suggestions are all based on true events, except for *The Hate U Give*, which is nonetheless true to life.

A series of viewings might begin with *Belle* (2014), directed by Amma Asante, a love story set in England against the background of the massacre of enslaved Africans on the British slave ship *Zong* in 1781. This could be followed by *12 Years a Slave* (2013), directed by Steve McQueen, about a free-born violinist from New York who was kidnapped and sold as a slave in 1841. After watching this film, it could be discussed whether the appalling experiences of female slaves, which often included rape, refusing time for critical childcare and abuse of their children, in addition to the evil of slave labour, are less often focused on than male slave narratives. *The Butler* (2013), by Lee Daniels, covers key twentieth-century events of US and world history, and *BlacKkKlansman* (2018), directed by Spike Lee, tells the story of an African American detective who exposed a Ku Klux Klan chapter in the 1970s. The film *Mangrove* (2020), directed by Steve McQueen, portrays the 1971 trial of the Mangrove Nine, reveals widespread institutional racism and offers a long overdue alternative position on UK history. *The Hate U Give* (2018), directed by George Tillman Jr., is a highly topical story of police violence against African Americans, based on the young adult novel by Angie Thomas.

Further films on this topic directed by Ava DuVernay, centring on or documenting real events, are highly recommended for students who are sixteen or older. These include *Selma* (2015), which shows the perils for peaceful protesters on the marches led by Martin Luther King and his co-activists on the right to vote for African Americans in the southern states. DuVernay's impressive documentary *13th* (2016) reveals a shocking pattern of cycles of oppression of African Americans and minoritized people of poverty that followed slavery and continues until the present day. Netflix has made the compelling and troubling documentary freely accessible on YouTube, with a choice of subtitles in sixteen languages. DuVernay's mini-Netflix series, *When They See Us* (2019), is the devastating and true story of a miscarriage of justice in the United States, a genuine education on systemic racism that could be relevant in many countries, not the United States alone. We observe the shattering effect of a wrongful (and brazenly manipulated) conviction for rape on the lives of five Black and Latino schoolboys, who are only exonerated thirteen years later. Hogan uses the term *outcome emotions* for 'emotions that are relatively enduring at the end of the story' (2014: 517). DuVernay's *When They See Us* shows the terror and damage to the fourteen- to sixteen-year-old boys and their families; films such as this elicit empathy as well as conceptual and perceptual perspective-taking at the time of viewing, leading to outcome emotions, which help us to learn more deeply.

Films that are not #ownvoices might be compared to the narratives above. *The Help* (2011), directed by Tate Taylor, and *Green Book* (2018), directed by Peter Farrelly, are illuminating on the Jim Crow laws as well as compelling narratives, and *Green Book* is also based on a true story. However, some critics have detected the White saviour narrative in *The Help*, for example. Comparing #ownvoices films with films by White directors – and female and male directors – can lead to an interesting discussion on the importance of including #ownvoices and all voices – the principle of multivoicedness – and learning to read against the text where there is bias, a topic I take up again in Chapter 11 on the White saviour narrative in *The Hunger Games* films.

A Highly Interwoven Text: Brian Selznick's *The Invention of Hugo Cabret*

While classrooms across the world are increasingly characterized by cultural diversity and readers by complex sociocultural identities (see Figure 10.1, in Chapter 10), serious literary texts are increasingly diverging from the monomodal novel format, and not only for children and young adults. As Roderick McGillis suggests (2011: 349): 'Literature and the other arts now consist of "texts". [...] "Text", however, suggests something woven, textured, connected to strands that may lead beyond the single text to contexts, intertexts, and subtexts.' So the opportunities for talking around texts in the classroom – with potential for acquisition of multiple literacies through cognitively demanding deep-reading processes – can be increased both through text ensembles as suggested throughout this book, and complex, interwoven multimodal texts such as Brian Selznick's *The Invention of Hugo Cabret*. However, while widening the canon of language education to include far more multimodal literature makes absolute sense, both artistry and craft in the matter of storytelling remain crucial, which is a leitmotiv in *Hugo Cabret*.

Hugo Cabret (2007) won the Caldecott Medal for best picturebook in 2008. Selznick entitled his book *The Invention of Hugo Cabret* possibly because the multimodal format he uses is an invention that blurs the boundary between picturebooks, novels and silent film. Oziewicz (2018: 30) argues with many examples that graphic novels display 'fewer restrictions on design, style, content and formula of picture-word interaction' in comparison to the related formats of the picturebook, comic books and comic strips. According to Oziewicz, Selznick's complex multimodal narratives, for example, are to be considered graphic novels, even though they do not feature speech balloons or multiple panels to a page. *Hugo Cabret* is an exhilarating and moving story, and while long passages are, like a conventional novel, told in words, much of the story is told through pictures. As a novel, *The Invention of Hugo Cabret* would be considered short. The book has 26,159 words, and a novel is said to be between 60,000 and 200,000 words. However, the book has no fewer than 284 pictures. There are no panels, narrated captions or speech balloons filled with dialogue, and the pictures are spread across facing pages – in this respect like picturebooks that usually feature double-page spreads – and the spreads additionally have a striking black surround. Consequently, the beautifully drawn black-and-white pictures are like film images that fill the whole screen in a cinema.

The narrator of the story begins, in a brief introduction, exactly as if we were going to watch a movie (I always ask my student teachers to close their eyes while I read this passage aloud):

> I want you to picture yourself sitting in the darkness, like the beginning of a movie. On screen, the sun will soon rise, and you will find yourself zooming toward a train station in the middle of the city. You will rush through the doors into a crowded lobby. You will eventually spot a boy amid the crowd, and he will start to move through the train station. Follow him, because this is Hugo Cabret. His head is full of secrets.
> (Selznick 2007: ix)

We are asked to visualize the story of *Hugo Cabret* from the outset as if it were a film, before we see the first picture of the book. This beginning explicitly helps struggling and reluctant readers to create a mental representation, and the ability to create a mental model of the storyworld is the hallmark of a fluent reader. McTaggart (2008: 33) maintains that reading graphic novels in the classroom 'promotes better reading skills, improves comprehension, and complements other areas of the curriculum'. She goes on to argue that the student who 'is unable to form pictures in his [*sic*] head while reading the printed word is not really reading. [...] The words give him no message, and they bring him no joy.'

The pictures that follow the introduction continue to support mental imagery, as the story is told through pictures wordlessly for the first forty-five pages. Importantly, indeterminacy is maintained – the pictures are mysterious and provide an ambiguous partly determining context (Krashen 1999: 12–14; see also Chapter 3) – so that while they support visualization, they do not block an individual imaginative mental representation of the story. The active participation of the reader is all important for the deep reading of texts: 'If the experience of literature is genuinely transactional, it always represents a meeting point of what texts invite from readers and what readers do in response to the invitation' (Nodelman and Reimer 2003: 24).

On page 46 the verbal text takes up the narrative, and continues the story for several pages, but soon pictures take over from the words again. The pictures rush the enigmatic telling onwards, so that readers simply have no choice but to proceed by reading the pictures and words in turn. Neither the verbal text nor the pictures can be skipped, or the reader will lose whole chunks of the compelling story. The book is a puzzle, and as with the best of stories unravelling the mystery is a joy; as Lisa Cron writes (2012: 194): 'a big part of the pleasure of reading is recognizing, interpreting, and then connecting the dots so the pattern emerges'. The pictorial narrative creates meanings that can be explored in groupwork around pictures, for they are physically present as the students think and talk around the text, providing a sensory anchor while details are examined and discussed.

Hugo Cabret is 12 years old when the reader first meets him as a homeless orphan living in a Paris train station, Gare Montparnasse, in the year 1931. Hugo's life is a lonely struggle, with which readers readily empathize. Nikolajeva (2014: 23) contends, 'our brains are capable of responding to fictional worlds as if they were actual; capable of making sense of a linguistically constructed world by connecting it to our empirical or mediated knowledge of the actual world.' The neuroscientific evidence for the ability of the human species to learn vicariously through empathy has profound educational significance. At the same time, the age gap between the protagonist Hugo and an adolescent reader – for in an English language learning context, the readers are likely to be at least three or four years older than Hugo – is an advantage for the opportunities of deep reading. Students will be able to identify and discuss the weaknesses and confusion in young Hugo's beliefs that drive the action and nearly lead to catastrophe. One example of this is Hugo's obsession with fixing an automaton – a wind-up mechanical man – believing it will write a message from his father who had perished in a fire. Enigmatically, it transpires that the message does seem to be inspired by his father, for mysteriously the mended automaton draws 'the scene his father had described from his favourite childhood film' (Selznick 2007: 259).

Artefact Emotion: The Pleasure of Reading and Viewing Aesthetically Crafted Narrative

Hugo Cabret is a thrilling multimodal celebration of the magic of story in books and films. The theme is the unlocking of the story of two individuals, Hugo the lonely child of poverty, and Papa Georges, an old man selling toys in a station booth who is mysteriously connected to the automaton, which is all that Hugo has left of the possessions of his beloved father, a gifted clockmaker. Both Hugo and Papa Georges are trapped by their poverty and by their past, and Hugo is also trapped in the train station, as a homeless boy with nowhere else to go and belonging to nobody. The boy is a vulnerable, yet tough, character who lives on the edge. He thus represents the threshold of pre-adolescence while he haunts threshold situations – stairs, corridors, towers and hidden passages behind the station walls.

But whereas Papa Georges and his wife try to forget their memories and leave the past buried, Hugo and Isabelle, the young girl who befriends him, try to uncover the past through their ingenuity and vigorous efforts to unravel mysteries and follow all the clues. The motif of finding the key to the past (both literally important to the story – for the key to wind up the automaton is missing – and metaphorically important to Hugo and Papa Georges) is pictured on the cover of Hugo Cabret, which shows a lock in the shape of a key. We might also wonder whether the lock refers to the way Papa Georges has tried to lock away his past, and the way Hugo and

Isabelle successfully unlock it, setting him (and themselves) free. Here are many opportunities for interpretation while talking around the text.

Despite their hardships, Hugo and Isabelle show bravery, tenacity, perseverance and imagination. They find that both books and films can transport them to other worlds. This demonstrates that fiction is a journey that all can undertake – as Cron (2012: 11) has indicated, fiction is 'an internal journey, not an external one'. While living in the station, Hugo maintains the colossal station clocks, and helps Isabelle discover the magical night world of Paris from a tall clock tower: ' "It's so beautiful," said Isabelle. "It looks like the whole city is made out of stars" ' (Selznick 2007: 378).

Above all, they discover the magic of the early silver screen as well as the true identity of Papa Georges – Georges Méliès. Far from being a thief, Hugo (who is pursued by the Station Inspector because he steals food for survival) gives Georges Méliès (1861–1938), an acclaimed pioneer of film in the silent era, back his life. David Robinson (2015: np) describes Méliès as: 'At once the cinema's first true artist and the most prolific technical innovator of the early years, Georges Méliès was a pioneer in recognising the possibilities of the medium for narrative and spectacle. He created the basic vocabulary of special effects, and built the first studio of glass-house form, the prototype of European studios of the silent era.'

Hugo's determination when the cards are stacked against him contributes to the power of this story. Books (in the station bookshop and research literature in the Film Academy library) and movies (the many still frames of silent films) enrich the narrative, and this culminates in the discovery of Georges Méliès' artistic past through the fictional textbook, *The Invention of Dreams: The Story of the First Movies Ever Made*, in the film library. Stories are repeatedly associated with dreams in *Hugo Cabret* – however, the aspect of craftsmanship for the invention of good stories is also accentuated. For Hugo is a skilled craftsman due to a great deal of hard work. He is as talented as a clockmaker as his father was, and throughout the narrative he is seen fixing and attempting to fix broken clocks, machines, toys – and broken people (see Figure 6.4).

Hugo also painstakingly fixes the complex automaton, so that it begins to create the hoped-for message: 'A cascade of perfect movements, with hundreds of brilliantly calibrated actions, coursed through the mechanical man' (Selznick 2007: 240). Unexpectedly, it is the restored automaton that provides the clue that enables Hugo and Isabelle to discover the identity of Méliès. The automaton draws an iconic image from Méliès' early film, which was the world's first science fiction movie: *Le Voyage Dans la Lune* (1902), and signs the name Georges Méliès – symbolizing the significant interaction of pictures, words, movies and meticulous craft. The huge pleasure that my student teachers and their own school students have experienced while reading *The Invention of Hugo Cabret* is an aesthetic response to the work as a meticulously crafted object. This has been termed artefact emotion by Hogan (2014: 523), 'the most important form of

FIGURE 6.4 *Hugo fixing a mechanical mouse (Selznick 2007: 158–9). From* The Invention of Hugo Cabret *by Brian Selznick © 2007. Reprinted by permission of Scholastic Inc.*

artefact emotion is aesthetic, prominently the feeling of beauty, although also the feeling of sublimity'.

Georges Méliès was well aware of the magic of stories as a young magician and filmmaker in his earlier life, before he worked in the tiny boutique selling toys at Gare Montparnasse (this thread of *Hugo Cabret* is historically accurate). The professor of film who, together with the children, persuades Méliès to accept the acclaim of the French Film Academy and return to public life, remembers how Méliès had influenced him as a child to admire the wonder of cinema. A present-day magician of words, Neil Gaiman, emphasizes the importance of dreams:

> We all – adults and children, writers and readers – have an obligation to daydream. We have an obligation to imagine. It is easy to pretend that nobody can change anything, that we are in a world in which society is huge and the individual is less than nothing: an atom in a wall, a grain of rice in a rice field. But the truth is, individuals change their world over and over, individuals make the future, and they do it by imagining that things can be different.
>
> (Gaiman 2013: np)

Hugo Cabret teaches how stories can be told effectively yet differently in the verbal and pictorial mode. The pictorial text shows, rather than tells, action sequences without dialogue. The chase scenes, for example, are shown in pictures, such as when Hugo is being hunted by an irate Station Inspector through the imposing hall of the Paris train station. We see their running feet, pounding up ladders and down the stairs, along dark passageways and in and out through metal vents in the walls. Hugo slips through fingers and melts through crowds as suspense is created over pages and pages of pictures (Selznick 2007: 416–51). Students can be asked to create a written version of the scene that is presented in these pictures, in order to discover and experience the huge differences between the modes.

When Hugo is nearly run over by a train (2007: 460–9), the almost slow-motion effect of the looming train, shown in pictures from Hugo's perspective on the tracks, reminds us of cinematic cliffhangers. The scene is introduced by writing that is rich in sense perception:

> The horrible sound of the brakes being pulled, coupled with the metallic screech of the wheels against the rails, made it seem like the whole station was about to collapse around him. The black engine was zooming right towards Hugo and he was caught, unable to look away, as though he were watching a film.
>
> (2007: 459)

This is followed by four spreads of the huge oncoming steam train – every detail increasingly enlarged. The fifth spread shows the hand of the Station Inspector as he yanks Hugo off the tracks in the nick of time. An inspiring creative writing task is to recreate verbally the horrifying experience encapsulated in the five spreads, from Hugo's, the Station Inspector's, the train driver's or a traveller's perspective.

The Invention of Hugo Cabret Celebrates Both Print-based and Screen-based Story

We talk of story threads, and about weaving or spinning stories, which emphasizes how stories are always interwoven with other stories. Storytelling is inventing and reinventing: 'In the workings of the human imagination, adaptation is the norm, not the exception' as Linda Hutcheon maintains (2012: 177). Imitation and invention go hand in hand: 'we *need* to imitate in order to innovate. Building on what came before underlies all creativity, in biology and culture' (Boyd 2009: 122, emphasis in original). *The Invention of Hugo Cabret* is woven throughout the narrative with references to books and films (see Figure 6.5). The numerous references to story, including abundant still frames from Méliès' and other silent films, slowly build to an exciting introduction to the first years of motion pictures. The book

FIGURE 6.5 *The significance of story (Selznick 2007: 178–9). From* The Invention of Hugo Cabret *by Brian Selznick* © *2007. Reprinted by permission of Scholastic Inc.*

chronicles Hugo and Isabelle's discovery of early film history – using still frames to show and share – so that the reader discovers the silent era of the movies along with the two children, and the book also works as a homage to pioneer cinema.

In addition to intertextuality, *The Invention of Hugo Cabret* features intermediality, meaning the materiality of the book itself is an evocation of a different medium – that of film. By including a transposition of filmic techniques, the book recalls the cinematography of silent movies. The opening invitation to 'picture yourself sitting in the darkness, like the beginning of a movie' (Selznick 2007: ix), is followed by a series of pictures that resemble an establishing shot – the initial uncut strip of film, often a long take, before the first edit. The first picture sequence, mimicking cinematic mise-en-scène, seems to begin with a high-angle shot, taken from an extreme long shot range, which gradually zooms in on the action. This 'establishing shot' sets the scene: the location of the story – indicated by the Eiffel Tower, as well as the time of day – shown by a night sky being gradually replaced by a rising sun and travellers entering the station. Following the establishing shot, a number of close-ups reveal some kind of a connection between Hugo and an old man selling toys in a station toy booth. The scene closes with a pictorial representation of the concepts of secrecy and mystery that dominate the plot – as Hugo spies on the toy booth from his hiding place behind the huge clock face of a station clock.

Throughout the book, close-ups and extreme close-ups, cliffhangers, chase scenes, flashbacks and juxtaposition effects of double-page spreads in an expressive continuum that recalls the editing of films maintain the resemblance to silent film. This is complemented by a suggestion of intertitles – though most passages of verbal text in *The Invention of Hugo Cabret* are far longer and all are vastly more descriptive than the brief intertitles of silent film. The pages are edged in black, as if we were watching the story in a darkened cinema; thus, the book itself is designed to resemble silent film. Like many great works of children's literature, *The Invention of Hugo Cabret* can be studied in different creative ways at different levels of competence, including language competence. Students in higher grades in secondary school might be challenged to investigate techniques of cinematography, and filmic effects on the page as well as on the screen. Episodes of the film version *Hugo* (2011), directed by Martin Scorsese, can then be studied to compare the effect of camerawork in film narrative.

Story is often considered to be the training of the imagination to mentally represent alternative visions and ideas. Scorsese's *Hugo*, though a story told in the very different medium of film, no less focuses on the power of stories. Clement and Long (2012: np) emphasize this point: 'But in the remediated relationship between movies and the more established medium of books so important to Selznick's novel and Scorsese's film, what matters most is the collaboration between these media in an openly nostalgic recuperation of the power of story. [...] the image and the word are imagined as harmonious collaborators.'

In fact, it was Georges Méliès himself who invented storying as an aspect of cinema. Before Méliès produced his fantasy films, the very earliest movies showed short real-life events, such as *The Arrival of a Train at La Ciotat Station* (1895), directed by Auguste and Louis Lumière. However, stories soon became the most popular form of cinema, and while the early movies were silent, they had key lines of dialogue appearing in the film as intertitles. According to Robinson (1973: 46) 'cinema found its audiences largely in the poorer urban communities; this form of mute drama was especially attractive to the vast immigrant population with neither money nor a strong command of the English language.' A century later, graphic novels are analogously supportive of English language learners, and equally inventive as many film narratives of the silent era.

Stories can simulate the multisensory nature of experience, and for digital natives this may be particularly true of multimodal stories like film, picturebooks and graphic novels. Well before the supporting empirical evidence of neuroscience, Kieran Egan (1986: 2) contended that story 'is not just some casual entertainment; it reflects a basic and powerful form in which we make sense of the world and experience'. Sharing stories is undoubtedly the oldest form of teaching, one at which the human species became particularly adept, for, as Ursula Le Guin (1985: 31) reveals: 'There have been great societies that did not use the wheel, but there have been no societies that did not tell stories.'

Brian Selznick has called his book *The Invention of Hugo Cabret*, possibly because the precise multimodal format he uses is rather a new invention. Patterning is extremely important in creative work, but so are unexpected pattern transformations. Deviation and invention often lead to artefact emotion in the reader; as Hogan (2014: 525) writes, 'the aesthetic response to beauty appears to be, first of all, a matter of reward response to unexpected patterning.' Georges Méliès invented a new form of movie, the fantasy film, and began a fashion that is still gripping moviegoers all over the world a century later. At the end of *The Invention of Hugo Cabret*, after a gala evening at the French Film Academy to celebrate his work, Méliès himself appears and is lauded by the audience of Parisians. In this final scene, Méliès accentuates how the magic of story must indeed belong to everyone: 'I address you all tonight as you truly are: wizards, mermaids, travellers, adventurers, and magicians. You are the true dreamers' (Selznick 2007: 506).

PART THREE
Participation in Literature and Creativity

CHAPTER SEVEN

Responding to Literature with Creative Writing

When employing creative writing in English language education, teachers give their students a reason to invest thoughtfulness, personal significance and feelings in their writing, awakening intrinsic motivation, and aspiration to write well. Creative writing with children and adolescents should be process-oriented so that the emphasis is on stepping-stones that support them as they develop. While creative writing focuses on self-expression and the pleasure of language, there are certain techniques that can help students articulate their thoughts persuasively and find formulations to express ideas and thoughtful feelings with nuance. This chapter deals with such techniques, suggests how mentor texts can be used to develop metalinguistic awareness, offers insight into how emotional and musical intensity is created and demonstrates some of the mechanics of creating writing. A fascination with language includes the understanding of poetic devices, and how language and meaning can be shaped by consciously and carefully connecting choices of words, formulaic sequences, and poetic images with a rhetorical objective. With this explicit knowledge, students can be in a better position to respond to different kinds of literary text with their own creative writing.

Opportunities for creativity can empower students who easily lack agency while trying to communicate in English when it is not their home language. As Scott Thornbury writes (2002: 30), 'memory of new words can be reinforced if they are used to express personally relevant meanings.' With reference to students struggling to rediscover their voice in multilingual classrooms, Jim Cummins maintains (2014: 6-7): 'Creative writing and other forms of cultural production (e.g. art, drama, music, etc.) represent an *expression* of identity, a *projection* of identity into new social spheres and a *re-creation* of identity as a result of feedback from and dialogue with multiple audiences' (emphasis in original). Whether knowingly made or not, linguistic choices govern rhetorical meaning, and Debra Myhill asserts

(2020: 199), 'that linguistic development might be more effectively enabled if we connect linguistic choice and rhetorical purpose'.

The processes of creative writing include students exchanging their ideas with peers, crafting a first version, then editing, polishing, attending to layout and presentation, editing again and finally sharing. This is a complete reversal of the current trend, influenced by online browsing, that encourages students to understand reading – and writing – as fleeting activities. Naomi Baron (2015: xiii) emphasizes how reading and writing are intertwined, and ephemeral online reading habits lead to less formality, precision and stamina in writing: 'Computers, and now portable digital devices, coax us to skim rather than read in depth, search rather than traverse continuous prose. As a result, how – and how much – we write is already shifting.' In contrast to short-lived writing tasks, students' carefully edited and polished creative writing could be kept as individual collections, as a class anthology or as part of a school online presence. Creative texts may be displayed on school walls or performed in the classroom and at school events, with potentially considerable increases in resultative motivation and self-efficacy. In addition, creative writing, according to Jane Spiro (2004: 5), 'is for teachers who wish to add a sense of production, excitement, and performance to the language classroom, to give students the opportunity to say something surprising and original, even while they practice new aspects of language'.

The Mechanics of Creative Writing

There are procedures to scaffolding creative writing that, if followed, can hugely contribute to students' success in creatively crafting their use of language. Alan Maley (2004: 3) refutes a common objection 'that "creative" writing is a waste of time because it appears to be unfocused and undisciplined', and Myhill (2020: 194) counters with the claim that 'the capacity to write well is fundamental to educational success'. In her doctoral research on singing, storytelling and chanting with young language learners, Annett Kaminski evidences: 'It is ironic that by trying to make a language lesson more efficient and not to "waste" time on enjoying the story and indulging in its aesthetic qualities, language learning actually becomes less likely' (2016: 180). The next sections outline features of language creativity that can be introduced to help students work on the craft of creative writing and achieve an aesthetic response.

Semantic and Phonological Patterns Connecting Orality and Creative Writing

The notion of orality refers to verbal expression that does not depend on writing, especially when functional literacy is not available to the majority of the people. Orality is characterized by memorization of cultural knowledge, incorporating, for example, folktales, mythologies, rituals, chants, songs and poetry. Randy Bomer (2010: 205–6) differentiates the mode of orality from the skill of oracy, which is the development of spoken language in children: 'While *oracy*, a term coined in recent decades, has been used almost exclusively in educational settings to describe students' oral language as something to be developed or improved – like literacy or numeracy – *orality* [...] is a much older and broader term referring to the overall use of spoken language, especially in a culture.' Even in predominantly literate societies, aspects of pre-literate orality still strongly influence poetry, speech writing and other creative uses of contemporary written language and can be clearly identified in children's literature as a cohesive rhetorical force.

A key feature of orality is *repetitive and patterned language*. Repetition and near repetition are important for the storyteller as a mnemonic tool and crucial to enable the listener to follow the story with ease. Patterned language refers to both phonological and semantic levels, both repetitive sounds and meanings. Orality researcher Walter Ong (2002: 34) refers to serious thought being intertwined with methods of remembering, such as 'heavily rhythmic, balanced patterns, in repetitions or antitheses, in alliterations and assonances'. Repetitive, patterned language is not confined to oral literature, but is an important component in many fields. Linguist Jean Aitchison (1994: 15) suggests a list of different names for repetition, which she considers a ubiquitous phenomenon, including:

> When advertisers do it, it's reinforcement.
> When children do it, it's imitation. [...]
> When novelists do it, it's cohesion.
> When poets do it, it's alliteration, chiming, rhyme, or parallelism.
> When priests do it, it's ritual.

There is frequently strong sound patterning in children's literary texts, and the mentor texts introduced in this chapter illustrate the rhetorical power of repetition. Mentor texts can provide a literary model for different proficiencies and possibilities of creative writing and can guide students to recreate the energy of rhetorical strategies.

Another fundamental feature of orality is *additive language* and an avoidance of complex sentences. This is clearly important for English language learners, for complex sentences, which contain subordinate clauses, are difficult for novices to master. Expert children's literature authors also make use of the additive characteristic of oral tales, as the multiple 'ands'– or *polysyndeton* – in the extract from Pullman's *The Firework-Maker's Daughter* show (see p. 163). Used in close sequence, polysyndeton can generate intensity and determination.

Playful Use of Language

David Crystal argues (1998: 1) that the playful or ludic function is central to language, and therefore 'should be at the heart of any thinking we do about linguistic issues'. That adult native speakers of English can generally quote far more nursery and playground rhymes than Shakespeare or the Bible testifies to the seductiveness of musical rhythms and jingling rhymes, which leads incidentally to learning by heart. Spiro (2004: 5) deems these are the first poems many children hear, 'the words of favourite songs, the jingles of advertisements, nursery rhymes and the spells of wizards in fairy tales'. According to Spiro (2004: 10), creative writing activities will help students 'develop an appreciation of the sounds and rhythms of language, sentences patterns, the shape and meaning of words, how words and sentences connect with one another to form texts, and the features of different text types. All of these are the skills of the confident reader too.' Fleming and Schofer (2013: 445) similarly highlight that 'literary texts are part of pleasurable games of the imagination, where children enjoy creating verbal associations which become the foundation for imaginary stories. The pleasure of reading is closely related to the pleasures of creating.'

The *tricolon* is a playful but also extremely effective rhetorical device that students can employ to enrich their creative writing. Also known as the rule of three, the tricolon provides tension, rhythm and a pleasing pattern to a text or speech. The power of the threefold pattern may in part emanate from the magical triples of fairy tales and oral storytelling, and the third of the triple often provides the climax. Encouraging students to use the tricolon means inspiring them to make use of synonyms to enrich their vocabulary and create a powerful textual rhythm. A castle, for example, is not just big, it can be *vast, grandiose, and with an infinity of strangely shaped towers*. The forest can be *deep, dark, and with dense, melancholy shadows*. Creative writing is not a silent mode; language learners can better attend to the rhythm of their writing if they read their texts aloud. This also allows them to focus on the poetic and other auditory aspects of the text, just like listeners of oral storytelling.

Sensory Imagery

For the reader to be able to visualize characters and the setting, novice writers need to focus on providing sensory details, so that the reader can experience the setting and engage with the characters in a multisensory way. The embodied simulation hypothesis postulates that we recreate the scene the writer evokes bodily in our perceptions, our emotions and our thoughts. Lynell Burmark makes the point (2008: 11) that language is employed 'to *recall* things we have already seen and experienced. This is why writing is so much more detailed and evocative when students can look at an image before they start writing' (emphasis in original). This is helpful

FIGURE 7.1 *The unicorn at the lake.* © *Elisabeth Lottermoser, Contour Illustration & Grafik.*

advice to enable a student writer to imagine and create the sensory imagery that is the hallmark of effective writing. For example, a student teacher (Nord University, Norway, 2021) wrote the following passage as a creative description of a forest setting with a unicorn (see Figure 7.1), including visual, aural, kinaesthetic, tactile and olfactory sense impressions:

> You could hear the silence. The atmosphere was gloomy and ghostly, and the lake was gleaming. […] The wind was silent, but you could feel it brushing against your skin, the icy air blistering on red lips. You could smell the sweet, sharp, and eccentric aroma of conifer trees. From between the trees a unicorn emerged and dashed gracefully towards the lake. Its fur was glistening. […] Its horn looked like it was made of icicle spears and its hooves were as black as the midnight winter sky. You could see warm air blowing from its nostrils.

Cohesion and Lexical Chains

Synonyms, collocations and ellipsis help to provide cohesion, so that a text glues well together. In the following example from *Catching Fire* (Collins 2009: 410), the words 'Closer. Very close now' illustrate ellipsis, when unnecessary words are omitted in the urgency of the moment: 'Vines cut into my face and arms, creepers grab my feet. But I am getting closer to her. Closer. Very close now.' This use of ellipsis draws the text tightly together. Using synonyms and formulaic sequences helps creative writers avoid overused and almost meaningless words like *big*, *nice* or *great*, instead employing words that fit together more naturally and with a more exact and thought-provoking meaning. While synonyms create redundancy, they also create layers of nuanced meaning and lexical density, and 'redundancy, repetition of the just said, keeps both speaker and hearer surely on the track' (Ong 2002: 39).

Lexical chains are a particularly powerful way to create cohesion in a creative writing task. In Thornbury's words (2002: 53), 'a characteristic feature of cohesive texts is that they are threaded through with words that relate to the same topic – what are sometimes called lexical chains. This is even more likely if the text is authentic – that is, if it has not been specially written or doctored for the language classroom.' A lexical chain refers to a string of words in proximity that add semantic depth and cohesion to the text by an accumulation of related meaning.

The following words spoken by the sloth in Eric Carle's picturebook, *'Slowly, Slowly, Slowly,' said the Sloth* (2002), exemplify cohesion – through alliteration (lackadaisical, dawdle, dillydally), rich lexical density due to the many synonyms suggesting degrees of lethargy and calm, and finally a lexical chain around tranquillity (relaxed, tranquil, live in peace):

> Finally, the sloth replied, 'It is true that I am slow, quiet and boring. I am lackadaisical, I dawdle and I dillydally. I am also unflappable, languid, stoic, impassive, sluggish, lethargic, placid, calm, mellow, laid-back and, well, slothful! I am relaxed and tranquil, and I like to live in peace.'

Variation

While poetic-repetitive patterns are important in creative writing, so is variation. This includes innovative metaphors and lexical expressions as well as variation in style. Geoff Hall writes (2018: 266), 'Variation is the most basic characteristic of language use in literature and a wider range of variation is typically found in literary texts than in any other text type or [discourse] genre.' Toolan (2012: 18) writes of the 'urge to hybridise' and the breaking of rules regarding format and literary genre, offering new opportunities for originality in creating inventive texts.

Novice creative writers can be challenged to give rhythm to their writing by varying the tempo; flashes of brevity should be juxtaposed with longer, descriptive detail. Gary Provost (2019: 60–1) illustrates the power that variation of sentence length can have to enliven writing, to slow down or accelerate the pace:

This sentence has five words. Here are five more words. Five-word sentences are fine. But several together become monotonous. Listen to what is happening. The writing is getting boring. The sound of it drones. It's like a stuck record. The ear demands some variety.

Now listen. I vary the sentence length, and I create music. Music. The writing sings. It has a pleasant rhythm, a lilt, a harmony. I use short sentences. And I use sentences of medium length. And sometimes when I am certain the reader is rested, I will engage him with a sentence of considerable length, a sentence that burns with energy and builds with all the impetus of a crescendo, the roll of the drums, the crash of the cymbals – sounds that say listen to this, it is important.

This is persuasive advice on varying sentence length, and it holds true for academic writing as well as creative writing.

Another kind of variation that is fitting for creative writing, but not for academic writing, is the use of incomplete sentences. Fragmentary utterances that lack a finite verb can be found everywhere in masterful creative writing, but this is not normally acceptable in more formal writing. In the Provost text, for example, the single word that stands alone (*Music*) is not a full sentence. Used perceptively (students should read aloud and attend closely to the sound and rhythm of their text), fragmentary utterances can help create a pleasing percussion effect and further accentuate meanings.

Lexical variation can generate a deviant and striking use of language in creative writing. Speculative fiction shows again and again how words can be used in fresh and inventive ways. The word muggle, for example, is not entirely new, but given a wholly new meaning by J. K. Rowling. Neologisms often originate in fiction and the arts, expressions such as scrooge, chortle, Orwellian and cyberspace, for instance. There is even an inventive and humorous chapter book about the successful creation of a neologism: Andrew Clements's *Frindle* (1996). In recent years, due to the internet and social media, countless neologisms and portmanteau or blend words have reached a lexicographical tipping point and become new dictionary words. Just two examples are *bromance*, which a student group used in their role-on-the-wall activity (see Figure 8.5, Chapter 8), to describe a very close friendship between boys and *infodemic*, a neologism that has gained in popularity due to Covid-19, as it refers to the wide-reaching spread of both accurate and false information, blurring distinctions between information and disinformation. Using nouns as verbs can result in playful and imaginative writing – animal nouns can be used inventively in this way, the footpath *snaked* up to the peak, the newcomer *moused* meekly into the meeting, for instance.

While lexical variation can work well in creative writing, grammatical variation is much trickier, especially for English language learners. For example, some expert authors are able to create urgency and suspense by telling a story unusually in the present tense, a well-known example is Collins's *The Hunger Games* trilogy. This is an undertaking that requires high proficiency. In creative writing classes, students who try to write stories in the present – usually because they have had more exercise in writing present-tense summaries than any other kind of writing – almost invariably muddle the tenses and grammatical aspect in their texts. The seeming simplicity is deceptive; present tense narration requires an exceptional command of tense and aspect. Consequently, novice creative writers should write using past tense narration, which is the usual tense for stories in English. Past tense narration involves all aspects of the past – including past perfect and past progressive – but excludes all aspects of the present, such as present perfect and present progressive, except in dialogue. As the present perfect cannot be used when a story is told in the past, a common confusion in the English language learning context – present perfect or past tense? – is easy to resolve.

The Role of Mentor Texts

A mentor text is said to teach readers and writers by providing a model, and by helping students to read like a writer (Moses 2014). Myhill, Lines and Jones (2018: 7) point to the use of a literary model as scaffolding for the novice writer, in that a degree of freedom is reduced, so reducing the scope for failure, while potentially deepening students' acquisition of 'metalinguistic awareness of the repertoire of possibilities of language choices'. Responding to literary texts with scaffolded creative writing, integrating inventive recreation and the urge to explore further, language learners may not only become more confident writers, but more confident readers as well. Maley (2013: 164) emphasizes the connection between reading and writing skills for language learners: 'Creative writing also feeds into more creative reading. It is as if, by getting inside the process of creating the text, learners come to intuitively understand how such texts work, and this makes them easier to read. Likewise, the development of aesthetic reading skills provides the learner with a better understanding of textual construction, and this feeds into their writing.'

Creative writing, then, could be a highly beneficial component of a literary apprenticeship. I also strongly advocate creative writing for student teachers, who, if they become confident creative writers themselves, could create their own purpose-built mentor texts, to guide and support the creative writing of their future language learners.

Rhyme, Rhythm and Rap

Inventive repetition is the literary feature that is the most prominent in children's literature: the enlivening effect of anaphora and refrains, and the impact of playing with sounds such as alliteration, assonance, and onomatopoeia. Re-formulations in literature are far more than mere duplications of language; they can be a means of foregrounding language, making language noticeable and catching the reader's attention. While this may not be sound driving sense, it is certainly sound enriching and extending the sense. Students can best recognize and grasp the power of phonological and semantic repetition through their own efforts in creative writing.

Roger McGough's 'The Sound Collector'

The topic of McGough's 'The Sound Collector' is how sound richly contributes to the meaning and experience of everyday existence. Daily noises of a family breakfast are foregrounded in this poem, with persistent use of the gerund that lends the poem humour as well as urgency, as all the family's sounds are stolen by a stranger:

> The crying of the baby
> The squeaking of the chair
> The swishing of the curtain
> The creaking of the stair

Despite the salient pattern and familiarity of the scene, there is also a tantalizing gap, an unexplained puzzle that begins and ends the story of the poem intriguingly, finally defamiliarizing the happening around the shadowy stranger: 'Left us only silence/Life will never be the same.'

The 'The Sound Collector' has such a clear, repetitive structure, and with a valuable illustration of the usefulness of the gerund, that it is highly suitable as a mentor text. Based on McGough's poem, a student teacher (Norway, 2021) created her own text that likewise uses the gerund in a highly patterned way:

> I prepared all night
> For this class we'll have today
> Will the pupils listen?
> I think as I make my way
>
> The singing of that pupil
> The tapping on the screens
> The silence of their gaze
> The talking of the teens
>
> The fumbling in their bags
> The creaking of their chairs
> The slamming of their books
> The pupil as he swears

> Suddenly, silence
> My task begins now
> I must break this sudden silence
> But do I know the best way how?

In L1 classrooms, elementary students are frequently introduced to the creativity of language and the opportunities to write creatively themselves, inspired by the wonderland of children's poetry. My emphasis here is that creative writing is equally important and productive in L2 classrooms and in teacher education, thus making most of 'the strong relationships that exist between identity investment and literacy engagement' (Cummins 2014: 5). The scaffolding effect of mentor texts can heighten the chances of success and lower the affective filter while sensitising learners to language possibilities, choices and constraints.

MC Grammar's 'Save the Planet'

Rhythm is a fundamental feature of dance and music as well as language, and there is a universal pleasure in participation in rhythmic dance. A rap echoes features of poetry, dance and song, combined with the natural rhythms of spoken language. It is a prose-like, but poetic, format with an insistent pattern – a 4/4 time signature – that needs to be heard in performance, as the rhythmic delivery by the rapper and strongly rhythmic accompaniment are key features. Rap energizes through its embodied rhythms and dynamic but chant-like performance, including rhyme that may be multisyllabic, and a strong metronomic beat, to create a flowing delivery. According to Derek Attridge (1995: 90), the metrical structure of rap consists of 'lines with four stressed beats […], separated by other syllables that may vary in number and may include other stressed syllables. The strong beat of the accompaniment coincides with the stressed beats of the verse, and the rapper organizes the rhythms of the intervening syllables to provide variety and surprise.' Referring to the pulsating rhythm of nursery rhymes, Guy Cook (2000: 18–19) discusses this kind of 'stress verse' as a potentially innate and pleasurable form:

> In stress verse, a steady beat emphasizes the syllables on which it falls. Between the beats, up to four unstressed syllables either bunch up together (if there are several)or stretch out (if there are only a few) to maintain a steady rhythm. [… Many rhymes in English] are most satisfactorily scanned as following an absolutely regular 4/4 rhythm (of the same kind as is found in music) with a very heavy initial beat in each bar, and the option of a 'rest' in which the beat continues through a pause.

Any topic can be rapped, and adding a catchy rhythm and movement to a message creates powerful multisensory learning. Rhythmical repetition can create a shared social experience, a sense of well-being, and a sensuous pleasure in words and rhythm. A mentor text could be the impressive three-minute 'Save the Planet' song, created by Wonder Raps (MC Grammar 2021), which is available on YouTube. In the following excerpt from the lyrics, the primary beats are indicated as a forward slash <u>/</u> with a single underlining, and / indicates the secondary beats.

<u>/</u> /   /   /
Reduce, reuse, recycle –
  <u>/</u> /   /   /
's vital for the planet's survival,
<u>/</u> /   /   /
climate change has spiralled
   <u>/</u> /   /   /
and I won't stop ringing the sirens.
<u>/</u> / /   /
Wow, wow, wow,
<u>/</u> /   /   /
wow, the time for the change is
<u>/</u> / /   /
now, now, now,
  <u>/</u> /   /   /
now, and I'm gonna show you
<u>/</u>
how.

The topic is very important for adolescents (and for us all), and in this case both the topic and poetic format coincide as motivating encouragement for creative writing and performance. If student groups create their own raps, the class can easily supply the regular backing rhythm. Alternatively, students could film their raps to backing music and show the recorded performance in class.

Narrative Creative Writing – the Central Role of Setting and Characterization

Using award-winning chapter books to inspire students to creative tasks and creative writing is a way of avoiding the more mundane activities that are common in language learning, for example when language learners should answer true or false statements about a book, answer comprehension questions, skim through the story to match headings to paragraphs, fill gaps in a summary or write summaries themselves. The chapter book (or middle-grade fiction) is a format for those students who can read independently, but still need very short chapters, 'for children who have mastered basic reading skills but still require simple, illustrated texts' (Agnew 2001: 139). Although primarily aimed at younger readers or reluctant readers, chapter books can be as expertly written as the best literature aimed at adults. The 2020 CILIP Carnegie Medal, for example, was won by a chapter book (Anthony McGowan's *Lark*; see Chapter 10). Philip Pullman, himself having won the Carnegie Medal in 1995 and Carnegie of Carnegies in 2007, has composed a number of beautifully written chapter books that are well suited as mentor texts.

Philip Pullman's *The Firework-Maker's Daughter*

Myhill (2020: 204) refers to a weakness in secondary school writing as 'over-emphasis on plot, resulting in plot-driven narratives with much weaker characterisation, and establishment of setting'. Pullman's writing can be used to illustrate the central role of sensory imagery, for example when he evokes a vivid setting for his protagonist Lila, a young girl who wishes to become a Firework-Maker, in *The Firework-Maker's Daughter* (1995: 64):

> All the jungle sounds, the clicking and buzzing of the insects, the cries of the birds and monkeys, the drip of water off the leaves, the croaking of the little frogs, were behind her now. [...] now there was nothing except the sound of her foot on the path and the occasional rumble from the mountain, which was so deep that she felt it through her feet as much as she heard it through her ears.

As students read this passage, they can reflect on the sensory imagery – how they can visualize the insects, birds, monkeys and frogs, hear the sounds they make, feel the drips of water on their skin and the rumble of the volcano reverberating through their frame.

A little further on in the story, Lila's journey is becoming increasingly desperate, for she has been told she must step deep inside the volcano if she wants to become a firework-maker. The next excerpt illustrates how an emotional response can be created through language choices. Lila is in deadly earnest in her intention to reach the Grotto of Razvani, the great Fire-Fiend. However, there are many stones in her path, both metaphorically and literally:

> On she climbed, higher and higher. Before long she came to a part of the slope where the stones were loose, and where she slid back two steps for every three she took upwards. Her feet and legs were bruised and battered, and then she lost her other sandal; and she nearly cried out in despair, because there was no sign of the Grotto – just an endless slope of hot rough stones that tumbled and rolled underfoot.

And her throat was parched and her lungs were panting in the hot thin air, and she fell to her knees and clung with trembling fingers as the stones began to roll under her again. [...] She dragged herself on bleeding knees up and up, until every muscle hurt, until she had no breath left in her lungs, until she thought she was going to die; and still she went on.

(Pullman 1995: 68–9)

With this writing, we are made to feel with Lila how the painful ascent of the volcano Mount Merapi batters and burns her feet, her legs, her throat, her knees, and fingers. Polysyndeton – repetition of conjunctions, a rhetorical device that young children often use in their own storytelling – emphasizes the inexorable painfulness of the climb: *And her throat/and her lungs/and she fell/and clung*. Finally, the threefold repetition of *until* in the last sentence relentlessly builds up to the climax 'and still she went on', illustrating the power of the tricolon, or rhetorical rule of three.

I find that students become very resourceful when producing hybrid texts of creative writing combined with artwork, which enhances the effect and adds layers to the meaning. I have included some examples from teacher education – student teachers for elementary and secondary school in Germany and Norway – in this chapter. Figures 7.2 and 7.3 provide examples of hybrid creative writing texts produced by student teachers in Germany on *The Firework-Maker's Daughter*.

Philip Pullman's *Clockwork*

Skilfully written literature, whether aimed at adults or children, can create an aesthetic response in the reader that Patrick Hogan (2014: 523) calls artefact emotion. This seems to be inspired by painstaking craft combined with unexpected, sometimes schema-refreshing elements. I have chosen another Pullman book as mentor text for setting and characterization, not only for the superb craftsmanship (the topic of dedicated hard work and craft in creative writing is also a theme in the story of *Clockwork*), but also for the genre of horror, which adolescents find fascinating. With highly unusual story elements that interlock yet move in different directions, this is an uncanny fairy tale with a story within the story that seems to come true, and automata that come alive. *Clockwork* is a chapter book and moderately easy to read – despite its echoes of E.T.A. Hoffmann's (1816) *Der Sandmann* and Mary Shelley's (1818) *Frankenstein* – but it is slightly more challenging and certainly more mysterious than *The Firework-Maker's Daughter*. The topic of *Clockwork* is particularly suitable for dark winter months, and then the teacher could make a powerful impression by reading aloud some of the eerie chapters in a shadowy classroom, lit only by candlelight, rather like tales around a wintry campfire. The setting of Pullman's *Clockwork* is again established with rich sensory imagery:

FIGURE 7.2 *Lila shape poem, based on* The Firework-Maker's Daughter.

It began on a winter's evening, when the townsfolk were gathering in the White Horse Tavern. The snow was blowing down from the mountains, and the wind was making the bells shift restlessly in the church tower. The windows were steamed up, the stove was blazing brightly, Putzi the old black cat was snoozing on the hearth; and the air was full of the rich smells of sausage and sauerkraut, of tobacco and beer.

(Pullman 1996: 11–12)

The first creative task could be for students to try to emulate the generation of sense impressions in Pullman's setting – of sight, sound, movement, touch, taste and smell – in their own creative writing, especially when crafting the beginning of a story and establishing the setting.

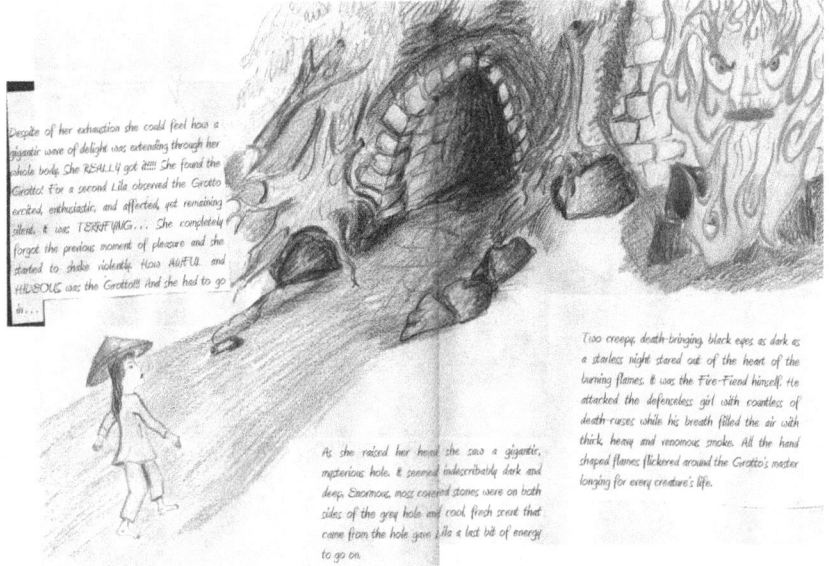

FIGURE 7.3 *At the mouth of the volcano grotto, based on* The Firework-Maker's Daughter.

Contemporary compelling narratives are generally character-centred and not plot driven; Brown et al. (2019) have called this protagonism (see Chapter 2: 44–6). A simple creative writing task that gives students the opportunity to reflect on character is the acrostic. The following examples show acrostics student teachers have written on *Clockwork* characters (their names are read vertically):

Knowing his iniquity
Apprentice with dishonest ambitions
Resentful of his fate
Lost his heart to greediness

Pretty, black and
Unnoticeable in the dark.
The tavern cat.
Zig-zagging along Karl's feet, as a thank you for being
Ill-treated by him.

Good hearted, young child
Running to serve her father, the landlord's friends and guests
Eager to find unknown answers
Took care of a helpless, dying child
Little she was, yet had the biggest, bravest heart

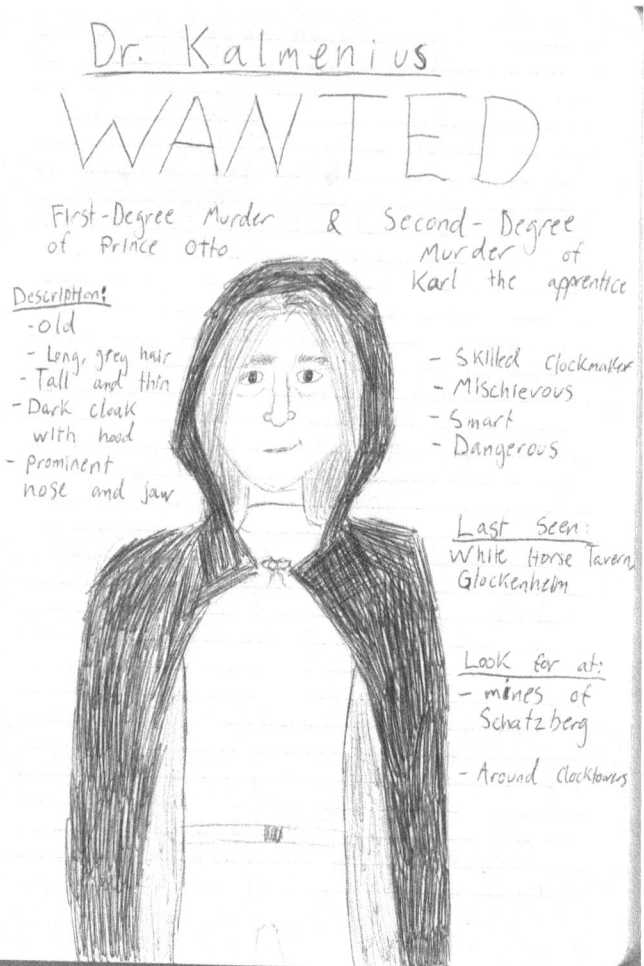

FIGURE 7.4 *Dr Kalmenius – Wanted poster, based on* Clockwork.

The enigmatic, iniquitous villain in *Clockwork* is Dr Kalmenius, a 'philosopher of the night' (Pullman 1996: 27). Tasking students with creating a WANTED poster will challenge them to explore details of his appearance, his characteristics, and his misdemeanours (see Figure 7.4).

Clockwork offers many opportunities for creative response. The following tasks are some of the motivating ideas fashioned by my student teachers (Norway 2021):

1 Use your imagination to describe mysterious Dr Kalmenius's workshop. Remember that he is a clever man and a marvellous clockmaker who can make just about anything with clockwork. Describe how it looks, what you can see, smell, hear and how you feel when you're walking around in the workshop. Focus on your descriptive words to create a picture of what you see in the workshop.

RESPONDING TO LITERATURE WITH CREATIVE WRITING   167

2 Create a crime board featuring one of the crimes in the story. Include where the crime takes place, a map, the murder weapon, and some of the main characters. Mark the characters as victim, suspect(s) and witness(es). (See Figure 7.5 for an example of a crime board based on *Clockwork*.)

3 Create a comic strip (pictures that together tell a story) of a scene in *Clockwork* that stood out for you. Create one strip with at least three panels telling the story of the moment you have chosen. Use literary devices that are typical for comics, like onomatopoeia, speech and thought balloons. Scenes you could use: Fritz's story, Dr Kalmenius creating Prince Florian, Karl's death, Gretl saving Prince Florian, etc. (See Figure 7.6 for a comic strip based on *Clockwork*.)

FIGURE 7.5 *Crime board, based on* Clockwork.

FIGURE 7.6 *Comic strip based on* Clockwork.

Epistolary Writing – Letters, Emails, Blogs

The important aspect of epistolary writing as a discourse genre is effectiveness of language use, register and rhetorical choices for audience and purpose. While letter writing may be on the decline, communicating formally or informally with a correspondent, on paper or by email, as an open letter to a newspaper or a multimodal post on a blog, are the most common means of expressing information, opinions, thoughts and feelings in writing. Novels, poems and picturebooks can be in the epistolary genre, and I propose two humorous epistolary picturebooks as motivating mentor texts for elementary school children.

Darcy Pattison and Joe Cepeda's *The Journey of Oliver K. Woodman*

The Journey of Oliver K. Woodman (2003) is a hilarious epistolary picturebook, cleverly written by Pattison and with stunning illustrations by Cepeda. It is better known in the United States than Europe, unsurprisingly as it tells in a series of letters and postcards of a fantastic journey across the United States from east to west. Tameka, who lives in California, writes to invite her favourite uncle in South Carolina to visit. He is too busy, so he builds instead the enigmatic Oliver K. Woodman to visit Tameka in his place. He sends Oliver on the road with a letter in his backpack asking for a ride and help to reach his destination (see Figure 7.7).

The coast-to-coast journey progresses amid breathtaking landscapes and told through the humorous correspondence, written in assorted styles and typefaces or lettering, by helpful drivers and families who give Oliver a lift part of the way, then write back to Raymond to update him on his friend's adventures. The final pages chronical a happy reunion and the endpapers trace Oliver's journey from state to state, supplementing the letter writing fun with a helpful geography lesson.

The students could similarly create a class mascot then send it on a virtual journey in their own country and to the heritage countries or regions of classmates with parents or grandparents from other nations. The class decides together on their mascot's destination and gathers suggestions for the en route stops. The students then write letters and include pictures sent by fictitious individuals who discover their mascot at the roadside, on the

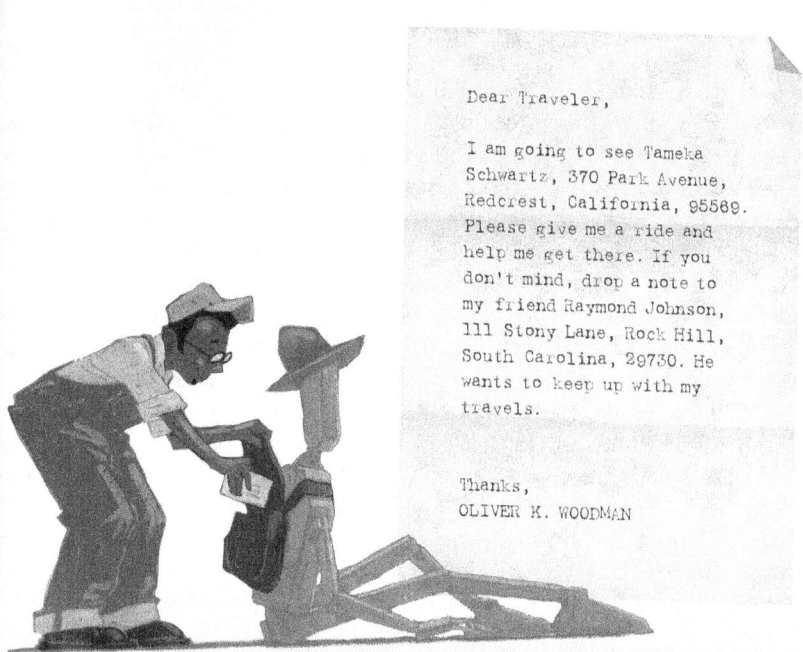

FIGURE 7.7 *Oliver Woodman's letter. From* The Journey of Oliver K. Woodman *by Darcy Pattison © 2003, and illustrated by Joe Cepeda © 2003. Reprinted by permission of Clarion Books, an imprint of HarperCollins Publishers. All rights reserved.*

shore or at sea and are happy to offer a lift – by car, helicopter, boat and so forth. This is a similar concept to the successful Flat Stanley project; however, it activates all students at the same time as the journeying is fictitious, and it takes advantage of the background knowledge and potentially heritage languages represented in multicultural classrooms.

Drew Daywalt and Oliver Jeffers' *The Day the Crayons Quit*

This is a witty picturebook that tells a story through letters written by warring crayons (Daywalt and Jeffers 2013). Each crayon has a personality visually communicated in their facial expressions and cleverly minimalized body language. Of course, the appearance of crayons can be individualized in the images only minimally, but this is expertly done by Oliver Jeffers, and it only increases the opportunity for character interpretation. This is another example of amplification through simplification (McCloud 1993), as discussed in Chapter 5. Thus, the expressive artwork has immediate impact, for 'we recognize emotions, in real life as well as in visual representations, through body language' (Nikolajeva 2018: 116).

However, the characterization is also well developed by Drew Daywalt's text, featuring letters the crayons write to their owner, Duncan. These are hand-lettered, in childlike, irregular handwriting, using the colour of each crayon-sender on different kinds of notepaper, with idiosyncratic word choices and integrated into the design of each verso page. They are letters of protest, altogether twelve letters from twelve crayons, telling of overwork, neglect or envy of another colour. The recto pages show the complaining crayons and an example of Duncan's drawings hitherto. For example, a red fire engine, a Santa, many hearts, and an exhausted red crayon are depicted on the opposite page to Red crayon's letter of complaint (see Figure 7.8). Pink crayon is dissatisfied with Duncan's artwork: 'Could you PLEASE use me sometime to colour the occasional PINK DINOSAUR or MONSTER or CowBoy? Goodness knows they could use a splash of colour.'

The proliferation of crayons on the endpapers seems to suggest a celebration of their creative potential in the hands of the implied reader. The title page features a closed box of crayons, so that all could be in good order. But, on careful inspection, the reader sees some interest-evoking protest placards: *WE'RE NOT HAPPY* and *DOWN with this sort of THING*. The reader is thus challenged to enter the story – what has caused the protests, and why is the language on the placards rather comical, even ineffectual? Many school children worldwide are now joining in demonstrations in the Fridays for Future movement and school strikes for climate justice, often creating banners and placards in the classroom before they leave for the streets. While the concept of peaceful and urgent protest is familiar and relevant to today's children, *The Day the Crayons Quit* offers the opportunity

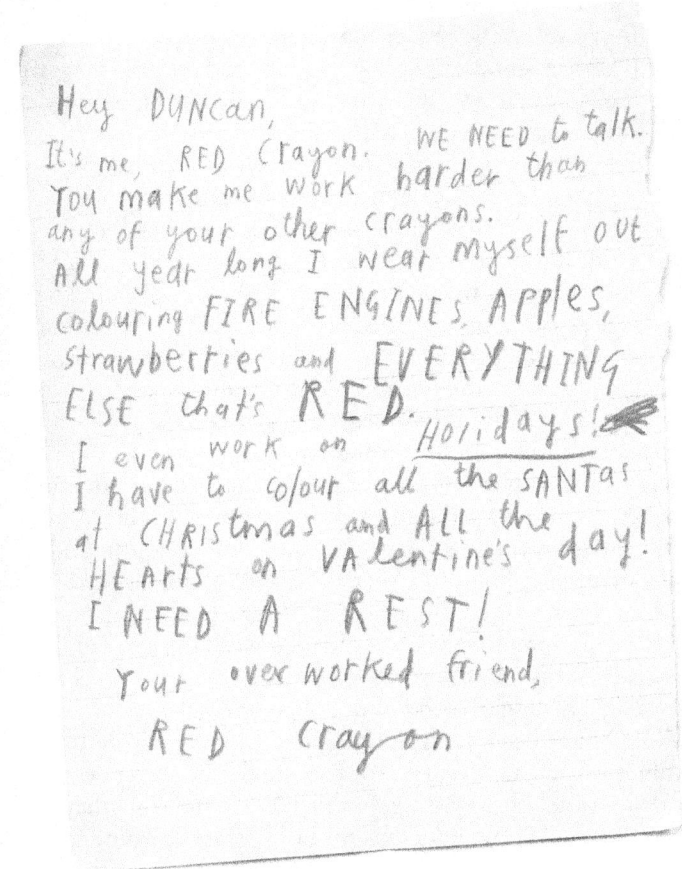

FIGURE 7.8 *Red crayon's letter. Excerpt from* The Day the Crayons Quit *(2013) by Drew Daywalt, and illustrated by Oliver Jeffers. Used by permission of Philomel, an imprint of Penguin Young Readers Group, a division of Penguin Random House LLC. All rights reserved. Reprinted by Permission of HarperCollins Publishers Ltd © 2013, Drew Daywalt and Oliver Jeffers.*

to think through the significance of constructive participation in democracy, and the importance of carefully worded messages.

The crayons' entertaining letters of complaint to Duncan are each written from a very idiosyncratic point of view, but with a lack of understanding or tolerance for others' perspectives. For example, Yellow crayon and Orange crayon squabble over who is the colour of the sun, and they each write to Duncan to solicit his support for their side of the argument: 'Dear Duncan,

Yellow crayon here. I need you to tell orange crayon that I am the colour of the sun. I would tell him but we are no longer speaking.' This comic depiction of the problematic reality that there are frequently two sides to a story can help prepare children for compromise and the challenging concept of agree to disagree, that an argument cannot always be won by one side and disagreement must be respected. This is important, for blog writing and other online communication platforms are too often misused to spread intolerance and hate, as well as dangerous disinformation.

The class should first enjoy a shared picturebook reading of *The Day the Crayons Quit*, while the teacher leads explorative talk around the many details of the picturebook: the protest pictured on the cover, the letters that the crayons write, and Duncan's disputed pictures. The class might then divide into twelve small groups, each group working on one double-page spread dedicated to one of the twelve colour crayons. In order to encourage reading as a social activity, and also reading as detective work, the children then identify and list the complaints and issues of their chosen crayon. After sharing their results with the other groups, the children can attempt to draw their own pictures using all the different colours, with due regard for the wishes of the different crayons. They give their pictures a title, and they give the animals, objects or figures in their drawings a speech bubble each, in which they can express their feelings with regard to their unusual colours. This is, then, an interpretative task (reading between the lines) and a creative writing task, while also an opportunity for children to be experimental in their artwork and imaginative in the use of colour.

The children can then be invited to write letters of protest from other everyday objects, such as toys, furniture or modes of transport. This is not studied and laborious letter writing, but incidental and empathetic learning. Frank Smith (2015: 75) suggests this kind of literacy learning is 'incidental because we learn when learning is not our primary intention, vicarious because we learn from what someone else does, and collaborative because we learn through others who help us achieve our own ends'. The creative nature of the challenge can lead to children feeling fully immersed in their learning and with energized focus, deep involvement and enjoyment in the process of creativity.

A double-page spread near the end of *The Day the Crayons Quit* shows the innovative picture Duncan draws after reading all the letters from his crayons. He draws his dragon violet, his monster pink, his crocodile blue, his whale orange, and with a green sea, a yellow sky and much more. As a result, he receives a 'good work' sticker from his teacher for colouring, and on the final page he receives a gold star for creativity. The students can now try writing a happy thank-you letter from their favourite crayon to Duncan.

The Day the Crayons Quit is empowering because it allows reflective participation and space for personal development. It illustrates the importance of being flexible, tolerant and learning to solve conflicts peacefully while understanding that people are different. Importantly, it bestows agency on students even when they are communicating in a language not their own. It signals an important educational goal, that children's voices can be heard, and complaints will be listened to.

Fantasy Writing

Fantasy is perhaps the most motivating imaginative impulse for novice creative writing. Nonsense and fantasy texts break rules; while rules are like a safety net, rule breaking provides the shock of novelty. When things are incongruous or out of place creativity and originality are exercised, and encouraging fantasy texts supports the inventive, the implausible and the bizarre. Young students love to create their own figures of fantasy. We know that 'children are both problem solvers and problem generators: children attempt to solve problems presented to them, and they also seek novel challenges. [...] They persist because success and understanding are motivating in their own right' (Bransford, Brown and Cocking 1999: 100).

The opportunity to create a fantasy scenario can both motivate and challenge secondary school students. Paul Morris, a teacher who has researched Swedish adolescents who write creatively in English outside of their English lessons, reports that 'the two most commonly repeated insights regarding creative writing and challenge in-class were that there needed to be more of both. Such insights indicate that the gap between informal and formal L2 English learning is such that it needs to be better bridged' (2022: 121). Morris uses the term *outlandish* 'to describe the imaginative and even bizarre stories, or story elements, created by some participants' (2022: 121), and derives the pedagogical implication from his study that, for many school students, opportunities for 'outlandishness and vivid imagination are most welcome' (2022: 144). According to this research, adolescents – just as much as children – derive enjoyment and satisfaction from challenge, and 'this tension between seriousness and play, or imagination and realism, or outlandishness and our lives' (2022: 134).

Fantastic Beasts of the Wizarding World

J. K. Rowling has provided much inspiration for creative writing among fans, leading to extensive fanfiction on the web. *Fantastic Beasts and Where to Find Them, Newt Scamander* (2nd edition 2017) offers a cohesive and playful stimulus for creative writing in the classroom. Purporting to be based on the fictional Newt Scamander's research, and read at Hogwarts as a textbook classic, the ideas for the fantastic beasts are rich in variation, innovation and comedy. Feigning the discourse genre of the school textbook, the descriptions are quasi factual and concise. Thus, Rowling's texts offer an enticing source of ideas for creative writing. The black and fluffy Niffler,

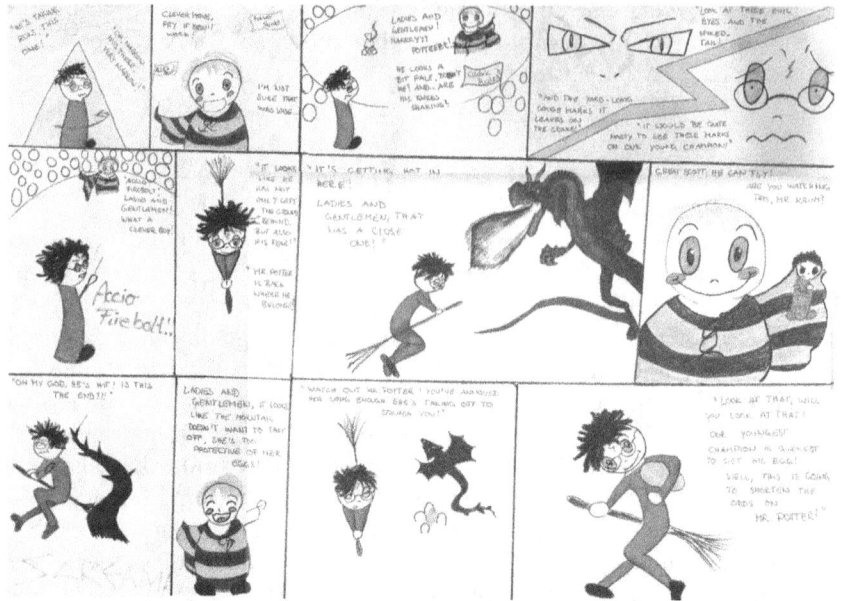

FIGURE 7.9 *Harry Potter and the Hungarian Horntail.*

for example, with its predilection for glittery items, is an affectionate beast. The Acromantula, on the other hand, with the Ministry of Magic (M.O.M.) classification XXXXX (meaning a known wizard killer that is impossible to train), is a monstrous carnivorous talking spider.

Dragons are another XXXXX classification, with ten different breeds, according to Newt Scamander. The Hungarian Horntail is said to be the deadliest. With yellow eyes, a spiked tail, lizard-like in appearance and a spectacularly long fire-breathing range, it is the dragon breed that Harry faced in *Harry Potter and the Goblet of Fire*. Figure 7.9 provides an example of a student teacher's comic-strip creative writing text, on Harry Potter and the Hungarian Horntail.

Students invariably enjoy inventing their own fantastic beast, and adding their own illustration (see Figure 7.10), which also helps them to focus on writing a detailed description. This can be seen in the following imaginative example, a student teacher's creation:

Nayseer (*Невиђени*)
M.O.M CLASSIFICATION: XXXXX

The Nayseer is a blind beast that has its origins in eastern Europe but has been mostly sighted around Serbia. Its eyes are sunken, spider like. And it has really thin and long arms, and a huge gaping jaw.

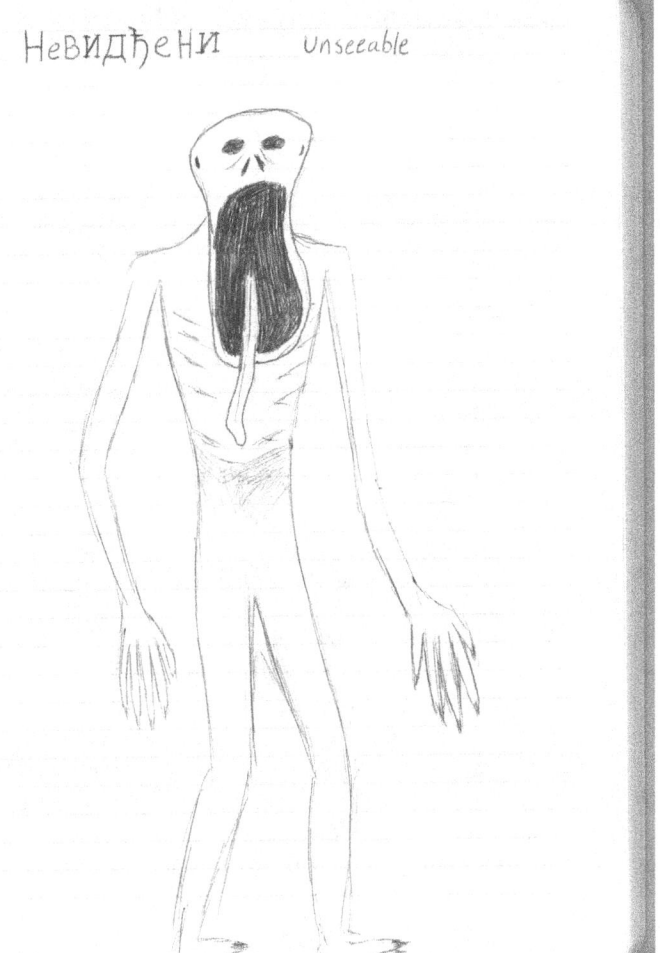

FIGURE 7.10 *Fantastic Beast – The Nayseer.*

The Nayseer has no teeth, so it swallows its victims whole. Inside its enormous mouth, it has vocal organs that can mimic human sound, like human screams and voices of your loved ones. It mimics sound to intimidate and lure prey. Once the Nayseer has you in its long grip, you will never escape.

Due to the beast's blindness, other senses like smell and hearing are heightened. This gives the Nayseer the ability to hear and smell almost anything within its range, BUT its hearing is also its ONLY weakness. Anything too loud will paralyse it due to its sensitive hearing. If you ever come too close, make sure you make as much noise as possible, maybe then you will have a chance.

David Almond and Dave McKean's
Mouse Bird Snake Wolf

Almond's *Mouse Bird Snake Wolf* (2013), vibrantly and powerfully illustrated by McKean, is an unusual literary format; it is smaller than a picturebook and more detailed than most fairy tales. It is a mystical tale about mankind's creative power, but with a dangerous edge that is highly topical, that destruction will follow hubristic anthropocentric creativity. Can anything be done to rid the world of a dangerous thing once it has been created? The book begins: 'Long ago and far away', and it tells of a world not quite finished. 'Like many worlds, the world they lived in was a marvellous place filled with marvellous things. It was safe and calm and rather wonderful' (Almond 2013: np).

The gods who created this world became complacent and inept, so one day, three children are inspired to creativity themselves, and invent some missing animals: a mouse, a bird, a snake, and a wolf. Inventing a wolf in a fairy tale is, of course, asking for trouble – this is a hauntingly illustrated tale on the hope, the beauty, and the danger of creativity. The language, apparently simple in the style of an oral tale, illustrates the power and suggestiveness of rhythmical repetition and storytelling rich with sensory imagery. A young boy begins by creating a mouse: 'The mouse tottered to its tiny feet; it sniffed the air; it peeped into the sky with its little bright eyes. It squeaked, and squeaked again, and squeaked again, and scampered right away.' All at once ambitious, an older boy becomes creative and conjures a twisty, legless thing: 'And yes! The snake hissed. It lifted its head and it hissed again. It slithered towards them across the grass. Its scales glittered. Its eyes gleamed. It bared its sharp little teeth. It flicked its forked little tongue' (Almond 2013).

Almond's writing evokes an embodied response, a theme which he echoes in his acceptance speech for the *Hans Christian Andersen Award*: 'For children, words don't sit still in orderly lines on the page. They work on the body and the senses. They move fluently into drama, into movement, into dance, into song. And the books that they read and love are similarly multi-faceted. [...] The children's book world is a place of abundance, abandon, experiment and play' (Almond 2010, np).

The innovation of the author and illustrator in *Mouse Bird Snake Wolf* can inspire both teacher and student to ingenuity. Exploiting the horrifying illustration of the wolf with its blood red eyes (see Figure 7.11), teachers can use their inventiveness to develop tasks for young creative writers. Ideally, creative writing tasks should encourage imagination and encompass vastly more stimulating opportunities than asking students to simply describe a picture. The following examples illustrate the potential:

FIGURE 7.11 *And it gobbled them up*. Excerpt from Mouse Bird Snake Wolf *by David Almond © 2013, and illustrated by Dave McKean © 2013. Reproduced by permission of Walker Books Ltd, London SE11 5HJ www.walker.co.uk.*

1 The wolf in *Mouse Bird Snake Wolf* is quite scary. In *Harry Potter and the Prisoner of Azkaban*, Harry is taught how to transform a terrifying boggart (a shapeshifter that portrays the beholder's worst fear) into something funny. Create a description and illustration of what you would transform the wolf into if you had the magic to do so.

2 What was the wolf's backstory? Why did she turn ferocious? Write half a page about the wolf's previous experience, including an event which led to her turning savage. Feel free to draw the wolf as well.

Writing on creativity and education, Dominic Wyse and Anusca Ferrari (2015: 43) refer to 'evidence that creative thinking is a feature of children's development from the early years onwards'. Creative writing tasks exploit and extend the role of a mentor text in supporting creativity, critical thinking, cognitive and affective involvement. This is particularly important in English language education, where motivation and self-efficacy are all important for children's confidence in the new role of speaking and writing in another language. Cummins (2014: 4) highlights the importance of enhancing L2 students' literacy engagement: 'Literacy engagement has emerged in multiple studies (both quantitative and qualitative) as perhaps the most significant determinant of literacy attainment.' Creative writing tasks help students to write effectively, to express their astuteness at an age-appropriate level, to take care in their language choices and pride in their work. The cognitive depth is far greater than gap-filling exercises could possibly achieve. And, as Fullan, Gardner and Drummy point out, 'filling in the blanks on a laptop is no more cognitively challenging than doing so on paper' (2019: 65).

CHAPTER EIGHT

Experiential Learning with Plays and Drama

Cecily O'Neill (2013: xix) writes: 'Study after study has shown that when the arts are given space in the curriculum, there are immediate benefits to students, schools and the wider community.' Worldwide, unfortunately, there is frequently little official space for the arts, including drama, but only absences. For this reason alone, it is important to include drama methodology in teacher education, so that language teachers can begin to acquire the expertise and experience needed to help compensate for restrictive school curricula, at least to some extent, by exploiting all the potential flexibility of the subject of English.

In some countries language gains are solely measured through narrow language proficiency testing, with broader educational goals of language development and communication skills scarcely afforded any weight. Fortunately, recent research from Asian contexts, where high-stakes language testing tends to be widespread, has shown that drama can be a superior method for increasing language skills as well as educational goals such as learner autonomy, confidence and critical thinking. Nasser Alasmari and Amal Alshae'el (2020: 61) have investigated the outcomes of teaching English through drama with ten- to twelve-year-olds in Saudi Arabia and found in the context they were studying that 'drama develops participants' language skills, especially the communicative ones such as interactions and conversations, and yields higher proficiency levels as it motivates them to become more engaged in the learning process'. Bünyamin Celik (2019) conducted research with university students on a preparatory language course in Iraq. It was found that a higher level of L2 acquisition was achieved through drama techniques than in the control group, a deeper experience of language learning and positive student feedback.

Creativity in the Language Classroom

Despite the various constraints of school curricula, creative processes, especially those without an emphasis on specific creative products, could be woven into a great deal of school subject teaching. The teaching of English offers many opportunities for communication, collaboration, critical thinking and creativity – often called the Four Cs of twenty-first-century education. But whereas communicative language teaching – the dominant paradigm of language teaching in many parts of the world for much of the last four decades – involves communication and collaboration as essential ingredients, critical thinking and especially creativity are more likely to be neglected. Kyung Hee Kim has shown (2016) how creativity – and the important development of creative climates in education, creative attitudes and creative thinking – is on the decline. Dean Simonton (2006: 492) refers to mental operations underlying the creative process such as 'remote association, defocused attention, intuition, incubation, imagination, insight, heuristic thinking and divergent thinking'. While there are usually a variety of reasons given for the many years of English as a school subject, opportunities for increased language creativity is probably not one of the first. Yet, it is faulty thinking that sees the demands of cognitive learning in opposition to story, creativity and the well-being of children and adolescents. Conversely, performative approaches to language education (Winston 2022: 192) may 'bring together physical and mental activity, aesthetic enjoyment and cognitive challenge, language play and language learning'.

Drama is a holistic method, both in the sense of whole language – learning whole language fully embedded in context and usage-based – and holistic in the sense of the whole person. Drama, in the first sense, avoids decontextualized language that is abstracted from any sociocultural context. Drama thus avoids monodimensional activities, for example filling gaps in worksheets, which inhibit multisensory encounters with language. In the second sense, drama aims to achieve 'learning as a whole person, with body, mind, and emotions in harmony with one another' (Stevick 1980: 11). Students can identify with their language learning – so achieving a positive mindset – if they can emotionally engage with it. Many scholars consider the affective dimension of central importance in language teaching, which drama certainly addresses, as well as the cognitive dimension, sociocultural dimension and physiological dimension of language learning.

Creating a motivating classroom environment is of constant importance, and drama activities can help to achieve this. Drama promotes students' self-confidence and self-efficacy as well as thoughtful feelings and group cohesion. Working towards a whole-group goal, such as a performance in the classroom or before an external audience, adds opportunities for resultative motivation, when students are further motivated by their success. Zoltán Dörnyei (2007: 721–2) has listed criteria for a motivating classroom environment. These include proximity, contact and interaction, the rewarding nature of group activities, investing in the group and cooperation towards common goals, as well as extracurricular activities, whereby 'students lower their "school filter" and relate to each other as "civilians" rather than students'. Successful drama teaching can help to accomplish all these elements of a motivating classroom environment.

Achieving a Balance in Drama Work

In drama, achieving a creative balance between almost contradictory elements is a key aspect. Drama educationalist Jonothan Neelands (2004: 16) argues: 'Too mindful and the work will become dull and uninspiring; too playful and nothing gets done or learnt.' As in all teaching methodology, the quality of teaching very much counts in addition to the chosen approach; concentration and informed focus must be balanced with flexibility and creativity for a performative approach to be truly useful. Teacher education has an important role to play here; where expertise is lacking drama pedagogy experts should, if possible, be invited to hold workshops to help train teacher educators.

It is advisable for a pedagogic contract to be negotiated at the outset of drama work to support students in fully – imaginatively and critically – engaging in the creative teaching and learning partnership that drama represents. The fundamentals in Table 8.1 are adapted from Neelands's suggestion for a pedagogic contract that could be negotiated with the school students or student teachers so that drama work can take on a powerful educational role.

The next sections in this chapter focus on scripted and unscripted drama with adolescent school students. Drama teaching can be immensely fruitful

TABLE 8.1 A Pedagogic Contract for Drama (adapted from Neelands 2004: 16)

Drama work should attempt to achieve a balance between:	
Mindfulness. We are mindful of self, others, and the world. We take the content and context seriously and aim for criticality and thoughtful feelings.	**Playfulness.** We play with language and other sign systems to find the new, the unspoken, the fresh voice. We are creative and feel safe to experiment.
Planned experience. We are entitled to the knowledge that will give us power.	**Lived experience.** Our lived differences are an asset and our strength.
Necessary constraint. We embrace and grow with the necessary structures.	**Necessary freedom.** We must have new openings and choices in our learning.
Knowledge. We realize that what we think we know is often a cultural imaginary.	**Imagination.** We are free from ideologies that replace the imagination.

in the elementary school too, and equally important in that context, as Alasmari and Alshae'el (2020: 67) maintain, 'drama activities generate a greater output of authentic language through interactive, hands-on activities, which are highly relevant to young learners.' For more guidance on language learning through drama with young learners, see Winston (2022), who explores drama with three- to seven-year-olds, and Bland (2015a) on drama with six- to twelve-year-olds.

Using the Deep Reading Framework with Beverley Naidoo's *The Playground*

The Playground (2006) is a short play in three Acts, set in South Africa against the background of Nelson Mandela's release from prison after twenty-seven years, his presidency of South Africa and the admission of Black students and children of colour to formerly all-White schools. This is very recent history, as former president De Klerk's video apology indicates, released posthumously on the day of his death on 11 November 2021, in which he apologizes without qualification, 'for the pain and the hurt and the indignity and the damage that apartheid has done to Black, Brown, and Indians in South Africa'.

Act One (scenes 1–16) of *The Playground* begins in 1989, when the main characters – Rosa, a Black girl, and Hennie, a White boy – are five years old, and ends in 1994 when they are ten. Act Two (scenes 17–19) takes place in 1995 on Rosa's first day at a White school, when Rosa and Hennie are eleven. Act Three (scenes 20–21) takes place in 2000, at the school Annual Prize-Giving and the following day, when Rosa and Hennie are sixteen. The language level and subject matter of this play make it suitable for language learners who are also approximately sixteen or older.

Unpuzzle and Explore

The Playground (Naidoo 2006) is based on a short story with the same title (Naidoo 2001). The short story is naturally far more compressed, illuminating a certain traumatic event in Rosa's life, when she started in an all-White school knowing that neither the schools' White parents and principal, nor many of the other students, would welcome her. *The Playground* as a stage play is more complex, and the characters develop over eleven years. The action in Act One moves swiftly with many short scenes, and a whoosh would be a good way to introduce the story and the characters to the students.

Whoosh

This drama convention will help the students enter into the story, with its background in apartheid, before they read the play. A whoosh provides a way of improvising characters using mime and dialogue according to the directions of the teacher. The class stands in a large circle and the teacher invites individual students to enter the circle, to improvise the characters in action and words according to her brief description. The teacher waves her arms and calls out 'whoosh' when any or all of the characters should leave the scene and return to their places in the circle. The characters in the whoosh that follows, based on Act One, are Hennie van Niekerk, Mevrou (Mrs) van Niekerk, Meneer (Mr) van Niekerk, Rosa Mogale and her Mama. The teacher tells the story, and the students improvise when they are called into the circle:

The play is about a Black and a White family living in a small town in South Africa. Rosa lives with her Mama, who is a servant to Meneer and Mevrou van Niekerk. When Rosa is five years old, she plays in the van Niekerk's garden with Hennie, their son who is the same age. (The teacher chooses two students to enter the circle as Rosa and Hennie.) *Rosa and Hennie often play tag.* (The teacher encourages the students to improvise the actions, here chasing each other in the circle.) *When Hennie falls over* (Hennie pretends to be hurt, while the teacher chooses a student to enter the circle as Mama), *Rosa's Mama mothers him until he feels better.* (Teacher whooshes Rosa and Hennie out of the circle, then chooses a student for Hennie's mother, Mevrou van Niekerk.) *Mevrou van Niekerk gives Rosa's Mama many tasks to fulfil around the big house: dusting, sweeping, making the beds, washing, ironing, cleaning the tiles in the bathroom, cooking, baking cakes and preparing drinks for the family.* (Mama mimes all the tasks.) *One day, Meneer van Niekerk, a man of business, comes home early when he hears Nelson Mandela is to be let out of prison.* (The teacher chooses a student for Hennie's father.) *He roars his rage to his wife, who is distressed. But Mama smiles while she goes on working.* (The teacher whooshes Mevrou van Niekerk out of the circle and brings Rosa and Hennie back in.) *Rosa and Hennie chase each other in the garden again. When Meneer van Niekerk sees them, he shouts in anger at Hennie and spanks him hard for playing with a Black girl.* (The teacher whooshes Hennie and Meneer van Niekerk out of the circle.) *Rosa is frightened and begins to cry. Her Mama comforts her but tells her she cannot play with Hennie anymore. Anyway, it is soon time for Rosa to begin school. Mama helps Rosa dress in her school uniform. She looks very smart and is very excited!* (The teacher chooses a student for the principal at the township primary school.) *The school principal is sorry, but she must send Rosa away, because the township school for Black children is already overcrowded with too few classrooms, desks, and teachers and nearly no books or equipment. Rosa and Mama are very disappointed.* (The teacher whooshes the school principal, Rosa, and Mama out of the circle and brings Meneer van Niekerk and Hennie back in.) *Meneer van Niekerk is very fond of rugby.* (The teacher gives Meneer a ball.) *He tries to teach Hennie to tackle him to get the ball. He wants his son to be rugby-loving and tough, to be a leader like himself.*

The whoosh is always a popular activity, for it is exhilarating and students can communicate with movements and gestures as well as language, thus lessening pressure on them to speak. The teacher can avoid a hectic whoosh (and stress for themselves) by preparing in advance a concise summary of a new text they wish to introduce.

Warming up, using features of the stage play

The Playground was first professionally performed at the Polka Theatre in London in 2004; this is a theatre that specializes in work for young people. As a stage play, *The Playground* is constructed to be alive and thrilling, and includes not only swift action – particularly while setting the scene in Act One – but also rugby playing, singing, celebratory dancing and ululation. The historical background is accentuated by the street cries of the Black paper boys selling the latest news stories. These lively ingredients of the stage play for young people can also be used for warming up in the classroom, as warming up is essential before every episode of drama work. The male students particularly may enjoy explaining and demonstrating (in slow motion!) some rugby football tactics mentioned in the play, such as tackle and scrum. Some of the South African songs could be practised in the classroom, as they are easily available on YouTube, for example 'Bana ba sekolo' to the tune of *Frère Jacques*. South Africa is a multilingual country, with eleven official languages. This is reflected in the play, which includes some expressions in Afrikaans, while the children in the township primary school learn to count in Tswana. A glossary supplies English translations.

The students will enjoy practising ululation, which is a celebratory custom in many African and Asian contexts. A three-minute film created by the Kenyan musician Wambura Mitaru (2012), *Ululate:)*, introduces ululating, and presents many hilarious examples that can be emulated in the classroom. The toyi-toyi is a South African protest dance, a rhythmical jogging with knees high often accompanied by chanting. When the news breaks that Nelson Mandela is out of jail, the toyi-toyi is danced joyfully. Paper boys calling out newspaper headlines provide a kind of chorus that informs the audience of the dramatic political events centring around Mandela, which creates the background to the play. These brief, but important, moments could also be used as a warming-up exercise, with groups of students practising toyi-toying and calling out the different headlines.

Activate and Investigate

Topics that could be investigated and prepared as a slideshow or poster presentation by different student groups might include: the system of Apartheid, Nelson Mandela's role leading to the first free democratic elections in South Africa, an introduction to Desmond Tutu (South African theologian, anti-apartheid and human rights activist), the Nobel Peace Prize (won by both Desmond Tutu and Nelson Mandela), the Springboks rugby team, South Africa today and even an overview of English-speaking countries in Africa (the largest being Nigeria, Ethiopia, South Africa, Tanzania and Kenya, but twenty-four African countries recognize English as an official language). This last topic could be included, as, due to Western native-speakerism, there is a tendency to focus too much on BANA countries – Britain, Australasia and North America (Holliday 1994) – in English language and literature education.

An understanding of Apartheid is an important background for students to recognize how the characters develop. Rosa's Mama explains something of her own past and obstructed opportunities in order to help her daughter find the courage to change from the overcrowded but friendly township school to the formerly all-White school that Hennie attends, despite expecting and experiencing bullying and abuse. In Act Three, we see a slight development away from racism in Hennie's parents, influenced by Rosa's exceptional school progress. Finally, Rosa opens Hennie's eyes, helping him, now her boyfriend, to begin to understand that racism is not only institutional, but is also deeply involved in 'discourse, knowledge, and social practices' (Kubota 2020: 712).

Critically Engage

Critical engagement requires a safe classroom climate, further enhancing a motivating classroom environment. The pedagogic contract introduced in Table 8.1 is proposed as supportive of an imaginative and critical learning partnership through drama.

The Playground throws light on racism, and the power racist societies tend to exercise over education, including the obstruction of knowledge equity, functional and information literacy, the barring of access to equipment, the denial of agency and the hindrance of learner autonomy. Such conditions also tend to characterize societies where misogynistic attitudes are deeply ingrained. As long as examination criteria and procedures, for example, are solely in the hands of a hegemony, minoritized groups will be disadvantaged.

The students could list the differences they discover between Rosa's township school and the all-White school. Large differences are mentioned in teacher–pupil ratios, with eighty children in the first class of the township school, so that Rosa must start school one year later. The township school has too few classrooms, and the children must take turns in going to school – either mornings or afternoons. Rosa complains that between ten and thirty children share one book, the board is too far away for her to see and, of course, the school lacks facilities and space.

Students might also investigate and report on disparities in their own country or region regarding access to education, the arts and the internet, school buildings and community facilities, sports and playing fields, science and other equipment, technology, stationery, coursebooks, school libraries and qualified school librarians. How do discrepancies affect knowledge equity? The class could role-play a formal meeting between citizens, local authorities and political representatives to address a problem such as inequities in educational provision. Using the teacher-in-role convention, the teacher can input information and encourage the students' ideas. As Sabina Li-Yu Chang (2009: 63) writes, 'taking on roles enable(s) teachers to work collaboratively with children to shape the fiction as it proceeds, which naturally generates a sense of immediacy and spontaneity.'

Experiment with Creative Response

Robert Sternberg (2006: 2) argues that creativity is 'neither wholly domain specific nor wholly domain general'. And, although domain-general elements are involved, 'to gain the knowledge one needs to make creative contributions, one must develop knowledge and skills within a particular domain in which one is to make one's creative contribution' (2006: 2). While the domain of English language and literature education offers many opportunities for creativity, this creativity may often be cross-curricular, particularly in the case of drama.

When working on a stage play in the classroom, the most dynamic creative opportunity is bringing aspects of the play to life. After warming-up activities, the students could work in groups on different scenes, and then act them out for the class, script in hand, either in the manner of readers theatre without physical action, or fully enacted using all the means of communication drama can offer. When students use their whole bodies and their physical space to communicate, they can fully employ the different meaning-making semiotic modes:

- the linguistic or verbal system – this comprises the written script with stage directions and the spoken dialogue.
- the visual system – this can include a minimal set, as well as lighting and possibly a suggestion of costumes.
- the touch-related system – acting out a scene involves physical contact and props.
- the gestural system – this includes facial expressions, body language, dancing and at times freezing the action.
- the auditory system – this will include sound effects and music as well as the prosodic features the actors employ: their intonation, stress, tone of voice, tempo, volume and rhythm.

- the spatial system – this comprises the design of the physical spacing where a scene is acted out, and the positioning of the characters to each other and to the audience.

Some of the scenes in *The Playground* would work best if the whole class took part, adding improvised role-play to the written script. Scene 17 in Act Two is a good example: as well as the characters with lines, some students could play the White parents who chant racist protests outside the formerly all-White school. Other students could play policemen who are standing nearby for security, and reporters with microphones who battle to interview Meneer van Niekerk who is among the protesters, Mama as she tries to enrol her daughter, as well as Rosa and the reluctant White principal.

The Playground is also a play that could be performed for parents and the local community, though in this case much of the hard but rewarding work is likely to be realized as an extra-curricular option. A school production is a community event, involving the strengths and commitment of teachers in other subjects as well as English, particularly Art and Music. Teacher colleagues and members of the students' families who can offer help with lighting, music, set design, stage management, scenery and costumes, as well as cultural advice, would be invaluable. The script of *The Playground* could be used very flexibly. The cast list includes fourteen characters; however, this list can easily be extended to include more children in the classroom scenes at the township and all-White schools, more parents at the school Open Day and Annual Prize-Giving, more protesting parents, and more reporters. The principal roles of Rosa and Hennie could also be divided, as they are aged five at the beginning of the story, but sixteen at the end. Working towards such a cross-curricular drama event has been shown to strongly increase the motivating classroom environment effect (Bland 2014).

Drama, a Learning Approach without Walls

Drama processes are not linear, routine or predictable. In this sense, drama methodology could jeopardize established routines and preordained outcomes. However, the rewards of drama – particularly if supported through teacher education – in terms of creativity, motivation and flexibility for all participants are considerable. Drama process work can be used without a playscript or any kind of script, or with a story the class is reading or viewing, including young adult novels, fairy tales and films. Carol Read (2008: 8) argues for the use of drama activities following the sharing of a picturebook, for example, to 'think from within the story and explore significant issues'. In this way, the characters' thoughts can be explored, and the plots can be investigated, with a multiplicity of potential outcomes. It is the context-embedded, open and collaborative nature of drama process work that makes it so rewarding and satisfying.

As a teaching and learning approach without walls, drama is an extremely flexible methodology, and ideally unscripted, small-scale drama activities should be used in the regular classroom. Following their comparative study involving sixth-grade students of English in a Saudi Arabian school, Alasmari and Alshae'el concluded (2020: 67), 'if implemented effectively, drama promotes learning in language classrooms. Therefore, language teachers should be aware of the importance of drama and are recommended to use this tool as a challenging task in order to increase their learners' motivation and thus their academic achievements.' Still, all participants of their study were female, and research conducted in Germany has shown that boys in the sixth grade tend to show somewhat less enthusiasm for drama in comparison with girls, while there is no difference when they are younger (Bland 2014). For this reason, I contend it is preferable for children to become accustomed to drama methodology in the elementary school, for example around picturebook stories or fairy tales, and before adolescence, which is so often characterized by inhibitions and bashfulness, begins. Joe Winston (2022: 5) explores performative language teaching with very young children, as embracing 'a range of strategies that include the dramatic but also make use of music, art, movement, games, storytelling'. Preferably introduced early on in students' school careers, drama can transcend into 'a magical box of tools; the more you take out of it, the more you find inside for future use' (Bland 2015a: 219). Once the teacher initiates the start, many of the students are themselves likely to help develop the ideas, activities and accomplishments.

Thorne, Rowling and Tiffany's *Harry Potter and the Cursed Child*

One of the most attractive aspects of J. K. Rowling's Wizarding World for adolescents is its familiarity. This still expanding storyworld is full of characters intimate and dear to huge numbers of readers and cinemagoers worldwide. As the series progressed in the early twentieth century, parents (many now grandparents) often read the books alongside their children. Those adolescents who grew up together with the heroes of the seven *Harry Potter* books are frequently the greatest fans, and now their own children may have joined this community. Current school students, if *Harry Potter* readers, are already the third generation. Moreover, many of the millennial generation of teachers attest to the influence of *Harry Potter* on their well-being while at vulnerable stages in their lives.

Doors are magically opened in *Harry Potter and the Cursed Child* (Thorne 2016) and metaphorically speaking, the immensely popular series can open doors to the world of story. Popular books such as these form a young adult canon and offer an opportunity for bonding between teachers and their students around a tale that is becoming as familiar as our older shared stories, such as myths and fairy tales. This should not be a cause for regret, derision or disrespect, for stories become a part of our world picture because they fulfil a need. Salman Rushdie (2021: 24) expertly expresses the real power of wonder tales: 'We know, when we hear these tales, that even though they are "unreal", because carpets do not fly and witches in gingerbread houses do not exist, they are also "real", because they are about real things: love, hatred, fear, power, cowardice, death. They simply arrive at the real by a different route.'

Friederike Klippel (2006: 89) suggests that story can create 'bonds between the teacher and her class, but also bonds between the text and its audience. These bonds function on a number of levels, the cognitive one, the social one, the affective one, the aesthetic one.' The characters Harry Potter, Hermione Granger, and Ron Weasley will probably become as long-lasting as Alice, Jim Hawkins, Dorothy, Peter Pan, Anne of Green Gables, Christopher Robin, Pippi and Matilda. There certainly seems to be a need for enduring boy heroes. Such stories can be enjoyed while simultaneously applying critical literacy and reading against the text (see Bland 2013, chapter 8). Meanwhile, the eagerness and curiosity of the students may surprise and animate their teachers. In addition, the enthusiasm of students and teachers combined may ignite those adolescents who have not hitherto discovered that books can be a source of joy.

Harry Potter and the Cursed Child is a playscript written by Jack Thorne, based on a story by Thorne, J. K. Rowling, and John Tiffany. The play production has been massively popular in London, Australia, the United States and Germany, with more productions in planning. However, only a tiny minority of students are ever likely to have the opportunity to see the play as live theatre. Therefore, the motivation to read the playscript may be correspondingly high. I found this to be the case with my student teachers and in-service teachers in Germany and Norway, with the consensus that, despite its length, the material could be suitable to use in mid-secondary school, with approximately fifteen- to sixteen-year-olds in English language education.

In teacher education, I find *Harry Potter and the Cursed Child* highly useful for four main reasons:

- It is increasingly common that student teachers enter university without having discovered the pleasures of reading. *Harry Potter and the Cursed Child* might not be the right choice for a home run book – by which is meant the first really positive reading experience that creates a reading habit (Krashen 2013: 20) – but the playscript can introduce student teachers to the joys of a fantasy-rich, collectively imagined storyworld, so a step towards pleasure in reading.

- Teachers of English should ideally be acquainted with texts that mean a great deal to large numbers of their school students. Reading the playscript opens the door to the shared fictional universe of *Harry Potter* for ongoing teachers.

- Introducing and experimenting with different drama conventions highly suitable for English learners works well with *Harry Potter and the Cursed Child*, even when (unfortunately this also happens) not all student teachers actually read the play.

- The *Harry Potter* series offers elements to enjoy and appreciate (skilful characterizations, clever plot twists, some very funny dialogue), but also offers opportunities to read against the text.

Age Appropriateness

The playscript, set nineteen years after the defeat of Voldemort, has been promoted as the eighth book in the *Harry Potter* series – which has given rise to some controversy among fans who are not keen on the stage play format, with its lack of a narrator's voice. However, studying a play in secondary-school English has a tradition in many countries worldwide, often with a particular focus on Shakespeare. Due to the difficulty of the adult canon, plays by Shakespeare, or other playwrights such as Oscar Wilde, Tennessee Williams or Arthur Miller, are generally studied as literary works on the page in the most advanced grades of secondary school, or not at all. *Harry Potter and the Cursed Child* is far more accessible for a combination of reasons. The setting is the familiar Wizarding World – students will find old friends among the characters, with dialogue not too distant from the language of contemporary adolescents. Moreover, the story includes events, places, fantastic methods of travel, paraphernalia (wands, broomsticks, potions, spells) and artefacts (the Sorting Hat, Cloak of Invisibility, Marauder's Map and Time-Turner) that are familiar from the *Harry Potter* series. Students could use the back-and-forth technique to check the meaning of these magical artefacts and memorabilia. In the back-and-forth technique, student pairs take turns to act as teacher and learner. The student playing the teacher first explains the artefact to their partner, who listens and takes notes. They then together check the meaning.

Knowledge of the *Harry Potter* films also supports readers in English language learning situations in generating a mental model of the text they are reading – a creative process of seeing, hearing, feeling and enacting the storyworld in the mind. Schmitt, Jiang and Grabe (2011: 30) refer to adult students learning English in their study of the percentage of words known in a text and reading comprehension: 'Readers with much greater knowledge of a topic, greater expertise in an academic domain, or relevant social and cultural knowledge understand a text better than readers who do not have these resources.' A literature review on second-language reading comprehension conducted by Siping Liu also found that familiarity was shown to be a decisive factor in supporting less proficient L2 readers (2014: 1087). Background knowledge contributes very significantly to reading comprehension, as prior knowledge encourages connecting and inferencing.

The play format supports the organizing of groupwork around scenes in preparation for the pleasure of reading roles aloud in class. This was found to be a favourite activity among students in advanced grades, as a teacher quoted in Duncan and Paran (2018: 255) explained: 'they loved reading, they're fighting over who gets to read which part [...] I think actually reading aloud gives them a sense of security so that even kids who are very very shy feel that they can participate and join in and have a voice but don't need to worry about what they're going to say.' Reading a playscript aloud is a collaborative activity, with different students embodying the different roles. Reading aloud in this prepared way – specifically with drama, poetry and verse novels – can be a lively and meaningful activity.

Drama Conventions

During the plot of *Harry Potter and the Cursed Child*, with the help of a Time-Turner, some events of the *Harry Potter* world of the original series are revisited – particularly the Triwizard Tournament in Harry's fourth year at Hogwarts, and the scene in Godric's Hollow at the time when Harry's parents were killed. However, the play mostly centres on the close friendship between Harry's son Albus and Draco's son Scorpius, as well as difficulties between the generations, which nearly have fatal consequences. Diverse drama conventions can be employed in the classroom to discover richer details of characterization and theme, to add new voices, deepen the reading of the play, and potentially reveal absences. Critical literacy is practised when the absences that have been revealed by the drama conventions are analysed. Students can respond with creative writing from different perspectives, potentially resisting the subliminal ideology of the text. Reading *against* a contemporary text is even more challenging than resistant reading of a canonical text, for in a contemporary text the ideology may be so close to that of the reader that it seems invisible and consequently non-existent.

Warming up

It is a good idea for a group to warm up before any focused work, but vital before working with drama. As adolescent students may be initially shy about using physical actions and movement in English language education, it is helpful to take a warming up activity from the script itself, so that the connection to the topic remains clear. While useful for warming up, playing with language also helps internalize the rhythms of contemporary spoken English. The dark prophecy introduced in Act 3, Scene 21, for example, is exhilarating when performed as a crescendo echo with slow, symbolic gestures. The teacher speaks the words of the prophecy, and these are echoed by the students – but unlike a natural echo increasing in volume:

When spares are spared,
*(... spares are spared, SPARES ARE SPARED, **SPARES ARE SPARED**)*
when time is turned,
*(... time is turned, TIME IS TURNED, **TIME IS TURNED**)*
when unseen children murder their fathers:
*(... murder their fathers, MURDER THEIR FATHERS, **MURDER THEIR FATHERS**)*
then will the Dark Lord return.
*(... Dark Lord return, DARK LORD RETURN, **DARK LORD RETURN**)*

On other occasions students might perform one of the Sorting Hat rhymes as a rhythmical dance, for example the rhyme from Act 1, Scene 4:

I've done this job for centuries
On every student's head I've sat
Of thoughts I take inventories
For I'm the famous Sorting Hat.

Certain drama activities, strategies or conventions can be used as building blocks to help readers into a story (such as a *whoosh*; see example earlier in this chapter). Drama conventions can also encourage thoughtful feelings in reaction to storytelling (*total physical response* can be employed in this way; see examples of TPR in Chapters 4 and 5), and investigate characters and their interactions more deeply (such as *gossip circle*, *intrapersonal role-play*, *subtext strategy* and *role-on-the-wall*, which are introduced in this chapter, and *hot-seating* introduced in Chapters 6 and 9). Critical literacy, which Hilary Janks (2019: 563) has defined as 'understanding the ways in which a text is positioned and is working to position us, the readers', can be supported by using drama conventions. The use of intrapersonal role-play and subtext strategy with *Harry Potter and the Cursed Child* disclosed absences to my student teachers, and once revealed, these absences seemed glaring to the whole class. Using the *teacher-in-role* strategy, the teacher can beneficially take part in these drama activities to guide, provide fresh input, prompt more active participation (for example by pretending to need help), model language and create renewed tension (see also Chapter 9).

Gossip circle

The gossip circle is a drama convention that can also be used as a warming up activity. Neelands designates this as an exercise whereby the 'behaviour of characters is commented on in the form of rumours and gossip circulating in the community; as the rumours spread around the circle they become exaggerated and distorted' (2004: 102). This technique works very well with the tensions and conflicts in *Harry Potter and the Cursed Child*. Students could, for example, explore the bullying experienced by Scorpius, who is rumoured to be the son of Voldemort: 'I mean – father-son issues, I have them. But, on the whole, I'd rather be a Malfoy than, you know, the son of the Dark Lord' (Act 1, Scene 3), and also experienced by his best friend Albus: 'Albus Potter, the Slytherin Squib' (Act 1, Scene 4). As the students become more familiar with the play, the gossip circle should be repeated in order to investigate any character development and the many other conflicts and rumours. The gossip circle works well when a soft ball is thrown around the circle to indicate who should speak next, adding the element of surprise.

As a warming-up activity, the gossip circle is creative as well as safe for students feeling vulnerable to peer pressure: the students are allowed and encouraged to exaggerate and distort the conflicts in the play, leading to later reflection. Such processes have been defined by Freebody and Finneran (2013: 61) as the 'opportunity afforded by the safe and imaginary world of drama, and the reflective space between the fictional world and the real world'. Nonetheless, it is supportive of a motivating classroom environment to always end the activity with friendly gossip – saying nice things about a character – such as 'Ron is always loyal to his friends', 'Ron is an affectionate husband', 'Ron has good sense of humour', 'he knows his weaknesses'. This activity also helps the reluctant readers build a better sense of character within the classroom community.

Intrapersonal role-play

This is an interpretative drama convention that encourages deep thinking about complex behaviour. Certain characters and pivotal decision-making moments are chosen. Two students portray a single figure from the play, trying to express different angles of their character. Figure 8.1 shows student teachers' ideas for intrapersonal role-play based on *Harry Potter and the*

	Intrapersonal role-play: Inner conflict	
	Group 1: Discuss then act out Draco's inner conflict about asking Harry for help with the rumours about Scorpius. (pp. 24-25)	Group 3: Discuss then act out Scorpius's inner conflict about helping Albus to bring back Cedric. (pp. 69-71)
	Group 2: Discuss then act out Albus's inner conflict after his decision to help Amos. (p. 57)	Group 4: Discuss then act out Snape's inner conflict at his decision to help Scorpius. (p. 192)

FIGURE 8.1 *Preparation for intrapersonal role-play (student teachers' design).*

Cursed Child. The intrapersonal role-play was discussed in groupwork first, for reflective preparation for improvisation tasks and the chance to try out dialogue first in small groups is always advantageous, even for student teachers fluent in English.

After the student teachers had improvised a number of intrapersonal role-plays, they realized that the chosen pivotal scenes portrayed only male characters. This point is further discussed in the section on critical literacy.

Role-on-the-wall

This is an activity that explores characters from the perspective of other characters. Two or three students create a large group poster of a chosen character, selecting a colour to represent their character. They then draw a spacious outline for the character, and fill the outline with snippets of information, qualities and thoughts, using pens of the same colour. When the outlines are full of ideas, the groups swap posters in order to annotate the other role posters – each group using the colour of their own figure and writing from their own figure's perspective – but on the outside of the other character outlines. Finally, the role posters are attached to the wall, for the annotations on the various characters may be further developed as more insights arise.

The theme of father-son generational conflict became very apparent with this task. The groups wrote either 'father issues' or 'daddy issues' within the outlines of all characters and Scorpius was even given the words DADDY ISSUES in place of eyes (see Figures 8.2–8.5).

Subtext strategy

This is a convention in drama teaching that allows students to collaboratively create and voice characters' thoughts in pivotal moments. In groups, students first reflect on, then script the thoughts of characters in a chosen scene before presenting them to other members of the class. Characters seldom say exactly what they mean, nor do they express all their thoughts in words. In the theatre or on film, actors' facial expressions and body language will help to reveal their thoughts. On paper, and without a narrator, there are often blanks that need to be interpreted. Creating subtexts offers the opportunity to fill these spaces, revealing the unspoken. Fleming (2013: 211) describes the strategy as 'freezing a moment in time, exploring subtexts, voicing characters' inner thoughts and intentions'.

Working in small groups, students could begin by creating an iceberg poster for each character. They write down a character's key lines in the space above the waterline, and then create the subtext together in the bulk of the iceberg below the waterline (see Figure 9.1 for an iceberg task template and Figure 11.4 for an example of the iceberg task related to *The Hunger Games*). The students subsequently rehearse the scene, while

FIGURE 8.2 *Role-on-the-wall – Harry Potter.*

deciding on moments when the characters' thoughts could be expressed. Finally, two students perform each character in the scene: one reading aloud the character's lines, the other voicing the character's inner thoughts. This works well at climactic moments, such as the following momentous altercation between Harry and his younger son, in Act 1, Scene 7:

> Harry (*finally losing his temper*): You know what? I'm done with being made responsible for your unhappiness. At least you've got a dad. Because I didn't, okay?
> Albus: And you think that was unlucky? I don't.
> Harry: You wish me dead?

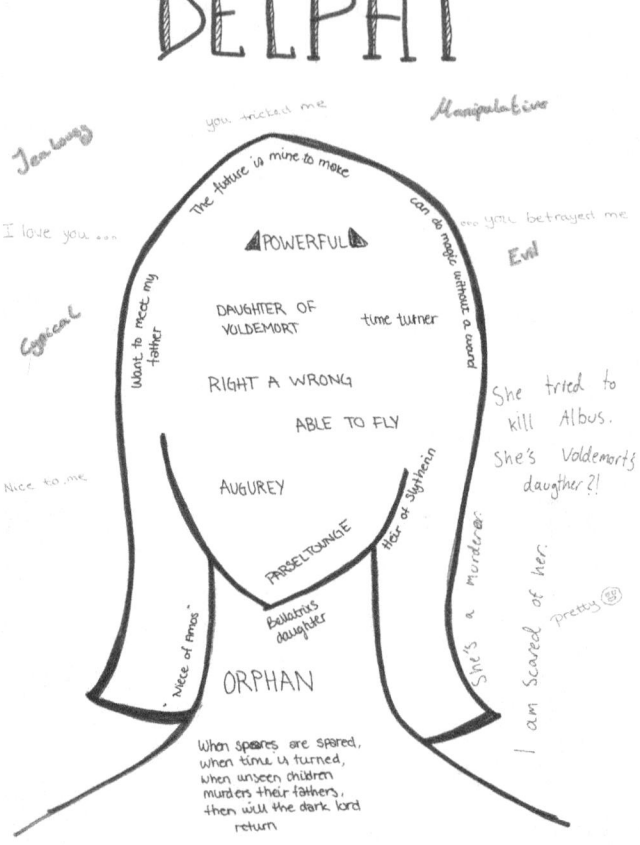

FIGURE 8.3 *Role-on-the-wall – Delphi.*

Albus: No! I just wish you weren't my dad.
Harry (*seeing red*): Well, there are times I wish you weren't my son.
There's a silence. Albus *nods. Pause.* Harry *realises what he's said.*
No, I didn't mean that...
Albus: Yes. You did.

This is a devastating scene between father and son. Watching students perform the characters and their thoughts in this scene can be a very moving experience. Extending and examining the moment by creating subtexts takes us right inside the characters, potentially revealing troubling and very personal real-life echoes.

FIGURE 8.4 *Role-on-the-wall – Albus.*

Critical Literacy – Female Agency, Queer Agency and Reading against the Text

As we have seen, there is human conflict as well as dark magic, wonder and awe in *Harry Potter and the Cursed Child*, as in the entire *Harry Potter* series. The speculative aspect of the play is imagining what might happen if we could really turn back the clock. The resulting drama is reminiscent of the butterfly effect as it appears for the first time in fiction in Ray Bradbury's short story *A Sound of Thunder* (1952), which might be read as an introduction to a central theme of the play. *Harry Potter and the Cursed Child* explores both figuratively and literally the many perils of being stuck in the past, for example because Harry cannot imagine that being at Hogwarts is so completely different for his son than it was for himself. As Delphi remarks (Act 1, Scene 6): 'It's tough to live with people stuck in the past, isn't it?' The present-day fixation – which likewise seems to have seized the older generation more than the younger generation – on

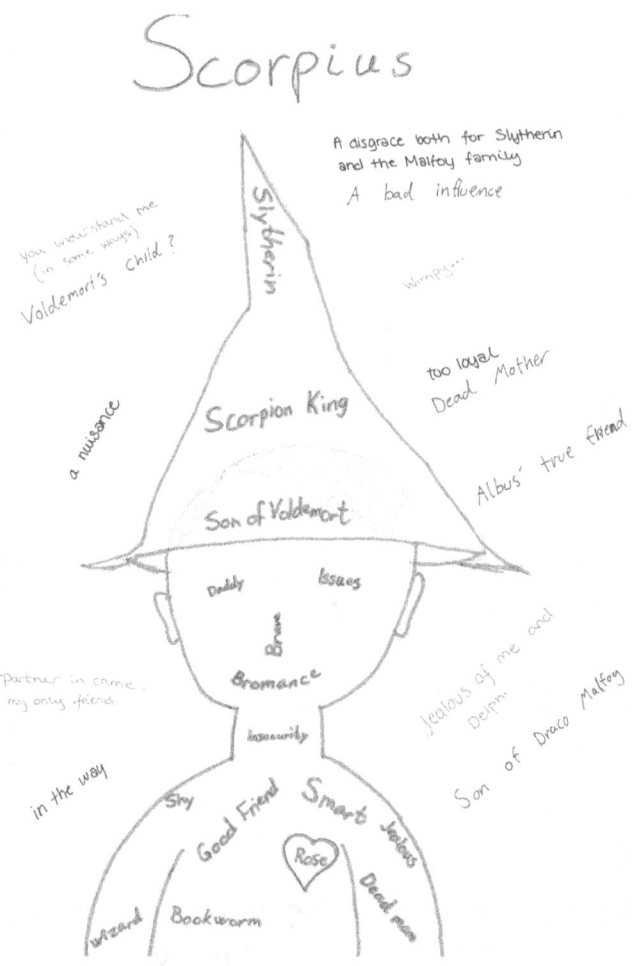

FIGURE 8.5 *Role-on-the-wall – Scorpius.*

living in an imagined past, demanding the rebuilding of walls and barriers as attempts to regain a supposed past stability and serenity, might be discussed in this context.

During the previously described drama conventions of intrapersonal role-play, role-on-the-wall and subtext strategy, a specific absence was noted by the student teachers: the lack of interactions between the female characters. This absence has been studied in movies particularly and found to be extremely common. This has become widely known as the Bechdel test – due to its association with critical commentator, graphic artist and novelist Alison Bechdel – as a way of gauging the agency of women and girls in narratives. Jill Dolan (2013: 3) states the test is 'for assessing whether a film is worth watching for feminist men and women. The test assesses whether a film has at least two named women in it who talk to each other about something besides a man.' In *Harry Potter and the Cursed Child* there are several named women, but they hardly talk to each other. There is no scene between sisters-in-law Hermione and Ginny, no scene between cousins Rose and Lily, no scene between teachers Professor McGonagall and Madam Hooch, and not even a scene between mothers and daughters Hermione and Rose or Ginny and Lily. This is disturbing, for as Fleming points out: 'Drama's primary language mode is dialogue and it is more evident that meaning is created "between" rather than "within" people' (2001: 104). That Delphi only ever interacts with boys and men is less surprising for the sake of the plot – a woman would surely have seen through her machinations.

Such absences can be filled creatively and animated by having groups of students script the missing scenes – also the boys can practise writing dialogue for girls. This may help to surface any stereotypes or prejudices amongst students – it may be revealing, for example, when girls act out scenes scripted by boys. Howard Gardner suggests taking risks in order to cultivate a creative mind, and recommends supporting 'exploration, challenging problems, and the tolerance, if not the active encouragement, of productive mistakes' (2006: 85). By such trial and error, young people should be given the opportunity to resist cultural conditioning.

Harry Potter and the Cursed Child has been accused of queerbaiting. The play provides a hint of LGBTQ+ portrayal with the characters Albus and Scorpius, and could imply a normalizing of queer representation, but the depiction so far on the commercial stage is heteronormative. The play is ultimately only really completed in each performance – to the extent that students might choose for themselves to portray either *bromance* for the close friends Albus and Scorpius, or romance and resistance to the heteronormativity suggested in the penultimate scene when Albus and Scorpius discuss their future girlfriends (Act 4, Scene 14). Thus, scripted drama can be considered a particularly powerful kind of 'literature as "doing", something to try for yourself' (Hall 2016: 465). In this way, the artistic process goes beyond a learning device; it also provides potential for transformative experiences, as Jessica Whitelaw proposes (2017: 66), 'by positioning art as the material and processes through which to engage the work of ongoing inquiry'. This suggests trial and error, searching for subtexts, students thinking critically and creatively, reading against the text, and being challenged to discover their own and others' voices.

Texts for deep reading should be authentic to the learner group, they should be within reach of their area of expertise and challenging – but not too challenging. As Gardner (2006: 87) points out, during adolescence 'students need to be posed challenges where they stand a reasonable chance of success'. Certainly, the playscript format demands active and curious reading – for it is challenging to conjure the staging, choreography, and dramatic effects of a complex stage play in the mind. The mixed responses to *Harry Potter and the Cursed Child* illustrate that readers need help in acquiring these skills. There are important reasons to include creativity wherever possible in the curriculum, and English offers opportunities to introduce 'new pursuits that are removed from the academic treadmill and that reward innovation and look benignly on errors' (Gardner 2006: 86). Focused attention on language learning is important, of course, but so is creativity, defocused attention, imagination, heuristic and divergent thinking. As Gardner (2006: 84) asserts: 'Options need to be kept open – a straight trajectory is less effective than one entailing numerous bypaths, and even a few disappointing but instructive cul-de-sacs.'

CHAPTER NINE

The Versatility of Verse Novels

A literary format that is highly promising for language education but has received very little critical attention as yet is the verse novel. Verse novels are frequently intimate stories of struggle set in contexts of sociocultural and political conflict or unrest. The textual hybridity of verse novels – neither a novel nor poetry in the traditional sense – and suggestive layout on the page seem to echo cultural hybridity and disrupted experience. Longer than a short story, the verse novel does not recount a brief epiphanic episode as the short story might but is usually a fully rounded narrative. However, and this is important for school language education, the verse novel is generally far shorter than a traditional novel, but is, in contrast to the excerpts from novels often included in coursebooks, nonetheless a complete artistic whole. Often the length of a novella, verse novels tend to be more immersive than poems – they allow readers to empathize with fully developed characters and may introduce several different perspectives.

The verse novel is not the first format to tell stories using verse. Epic poetry has existed in many cultures and languages for millennia, and thus originated before the appearance of writing. Later, when most poets were literate, the bards and performers still shared their poetry with their usually illiterate audiences through purely oral means. Repetition and other forms of patterned language facilitate memorization (Ong 2002, see Chapter 7). In this way, the language of epic poetry displays some features of everyday speech, such as redundancy, repetition and additive language. Verse novels share some of these characteristics of oral literature.

The Verse Novel Format

The most accessible verse novels come across as spontaneous and direct. They may have staccato rhythms not unlike children's talk, who express their thoughts as they come to them, in short bursts and cumulatively, one by one until they are understood. But this is only seeming spontaneity; the best verse novels are very carefully crafted and increasingly achieve critical acclaim by winning prestigious children's literature awards, such as the Carnegie Medal and the Newbery.

Verse novels typically tell their stories using a persona as in poetry rather than extended narration. They use a variety of poetic forms, most frequently unrhymed free verse, and often with a title to each poem, which may be an evocative vignette taking up only a few lines on the page or may extend over several pages. Sometimes these poems are both beautiful and meaningful even outside of the story and can be individually chosen for discussion in the classroom, for unrhymed free verse tends to be a meditative kind of writing that can carry the flow of emotions and fiercely felt experience. Verse novels tend to be stories of marginalized peoples, and the feeling comes across that the tales they tell are too deeply felt for prose. Their haunting, evocative language and moving musicality communicate sensory, embodied experience as well as understanding.

Ideas, thoughts and scenes in verse novels tend to be juxtaposed episodically. Brief episodes – from just a few lines on the page to several pages – accumulate to a multi-layered collage of the storyworld. Mike Cadden (2011: 26) expresses this as 'rather like one of those picture mosaics that create from individual and unrelated pictures a larger image'. Joy Alexander (2005: 271) suggests the format is 'cinematic in style, as a succession of scenes are presented to the visual imagination with the "voice-over" heard simultaneously in the mind'.

While the episodic structure of the verse novel leaves gaps in the narrative, the verses also leave spaces on the page. Such gaps and spaces invite deep reading, for they encourage, as Cadden (2011: 24) suggests, 'imaginative speculation about the things that are left unsaid by either characters or absent narrators – the descriptions of characters, settings, movements, and background information provided in the traditional prose novel that here are gaps, white or negative spaces, silences'. The silent, white spaces on the pages often encourage the reader to muse on the reflections of the speaker, while in other scenes the rhythms, the flow of the lines (enjambment) and emphases seem to demand reading aloud.

Deeply felt refugee and minoritized perspectives are very common in verse novels, perhaps because of the hybrid format itself that is a composite of different elements. This speaks to the affective dimension of language education and affords the opportunity to build a better understanding of different cultural groups, enhancing mutual respect and interculturality. Yet verse novels are also story, and as such can work as a training ground for ToM, learning empathy and acting with an intercultural disposition.

Using the Deep Reading Framework with Helen Frost's *The Braid*

Helen Frost's *The Braid* (2006) is a compact verse novel, less than 100 pages, that has as its main characters two sisters, Jeannie and Sarah, who are 14 and 15 years old at the beginning of the narrative and 16 and 17 years old at the end. The potential for dialogue on historical as well as global issues renders the book better suited for higher grades in secondary school.

Unpuzzle and Explore

This first step of the deep reading framework (see Figure 1.1: 26) helps students gain literary literacy, for example recognizing the conventions and patterns of different genres and formats. Frost's *The Braid* displays characteristics of several genres: historical fiction, refugee narrative and love story. The family drama takes place in mid-nineteenth-century Scotland, bringing to life the Zeitgeist of the period, when many tenants were evicted from their homes to make way for more profitable sheep farming, now known as the Highland Clearances. The verse novel format perfectly suits the anguish of the family, with some members becoming refugees and others internally displaced. Features of orality in the verse novel beautifully express the alternating inner voices of the two sisters as they tell their story, separated and divided by the Atlantic Ocean.

The communication seems at times almost telepathic, as none of the family members or divided lovers can read or write. The class could first explore the importance of literacy by working together on a mind map (see example on p. 83). They could then explore illiteracy amongst rural and industrial workers in nineteenth-century Britain, which made separations far worse as there were no alternative means of communication to letter writing. Some of the poetry of *The Braid* invites reading aloud in addition to silent reading, and in this way the text becomes multimodal. Mostly used with drama and poetry, carefully prepared reading aloud can turn prose into a multisensory and animating experience.

Activate and Investigate

In this second step, a jigsaw activity could be organized to activate prior knowledge and investigate topics relevant to the storyworld of *The Braid*. Topics could be connected to the plot (expulsion and separation of families), or the settings (the wild Western Isles of Scotland and Cape Breton Island in Canada). Students could investigate the mass evictions from the Scottish Highlands and Islands, which took place approximately 1750 to 1860.

Students could try to connect the storyworld with the contemporary world and investigate, for example, the past and present of the Gaelic language in Nova Scotia and Scotland, or issues around adult literacy in the twenty-first century. If these topics are dealt with as a jigsaw activity, the class is first divided into home groups with one student per topic in each group. In the home groups, each student first decides which topic to explore, then students regroup into teams that focus on the same issue, and this becomes the expert group. After working on their topic, the students return to their home groups and teach each other what they have learned.

In deep reading, empathy is activated through the characters: Sarah and Jeannie, the courageous and resilient sisters, and Murdo, Sarah's strong and faithful lover. The title, *The Braid*, refers to Jeannie and Sarah's hair, which they braid together before they are parted when evicted from their home. Sarah then cuts the braid, and each takes a part of their braided hair with them. Sarah stays behind with her grandmother, and they take refuge on windswept Mingulay, a small and inaccessible island with ferocious weather and no sheltered landing for boats. With a tiny Gaelic-speaking population, and unreachable for weeks at a time due to severe weather conditions, the island of Mingulay was not targeted by the mass evictions.

Critically Engage

In the third step, students exchange understandings on how the novel affects them emotionally and cognitively. Verse novels usually mirror thoughts or inner speech, and therefore there are always gaps, allowing students the opportunity to read between the lines. Critically engaged students speculate on some of the missing elements, for example the fearful details of the Atlantic crossing, during which two of Jeannie's younger siblings and her father die of cholera. The stories of the sisters are often expressed in incomplete sentences, their thoughts appear to spring spontaneously from one impression to the next, aware of the dangers but avoiding naming them explicitly. Instead, the sisters use imagery, which help the reader imagine, for example the ship that is 'like Grandma's salted herring' (Frost 2006: 12):

> *Jeannie*
> *Crossing the Atlantic*
> So many people in so small a space. This ship is like
> Grandma's salted herring, people packed that tight, everyone
> hungry, cranky, some sick – a man died yesterday. I go
> out to the windy upper deck, taking Willie, leaving
> behind our crowded sleeping quarters down below. That air –
> the stench of it won't leave my hair and clothes.

Referring back to the title, *The Braid*, words and phrases in the verse novel are also braided or interwoven, inspired by the image of Celtic knots. The alternating internal monologues of the sisters are interspersed with short poems (praise poems) that are cohesively connected to the narrative by word repetition from poem to poem, like an echo across the ocean, on themes of home, shelter, family and heritage. This is an adventurous use of language and imagery, creating symmetry while symbolizing the strong bond between the parted sisters. Students might compare *The Braid* with refugee narratives of young people in the contemporary refugee crisis (see Chapter 5). In stories set in the present, the focus is often more on the reasons for the flight and the circumstances of the refugee journey. Does it matter that refugee stories are sometimes primarily plot driven rather than character driven? Do the students find the focus on characterization and plot events are well balanced in this verse novel?

Experiment with Creative Response

Literature as doing, including creative writing and performance, such as recreating a text in another format or making use of audience involvement, represents an ongoing transaction between text and readers. The twenty-eight praise poems interwoven throughout the sisters' narratives offer an opportunity for creative writing, such as when students create their own praise poems on topics from their lived experience. All creative writing must have rules, as this helps the students structure their work and achieve literary cohesion. The rules governing these praise poems are that they are made up of eight lines, and eight syllables in each line, and they praise something named in Sarah or Jeannie's narrative. In addition, something named in the last line of each poem is echoed in the first line of the following praise poem, several pages later.

As a preparation for writing their own poems, each student could be given a copy of a different praise poem (each poem is printed on a separate page in the verse novel), which they read carefully, before standing in a circle. The teacher reads aloud the first praise poem in *The Braid*, and the students listen closely in order to discover if their poem is next. When a student hears the words that are reiterated at the beginning of the praise poem they have been given, this means their poem is next in sequence and they read it aloud, until all twenty-eight poems have been recited. Here are three examples of praise poems from *The Braid* that illustrate the word braiding (underlining added):

Table
A table absorbs written thoughts
(slight indentations in its wood),
and holds within its sturdiness
echoes of the conversations
that go on around it: laughter,
mealtime chatter, words of comfort.

It's part of all the stories, like
the constant <u>kettle on the stove</u>.

(Frost 2006: 50)

Kettle
The iron <u>kettle on the stove</u>
sings a low song, deep in its throat.
We pour the substance of the song
into a teacup: *Drink slowly,*
sit awhile, it croons, *remember,*
drink deep, and fill me up again.
It sends its heat into the world
while it <u>holds one still central place</u>.

(Frost 2006: 53)

Trees
Each tree <u>holds one still central place</u>
with its deep roots. Shelter for birds,
squirrels. Branches for climbers, fruit
in its season, and later, boards –
the sweet smell of lumber, fresh-cut,
solidity of wood-made things
(a bowl, a house, a rocking horse).
Shadows of leaves like passing thoughts.

(Frost 2006: 56)

The rule connected to the sisters' narratives is that the line lengths are based on syllable counts according to the sisters' ages. Sarah, the elder sister, is seventeen by the end of the story:

Sarah
Mingulay

I look
up as Murdo steps ashore and strides towards me. *Sarah! I tried to send word that I was coming, but –* He stops and stares at Jeannie. At me. Something huge and silent holds us and surrounds us. Uncle Allen says, *Why don't we get this boat up before we begin our telling and our asking – it is clear there will be stories here this evening.*

(Frost 2006: 81)

Murdo is as much caught up in the traumatic events as the sisters, so that students could provide his perspective by writing or dramatizing his role in the story, for example how he was brutally forced onto a ship bound for Canada by the landowner's men and dogs, '*he was bellowing and crying as if his heart was torn in half when they took him on that ship*' (2006: 58, italics in original), how he managed to find Sarah's sister, mother and little brother in Cape Breton, or his long and determined struggle to get back to Mingulay.

Promoting Interculturality, Creativity and Critical Literacy with Verse Novels

Further moving and appealing verse novels that are apposite for language education with younger and older adolescents are introduced in this section: *Hidden* (Frost 2011), *Home of the Brave* (Applegate 2007), *The Crazy Man* (Porter 2005), *Aleutian Sparrow* (Hesse 2003), *The Crossover* (Alexander 2014), *Inside Out & Back Again* (Lai 2011) and *Brown Girl Dreaming* (Woodson 2014).

Helen Frost's *Hidden*

Another verse novel by Helen Frost, *Hidden* (2011), set in the present, tells a gripping story of traumatic childhood memories and social-class differences. *Hidden* illustrates a quite common characteristic of the verse novel – the presentation of alternating voices that directly offer different points of view, unmediated by a narrator. This is very relevant for the educational goal of interculturality, with the aim of building links between sociocultural groups based on mutual respect.

In *Hidden*, the story is told in the alternating voices of two fourteen-year-old girls, Darra and Wren, bound together by a crime that happened when they were eight years old, partly accidental and for which neither girl is responsible. Now, six years later we discover that each of them still suffers feelings of blame, guilt, and unresolved anguish. Having heard a gunshot, eight-year-old Wren was hiding in her mother's car when Darra's father stole the car to escape from an attempted robbery that ended in disaster. The little girl found herself trapped in a garage where the stolen car was parked. Darra discovered Wren, concealed in a small fishing boat in the garage, but feared to reveal this to her father. She left Wren food and water and meant to help her escape, while also doing her best to protect her father from arrest and inevitable prison. The ordeal was horrifying for eight-year-old Wren, who was hiding in the home of a thief, whom she thought might have shot her mother. Terrified, hungry, thirsty, cold and needing a toilet, Wren struggled with basic needs:

> When the cat
> jumped out of the boat,
> I watched it.

>   A litter box?
>   Not too far away.
>   Maybe I could…
>   I had to.
>   I did.
>   I got back in the boat. The cat came too.
>   It settled beside me.
>   We fell asleep.
>
>   (Frost 2011: 18–19)

Darra and Wren never came face to face in the garage; however, when they met at a summer camp after six years had passed, they recognized each other's names from the media broadcasts at the time of the accidental kidnapping. Darra's father was still in prison, her parents were now divorced and fishing on the lake with her father had vanished for ever:

> What do you do when all of a sudden your dad is gone and the
> rest of your life is nothing
> like it was before?
>
>   (2011: 43)

Wren had likewise not entirely overcome the traumatic episode that occurred when she was eight, though coming from an intact and wealthy family she had had more support to deal with the trauma than Darra. The duality of perspective in the verse novel gradually reveals the complexity of their life stories, their multifaceted identities, their very different family backgrounds, and how subjective our notion of the truth can be. At a summer camp, the girls avoid each other at first, then cautiously learn to comprehend the events through the other's eyes, understanding how the past hurt the other too in ways they had not imagined, and to value their different perspectives.

Some editions of *Hidden* picture Darra and Wren on the cover, as young adolescents, one dark-haired, one with red hair. As we do not learn that Darra is red-headed until the last part of the story (2011: 103), we only discover quite close to the end that the daughter of privilege and a happy family is Black, and the daughter of poverty and a broken family is White. For some students this could be schema refreshing: disrupting expectations and shattering a stereotype. As Darra and Wren reconcile, they truly model perspective-taking, by observing, listening, trying to understand how each has suffered and how, in fact, each had tried to help the other all those years ago.

As with *The Braid*, though for a younger readership, Frost has lain a treasure hunt of words for readers to find a hidden story; the puzzle is explained at the end of the book. Stringing together the extra story by finding these hidden words is an engaging task for young adolescent readers, but not essential to the meaning of the verse novel. This hidden story is one explanation for the title, *Hidden*, as well as the dramatic opening of the narrative when Wren is hidden inside the boat. In addition, the girls have hidden the past inside their unhappiest memories, and kept it locked away. When they have the opportunity to share their experience at the summer camp, and to see it with the other's eyes and from the perspective of the other's family, the healing process can begin.

The story is compelling for reluctant readers – both the suspenseful incident six years previously and the surprise meeting at the summer camp – but is also thought-provoking. Group hot-seating is an excellent student activating task that works well with *Hidden*. Students who are hot-seated sit at the front of the class in the role of a story character, and answer questions about their feelings. After reading the beginning of the story, for example, six students could be hot-seated in the following roles: eight-year-old Wren and eight-year-old Darra, Wren's parents, who are terrified for they believe their daughter has been kidnapped, Darra's father who is horrified and panicked as his partner was shot and killed during the robbery attempt, and Darra's mother who is abused by Darra's father, alarmed when she hears the media reports that a young girl was in the stolen car, and fears her husband's actions. The students playing characters always answer in role.

It is important that the class has time to first prepare questions in groups. The questioning students could also take on the role of reporters, others could be witnesses and either a student or the teacher could be the police detective. The teacher-in-role convention is an admirable strategy for adding tension and energy to any drama work. Drama educationalist Neelands (2004: 104) writes: 'Teachers often feel extremely reticent, for a variety of reasons, about joining in alongside the pupils but there is no doubt at all that they [the students] respond very positively indeed to their teacher becoming part of the shared act of creating a drama.'

Kwame Alexander's *The Crossover*

The Crossover (2014) is a multiple award–winning book by Kwame Alexander. Dynamic, motivating and emotional, the verse novel moves forward swiftly like a ball in play. There is just no time for reluctant readers to get bored – the poetry embraces urgent themes of family and sportsmanship, friendship, young love, jealousy, learning and fairness, and all the while the twin thirteen-year-old brothers Josh and Jorden Bell play basketball as an art form to the beat of the rhythmic verse. Josh is the persona, and basketball magic powers the story in tune with the serious themes; there is excitement and joy, but also anger and grief when their father, a basketball star in former days, is taken seriously ill.

It is important that this is a portrait of a loving African American family that is successful in education as well as sport. The twins' mother is an assistant school principal, and Josh learns new words throughout the tale, and ponders their meaning:

pul-chri-tu-di-nous

[PALL-KRE-TOO-DEN-NUS] *adjective*

Having great physical
beauty and appeal.

As in: Every guy
in the lunchroom
is trying to flirt
with the new girl
because she's so *pulchritudinous*.
[…]
As in: Wait a minute –
why is the *pulchritudinous* new girl
now talking to my brother?

(2014: 55)

The Crossover is creative in every way – interweaving its themes creatively, with ingenious rhythms, word choices and inventive metaphors, and often using typographic creativity. This may well inspire students to create a page of verse about their own favourite sport, with invented words and similarly playful lettering. While *The Crossover* is funny, it is also a sad story about family and basketball, about grief and growing up. The 'basketball rules' Josh invents always seem to apply both to the sport and to life:

Basketball Rule #10

A loss is inevitable,
like snow in winter.
True champions
learn
to dance
through
the storm.

(2014: 230)

An enjoyable and creative task is to ask the class, divided into groups, to choose and prepare a poem for choral speaking. While choral speaking works well with many of Kwame Alexander's poems, the four poems entitled Josh's Play-by-Play are ideal for this. Each group decides which lines, or parts of lines, are spoken by one or two students, and which are spoken by the whole group in unison. Choral speaking can use orchestrated volume, tempo, and other prosodic features, plenty of sound effects, facial expressions and dynamic body language, but the speakers remain in the same space!

Katherine Applegate's *Home of the Brave*

Applegate's *Home of the Brave* (2007) is an endearing and very accessible refugee story, written in free verse with humour and humanity. The verses deliver wonderfully strange images of Minnesota, told from the puzzled perspective of a ten-year-old Sudanese boy, Kek, who has been rescued from a refugee camp after having escaped horrific violence that robbed him of his family. The power of the story lies in Kek's courage and strength in learning to live in the United States and start life anew amongst so much that he cannot understand, while still in mourning for his father and brother, and not knowing whether his mother has survived.

The foreignness of the new world is often expressed in images from the land Kek has left behind, for example when he is confronted by the paperwork of the Refugee Resettlement Centre:

PAPERWORK
Soon I grow sleepy,
and after a while her words
begin to fall like raindrops on the floor.
I try to understand,
but all I hear is a river of words,
rushing and thundering
and pushing me beneath the surface.
Now and then a word I know
darts up like a sparkling fish,
but then it's all dark
moving water again.

We are there a long time.
I don't think
I like this America paperwork,
I whisper to Dave.
It makes for
too many yawnings.

(Applegate 2007: 54–5)

The focus is on the introspective rhythms of Kek's voice, so that we hear him speaking to himself as we read. This orality creates a similar effect to a soliloquy spoken on stage: we are overhearing Kek's thoughts. Cadden (2011: 24) maintains the verse novel is written for the ear, 'making it a bridge between the orality of poetry and silence of novelistic prose'. Later, when on a field trip to the zoo with his English class, Kek is amazed at 'so many tribes from all over the world' who can share the same spaces without strife:

Of all the things I didn't know
about America,
this is the most amazing:
I didn't know
there would be so many tribes
from all over the world.
How could I have imagined
the way they walk through the world
side by side
without fear,
all free to gaze at the same sky
with the same hopes?
[...]

I walk behind my classmates to the next exhibit,
but I am not alone.
My family is with me,
and every sight is something they cannot see,
and every hope is something they cannot feel.

To carry them, unseen as wind,
is a heavy burden.

(2007: 148–9)

Overwhelmed by Western affluence, Kek begins to weep in the opulent, colour- and light-filled grocery store, 'with its answers to prayers on every shelf' (156). At the library he is abruptly reminded how his mother had

always wanted to learn to read,
to own a book,
to open one of these magical presents
and see what's inside.

(160)

Instances such as these are powerful and pivotal moments in a story. Students can be invited to choose a key experience in the verse novel and create a *pivotal moment* group poster:

- Students select a quotation from the text that captures the pivotal moment.
- They annotate the quotation, in a different colour, noting how this reveals Kek's thoughtful feelings.
- They specify, in another colour, how the pivotal moment could support interculturality in the reader.
- The students may like to add their own illustrations.

Home of the Brave was published before South Sudan gained independence from the Republic of the Sudan, after one of the longest civil wars on record, during which some two million people died as a result of the fighting, famine and disease. Kek is one of the Lost Boys of Sudan, and their suffering is merely hinted at in *Home of the Brave*. In order to introduce a diversity of voices, the verse novel should be supplemented by the voices and perspectives of the victims themselves. For the author of *Home of the Brave*, Katherine Applegate, is a prizewinning US author and not herself a member of the Nuer people, the 3,500,000-strong ethnic group to which Kek belongs.

Voices of the Lost Boys as well as representatives of the tragically vulnerable and largely overlooked Lost Girls are easily accessible online through a number of inspiring TED Talks. Bringing a variety of oral renderings into the classroom in this way creates a text ensemble, which is recommended for intercultural learning in order to offer a nuanced picture with different voices and authentic perspectives. Particularly groups that are othered – the marginalized, refugees and migrants, people from the majority world or non-Western nations – should be able to contribute to their own representation. An ideal text ensemble highlights different perspectives, aiming 'to include many experiences from around the world, so that no one particular perspective predominates' (Bland 2018b: 3).

Pamela Porter's *The Crazy Man*

Porter's *The Crazy Man* (2005) is a multiple award–winning, outstanding historical study of life and social attitudes in a Saskatchewan farming community, in Canada of 1965. The first-person narrator is Emmaline, who turns twelve during the course of the events. The story begins when her leg is mangled by the tractor her father is driving. Waking up in hospital, Emmie learns how her father shot dead her beloved dog Prince, though the dog was not really the cause of the terrible accident. Then he left the farm:

> That day built a room inside my head
> where we all live – Daddy, Prince, Mum and me.
> I want to build a door for that room so I can shut it off,
> and if I think about it real hard, maybe
> I can build that door.
> Because that day's living in my brain now,
> and it's all colored red.
>
> (Porter 2005: 13)

Emmie and her mother are saved by the farming skills and humanity of Angus, a gentle giant they hire from the local institution for the mentally ill. Angus teaches Emmie to see the beauty in the world that seemed lost when her father left. However, Angus – the man from the Mental, as he is called – endures the irrational fears, prejudice and discrimination of neighbouring farming families, which nearly lead to tragedy. The brevity and suggestiveness of the verse in *The Crazy Man* allow time and space for the characters and insights to unfold over the change of seasons from spring to summer to deep winter. The characterization influences the highly emotive nature of this verse novel, especially the compassion of Angus, Emmie's teachers, Miss Tollofsen and Mr Liddle, and her friend, Mei Wang, whose family also suffers from the ethnocentrism of the community. The setting and existential struggles of the farming families shape the atmosphere of the novel:

> Me, I'm filled with the wind, sky, smell
> of ground, harvest dust in my nose,
> my lungs, the land in my skin and hair.
> I'm land, I'm sky.
> I'm Saskatchewan.

(Porter 2005: 173)

There are many opposing opinions in this verse novel, for instance those who view Angus as a 'sub-human', a 'gorilla' and the 'crazy man', and those who view him as a man of many talents and of great empathy. The students could conduct interviews with characters to elicit their opinions, motives and values. They could hold a formal community meeting in which different characters give evidence and express their needs and beliefs. They could also write reports for the local newspaper or create a video newscast, for example about the crime against Angus perpetrated by a bigoted farmer, and Angus's selfless rescue of the farmer's son during a dangerously severe Saskatchewan blizzard. Furthermore, students could consider the hostile ablism depicted in *The Crazy Man* and compare this to the present day. Does mental ablism – discrimination centring on cognitive differences and mental health conditions – exist in their current context?

Karen Hesse's *Aleutian Sparrow*

A powerful historical narrative, *Aleutian Sparrow* (2003) by verse novelist Karen Hesse tells of the evacuation of the Aleut people from their islands and forced relocation far from home in south-east Alaska. This took place in 1942 when the Japanese invaded two islands of the Aleutian Chain, an archipelago of mountainous, volcanic islands which stretches over 1,000 miles across the North Pacific Ocean like a broken bridge from North America to Russia. Although the Japanese were routed out of Alaska by 1943, the Aleuts had to remain in enforced internment and deplorably crowded conditions, without sanitation, medical care, or the means to support themselves, until the end of the Second World War. It is now estimated, according to Hesse (2003: 155), 'that by that time as many as one in every four evacuated Aleuts had died from tuberculosis, whooping cough, measles, mumps, pneumonia, or pain'.

Told through the voice of an adolescent Aleut girl, Vera, the poetry evokes the disruption of the Aleuts' groundedness in place: 'We never thought who we were was so dependent on where we were' (Hesse 2003: 139). In this verse novel, the world of the Aleuts is an ecosphere just as much as a social sphere. The following verses show glimpses of the internment camp and illustrate the unique imagery for nature that Hesse employs:

UNDER A CANOPY OF TREES
Around our crowded camp, everywhere we turn, green life
    rubs its moss skin against us.
The air steams green, and always the sound of dripping,
Always the smell of rot. Always green curtains smothering us.
On the Aleutians there are no trees.

(2003: 54).

WET
Our books ruined because the pages are too wet to turn.
    Everything stinks of mildew.
Our blankets, our hair. Our skin never dries, our clothes
    cling, our feet are damp, we are always coughing.
Perhaps somewhere people sleep in dry beds
And take the sunlight for granted.

(2003: 95)

The students could compare the setting of the internment camp with landscapes they may know, as well as the landscapes and seascapes of the Aleutian Islands. These too are described in numerous poems in the verse novel, such as:

UNALASKA MEMORY
Last year, in Unalaska village, when the fierce wind played the
    grass like a tempest of green violins,
When the waves crashed against the rocks and the spume
    rose like raging sea lions.

(2003: 86)

There are also interesting contemporary and historical images of the islands and the Aleut people on the internet, which can be described and compared to the mental representations created by the poems in *Aleutian Sparrow*. One example is the drawing of an Aleut paddling his *baidarka*, or Aleutian sea kayak, in the Bering Sea, by Louis Choris 1817 (public domain on the web).

The story of *Aleutian Sparrow* is informative and at times heart-breaking. In order to foster critical literacy, the class might discuss the injustices and discrimination that are often obliquely and metaphorically described. The following lines are part of a poem entitled 'THE VALUE OF AN ALEUT' (2003: 41):

> The man from Indian Affairs
> Stitches his net around us:
> Aleuts go nowhere without permission, he says.
> Aleuts go nowhere.

Hesse's free verse tends to follow and enhance the imagined rhythms of the unspoken thoughts of her protagonist. Vera's story tells of the tragedy of loss – of cultural heritage as well as loss of family and friends. Her best friend Pari does not survive the internment:

> Grief turns me invisible as I walk out of the camp, down the path.
> Water stretches between this shore and the wooded mountains
>   across the channel.
> The air is fur thick, damp and green,
> I sit on the sand in the rain,
>   and I scream.
>
>   (2003: 130)

Much of the Aleut's cultural heritage was wrecked while the islanders were detained 2000 miles away from their villages. On their long-awaited return to their islands, they meet with devastation:

> THE SPOILS OF WAR
> We cannot eat the war-poisoned clams and mussels; soldiers
>   murdered our foxes and our sea lions.
> Our very culture stolen or destroyed, not by the enemy, but
>   by our own countrymen.
>
>   (2003: 149)

As in many verse novels with a young persona, there is a tender love story. The verse novel format in the hands of a master like Karen Hesse is ideal for disclosing the inner thoughts and feelings of an insecure adolescent:

> THE TERRIBLE BEAUTY OF NIGHT
> Escaping outside to the cabin steps,
> Dim lights burning up and down the row,
> Alfred and I sit back-to-back and I tremble to be so near him,
>   forgetting for a moment the forest and its thousand
>   unnamed monsters, and Pari.
> 'Don't be afraid,' Alfred says, sounding like an old man. I put
>   my hand over my eyes so the light he makes shine
>   inside me won't leak out.
>
>   (2003: 67)

Asking the students to complete an *iceberg task* (see Figure 9.1) will help to promote deep reading and critical literacy. This works well for verse novels that are sparse and leave much space – also visually on the page – for reflection. In small groups, the students choose a poem or poems on a certain theme (such as the Aleutian Islands setting, internal displacement, the internment camp setting, discrimination, cultural destruction). They then copy the iceberg task template onto a large sheet of paper. On the ice mass above the waterline, students make notes on the text and quote brief passages, in the larger space below the waterline they write down their thoughts on the subtext, on the meanings that are found between the lines. (See also Figure 11.4 for an example of a completed iceberg task related to *The Hunger Games*.)

FIGURE 9.1 *Iceberg task template.*

Another task could be to translate the events of the verse novel into a documentary format, for example as a radio report with interviews, or as a short film. In the documentary, the students might question and discuss that the dangerous overcrowding of the Aleuts' internment and separation of family members is sadly echoed in the present, with migrants and refugees often interned in poorly equipped border detainment facilities.

Thanhha Lai's *Inside Out & Back Again*

Thanhha Lai crafted her multiple award-winning verse novel *Inside Out & Back Again* (2011) in a free-verse diary format. The book tells the story of her family's escape from Vietnam after the Fall of Saigon, and their new start in Alabama. The impressionistic verse is exactly right to express the conflicting emotions – anguish but also fun and humour – of the author as a ten-year-old refugee. Lai herself comments: 'I struggled for fifteen years to tell Hà's story in a voice that would be authentic. I tried long flowing sentences in third person, but that rang false because what distraught ten-year-old would think in long flowy sentences?' (2011: 268).

Inside Out & Back Again is an autobiographical story that is absorbing, shocking, funny and illuminating, with a persona who is a representation of the author as her ten-year-old self. The book chronicles her family's last weeks in Vietnam until the Fall of Saigon, their experience as Vietnamese boat people in 1975, their stay in two refugee camps, followed by their sponsorship to Alabama, where they can start making a new home. This is an inspiring story, and the verse is replete with sensory imagery of Vietnam. Hà's sad memories of the Vietnamese foods and fruits she later deeply misses are particularly evocative.

The family survived the escape from Saigon by managing to get a small space on an over-crowded navy ship:

One Mat Each
By sunset our space
is one straw mat,
enough for us five
to huddle together.

Bodies cram
every centimeter
below deck,
then every centimeter
on deck.

Everyone knows the ship
could sink,

unable to hold
the pile of bodies
that keep crawling on
like raging ants
from a disrupted nest.

April 29
Sunset. (Lai 2011: 63)

Every word counts in the evocation of this traumatic event, with the simile of a disrupted nest of ants creating a more powerful effect than a lengthy wordy description. Vivid spoken word scenery in Shakespearean drama similarly prompted Elizabethan audiences, in the absence of elaborate sets or painted scenery, to recreate the settings in their imagination.

In the following example from *Inside Out & Back Again*, the sparsity of words establishes the new setting in Alabama as so empty of life that it seems surreal to the refugee family from Saigon:

Out the Too-High Window
Green mats of grass
in front of every house.

Vast windows
in front of sealed curtains.

Cement lanes where
no one walks.
Big cars
pass not often.

Not a noise.

Clean, quiet
loneliness.

August 21 (2011: 122)

Despite being generously sponsored in Alabama, the family suffers severe culture shock and the pain of lost cultural identity, loss of status, loss of language and, above all, the loss of their father, who is missing in action. Hà expresses the frustration and humiliation of her descent from star pupil in Saigon, to feeling dumb at school in Alabama:

Feel Dumb
I'm furious,
unable to explain

I already learned
fractions
and how to purify
river water.

So this is
what dumb
feels like.

I hate, hate, hate it.

September 10 (2011: 156–7)

Most Alabama neighbours at first shun Hà, her three older brothers and their mother, until they convert to Christianity. The description of the ceremony of baptism (2011: 169–72) well illustrates, with delightful humour, the sensory disorientation of having an utterly strange cultural identity forced upon you. Notwithstanding their conversion, Hà still faces teasing and bullying every day at school:

Hiding
I'm hiding in class
by staring at my shoes.

I'm hiding during lunch
in the bathroom,
eating hard rolls
saved from dinner.

I'm hiding during outside time
in the same bathroom.

I'm hiding after school.

September 13. (2011: 160)

The absence of wordiness creates images that are all the more striking and disturbing. The empty spaces on the page that are characteristic of verse novels help students to pause, ponder and wonder:

No one would believe me
but at times
I would choose
wartime in Saigon
over
peacetime in Alabama.

October 29. (2011: 195)

Despite the episodes of prejudice, struggle and grief, this is a tale of resilience that finally strikes an uplifting note with the confidence that the family will regain their agency in full and, with the help of some generous neighbours and friends as well as their own energy and courage, learn to thrive again. This energy could be simulated in the classroom by inviting student groups to choose favourite scenes and create a dramatic reading with the script in hand (readers theatre). Changing reading roles frequently will echo the staccato effect of the short lines, and lively vocal expression will help to animate the chosen passage.

Further discussion in the classroom could centre on the reception of refugees in the present, for forty years after the end of the Vietnam War, in 2015, the total number of refugees, asylum seekers and internally displaced persons worldwide had reached the highest level on record, while the figures of the UN Refugee Agency reveal that 'children below 18 years of age constituted about half of the refugee population in 2017' (UNHCR 2018: 3). Disastrously, the refugee situation has, since 2021, deteriorated still further due to the tragic Afghan refugee situation and the catastrophic exodus of refugees from Ukraine.

Jacqueline Woodson's *Brown Girl Dreaming*

Brown Girl Dreaming (2014), an award-winning book by verse novelist Jacqueline Woodson, is a poetic, partly fictionalized memoir of Woodson's childhood in Greenville, South Carolina, and Brooklyn. Her memories, particularly those related to the injustices of the Jim Crow laws, and the civil rights movement in the 1960s and 1970s, are a touchstone for recent African American history. The repercussions of this shared history are demonstrated memorably in Woodson's following poem.

> *ghosts*
> In downtown Greenville,
> they painted over the WHITE ONLY signs,
> except on the bathroom doors,
> they didn't use a lot of paint
> so you can still see the words, right there
> like a ghost standing in front
> still keeping you out.
>
> (2014: 92)

There's a childlike scrapbook feel to *Brown Girl Dreaming*, snippets of musings and memories that tell story after story until they become an eloquent whole, the lens of the schoolgirl revealing how the future writer finds her voice and her vocation amidst a tale of US racial history. The slower reading of the poetry works well for deep reading and intercultural learning, for readers are forced to pay attention to every word. The following example illustrates the speed-bump effect of the verse, guiding readers to slow down their pace:

how to listen

Even the silence
has a story to tell you.
Just listen. Listen.

(2014: 278)

The autobiographic nature of this book calls for a scrapbook response or poster collage of students' own lives, interests, circumstances and cultural identities. Elements the students could include in their collage are photographs, magazine and newspaper cuttings, entrance tickets and postcards, found material, pieces of fabric, stamps, stickers and the like.

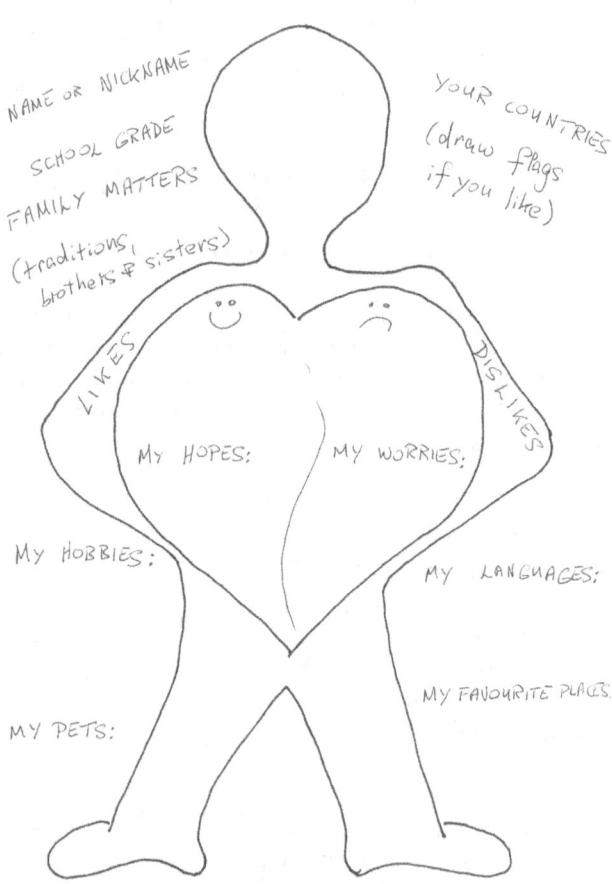

FIGURE 9.2 *Cultural X-ray template.*

The collage becomes even more personal if students incorporate their own drawings and poems, or other written texts.

As a complement to their collage or scrapbook, students could create a cultural X-ray (Short 2009) of their own cultural identity. The students should first discuss sociocultural phenomena that influence our lives, emotions and thought. Then each student creates a simple outline of a body shape with a huge heart. On the outside of the body shape, students write their name or nickname, and facets of their identities that can be seen from the outside, such as their age, school year/grade, family constellation, traditions, places they have lived, sports, hobbies and pets, languages they speak, places and people they love to visit. On the inside of the X-ray, in the huge heart, students write the facets of their identities that cannot be seen from the outside, such as likes and dislikes, their concerns and hopes, ideals and principles (see Figure 9.2). The teacher should also create their own cultural X-ray as an example. Cultural X-rays can also be created with younger grades – children's own identities (see for example Figure 10.4) as well as cultural X-rays of characters in books.

It has been argued in this chapter that verse novels can offer exciting advantages for language education that are currently practically unknown. Well-crafted verse novels are often characterized by orality, for this reason accessible and, with a gripping story, also compelling. The oral characteristics of the language help the reader to almost hear the voice of the speaker, supporting the flow of the reading and understanding. The episodic, mosaic structure of the verse novel, sometimes akin to a journal or diary, leaves gaps that can be filled by students' response. Some verse novels offer alternating voices with alternating points of view, and the excitement of unusual twists and puzzles. Verse novels can stimulate thoughtful feelings, speaking to the affective as well as cognitive dimension of language education, and afford the opportunity for a better insight into different cultural groups, enhancing mutual respect and interculturality. Finally, verse novels are also story, and as such can work as a training ground for creative language learning, empathy and acting with an intercultural disposition.

PART FOUR

In-Depth Learning and Critical Literacy

CHAPTER TEN

Encountering Global Issues in the Storyworld

Many key global issues might be topics in English language education, and some have already been encountered in other chapters, including racism and discrimination (Chapters 6, 8 and 9), migration and refugees (Chapters 5 and 9), literacy for all children (Chapters 4 and 11) and the climate crisis (Chapters 4 and 5). Shorter works of children's and young adult literature will be introduced in this chapter on issues of inclusivity, gender expression, poverty and inequality, ethnocentrism and prejudice, and environmentalism.

Cognitive Literary Criticism Means Involving Emotion as well as Cognition

Cognitive literary criticism means an interest in all aspects of cognition and young people's engagement with literary texts, including emotion, ethics, empathy and knowledge of the world, ideology and social justice issues. As an approach that studies the effects of literature in education, cognitive criticism claims literature as a powerful instrument of human thought that serves to expand cognitive abilities. Deep reading is important for intellectual, emotional, ethical and social development, for fiction offers vicarious ethical experience when, as Nikolajeva (2014: 178) writes, it 'puts its characters in situations where ethical issues are inescapable, and moreover, in fiction these issues can be amplified and become more tangible'. Thus, the process of deep reading frequently involves encouraging the community of readers to contemplate an ethical issue in empathy with a protagonist – rather than the teaching of a moral lesson through the text.

The theory of cognitive literary criticism makes use of recent advances in neuroscience to move decidedly beyond reader response: 'while reader-response theories deal with *how* readers interact or transact with fiction, cognitive criticism also encompasses the question of *why* this interaction/transaction is possible' (Nikolajeva 2014: 8, emphasis in original). Our response to narrative is embodied, involving emotions and cognition, for our brains react to the story as if it were real.

Neuroscientist Antonio Damasio (1999: 41) has demonstrated 'that emotion is integral to the processes of reasoning and decision making', and, moreover, 'well-targeted and well-deployed emotion seems to be a support system without which the edifice of reason cannot operate properly' (1999: 42). Carl Ratner (2000: 23) explains that, as well as the largely culture-dependent socializing or enculturation of emotions that caregivers typically deliver, 'emotions are also modeled in literature, plays, music, poetry, television and movies which children imitate to generate appropriate emotions in themselves'. Ratner refers to neurological evidence in support of his assertion 'that emotions are the feeling side of cognition rather than a singular, separate phenomenon' (2000: 27). An important point that Ratner makes (2000: 24), however, is that 'imagination and creativity are not necessarily emancipating. They only become so if they are cultivated and utilized to critically examine cultural phenomena.' If we choose the right compelling stories, with opportunities for different cultural perspectives and supporting knowledge equity, then we can help students' imagination, creativity and critical literacy to work outside of the constraining ideological, cultural context of a specific classroom and social group.

Inclusivity

Language education and literature teaching are clearly fields of global relevance. As Karen Risager writes (2021: 121), 'a great advantage of language learning is that it may offer new perspectives on the world, both because it is a new language for the learner, and because the language in question has developed in other parts of Europe or the world, characterised by particular geographical conditions, historical experiences and ideas.' English, of course, has developed in many different countries and in very diverse cultural contexts within countries. In order to take advantage of this local and global diversity, it is essential that the curriculum is not rigid or exclusionary, but rather includes consideration of the evolving nature of culture and the potential for change evident both inside and outside the classroom.

Our identities also change and develop. Reflecting on the discipline of cultural studies, Risager (2021: 126) refers to both cultural and social identities, 'cultural identities like social class, gender, sexuality, ethnicity, nationality, language, race, religion, education, age, etc., or [...] social identities like teachers, business people, workers, farmers, celebrities, refugees, engineers, school children, homeless, journalists, etc.' An attitude of acceptance that certain identities are influenced or impacted by culture,

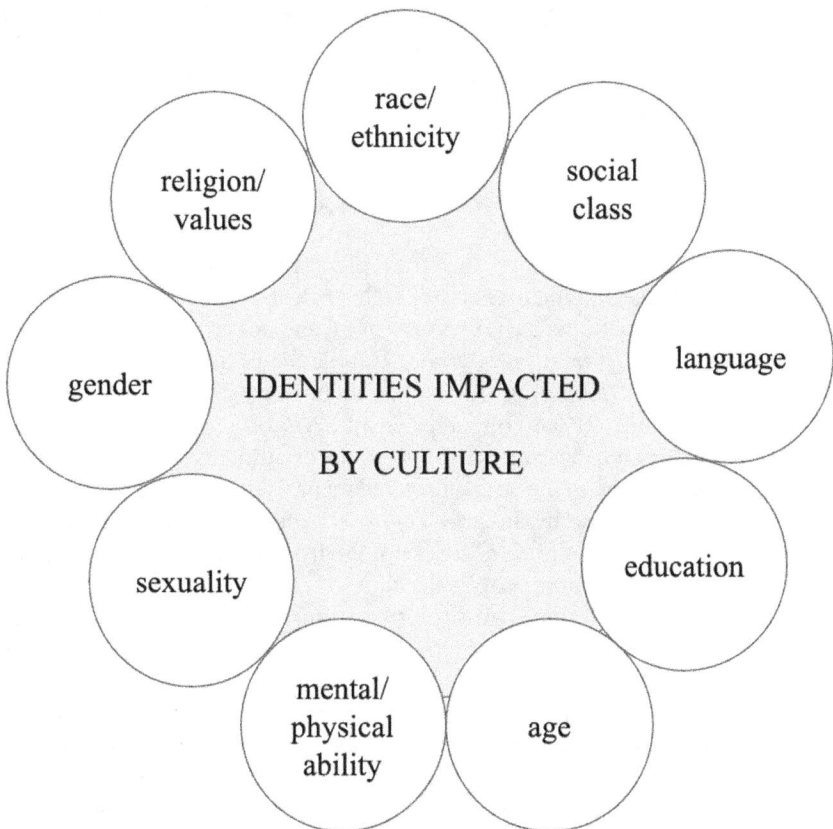

FIGURE 10.1 *Identities impacted by culture.*

as suggested in Figure 10.1, can be an important step in promoting inclusion and tolerance.

In contrast to earlier, more insular children's literature classics, twenty-first-century children's literature offers increased opportunities for purposeful involvement in both local and global diversity. Especially using more recent children's literature, we can expand limited subject knowledge to global education and worldmindedness (see also Chapters 2, 4, 5, 6, 8, 9 and 11).

Using the Deep Reading Framework with David Ouimet's *I Go Quiet*

Many young people experience loneliness and feel misunderstood, and some people experience the challenges of neurodiversity, being neurocognitively atypical. *I Go Quiet* by David Ouimet (2019), is about a child who feels different, feels an outcast and alone. *I Go Quiet* can be a puzzling, but meaningful and reassuring introduction to the topic of mental well-being – in these times very much a global issue – coping with stress and difference and developing resilience.

Unpuzzle and Explore

Ouimet's *I Go Quiet* is neither exactly a picturebook nor a graphic novel, though much of the significance is in the illustrations. The book is small and compact, and the poetic verbal text is very brief, and not difficult linguistically. It has been called an 'an all-ages work, suitable for both younger and older readers' (Gordon 2019: np). Other reviewers have concluded that the book is not really appropriate for younger, elementary-school readers. I found the book was fitting and meaningful for a group of students at the beginning of adolescence who were about to leave elementary school and move on to secondary school. Some in the group worried about being a misfit and an outsider in their approaching new school environment. The importance of this book is to give young people a feeling of sanctuary and comfort that they are not, after all, alone with their concerns. *I Go Quiet* can serve to begin a discussion and help to lighten dark feelings – which is what the book is all about.

After the first read-aloud of *I Go Quiet*, the students in small groups could choose to focus on different double-page spreads, which they explore for hidden details and potential meanings as well as the unspoken feelings on their spread. There are many minutiae to unpuzzle as each illustration seems to tell a story, so the students will need time to prepare. They could decide what they like about their picture and why, what they dislike and what they find puzzling. The groups should then reflect on the text on their chosen double-page spread and be prepared to comment on possible interpetations. Most spreads are accompanied by just one or two sentences, which are also often ambiguous, for example (Ouimet 2019: np), 'I sing silence as loud as I can'. A second read-through of *I Go Quiet* follows, and this time each group leads the discussion of their spread. The booktalk should come naturally, as the learners themselves have identified interesting and puzzling features to explore and question. From time to time the teacher could offer a summary of what seems to have been said to help find coherence and connections between the interpretative understandings.

Students may agree on some of the symbolisms in the pictures, for example a mouse mask for the protagonist who feels so different and small, and – from her subjective perspective – what appear to be cat masks for all the other children, from whom she feels estranged. For the most part, however, the pictures are open to interpretation, and the words leave space for thought, so there will be differing and conflicting answers. This makes sense for a book that is about valuing difference, the power of quiet reflection and the power of imagination through story.

Activate and Investigate

An important topic to investigate and deconstruct with young adolescents is the concept that there is a standard type of 'normal'. Many students will be able to relate to the girl who feels she is different from everybody else, and who is convinced, 'When I walk into a room I hear whispers' (see Figure 10.2). Likewise, many students will have felt alone even in a busy crowd. This already shows that a typical normal is an illusion. The students could try to find words to characterize the protagonist, such as shy, unsure, anxious, introverted. On the other hand, as the girl has no name, she could represent any child at a stage when they experience mental distress, which all adolescents (and adults) experience at times (see Figure 10.3 on the inter-relationship of mental health states).

The students could discuss why the other children seem to conform to a norm to such an extent, with expressionless faces, and many with hair gelled in the exact same style. Have they been intimidated, even indoctrinated by the school that looks like a forbidding factory? Do the darkness, smog and surreal industrial structures suggest pollution? Does the absence of teachers and instead the presence of large black ravens suggest a lack of care by adults? In German, the expression *Rabenmutter* refers to a mother and *Rabeneltern* to parents who do not look after their children. With this book

FIGURE 10.2 *When I walk into a room I hear whispers. From* I Go Quiet *by David Ouimet © 2019. Published by Canongate Books.*

there are more questions than answers. However, tolerance of ambiguity is an important personality trait to encourage and activate for various reasons, including intercultural competence (see Chapter 2), second language acquisition (see Chapter 3) and for a successful literary apprenticeship (see Chapter 4: 77, teachers as fellow speculators).

I Go Quiet celebrates difference and imagination. The girl begins her journey to resilience by imagining an escape on fantastic striped beasts. But then she discovers an amazing and eccentric library, and the solace of books. She climbs up several frighteningly tall ladders past countless shelves of books, climbing up out of her darkness, and taking her reading with her into the daylight. Through stories, she seems to become one with the landscape beyond the school: 'I read that every living thing is a part of me.'

Critically Engage

I Go Quiet is ultimately reassuring, for the world of books helps the protagonist discover an inner strength to be herself and begin to feel comfortable with difference. She now encounters other characters in the landscape, a flock of white birds wearing hoodies, who jostle forward to share in her stories. She is no longer alone in a crowd, and instead finds others want to listen to her. The book ends: 'Yes, sometimes I go quiet. But some day I will make a shimmering noise.' The students could reflect on the symbolism of the hoodie garment. For some, the hoodie represents defiance, mystery and detachment from any kind of uniform. However, hoodie wearers can be stereotyped by others as belonging to an impoverished social class, and likely to be troublemakers.

With this topic, clearly cultivating a safe classroom climate is essential (see Chapter 5: 102–104). The students could discuss who defines what represents normal behaviour? How are those who differ from a norm treated in the classroom and in society? *I Go Quiet* illustrates mental distress and not a mental disorder (see Figure 10.3). Everybody experiences mental distress at different times, and it is important to engage with stress and anxiety in order to learn how to become resilient and strong, developing the capacity to mature into a successful adult.

If *I Go Quiet* is discussed with adolescents who are in their early to mid-teen years, the different states of mental health and use of correct language could be debated. Mental health disorders frequently first begin in adolescence (Kessler et al. 2007). According to the World Health Organization (2020), 'Half of all mental health conditions start by 14 years of age but most cases are undetected and untreated.' It is important to clarify that everybody suffers from mental distress from time to time, and this is quite distinct from a mental illness (see Kutcher 2017 for a valuable clarification). However, the increase in numbers of adolescents that are affected by mental disorders such as depressive symptoms and social anxiety means that the well-being

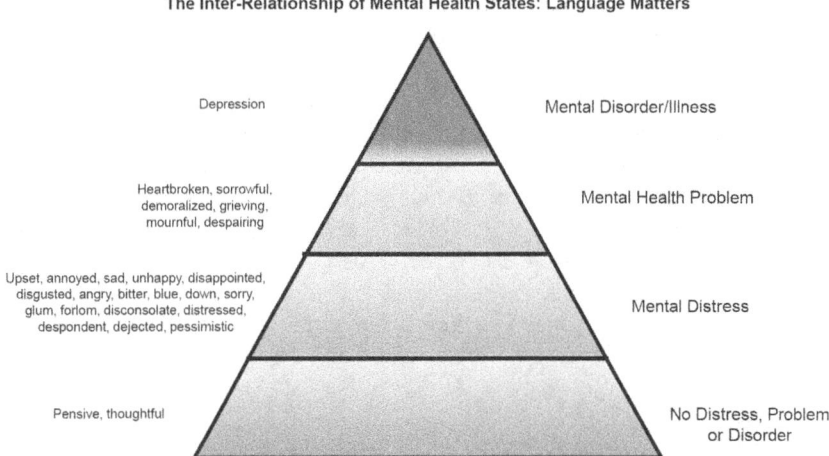

FIGURE 10.3 *Screen grab from* The Inter-Relationship of Mental Health States: Language Matters *[YouTube video blog]* © *Stan Kutcher (2017)*.

and mental health of young people is now a pressing global concern, and an early conversation may help prevent stigmatization.

A number of well-known individuals are now outspoken about mental health disorders, such as actors Daniel Radcliffe (Harry Potter), who has suffered from obsessive-compulsive disorder, and Mara Wilson (Matilda) who has suffered from anxiety and depression. Their courage in talking frankly about these conditions can encourage adolescents to be open to their care persons or teacher about any difficulties they may fear or already face, and help them understand that therapy and other support are very important means for developing coping strategies. A glance at successful adults like Radcliffe and Wilson may help destigmatize the conversation around mental health.

In reviewing *I Go Quiet*, Joe Gordon (2019: np) asserts the importance of compelling stories, for 'reading is not a retreat from the world, it is an engagement with it at the most fundamental level, an attempt to understand and articulate the human experience, and that reading can empower us to face the slings and arrows of the world, arming us with a shield made of book covers and a sword forged from words'.

Experiment with Creative Response

I Go Quiet is a very personal book, and a creative response through artwork is likely to help students who lack confidence in expressing their mindsets through spoken or written language. If all students have access to mobile phones, they could be invited to create a photo journal, *A Day in my Life*. For this activity, students create a series of photo collages with digital photography to tell the story of a single day. They could include shots of people who are important to them, objects, and places that they value, as well as activities that are special to them. The photo journals will not be shared beyond the classroom without permission, and photos can be edited using filters like Pop art and Magic pen to disguise faces, if necessary. Students give titles to each page in their A Day in my Life journal, much like each double-page spread in *I Go Quiet*. The first page of the photo journal could be a personal *cultural X-ray*; see Figure 10.4 for an example (see also Figure 9.2 for a cultural X-ray template).

In the following sections, I suggest a few glimpses into broad areas such as homophobia, xenophobia, social class and environmentalism through

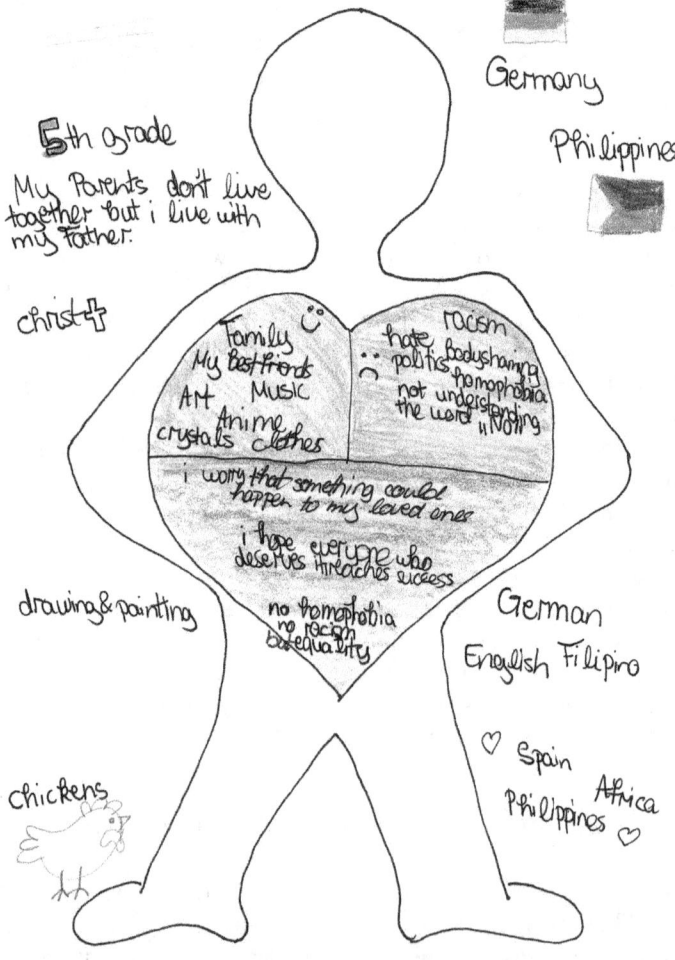

FIGURE 10.4 *Cultural X-ray, fifth grade student.*

literary texts. The texts included are picturebook exemplars for older grades, chapter books, poems, biography, an illustrated fairy tale reimagining and songs that tell important stories. I have chosen texts that might be most useful in elementary or lower secondary school / middle school, depending on context, as many teachers find it difficult to locate compelling literary texts for young adolescents, especially on serious themes and for English language learners.

Gender Expression

Baldacchino and Malenfant's *Morris Micklewhite and the Tangerine Dress*

Morris Micklewhite and the Tangerine Dress (2014) is a cleverly written story by Christine Baldacchino that deals with gender expression, individualism and bullying. The protagonist Morris Micklewhite is a strong and unique character. He lives with his mother Moira and Moo the cat: this is a picturebook with plentiful phonological language patterns such as alliteration, rhythmical repetition and onomatopoeia. Morris loves to wear a tangerine dress from his class 'dress-up center', and he 'takes turns wearing all the different shoes, but his most favorite ones go click, click, click across the floor' (Baldacchino 2014). The stunning artwork, by illustrator Isabelle Malenfant, emphasizes the colour tangerine, which reminds Morris of 'tigers, the sun and his mother's hair.' When his friends make fun of him,

> Morris pretends he can't hear their words
> over the swish, swish, swishes,
> crinkle, crinkle, crinkles,
> and click, click, clicks he makes when he walks.
> Morris pretends he can't hear their words, but he can.
>
> (Baldacchino 2014: np)

Formulaic sequences like 'he takes turns', 'the boys make fun of (Morris)' and 'his shoes go (click, click, click)' are highly useful – the story and illustrations help to make such idiomatic language salient and therefore more easily noticed. At the same time, children may warm to the theme of individuality and, finally, acceptance. After spending some initially sad days at home with his mother, reading, dreaming and then painting a wild and wonderful outer-space picture, Morris's amazing imagination helps him regain his strength and agency. When he returns to school, he decides to build his own spaceship as the other boys will not let him play on theirs (see Figure 10.5). Soon, however, they join in Morris's game of make-believe, for with him they discover that 'the best astronauts were the ones who knew where all the good adventures were hiding. Morris smiled. He already knew that.'

On Tuesday, Eli, Henry and the other boys wouldn't let Morris ride on their spaceship unless he took the dress off.
"Astronauts don't wear dresses."

FIGURE 10.5 *Astronauts don't wear dresses. From* Morris Micklewhite and the Tangerine Dress *by Christine Baldacchino © 2014, illustrated by Isabelle Malenfant © 2014, published by Groundwood Books.*

Picturebooks are frequently even more meaningful for an older age group than the publisher suggests. *Morris Micklewhite and the Tangerine Dress* might be most useful for the English language classroom with approximately nine- to ten-year-olds, when a heteronormative binary understanding of gender expression may be in the process of becoming entrenched. Younger children would probably not even think of bullying a child who loves cross-dressing. While the boys love playing spaceships and astronauts in *Morris Micklewhite and the Tangerine Dress*, it is Morris who is able to show his classmates how important a wild imagination is for this game.

Following a shared reading of the picturebook, the students could draw pictures of an amazing planet, with multicoloured animals and people of all shapes and sizes, and outlandish costumes. The students could help the depicted creatures and people communicate with each other by adding dialogue in speech balloons. *Morris Micklewhite and the Tangerine Dress* is all about the acceptance of difference. While heteronormativity may be an almost invisible ideology, it is not absence of ideology.

Neil Gaiman and Chris Riddell's
The Sleeper and the Spindle

The Sleeper and the Spindle (2014) by Neil Gaiman and illustrated by Chris Riddell is a reimagining of the fairy tale *Sleeping Beauty*, cunningly blended with *Snow White*, although this is only gradually, tantalizingly, revealed. It is a tale of an intrepid woman – a young queen – who succeeds through courage and wisdom (painfully gained through her past experiences with an evil stepmother), where many heroic princes have failed. When a sleeping sickness spreads beyond the walls of a cursed castle in a neighbouring kingdom, the queen immediately sets off with her loyal dwarf companions to investigate the threat.

This is not a lesbian love story, even though it is Snow White herself who kisses the beautiful sleeper awake. It is rather an affirmation that girls and women can and should take the initiative, and princes are anyway not always charming. It is disturbing that the boy-kisses-girl imperative of traditional fairy tales is still so strong that *The Sleeper and the Spindle* garnered much controversy for its same-sex kiss. Naturally, it also harvested much publicity, and the paperback edition of 2019 features the disputed and very strikingly drawn kiss on the cover of the book (which some would call queerbaiting as there is no queer representation in the story; see also Chapter 8 on *Harry Potter and the Cursed Child*). Comparing the hardback and paperback covers presents an opportunity for dialogue on gender expectations, gender fluidity, queerbaiting, gender stereotypes and gender inequality, for considering current concerns this discussion must surely begin in the classroom (see Figure 10.6).

Chris Riddell's pen-and-ink illustrations embellished with dramatic gold are stunning and sumptuous, but also melancholic and menacing. Neil Gaiman's short story is poetically told, and black and gold lettering adds an exquisite touch, however the language is quite challenging, and far more descriptive than Jacob and Wilhelm Grimm's fairy tales and other more traditional versions. For instance, the apparently sleep walking courtiers in the castle of the Sleeping Beauty are described in chilling detail: 'Sleeping people are not fast. They stumble, they stagger; they move like children wading through rivers of treacle, like old people whose feet are weighed down by thick, wet mud. [...] cobweb-shrouded, eyes tight closed or eyes

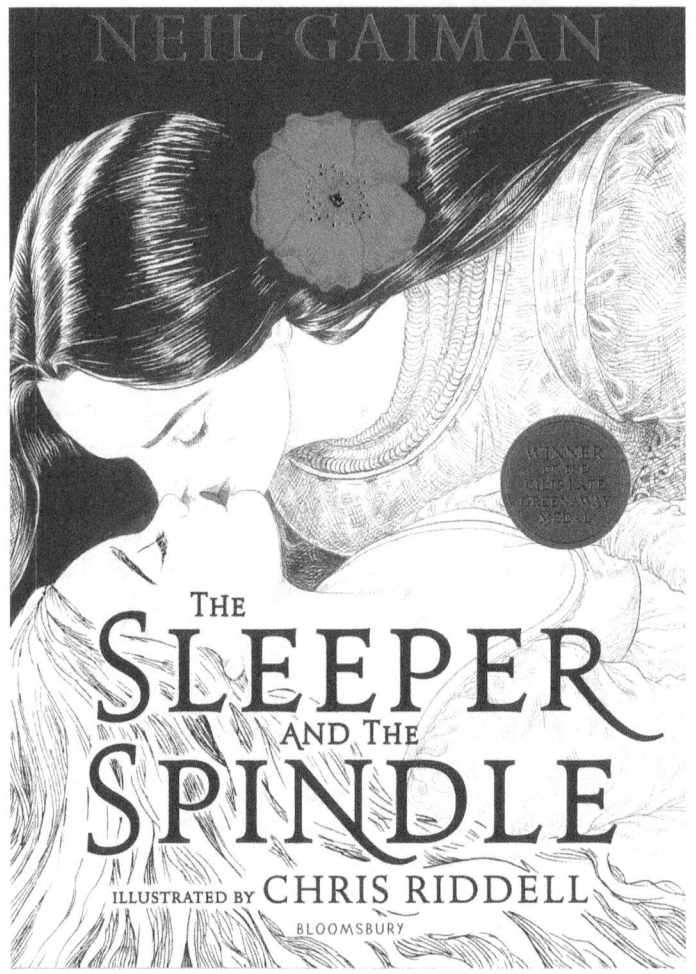

FIGURE 10.6 *Paperback cover of* The Sleeper and the Spindle *(2019) by Neil Gaiman. Illustration by Chris Riddell © 2014, Bloomsbury Publishing Plc.*

open and rolled back in their heads showing only the whites, all of them shuffling sleepily forwards' (Gaiman 2014: 35). Fairy tales have never been meant for younger children alone, they reflect the rich oral tradition of storytelling passed on and shared from generation to generation. *The Sleeper and the Spindle* is most appropriate for adolescents who can deal with the complexities of the language as well as the intertextuality.

If the students read through *The Sleeper and the Spindle* first at home, the in-depth work can take place in the lessons. The illustrations offer many opportunities for group work around the pictures, and this is important for this is a postmodern reimagining of the fairy tale that can be confusing to students who are not used to twists in traditional tales. Reciprocal teaching was introduced in Chapters 5 and 6, and this groupwork might, for example, take place around the double-page spread on pages 54–55 (see Figure 10.7). Groups of four students can divide between them the roles of summarizer, clarifier, predictor and questioner. The summarizer describes what is happening on the spread and suggests a suitable title for the picture. The clarifier describes what has led up to this spread and attempts to clarify any confusions. The predictor studies the picture to interpret the scene and to predict what will happen next. The questioner investigates the meaning of intertextuality and reimagining of fairy tales, for example making note of some recent film reinterpretations of *Sleeping Beauty*, *Snow White* or other fairy tales. Once each student has briefly discussed and understood his role in the group of four, the groups disperse and all the summarizers, clarifiers, predictors and questioners meet, compare notes, potentially revise their findings and then report back to their group, and to the class.

While the story has the bewitching 'Once upon a time' feel, both familiar and strange, the three strong central characters – two good and one bad – are all female, which already makes this a subversive fairy tale. Unorthodoxy is a common trait in postmodern literature, and the story disrupts and transforms older versions. This unsettling is appealing to adolescent students, as they reach the understanding that there are no straightforward

FIGURE 10.7 *She was sitting up in the bed. Pages 54–55 from* The Sleeper and the Spindle *(2014) © Chris Riddell (illustrator) and © Neil Gaiman (author), Bloomsbury Publishing Plc.*

solutions. The prince remains invisible throughout the plot, and once Snow White has overcome both the sleeping sickness and the wicked enchantress, she chooses to abandon her wedding plans (see Figure 10.8):

> She said nothing, but sat on the moss beneath an oak tree and tasted the stillness, heartbeat by heartbeat.
> *There are choices*, she thought, when she had sat long enough. *There are always choices.*
> She made one.
>
> (Gaiman 2014: 66)

FIGURE 10.8 There are choices, *she thought. Page 67 from* The Sleeper and the Spindle *(2014) © Chris Riddell (illustrator) and © Neil Gaiman (author), Bloomsbury Publishing Plc.*

A fairy tale reimagining is motivating in that it both affirms and interrogates students' pre-existing knowledge; they could contrast this version with more traditional retellings of *Snow White* and *Sleeping Beauty*. Philip Pullman's *Grimm Tales* (2012) is a collection of retellings that preserve the swift narration, plot-driven story and conventional flat characterization of the traditional fairy tale – the opposite of contemporary protagonism. Comparing Pullman's Snow White character with Gaiman's is revealing. Pullman's protagonist, like the Grimms' Snow White, is still a child and meekly tries to follow the dwarfs' instructions when they warn her not to let anyone in the house when she is alone. When she fails, she exclaims, 'Oh, dwarfs, I'm so stupid! She didn't look at all like she did before, and I thought it would be all right' (Pullman 2012: 214). Having failed to recognize the evil stepmother a second and third time, she has no say in the matter when the prince falls in love with her and carries her off in her glass coffin. As she is now a beautiful child corpse, from a twenty-first-century perspective this seems rather a worrying peculiarity in a future husband. True to the traditional tale, the wedding ceremony ends the story, so we cannot know whether they lived happily ever after – as a married couple.

The students could also compare Chris Riddell's illustrations with enduring scenes from fairy tales, for example comparing the image of the resolute queen helper in *The Sleeper and the Spindle* with that of the three good-fairy helpers in Walt Disney's (1959) animated *Sleeping Beauty*. The female helper is a traditional feminine role, but this role has developed hugely in postmodern literature from the stereotypical, matronly, inept and rather ridiculous helpers in the Disney classic; a film clip is freely available on YouTube Kids depicting the comical fight over the colour of the princess's dress – https://www.youtubekids.com/watch?v=D1fOLHnTlyA. The young queen in *The Sleeper and the Spindle* is in contrast determined, courageous and strong-minded, but also thoughtful and perceptive.

The author/illustrator team Neil Gaiman and Chris Riddell (both multiple award-winning creators) have dedicated this book to their respective daughters. The story is – due to its fairy tale nature and short story origin – immediate and condensed. The message that girls need resilience and self-confidence, and not meekness and intimidation, could be highlighted through discussion and comparison with traditional versions, as it is handled succinctly in *The Sleeper and the Spindle*. In the past, Gaiman's Snow White had learned a lesson about coercion from her malevolent stepmother: 'Learning how to be strong, to feel her own emotions and not another's, had been hard; but once you learned the trick of it, you did not forget' (Gaiman 2014: 59). This is, then, an almost complete reversal of the many stories that fail the Bechdel test (see Chapter 8: 198). While the three dwarfs may be the only male characters of significance, they certainly talk to each other and take initiative too.

It would be interesting to debate the lack of a prince, and why some male students find this concerning (as I have experienced in teacher education), when the lack of a female lead in narrative is still very much the norm, especially in popular fiction. Perhaps the best-known scene in the Disney classic is when the prince awakens Sleeping Beauty with a kiss (see Figure 10.9). We do not need to decide on the best version (comparing the Disney version of the kiss with Chris Riddell's version), but rather a discussion that there are alternatives, as Neil Gaiman's heroine says, '*There are always choices*'.

Jack Zipes (2007: 31) emphasizes the emancipating quality of fairy tales, and this seems particularly the case with postmodern versions: 'The worlds portrayed by the best of our fairy tales are like magic spells of enchantment that actually free us. Instead of petrifying our minds, they arouse our imagination and compel us to realise how we can fight terror and cunningly insert ourselves into our daily struggles, turning the course of the world's events in our favour.' The students themselves could take the debate on gender equality much further than *The Sleeper and the Spindle* offers, by investigating in groups and presenting concise information on important topics such as the following: the #MeToo movement, male privilege, coercive control, sexual objectification through social media and advertising, body shaming, sexual harassment, sexual abuse, victim blaming, rape culture, hegemonic masculinity and the *Everyone's Invited* website. It was significant that a 2021 cultural X-ray of a fifth grader – just ten years old – included 'body shaming' under her 'dislikes' (see Figure 10.4).

FIGURE 10.9 *Awakening Sleeping Beauty. Screen grab from Walt Disney's Sleeping Beauty (1959).*

Poverty and Inequality

The topics of social class, poverty and inequality have been somewhat neglected by children's literature scholarship as well as in the theory of teaching literature. This is surprising as class division and class conflict affect the life of every child and seem to be on the increase in many societies.

Anthony Browne's *Voices in the Park*

Voices in the Park (Browne 1998), with its heteroglossia of different voices, is a surreal picturebook that nonetheless speaks to the experience of many children in contemporary classrooms. It is full of stories within stories, hidden surprises and intertextuality, and thus highly suitable for booktalk in the English language classroom. Gradually and collectively, on repeated visits to the text, the students can investigate and discover all the visual jokes and metaphors and ponder the symbolic meanings. Due to the many layers, in most contexts where children are learning English as a second language, *Voices in the Park* is likely to be much more suitable for lower secondary school than elementary school. With the aid of scaffolding, the more mature students will be in a good position to discover the nuances of the commentary on social class and inequality.

The storyline is minimal, but repeated four times, using four voices and points of view that belong to a haughty lady gorilla, her tyrannized son Charles, a sadly demoralized unemployed male gorilla, and his vivacious warm-hearted daughter Smudge. The characters have human bodies with gorilla heads, so they are human beings imagined as animals. This zoomorphism encourages a critical distance to the fantasy storyworld. The students will notice social class differences such as the splendid house Charles lives in with his mother, the characters' clothes, language choices, behaviour and body language. The challenge of the picturebook is in the symbolism of the pictures, and the need to interpret them in order to grasp the social comment. According to Sylvia Pantaleo (2008: 61): 'The sophisticated and complex illustrations in Browne's book create an almost hypertextual viewing experience; there is much to choose from to "click on" with one's eyes.' The verbal text is less complex than the illustrations, but is also visually significant for it characterizes the two families as belonging to two different social classes already by their own individual type fonts as well as discourse styles.

The four different voices relate the events of one afternoon as in a journal, nuanced according to character and social class. While the children play together, and the adults keep their distance, there is much ingenious and humorous comment in the illustrations. This creates, according to Sandie Mourão (2015: 211), 'bridges linking the characters and events and forcing the reader to fill gaps and find the pieces to complete the puzzle in an attempt to understand the whole story.'

The characters (the four voices) recount the afternoon in the park each from their own perspective. Additionally, the colours, weather and even different seasons in the park – although they were all there at the same time and witnessed the same events – become metaphors for the characters' attitudes and moods. This unexplained symbolic connection between the season and each narrator's mood creates a challenging indeterminacy that adds to the puzzle that must be disentangled. Charles's arrogant mother is fiery, her hat a fierce red, and the park trees are richly autumnal. For Smudge's father the streets on the way to the park are dark and dreary, the park trees are wintry and leafless. Having been cheered up by his daughter in the park, sparkling fairy lights appear in the trees on their return home. The pavement scene, which young readers find bizarre, shows a street artist dressed as Father Christmas having now discarded his sign 'WIFE AND MILLIONS OF KIDS TO SUPPORT', and instead dancing with characters from his own paintings for sale on the pavement. Charles's park experience is first wintry and cloudy (the clouds, tree tops and even lamp posts are shaped like his domineering mother's hat). However, when he begins to play with merry Smudge, there is a break in the clouds and the trees can be seen covered in spring blossoms. Finally, when Smudge, the fourth voice, narrates the afternoon in the park, the scene is saturated with the brightest and friendliest of summer colours.

There are intertextual references to films and art. In various illustrations we can spot a King Kong, Mary Poppins flying high, Edvard Munch's *The Scream* just visible in the newspaper Smudge's father is reading and Rembrandt and Mona Lisa leaving their paintings to dance together. As Mourão (2015: 212) has written, 'this picturebook provides numerous opportunities for developing aesthetic understanding and the all-important ability to connect with, and recognize, references to other texts.' Thus, *Voices in the Park* can provide excellent lessons in literary literacy through its intertextuality and four very distinct points of view, as well as visual literacy through its use of visual metaphor as an oblique commentary on social class and inequality.

Anthony McGowan's *Lark*

Lark (McGowan 2019) is an award-winning chapter book that will appeal to younger adolescents, including struggling readers. It is the gripping adventure story of two brothers, published by Barrington Stoke, an independent publisher that publishes highly readable and well-written, compelling stories designed for reluctant, often under-confident or dyslexic children and adolescents. Many things about this compact novella make it special, above all that *Lark* won the oldest and most prestigious award for children's literature in the UK in 2020, the CILIP Carnegie Medal.

Although it is the last in a series of books about Nicky and Kenny, it can be read separately from the other books. We learn the most important things we need to know about the brothers through the deft first-person narration, in the voice of Nicky. He is the younger of the two brothers, who is devastated from having just lost his first ever girlfriend. However, Nicky tenderly looks after his older brother Kenny, who has learning difficulties, or special educational needs. The brothers have endured abject poverty after their mother left the family, which becomes clear through the memories Nicky shares with us. Even now, though they are no longer suffering extreme deprivation, the consequences of modern-day poverty form the backdrop to the predicament the boys get themselves into when they are overtaken by a blizzard during a hike on the moors.

Unexpectedly, what was meant to be a gentle ramble swiftly turns into a hazardous battle with life and death. *Lark* is a compelling story, written with humour, with an excellent rendering of brotherly love, and an understanding of the danger but also the solace of nature. This makes *Lark* extremely topical, for the era of Covid-19 has rediscovered the consolation of nature, while the climate crisis exposes mankind's vulnerability concerning extreme weather events. The writing is simple and elegant: 'The stream snaked back and forth as it ran down the side of the hill. There's something about walking along by the side of a stream or river that takes away your sadness and eases your fears. Rivers always go somewhere. Rivers never get lost. Follow it, and you'll be OK' (McGowan 2019: 45–46).

Before reading the story, the class could be asked to list the preparations they would make and equipment they should take on a trek over high ground when snowfall and icy wind are a possibility. Then, after finishing the story – which is dramatic and convincingly real – the students could try to recapitulate all the mistakes the boys make at the outset and during the hike. Some of their difficulties are due to Kenny's special educational needs, others because their father and his new partner must both work a night shift and are not at home to supervise their preparations and provisions. So, the boys set off too late to complete their hike in daylight, they are only wearing trainers and thin jackets, with one woolly hat, one scarf and one pair of gloves between them, insufficient water, no real map, and no clear direction that they must never leave the path in a blizzard. The escalating life-threatening situation is entirely credible and suspenseful, followed by a moving and satisfying ending, when the brothers shine with their care and support for each other.

Armin Greder's *Diamonds*

Diamonds by Armin Greder (2020) is a challenging, almost wordless picturebook. The topic is the dire poverty of African countries that have the rich mineral resources of diamonds, with no benefit to the people. The book also refers to the trade in diamonds for weapons: 'Conflict diamonds, also known as blood diamonds, are diamonds that are used by rebel groups to fuel conflict and civil wars. They have funded brutal conflicts in Africa that have resulted in the death and displacement of millions of people' (Global Witness 2006: 1).

The framing device that begins and ends the story features a brief dialogue between a mother and daughter about the diamond earrings the White European mother dons in preparation for an evening out. The child, Carolina, hopes to dig a hole in their garden to find a diamond, but her mother explains that diamonds are mined far away in Africa. Surprised, Carolina wonders why her nanny Armina, who is from Africa, is not rich. The stylishly dressed mother suddenly tires of answering her daughter's questions, and leaves: 'Armina will put you to bed. Be good' (Greder 2020).

The following pages of *Diamonds* show the practices of artisanal mining that is typical of many African countries, which means severely underpaid mining with inadequate equipment. We see the processes through a wordless sequence of images, and the challenge for adolescents reading the book is to make explicit through booktalk the implicit meanings in the illustrations. These seem to represent Armina's explanation for Carolina, who afterwards has a nightmare. We see men, women and children digging craters and searching laboriously by hand in dirty and dangerous conditions. We observe how they are vulnerable to shootings, murder and theft. We see the exchange of diamonds for arms, the wealthy middlemen and prosperous exporters taking the gems out of the country, jewellery makers, retailers and buyers, and finally we see the gift of earrings Carolina's mother receives. It becomes clear in the illustrations that 'most profit goes to middlemen, traders and exporters who regularly collude to cheat artisanal diggers in a market that is rigged so it is neither free nor fair' (Global Witness 2006: 3).

This picturebook connects to a critical tradition in narrative art that seeks to expose human rights abuses, exploitation, corruption and abuse of power. Stylistically, students could compare Greder's art with that of other committed artists who have depicted oppression, for example France's Honoré Daumier (1808–1879) and Germany's Käthe Kollwitz (1867–1945). This would be an excellent chance for Content and Language Integrated Learning, for example in the art lesson or social studies, and it is wonderful that high-quality contemporary picturebooks such as those of Armin Greder allow this opportunity.

A topic of debate could be whether diamond mining can be justified when it does not contribute to the wealth of local communities and their sustainable development. However, there are exceptions – according to Global Witness (2006: 3), Botswana benefits from their diamond resources, at least more than other diamond-rich African countries. Other considerations are the pollution of the earth, water and air, and the destruction of animal habitats, in common with other mining processes. Finally, in some African war zones conflict diamonds are still widely used to finance weapons and fighting.

Compelling stories like those of Armin Greder are needed that involve students in the experience of oppression and inequality, 'and where learners are emotionally touched or even disturbed and have to deal with controversial issues', as Laurenz Volkmann writes (2011: 30). Another of Greder's picturebooks, *The Island* (2007), is a well-known classic among challenging picturebooks. *The Island* forces the reader to live through the xenophobia of an ethnocentric island community, because we read in the narration, dialogue and pictures not the experience of the refugee, but the fears, prejudice and intolerance of the islanders, who convince themselves that their behaviour is reasonable normality. Despite the challenge of *The Island*, García-González, Véliz and Matus (2020) have been able to show how elementary students respond to the picturebook in a more embodied and dynamic way than in-service teachers. In contrast to the adults, the children in their study demonstrated 'an intensity, a capacity for being affected, of vibrating with the story' (2020: 558).

Ethnocentrism and Prejudice

David Almond's *Klaus Vogel and the Bad Lads*

Klaus Vogel and the Bad Lads (Almond 2014) is a very brief chapter book. The story was originally published in *Free?* (2009), an anthology of short stories compiled by Amnesty International. The publisher of the new edition of Almond's tale is Barrington Stoke, publisher of books for dyslexic and reluctant readers (see also *Lark*, this chapter).

As literary texts are characterized by gaps, which can be confusing for young adolescents, a good way to begin the discussion of any story is with the students' own questions, to find out which gaps interest and perplex them. The teacher can invite the students to consider and write down in pairs a question they would like to discuss. Students usually ask about the meaning of a pattern they've noticed, they may ask about something that puzzles them, or they may simply want clarification about the setting or the historical period of the storyworld. The following questions might be productive to gain a deeper understanding of *Klaus Vogel and the Bad Lads*:

1 The students may be puzzled as to **when** the story takes place.

Perceptive students may have found some of the clues in the text. The Bad Lads, a group of thirteen-year-old English school boys, meet to play football using the names of football stars of the sixties and early seventies of the twentieth century (Best, Pelé, Yashin and Müller). One day Klaus Vogel, a refugee from East Germany, joins their school; East Germany existed from 1949 to 1990. Klaus's father is in a prison camp in Russia and his mother has disappeared. There is also discrimination against Mr Eustace, including acts of vandalism led by an older boy, Joe. Mr Eustace was a conscientious objector (called a 'conchie') during the Second World War – the boys' parents had mostly fought during the war.

2 The students may want to know **where** the story takes place.

In this case the clues are mostly in the language. When Klaus arrived from East Germany, he spoke no English, 'but he was bright and he learned fast. Soon he could speak a few English words, in a weird Geordie-German accent' (Almond 2014: 23). Geordie is the dialect of the northeast of England. The boys laugh when Klaus translates *Ja!* using the Geordie *Aye!* Fifteen-year-old Joe exercises authority over the thirteen-year-old boys partly through his use of language. He calls individual boys *son*, as a Geordie adult would talk to a boy.

3 Another question might refer to Mr Eustace. **Why** does the gang persecute him?

Again, there are indications to be found in the text. First Joe criticizes the hedge surrounding Mr Eustace's front garden:

> 'Would *your* dads let *your* hedge get into a mess like this?' he said.
> 'No,' we answered.
> 'No,' Joe said. 'It's just like he is. Crazy and stupid and wild.'
> 'Like who is?' whispered Frank.
> 'Like him!' Joe said. 'Like Useless Eustace!'
> (2014: 12–13, emphasis in original)

Joe wants the Bad Lads to burn down Mr Eustace's hedge. He transfers the wildness of Mr Eustace's hedge to the cultural category of 'conchie', to stereotype a conscientious objector as freakish and uncivilized. Previously the Bad Lads had not done much harm, mere 'little kids' tricks' (2014: 7). They are described as 'mischief-makers, pests and scamps' (2014: 1), synonyms for children who enjoy a rather naughty joke. Using synonyms in triples, as in the above example, not only adds rhythm and reinforces the message but also helps students widen their vocabulary.

When the thirteen-year-old first-person narrator is reluctant to burn down the hedge, Joe turns on him at once:

> 'He was a coward and a conchie,' Joe said. And like me dad says – once a conchie…'
> 'Don't do it, Joe,' I begged.
> 'You gonna be a conchie too?' he said. '*Are* you?' He looked at all of us. 'Are *any* of you going to be conchies?'
> 'No,' we said.
> (2014: 17, emphasis in original)

The gang is afraid to be stigmatized by the older boy Joe, so they give in and join in the burning of the hedge.

4 What is the significance of introducing a German boy, Klaus Vogel, to join the Bad Lads gang?

Klaus Vogel has been taught by his father the importance of being free – physical freedom, but also freedom within the mental dimension of ideas and values. Klaus has experienced lack of physical freedom: 'The kid had been smuggled out in the boot of a car' (2014: 22). Having won his freedom, he refuses to submit to the peer pressure to join in the bullying of Mr Eustace. Joe tries to dominate him by stereotyping him, calling him Herr Vogel and mimicking his German accent: 'Joe laughed. He mocked the word – "*Nein! Nein! Nein!*" – as he stamped the earth and gave a Nazi salute' (2014: 48). Klaus's moral courage in standing up to Joe, despite expecting and getting a beating, gives the Bad Lads the example they need to break free of the older boy.

Both Klaus Vogel and Mr Eustace belong to an outgroup in *Klaus Vogel and the Bad Lads* and are stereotyped and Othered despite the courage they show. However, as stereotypes are socially and culturally constructed, they can be changed and reworked. The reader of the story bonds with the young narrator, who first admires Joe: 'But he was tall and strong. He smelled of aftershave, he wore a black Ben Sherman shirt, black jeans, black Chelsea boots. We hadn't broken free of him yet' (Almond 2014: 43). As his eyes are opened, so the reader with the narrator comes to see the importance of Klaus Vogel's sense of agency, his empowerment through learning and understanding the importance of freedom, even at a cost.

Zanib Mian's *Planet Omar. Accidental Trouble Magnet*

The huge benefit of this endearing and amusing book by Zanib Mian (2019), with its eye-catching typographic creativity and appealing illustrations by Nasaya Mafaridik, is that it portrays an adorable Muslim family and includes weighty topics smuggled in between all the fun. The clever protagonist Omar (see Figure 10.10) guides the reader through his story in twenty-three very short and playfully illustrated chapters. Omar lives in a suburb of London with his little brother, older sister and parents who are both scientists with a Pakistani background. *Planet Omar. Accidental Trouble Magnet* is easy to read and covers every-day topics of young family life as well as anti-Muslim bigotry and ethnocentrism.

Omar shows how he deals with his troubled feelings by using his imagination. For example, he conjures up 'a SUPER Awesome Magnificent DRAGON' (Mian 2019: 45) to help him start at a new school: 'Only two more sleeps before I had to walk into a brand-new classroom with everyone watching and a teacher who might or might not be an ALIEN ZOMBIE' (2019: 21).

In their neighbourhood the family experiences prejudice, and Omar faces bullying at school, connected to bigotry towards Muslims:

As we queued up to leave the classroom, he stood behind me and breathed down my neck.

'Don't think I don't know the worst thing about you. YOU'RE MUSLIM. I saw your mum the other day, looking like a witch, in black. You better go back to your country before we kick you all out'.

(2019: 89)

A thrilling sequence in the narrative is when Omar and the bully, Daniel, get lost in central London during a school trip. Their frightening adventure and Omar's resilience bring the boys together, and the ending of the book cleverly illustrates overcoming anti-Muslim xenophobia and fostering social cohesion. In between there are many amusing and informative episodes on Islamic values and teachings. Sharing this text in the classroom could be a wonderful opportunity to talk about the different celebrations of Islam, both as expressed in the story, for example Ramadan and Eid al-Fitr, but also asking children to offer their own experiences of these or any other religious festivals they may want to explain to their peers. The children could also create their own ME picture inspired by Omar's drawings of himself (see Figure 10.10), and other members of his family.

George the Poet's 'Hate Crime'

This poem exists as a short film (Hate Crime 2017), less than three minutes long, that was written and is performed by spoken-word artist George Mpanga. The film was commissioned by the Equality and Human Rights Commission (EHRC), as there have recently been increased instances of hate crime in the UK: 'Although the recent focus has been on hate crime towards immigrants and ethnic minorities it is also often directed at disabled people and the LGB&T community' (EHRC 2017).

George Mpanga, better known under his pen name George the Poet, is a young award-winning poet, rapper and podcast host. Born in the UK, with parents from Uganda, his poems usually focus on social and political issues, such as better education and fair wages. In 'Hate Crime', as other of his poems, Mpanga's social commentary highlights the need for grassroots activism, due to inept traditional power structures:

The defining characteristic of a hate crime is not actually hate.
It's prejudice.
We use the word 'hate' to define it,
because the prejudice is born of a hateful climate.
But a climate is a collective mood, it's not an individual selective move.
And in the face of political ineptitude, we only have one option:
Let's improve.

(Hate Crime 2017)

FIGURE 10.10 ME. Page 1 from Planet Omar. Accidental Trouble Magnet *(2019)* by Zanib Mian, illustrated by Nasaya Mafaridik. Reproduced by permission of Hodder Children's Books, an imprint of Hachette Children's Group, Carmelite House, 50 Victoria Embankment, London, EC4Y 0DZ.

It would be interesting to compare 'Hate Crime' with a song that was created by Rodgers and Hammerstein for their 1949 musical *South Pacific*: 'You've Got to Be Carefully Taught'. This significant song caused huge controversy more than seventy years ago, and has since been reinterpreted again and again, most recently by James Taylor (2020). Many of the different versions, including both the original and Taylor's rendering, are available on YouTube. The song explores the enculturation of prejudice that is passed down through generations, which sadly explains the song's continued relevance after nearly a century:

You've got to be taught to be afraid
Of people whose eyes are oddly made
And people whose skin is a different shade
You've got to be carefully taught

You've got to be taught before it's too late
Before you are six or seven or eight
To hate all the people your relatives hate
You've got to be carefully taught
(from 'You've Got to Be Carefully Taught',
lyrics by Oscar Hammerstein II)

George Mpanga has published a collection of poems entitled *Search Party* (George the Poet 2015) and has performed several of these and uploaded them to YouTube. One of my favourites is his moving tribute to Nelson Mandela, 'My Mandela', that he performs while walking to Mandela's bronze statue in Parliament Square, London.

The discipline of Cultural Studies has illustrated how some aspects of culture – for example mainstream art and traditional cultural narratives – can reproduce social power relations, whereas other aspects of culture – for example postcolonial texts and radical young adult literature – can challenge social power relations. As Chris Kearney writes (2003: 156): 'Fictional representations are also part of memory and a resource for analysing collective histories. [...] To be truly inclusive, a curriculum must consider ways to incorporate these alternative histories and viewpoints within the compass of schooled learning.'

Environmentalism

Areas within this urgent global issue are explored in Chapter 4: 86–93, Chapter 5: 108–110 and Chapter 7: 160–1 and 176–7. There, picturebooks are introduced that can immerse students in environmental awareness, or ecocentrism, through compelling and motivating story. Many literary texts can be explored with an ecocritical lens, which I also undertake with Collins's *The Hunger Games* in Chapter 11: 277–8. Ben Lerwill's *Climate Rebels* (2020) is a superb nonfiction book that collects twenty-five brief biographies of environmental activists. Their captivating stories, suitable for young adolescent language learners, are richly illustrated by Masha Ukhova, Stephanie Son, Chellie Carroll, Hannah Peck and Iratxe López de Munáin.

Ben Lerwill's *Climate Rebels*

This compilation of well-illustrated concise biographies of wildlife and climate champions includes well-known campaigners such as Jane Goodall,

David Attenborough, John Muir, the Greenpeace founders, Rachel Carson and Greta Thunberg. Other, lesser-known heroic figures are included, for example The Black Mambas, an all-female anti-poaching unit from South Africa that protects the rhino from the very real threat of extinction caused by poaching (see Figure 10.11).

Many of the featured climate rebels began their activism as children, such as Marinel Ubaldo from the Philippines, who as a youth leader helped to coordinate the first youth climate strike in her nation. Autumn Peltier, from Wikwemikoong First Nation, has been called a 'water warrior' for her mission to guard against water pollution, and was nominated chief water

FIGURE 10.11 *The Black Mambas. Page 71 from* Climate Rebels *(2020) by Ben Lerwill, published by Puffin Books.*

commissioner for the Anishinabek Nation at the young age of fourteen. Ridhima Pandey is an environmental activist who, with her father's help, has made a legal complaint against the Indian government for their inadequate protection of the environment – at the age of nine. Xiuhtezcatl Martinez is well known both as a hip-hop artist and as an environmental activist. From the United States and with Aztec ancestors, he began his public speaking career on environmental concerns at the age of six, and now uses his music to further spread the message of environmental awareness to young people. The Fridays for Future movement is also featured, emphasizing its important role in giving 'a voice to all schoolchildren, wherever they live. That includes you! [...] All around the world, organizations working to combat climate change now have a young army behind them' (Lerwill 2020: 60).

These biographies are written succinctly and clearly to appeal to a young audience, for example lower secondary/middle school. In pairs, students could study one of the twenty-five activists in more depth, then introduce their chosen activist to the class, including more information on the background of their activism, as many countries, cultures and different crises are represented in the collection. The students could role-play interviews with the rebels, several students playing the role of reporters who want to discover more about each activist.

A further sixteen campaigners and rebel groups who also contribute jigsaw pieces in the fight for the planet's survival are very briefly introduced at the end of the book. Working in pairs, students could choose to find out more about one of these activists and present their findings to the class. Students might additionally investigate other activists that work on issues that particularly interest them, such as fashions and smartphones. For example, Angel Chang, who is a womenswear designer and activist on applying indigenous knowledge to achieving sustainable fashions, has authored a must-see six-minute animated film, *The Life Cycle of a T-shirt* (2017). Chang's video explains the colossal carbon footprint of cotton, how clothing production generally accounts for 10 per cent of global carbon emissions and how we could become eco-friendly in our clothing choices.

Fairphone has created a four-minute short film, *The Hidden Impact of the Smartphone* (2021), that highlights the gigantic cost to the environment of this now indispensable device. Smartphones contain valuable materials including copper, silver and gold that are often mined under dangerous conditions, and smartphones frequently make use of conflict minerals. While consumers repeatedly replace and update their smartphones in wealthy countries, the vast resulting loads of e-waste are sent to countries like India and Ghana (see Figure 10.12). Unregulated recycling causes the release of toxic chemicals and heavy metals into soil, air and water and harms workers, who are often children and many times more vulnerable to e-waste exposure than adults.

FIGURE 10.12 *Sacks of mobile phones in Agbogbloshie, Ghana. Image created by Fairphone – Day 6 Warehouse, https://commons.wikimedia.org/w/index.php?curid=69191116.*

The award-winning website ELT Footprint (2019) is a very valuable site that shares projects, initiatives and resources on environmental issues from across the world of English language education. Finally, students can individually calculate their own environmental footprint with the World Wildlife Fund online carbon footprint calculator, which is informative on where and how each of us could improve (https://footprint.wwf.org.uk/#/).

CHAPTER ELEVEN

Speculative Fiction for Deep Reading

Speculative fiction refers to narrative where the storyworld is not restricted to a faithful reflection of the real world, but includes elements of fantasy – such as magic, the unreal, the more than real and technology that does not (yet) exist. Dystopian fiction, fantasy, science fiction and alternate history are included under the umbrella term of speculative fiction, but also horror fiction, which is popular with both girl and boy adolescent readers (Harmgarth 1999: 24). While fables and allegories often feature anthropomorphized animals and other symbolic characters as a way of channelling complex reflections on real-world issues, speculative fiction allows the reader to consider the world in a different light, to use imagination to mentally represent alternative visions, to reflect on the implications and potential results of current problems in the future, and to speculate on how things could be different. This is a central concern of education for creativity, as Wegerif (2013: 62) maintains: 'Widening, deepening and fully inhabiting the space of possibilities that opens up in dialogue is becoming a creative thinker. [...] using the language of "what might be the case" depending on perspective rather than "what is the case".'

Brian Boyd (2009: 49), as an evolutionary literary critic, argues that story sharing and play belong to adaptive human behaviour that tones neural wiring, rehearses cumulative creativity and offers advantages for human survival – stories 'engage our attention so compulsively [...] that over time their concentrated information patterns develop our facility for complex situational thought'. Boyd (2018: 13) also maintains that the successful effects of science depend partly on our adaptive predisposition for narrative, 'the effects of science depend on our sociality, our dispositions for language, for narrative, for fiction, for imagination, and for knowing the whole story'. Stories and narrative are central to humankind, helping us to learn from experience, and to Mark Currie (2011: 6), 'it does not seem at all exaggerated to view humans as narrative animals, as *homo fabulans* – the tellers and interpreters of narrative' (emphasis in original).

Nations as a whole tend to commemorate narratives of the past in a playful and subjective way, sharing and shaping a national story, through ceremonies and special events, monumentalizing glorified moments and historical personalities, for example. However, it is often the case that historic narratives and collective national memories are manipulated through the media, and hegemonic interests of the present may shape our understanding of the past. Literary narrative can provide fresh perspectives and opportunities for critical thinking and creative response, supporting schema refreshment and preparing for the future, often by better understanding the past.

In supporting this mission and other goals of language education, the integration of non-traditional texts does not necessitate sacrificing literary value, and can increase educational value, reinvigorate curricula and engage language learners as readers. For those school students who do not have the maturity, societal knowledge and advanced language competence to read literature aimed at an adult audience – quite naturally the huge majority – it is essential to open the canon of literature that is read in the classroom (see Chapter 3). Well-known, often older canonical literature is too often used in language education and teacher education out of cultural habit, ease, and familiarity, as well as conformity to a well-worn, recognizable model. Referring to the discussion of a canon in the global literary world, Peter Hunt (2014: 10) determines that choices by literary critics have been 'riddled with value judgements and appeals to canonicity, as if it were quite natural'. For the discussions in this chapter on the educational potential of speculative fiction, I have chosen Suzanne Collins's extremely popular and gripping dystopian series, *The Hunger Games*.

I begin, however, with a well-executed graphic novel version of a highly regarded canonical tale. When suitable canonical literature is reimagined into a more accessible format, mixing the old with the new can provide a rewarding experience that scaffolds language learners and is age appropriate for adolescents. Age appropriacy, even in higher school grades, should be considered equally important as language accessibility for enticing students to read. High-quality reimagined versions can also offer new insights for teachers, and this is the case with Odyr's graphic novel version of Orwell's *Animal Farm*.

Orwell and Odyr's *Animal Farm.*
The Graphic Novel

George Orwell's novella was originally published in 1945, and in 1996 won a Retrospective Hugo Award, an award which showcases works of outstanding speculative fiction, in the category Best Novella (for works of fiction of between 17,500 and 40,000 words). Odyr Fernando Bernardi's graphic novel version of *Animal Farm* was first published in Brazil in 2018, a year later in the United States, and likewise in the United Kingdom, where the story is set. In the graphic novel version, Orwell's text is much abbreviated, and the pictures express the action and strong emotions of the story, which are often deliberately understated by Orwell's narrator. Though truncated, Orwell's English is not distorted in the graphic novel version. This is important, as George Orwell's language is clear and direct, for he abhorred the use of language to confuse, deceive and manipulate – which is part of the message of his work. With powerful and dynamic illustrations, the graphic novel version captures the essence of the original and its political content (see Figure 11.1). Most importantly, it is far more accessible and appealing for adolescent readers than the original, as countless favourable reviews on GoodReads testify. Yet, it still provides the motivation of reading a classic, which many adolescent readers find alluring (Alfes et al. 2021).

While some high school or upper secondary school students may be interested in reading Orwell's original alongside the graphic novel, for most school students in L2 education – and especially for dialogic and agentic learning – the graphic novel version of *Animal Farm* will be more suitable than Orwell's original. The danger of expecting students who are too young to read literature aimed at adults is that, though they may well understand the surface level or referential meaning of the text, they are liable to rely on teachers to explain the political satire and allegorical references. When teachers (or model interpretations, which are all too readily available with canonical literature) provide ready-made answers, there are at least three problems:

1 Model interpretations discourage students from making their own investigations, explorations and discoveries, so disrupting an important process in learning to learn, practising information literacy and metacognitive strategies for learning, which are important for gaining learner autonomy and agency.

2 Model interpretations indicate a literary text is an artefact with clear boundaries and absolute meanings. There are reasons for the shifting meanings of texts, including readers' different sociocultural and political contexts, perspectives that have evolved since the text was written and have opened new pathways for exploration, and potentially unintended divisive meanings due to the author's time and place. As Mike Fleming writes (2007: 34), 'if a text has a different meaning to different generations, the idea of a static list of texts claiming universal quality must be open to question. It is also argued that the traditional idea of a canon does not acknowledge the significance of cultural differences sufficiently.'

FIGURE 11.1 *Cover of Orwell and Odyr's* Animal Farm, The Graphic Novel *by George Orwell, illustrated by Odyr (2019), published by Penguin Classics, © 2018 The Estate of Sonia Brownell Orwell and Odyr Fernando Bernardi.*

3. When teachers and students rely on model interpretations, this blocks the principle of multivoicedness, in that many literary critics are, like many authors, White, middleclass and from the West.

While Odyr's graphic novel version of *Animal Farm* can work well as a timely initiation into the dangers of disinformation, propaganda and corrupt political strategies, some finer nuances of the original are lost due to the condensing of the narrative. However, the brevity, succinct cohesion and urgency, as well as elegant introduction to how absolute power corrupts absolutely, remain. Some students may be inspired to listen to one or other of the many audio performances of Orwell's *Animal Farm*, which also works very well as an audiobook. These students could then supply some missing details; for example, the manipulations of Squealer are represented in greater detail and more clearly in the original text. It is always preferable if one or two students can take on the role of filling in extra details, rather than the teacher. In a classroom characterized by dialogic learning, students and the teacher learn together and, as Abednia writes (2015: 85), 'students feel like co-owners of the classroom process since their active involvement in dialog facilitates their contribution to the classroom content.'

Recently, in the *New York Times*, the headline of an article by literary scholar Hillary Chute (2019) proclaims: 'Graphic Novel Versions of Literary Classics Used to Seem Lowbrow. No More'. Chute is persuaded by the power of the illustrations in *Animal Farm, The Graphic Novel*: 'Instead of a reduction of the original, Odyr's imagined barnyard world adds to the depth of the characters: His pigs, horses, sheep and hens have expressive faces and postures, revealing both sweetness and malevolence.' While it may be questionable whether the majority of practised adult readers would concur with Chute on the *addition* of depth, for the majority of adolescents, who cannot yet be expert readers, and particularly for L2 readers, I have no doubt whatsoever that this is the case.

Using the Deep Reading Framework with Orwell and Odyr's *Animal Farm*

Unpuzzle and Explore

In order to explore the conventions of the graphic novel format, students can compare *Animal Farm, The Graphic Novel* with other graphic novels they have read. What are the communicative effects of the visual dimensions of Odyr's artwork? How is the illustration style different and distinctive and how do the choice of scenes, settings and colours effect the telling of the story? Compared to many comics, Odyr's illustration style is unusually painterly and realistic. It is also colourful and emotional. At the beginning of the tale, this style and the earthy colours seem to evoke a traditional pastoral farmyard setting. Students quickly notice that the human characters, in contrast, are relatively colourless, grubby and drab, in shades of brown and grey. The colours become brightest when the pigs, most intelligent of all the animals in Orwell's fable, create the system of thought they call ANIMALISM. Animalism upholds the superiority of animals over humans, and the conclusion that mankind is the enemy. This panel has colourful lines radiating out from a central group of animals, suggesting hope, strength and agency.

A striking feature of *Animal Farm, The Graphic Novel* is that the panels have no borders, they flow loosely and freely and sometimes overlap. This dynamic use of space creates the impression that not only the revolt of the animals but also the subsequent pig-directed events hurtle forward swiftly, with little time for the other animals to pause and reflect. With this fluid layout, the action moves fast, the darker episodes follow almost in a rush and soon the colourful, evocative art builds to a harsh dissonance when the cruelty of Napoleon and Squealer's tyrannical pig oligarchy takes over. This is particularly noticeable in chapter V, when a double-spread panel is devoted to the violent expulsion of Snowball through Napoleon's dogs, trained for aggression, and again in chapter VII, when the blood-red panels depict Napoleon's lethal purges.

While the format of this version of *Animal Farm* is a graphic novel, and the original is a novella, the genre does not, of course, change when the format changes. *Animal Farm* is a speculative fable with allegorical themes that can be understood historically in the context of the mid 1940s – Orwell made use of the animal fable genre to satirize Joseph Stalin's totalitarian Soviet Union – but can also be reinterpreted for twenty-first-century implications, for authoritarianism and manipulation of information do not seem to be decreasing (see Russian President Vladimir Putin's widely condemned invasion of Ukraine). Both the original and the graphic novel of *Animal Farm* are divided into ten chapters without chapter headings. A good reading tactic to help the students comprehend the plot from the outset while reading at home is to ask them to create chapter headings, and then the class decides together on the best choices. This is also an effective way of keeping track of what happens in the story.

Looking at the language, there is always a certain oral quality that attaches to a graphic novel, due to the use of dialogue in speech balloons (see Chapter 6). Usually this makes reading a graphic novel easier for language learners, quite apart from the motivating and scaffolding effect of pictures. In *Animal Farm, The Graphic Novel*, there are fewer speech balloons than usual and more narrated text, in Orwell's language that deliberately avoids convoluted sentence structures. The text flows in between the panels without caption borders, just as the panels are not framed, so creating an interwoven effect. The omniscient, third-person narrator relates the animals' thoughts, in a detached way that suggests inevitability, so that the physical intertwining of narrated text and pictures echoes how the narrator can weave in and out of the animals' heads. The narrator, however, never discloses the pigs' thoughts, but rather the collective perspective of the other animals, who are consistently puzzled by the machinations of the pigs.

The first betrayal of the hard-working animal comrades, as they call each other, is the disappearance of the cows' fresh milk, 'five buckets of frothing, creamy milk at which many of the animals looked with interest' (Orwell and Odyr 2019: 42). The style of the narration intimates that the animals notice happenings without quite understanding the proceedings: 'When they came back in the evening, it was noticed that the milk had disappeared.' It is up to the reader to interpret how the pigs manipulate the downtrodden animals – by confusing them, by taking advantage of their ignorance and illiteracy, and by terrorizing dissenters. The latter goal is achieved when Napoleon takes nine puppies from their mothers, 'saying he would make himself responsible for their education' and 'kept them in such seclusion that the rest of the farm soon forgot their existence' (2019: 56). The animals, and the reader, discover only later that the puppies have become Napoleon's own private army.

Activate and Investigate

While a deep reading of *Animal Farm* does not necessitate researching the *historical* allegorical references, if student groups are interested in doing so and have sufficient access to the internet, this would be a useful exercise in information literacy and how the past can inform the future. Indeed, the interdisciplinary field of Future Studies, a branch of the social sciences, is parallel to the field of history, and researches pattern-based insights into the past, the present and into potential futures. A quick internet check will inform students that with *Animal Farm*, Orwell meant to throw light on events before and then following the Russian Revolution of 1917.

The book opens with Old Major's speech addressed to his fellow pigs and all the animals of Manor Farm, 'to pass on to you such wisdom as I have acquired' (Orwell and Odyr 2019: 14). His message is a revolutionary one: 'No animal in England is free. The life of an animal is misery and slavery: that is the plain truth' (2019: 15). Old Major urges rebellion: 'a dream of the earth as it will be when Man has vanished' (2019: 19); Old Major stands for Karl Marx in this story, and the farm pigs' idealistic development of Animalism points to Marx and Friedrich Engels' *Communist Manifesto* (1848). The promising beginnings depicted in *Animal Farm* degenerate fast once the thinking and planning leader, the pig Snowball, is driven out, an allusion to Leon Trotsky. Snowball soon after becomes the scapegoat for all the following misfortunes. Napoleon takes over as dictator, representing Stalin. Here also Orwell was ahead of his time, as evidence that revealed the full horror of Stalin's show trials and purges (portrayed in *Animal Farm* through Napoleon's deadly purges) did not appear until after Stalin's death, and Stalin outlived Orwell.

Cult of personality

Students could investigate what is meant by the cult of personality. Stalin was an extreme example; he caused an overblown image of himself to be contrived through extravagant praise, rallies, spectacles and ubiquitous posters and portraits. This cult of personality is mirrored in *Animal*

Farm: Napoleon is given the credit for every success the other animals achieve, and the pigs 'invent for him such titles as "Father of All Animals" and "Terror of Mankind" ' (Orwell and Odyr 2019: 126). He is always accompanied by his retinue of vicious dogs and 'a black cockerel who marched in front of him and acted as a kind of trumpeter' (2019: 127), while speeches, songs, processions and Squealer's constant propaganda glorifying Napoleon maintain the deception.

The phenomenon of cult of personality has become even more acute since Orwell's times and may seem eerily reminiscent of current political developments due not only to populist and authoritarian leaders, but also to mainstream parties being drawn into populism involving incessant campaigning and public relations exercises, with the consequent endangering of democracy. Dangers associated with the cult of personality include the use of social media for disinformation, scapegoating outgroups and posturing as one of the people while delivering gross oversimplification of complex matters.

Further opportunist tactics that students can compare are lying, and blaming a past leader (Snowball is blamed), and using simplistic and hypnotic slogans that the crowd chants over and over again (the sheep bleating FOUR LEGS GOOD, TWO LEGS BAD). Populist politicians use these tactics too, for example the three-word slogans that are easily memorized: 'Lock her up!', 'Build that wall', 'Stop the steal' and 'Get Brexit done'. The fact that nearly all political leaders associated with the cult of personality phenomenon are male should not be unexpected, as still fewer than 10 per cent of national leaders are female. Unsurprisingly, female leaders never act as strongmen, but tend to work in partnership with their team, evidencing seriousness, compassion and good listening skills. In this context, students might discuss Allyson Bear and Roselle Agner's suggestion (2021), that the female heads of state in Denmark, Finland, Iceland, New Zealand, Germany and Slovakia managed the Covid-19 response better than male leaders, and were 'shining examples of vital and effective leadership in the pandemic response'.

Related world events, related texts

Animal Farm is a fable, and students may well have some prior knowledge of this genre that could be activated. The US cartoonist and author James Thurber was a contemporary of the UK author George Orwell, and some of Thurber's brief satirical fables have often been discussed in second language classrooms. Thurber's tale *The Rabbits Who Caused All the Trouble* was first published in 1939, so just a few years before *Animal Farm*. This is another allegorical fable with anthropomorphized animals and an urgent comment on the times Orwell and Thurber were living through. This might therefore be introduced as a comparison fable.

Thurber's *The Rabbits Who Caused All the Trouble* is a tale of wolves (representing German Nazis), rabbits (representing persecuted minorities, particularly the Jews) and other animals (representing all the nations of the world who delayed acting against the Nazi persecution). The rabbits were blamed for all misfortunes, as Snowball is on Animal Farm: 'One night several wolves were killed in an earthquake and this was blamed on the rabbits, for it is well known that rabbits pound on the ground with their hind legs and cause earthquakes.' Next the rabbits are blamed for a lightning strike that kills a wolf, because 'it is well known that lettuce-eaters cause lightning'. The rabbits decide to flee to a desert island, but the other animals, who live 'at a great distance', dissuade them from escaping: 'You must stay where you are and be brave. This is no world for escapists. If the wolves attack you, we will come to your aid, in all probability.' The rabbits are then blamed for a terrible flood, 'for it is well known that carrot-nibblers with long ears cause floods. [and] The wolves descended on the rabbits.' Weeks later the other animals question the wolves about the disappearance of the rabbits, learn the wolves have eaten them, and that 'the affair was a purely internal matter'. When an explanation is demanded: ' "They were trying to escape," said the wolves, "and, as you know, this is no world for escapists".' Thurber adds a message: 'Moral: Run, don't walk, to the nearest desert island', and the fable was published 26 August 1939, one week before the Second World War began on 1 September, when Germany invaded Poland and subsequently the UK and France declared war on Germany.

Students may well be surprised how much Thurber and Orwell were able to discover and understand without the help of the internet, mobile phones or even, in many cases, any kind of telephone, just as the Second World War was about to begin, before the genocide of the Holocaust began (*The Rabbits Who Caused All the Trouble*) and just before the Cold War began (*Animal Farm*). Indeed, it was Orwell himself who first used the term 'Cold War' in an essay entitled 'You and the Atom Bomb', published 19 October 1945 in the *Tribune*. He referred to the amassing of might by 'two or three monstrous super-states' that can afford this new bomb, as making the State 'at once unconquerable and in a permanent state of "cold war" with its neighbours' (Orwell 1945), and the consequent lack of any real democratic power for exploited classes and peoples. At the end of the original version of *Animal Farm*, but omitted from the graphic novel, Napoleon (representing Stalin) and neighbouring farmer Pilkington (representing the West) are seen cheating at cards – Orwell foresaw the tensions of the Cold War.

Critically Engage

George Orwell had a deep sense of social justice. His study of tyranny is forceful yet heart-breaking in how easily the animals are manipulated and exploited by the pig oligarchy that follows the animal rebellion. This needs to be closely investigated in the third step of the deep reading framework – how far is this applicable to our current world? The educational goals in the following discussion areas include critical thinking, multiple literacy (particularly information literacy and media literacy), metacognition, empathy, interculturality, learner autonomy, cross-curricular topics and global issues.

Manipulation and distortion of language as primary tool of tyranny

In *Animal Farm*, the central principles of Animalism that aim to build solidarity and avoid the evil ways of the human oppressor are inscribed on the wall of the big barn, and known as the Seven Commandments (Orwell and Odyr 2019: 40; the second commandment is slightly shortened from the original):

1 Whatever goes upon two legs is an enemy.
2 Four legs, or wings, a friend.
3 No animal shall wear clothes.
4 No animal shall sleep in a bed.
5 No animal shall drink alcohol.
6 No animal shall kill any other animal.
7 All animals are equal.

Over time, the pigs break all these commandments. Little by little, Squealer manipulates the language to confuse the animals. When the pigs take to living in the farmhouse and sleeping in beds, he claims: 'The rule was against sheets, a human invention. A bed merely means a place to sleep in. It's also more suited to the dignity of the Leader' (Orwell and Odyr 2019: 97). While lack of transparency, secrecy and manipulation of language comes across in the graphic novel, the deception of the pigs through their superior use of language is clearer in the original. There it is shown that Squealer, secretly and at night, adds extra words to three of the commandments (indicated in bold):

1 No animal shall sleep in a bed **with sheets**.
2 No animal shall drink alcohol **to excess**.
3 No animal shall kill any other animal **without cause**.

Most of the animals do not have even basic, functional literacy. This helps Squealer to manipulate their memories, claiming, 'Snowball was in league with Jones from the very start!' (Orwell and Odyr 2019: 112). The horse Boxer, a highly respected worker on the farm, attempts to resist, 'I do not believe that. Snowball fought bravely at the Battle of the Cowshed' (2019: 113). However, his illiteracy makes him dependent on Squealer's version of what happened: 'It is all written down in the secret documents. […] Our leader, Comrade Napoleon, has stated categorically that Snowball was Jones's agent from the very beginning,' and Boxer acquiesces: 'If Comrade Napoleon says it, it must be right.' Orwell further elaborates the theme of controlling the future by controlling the past, and controlling the past by controlling the present in his dystopian novel, *Nineteen Eighty-Four*.

Manipulation, equivocation and deception through language is as urgent an issue as ever, with numerous twenty-first-century political leaders locked into the hunt for favourable headlines while increasingly suppressing independent news media. Putin's rhetoric, and his determination to disguise the hostilities he has initiated by twisting language, illustrates how language can be used to obscure thought. In April 2020, a Fact Checker analysis in *The Washington Post* demonstrated that 'President Trump made 18,000 false or misleading claims in 1,170 days' (Kessler, Rizzo and Kelly 2020). Early in Trump's presidency, claims of the largest crowd size ever during his inauguration were called 'alternative facts' by a senior adviser, obviously as a way of disguising a falsehood. Using words to undermine meaning and to corrupt concepts, particularly facts and truth, is often referred to as Orwellian, in reference to his term doublethink, introduced in *Nineteen Eighty-Four*: 'Whatever the Party holds to be the truth, *is* truth. It is impossible to see reality except by looking through the eyes of the Party' (Orwell 1949: 200, emphasis in original).

Manipulating thought by manipulating language undermines nuanced and critical thinking, and preventing critical thinking is the desired goal in many regimes, as portrayed in *Animal Farm* and *Nineteen Eighty-Four*. The animals in *Animal Farm* do not understand their slavery as slavery, but rather as freedom due to the propaganda and manipulations of language: 'All that year, the animals worked like slaves. But they were happy in their work. They worked a sixty-hour week, and in August Napoleon announced that there would be work on Sunday afternoons as well. This work was strictly voluntary, but any animal who absented himself from it would have his rations reduced by half' (Orwell and Odyr 2019: 93). It is clear that 'strictly voluntary' is equivocal and deceptive use of language here, confusing the animals into thinking they had a choice.

Ecocentrism

As a political allegory, *Animal Farm* was not initially or primarily about the powerful adverse effect humans have on the natural world. However, Old Major's statement, 'all our problems can be summed up in a single word – Man. Man is the only real enemy we have' (Orwell and Odyr 2019: 16) can, additionally, be debated as an argument against anthropocentricism and speciesism, and for ecocentrism. Exploiting animals and treating them as slaves for the profit of mankind is a theme in the novella *Animal Farm*. It is significant that when Napoleon's dictatorship increasingly enslaves the animals once more, the pigs gradually become interchangeable with humans, in direct opposition to Old Major's warning: 'No animal must ever live in a house, sleep in a bed, wear clothes, drink alcohol, smoke, trade, or kill. All the habits of Man are evil.'

Students can share understandings on the emotional impact of the events of the plot, whereby the pigs increasingly abuse their power just as Manor Farm owner Mr Jones had done. They overwork the other animals, then sell much of the harvest for their own luxury and 'evil habits', while the worker animals slowly starve. The most disturbing abuse is when Napoleon sends Boxer to be slaughtered once he finally loses his strength, despite his gruelling work ethic, 'when the entire work of the farm seemed to rest on his mighty shoulders' (2019: 51). With the final betrayal of Animalism, the pigs learn to walk on two legs, and one species is back at the centre of all things. The sheep are taught to chant 'Four legs good. Two legs *better*. Four legs good! Two legs better!!' (2019: 166), and the Seven Commandments are replaced on the big barn with a single Commandment: 'ALL ANIMALS ARE EQUAL BUT SOME ANIMALS ARE MORE EQUAL THAN OTHERS' (see Figure 11.2).

FIGURE 11.2 *Page 166 from* Animal Farm, The Graphic Novel *by George Orwell, illustrated by Odyr (2019), published by Penguin Classics, © 2018 The Estate of Sonia Brownell Orwell and Odyr Fernando Bernardi.*

Questions that students might critically engage with could include:

1 How and when do all or some of the animals in *Animal Farm* behave like sheeple (a portmanteau word of sheep and people)? Is herd behaviour a problem for mankind generally?
2 Is the line between populism and mainstream politics becoming thinner? What consequences could there be?
3 Successful leadership – what is more significant, the gender of the leader or a country's culture with a more egalitarian society that is prepared to elect a female leader?
4 Does the 'some animals are more equal than others' mentality still thrive generally?

Experiment with Creative Response

The panels in *Animal Farm, The Graphic Novel* – from full-page panels to six panels on a page – are accompanied by the narrator's voice in brief captions and the main characters' dialogue in speech balloons. This is an arrangement that supports the creative response of readers theatre, dramatizing the different scenes after initial preparation in groups. Many of the animals appear collectively, the hens, pigeons and always the sheep, so that speaking in unison works well for the narration that refers to their activities, for the repetitive chants of the sheep and for the frequently repeated ceremonial song 'Beasts of England'. Some members of readers theatre groups could rehearse the sound effects (battles, wind and storm, animal noises, human cries and the blowing up of the windmill), though this must be carefully orchestrated, with one student per group directing, to give context but not drown out the voices of the narrator and animal characters.

The students might discuss a historical comic strip in cartoon style, based on Orwell's novella. In 1950, in the beginning of the Cold War between the Soviet Union and the United States and their allies, the British Foreign Office commissioned a comic strip version of *Animal Farm* (see Figure 11.3). *Animal Farm* was considered a useful propaganda tool in the Cold War, and the anti-communist strip was made available for publication in newspapers in several countries.

Students can be invited to create their own comic strip of a scene from *Animal Farm* that that they found particularly meaningful. They should design at least three panels with speech or thought balloons, captions and perhaps sound effects, to relate a significant moment from the story. This will encourage students to examine different scenes more closely in the book. Students could optionally add visual references and supply dialogue for farm animals that scarcely play a role in Orwell's narrative. If all students choose to illustrate different moments, the comic strips could appear as a continuous narrative around *Animal Farm* when displayed as a frieze in the classroom.

FIGURE 11.3 *Excerpt from* Animal Farm *1950 comic strip. From the National Archives UK, No restrictions, via Wikimedia Commons.*

Suzanne Collins's *The Hunger Games*

In August 2020 young pro-democracy protestors in Thailand chose to use the three-finger salute from *The Hunger Games* as their symbol of resistance against the entrenched inequality in the kingdom. The protest symbol spread to the schools, and 'pupils at more than a dozen Thai high schools raised the three-finger Hunger Games salute' in a show of support for Thai students' call for democracy and monarchy reform in Thailand (Rasheed 2020). The students' and adolescents' use of a symbol of protest from *The Hunger Games* series illustrates the sway that it has over young people, as a narrative of good versus evil, right versus wrong, young versus old. Lisa Miller (2018: np) considers the creation of a vision of youthful power is the pivotal role of young adult fiction: 'It's the main job of a YA author to make heroes and heroines of people who are accustomed to being powerless – kids – but also, increasingly, other kinds of social outcasts as well, creating in fiction a vision of equity and power that counters the reality in which so many kids live.' Through English, adolescents have now become more connected to the wider world and its problems, and the need for teamwork between young people and adults has become evident. Justyna Deszcz-Tryhubczak and Zoe Jaques (2021: xii) appeal for strong intergenerational engagement 'to enhance the relevance of this field [of children's literature scholarship] to current political, societal, and cultural needs and to strengthen its impact outside academia'.

Choosing the right compelling story with a storyworld that encourages discussion of pertinent global issues is likely to be empowering for young adults. In most countries, school language learners cannot manage texts considered to be classics of the adult literature canon until the end of their school career, if at all. There is also a danger in (over-)explaining literature meant for an adult audience to less experienced younger readers. This is counterproductive to the rich cognitive development literature can support when learners empathetically and critically interact with a narrative suited to their developmental level – age as well as language level – '*enter[ing] as a creator into what is seen, heard, or pronounced*' (Bakhtin 1990: 305, italics in original).

Sadly, reading a full-length book has become a challenge for most students, and as books must appeal both to teachers and learners it is imperative to introduce compelling texts in teacher education. Teachers in a recent study considered this factor to be key, 'one of the key ways that teachers in our study tried to manage or negotiate the challenges posed by literature was through choosing texts that they felt would appeal to their students, that is texts they felt students would enjoy, be interested in or motivated by' (Duncan and Paran 2018: 249). The trilogy *The Hunger Games* resonates with adolescents, for feelings of unease, helplessness and fear for the future have fuelled an appetite for dystopias. Sean Connors (2014: 139) highlights how a dystopia creates 'a deeper understanding of the human condition by exaggerating its flaws and imagining the consequences of their being taken to an extreme. In this way, though the genre ostensibly presents stories that are set in the future, young adult dystopian fiction is best understood as inviting readers to wrestle with, and interrogate, contemporary problems and issues.'

The books and films of *The Hunger Games* provide material for deep reading and genuine communication about complex dilemmas, and seem an ideal choice for language learners that are about the age of Katniss, the first-person narrator and focalizing character, who is sixteen when the story begins. Adolescents prefer books that have renown with their peer group, and that they can discuss with their friends (Smith and Wilhelm 2002). Together with Katniss, the reader vicariously experiences the fear, the heartbreak, the humour, the human warmth and love as well as the cruelty. *The Hunger Games* trilogy confronts issues such as celebrity worship and lookism, social media and reality television, compulsive consumerism, alienation from nature and anthropocentrism as well as the theme of social justice. Notwithstanding the wide range of challenging issues, as Brianna Burke (2014: 545) points out, the trilogy is 'a deceptively easy read, sweeping readers along with its suspenseful narrative, implanting its social and environmental message'. The teacher might decide to use the second book as an exemplar, *Catching Fire* (Collins 2009). This may bring about that some students read the first and third books in their own time, *The Hunger Games* (2008) and *Mockingjay* (2010).

Social Injustice and Violation of Human Rights

The Hunger Games series is set in a country called Panem, which suffers through despotic colonization, mass poverty and starvation, disenfranchisement and slavery. Panem is ruled by the elite in the Capitol, 'which is both a consumer-driven thinly-veiled version of the United States, now a dictatorship, and a nightmare vision of our future' (Burke 2014: 545). The three central characters, Katniss, Peeta and Gale, attend school in an outlying area, District 12. The school curriculum for the population of Panem is entirely under the control of the totalitarian dictatorship, and consequently distortions, false claims and misrepresentation hold sway. All narratives in Panem, whether through formal education or the state-controlled media, fit a widely accepted definition of propaganda: '*Propaganda is the deliberate and systematic attempt to shape perceptions, manipulate cognitions, and direct behavior to achieve a response that furthers the desired intent of the propagandist*' (Jowett and O'Donnell 2006: 7, italics in the original). The propaganda through the media, which is unquestioned by most of the privileged yet ignorant Capitol citizens, can be compared to unscrupulous political bluster and disinformation in the real world: in our times, it is ever more apparent that cautious and reflective decision-making 'is hampered by the seductive and one-sided solutions suggested by popular media, populist politicians, or fundamentalist groups' (Delanoy 2018: 148).

The following are all topics for class discussion and project work on contemporary issues in the real world that connect to the themes of exploitation and social injustice in the books of *The Hunger Games*:

- Economic disparity, unfair food distribution, hunger and starvation.
- Disenfranchisement, no free speech, no freedom of movement.
- No medical care or safe work environment.
- Child labour and use of children as soldiers.
- Slavery and sex slavery.
- Refugeeism and post-traumatic stress disorder.

The people of Panem have lost the knowledge of how to forage and hunt for food, as they are forbidden to enter the woods surrounding their fenced-in districts. The result is that they are dependent on the Capitol-controlled food system, which means they barely have enough to survive. Connections to corporate food systems in the real world are clearly also intended here: 'The blunt fact of the matter, both in the book and in real life, is that starvation is a cheap way to control the masses' (Burke 2014: 552). The woodland wilderness surrounding District 12, where Katniss and Gale hunt illegally in order to feed their starving families, serves as an important wild space for temporarily escaping the corrupt power of the Capitol. The themes of social injustice and human rights violations are woven throughout the books of *The Hunger Games*, though sex slavery is not exposed until *Mockingjay* (2010).

The White Saviour Script

There are conventional story tropes in *The Hunger Games*, including the love triangle, and reluctant hero/heroine. Sometimes the film version of a literary text introduces a new element that is not in the book. In order to reveal harmful ideological slants, such as the menace of epistemological racism and ethnocentrism (Gay 2010), it is often productive to compare both print and screen versions of the same story, as another kind of text ensemble. It has been shown that attitude formation on race issues, for example, can be influenced beneficially while students are still in school (Margaryan, Paul and Siedler 2018), and that limiting scripts should be interrogated in the classroom.

The White saviour script is a ubiquitous and damaging story trope, whereby a White character or characters are 'burdened' with a mission to save others, particularly non-White Others. This trope seems to be apparent in *The Hunger Games* films, but not in the books. The film *The Hunger Games* was released in 2012 (director Gary Ross), with the film sequels, *The Hunger Games: Catching Fire* and *Mockingjay – Part 1* and *Part 2*, released from 2013 to 2015 (director Francis Lawrence).

In the books, Katniss is described 'as having olive skin, gray eyes, and black hair, leaving her racialization open to a few possibilities (such as mixed race, Middle Eastern, Latina), but the film portrays Katniss as white' (Dubrofsky and Ryalls 2014: 400). Although there are some important and empathetic characters of colour in the films, such as Rue, Thresh and Cinna, these characters are all destroyed by the Capitol's vindictive Hunger Games before the midpoint of the series. The central heroic figures who inspire rebellion against the Capitol – Katniss, Peeta, Gale, Haymitch, Finnick, Johanna Mason and Plutarch Heavensbee – are all White in the films. This is an issue that clearly demands interrogation in teacher education and the language classroom, as the White saviour narrative is still a very common trope in movies (Hughey 2014).

Whereas *The Hunger Games* books do not reinforce essentialism, for the ethnic background of the characters remains unidentified as not of any special consequence to the story, the films offer a limiting script. The anthropologist Robin Bernstein, coining the phrase 'scriptive things', refers to objects of material culture that reveal how behaviour is often scripted by the stories that surround us – images and objects as well as oral and written narratives. Significantly, she argues that 'a resistant performer understands and exerts agency against the script' (2009: 75). Clare Bradford (2010: 254) states: 'It is a fundamental aspect of whiteness that it operates by being invisible.' This point can be debated in the classroom with the aid of the movie posters. Do they script a conscious or unconscious response? Cumulative limiting scripts are harmful, as they reinforce stereotypes. Do the victors as portrayed in the movie *Catching Fire* accurately represent the contemporary United States, with its mix of European Americans, African Americans, Native Americans, Asian Americans and Latinx? It can be quite schema refreshing for some students to notice, for the first time, the overrepresentation of White characters on a movie poster.

Celebrity Culture and the Cinderella Script

A further example of a popular and very familiar trope is an oppressed girl becoming beautiful and successful through magical transformation: the Cinderella script. To what extent is this patriarchal fairy-tale script revised or endorsed in the films and books of the trilogy? Linda Parsons (2004: 141) observes: 'It is extremely difficult to write completely outside the familiar and recognizable patterns of the discourses that shape how we think, how we view the world, and how we come to know ourselves. Thus, the writer must work simultaneously within and against dominant discourse.' This particular dominant discourse is troubling, for young adults must often make distressing decisions as to how far they allow invasive image-based social media culture, which tends to amplify competitiveness and exhibitionism among adolescents, determine the way they live their lives.

There are clear parallels between Panem and the United States (and other countries) of today, and meanwhile the consumerism critiqued by *The Hunger Games* has adapted the narrative to its own ends, for example with video games and a collection of Barbie Dolls based on the movies (see Bland and Strotmann 2014). Similarly, *The New York Times* published a disturbing article entitled 'Bridal Hunger Games' (Lee 2012), which describes the drastic measures US brides will follow to lose weight fast. In teacher education, therefore, it is important to prepare for critically aware classroom discourse on subjects like, for example, contemporary consumerism and consumer manipulation, reality television and a celebrity culture saturated with increasing self-promotion, even narcissism. An experienced teacher on my teacher development course (Norway 2020) reported on her work hitherto with fifteen-year-olds:

> Working with 10th grade last year, I would say that only a few higher-level students were able to question perspectives on their own. But with guidance and focus on the topic, and if they were motivated enough, I guess a lot more of the class would start questioning and develop critical literacy. But there has been little focus on these matters.

In *The Hunger Games*, sadistic Capitol gamemakers prepare the annual Hunger Games spectacular as a week-long battle, in a specially built, sprawling arena with omnipresent cameras providing for intense media coverage, until only one contestant survives. For the show one boy and one girl are randomly selected from each of the twelve subjugated districts. The twenty-four adolescents are extensively groomed (particularly the female victims) and trained to perform for the pampered Capitol citizens, who may sponsor their favoured tribute by sending gifts of food or medicine into the arena. Vivienne Muller (2012: 54) compares this to our current reality: 'violent video games and reality television shows serve much the same purpose; they are our modern bread and circuses and they are potentially dangerous detractors from what might really matter in terms of humanity's greater goals or the truths that their virtual mode so entertainingly conceals.' A search-and-define classroom task might highlight how new technologies are shaping the way we gain information, read and remember. The teacher invites students to create word definitions, choosing among new buzz words such as: *populism, fear appeal, truth decay, confirmation bias, disinformation, fake news, infodemic, echo chamber, edu-business, information literacy* and *knowledge equity*.

Made both strong and vulnerable by happenings beyond her control, Katniss acquires fearsome survival tactics brought on by bitterly unfair odds. She is forced to kill others who are hunting her, and then dwells on the aftermath until she becomes severely traumatized. Katniss must play several imposed roles to survive: the Cinderella-like princess, groomed and dressed in spectacular outfits and wedding gowns, the lethal warrior, a 'star-crossed lover', and, in the final book, the symbol of the revolution. The impossible weight of her responsibility as female protector in a brutal world results in severe post-traumatic stress disorder, by the end of the trilogy she is deeply scarred, both physically and mentally.

In the films, the characterization of Katniss in her performance of femininity is worryingly conventional: she remains stunning and perfectly unscarred to the end of the tale. It is interesting to compare with students whether Peeta's and Gale's roles change in the same way between the films and the books. This does not seem to be the case. In both books and films, for example, Peeta chooses obliteration through extreme camouflage, while Gale readily embraces the role of the warrior. In order to resist unwanted scripts, it is important to study with students how familiar patterns, such as the Cinderella script, dominate popular narratives.

Katniss is thus a complex character and seen in very contrasting ways by those around her. She tragically realizes that no matter how hard she tries, people will always get hurt, which resonates with the distress of contemporary adolescents as they discover there are no simple answers to complex problems. In order for students to explore the character of Katniss through the perspective of other characters, teachers might set the task to create an entirely subjective characterization of Katniss from the perspective of another, such as Peeta, Gale, Haymitch, President Snow, Madge Undersee, Prim, their mother, the District 8 runaways Bonnie and Twill, Effie Trinket, Cinna, Katniss's prep team, Finnick Odair, Johanna Mason, President Coin (if they know *Mockingjay*) or Prim's cat Buttercup. The students could then compare the different perspectives on Katniss in class.

To help students feel Katniss's experiences and develop thoughtful feelings, students can be invited to explore her relationship to Gale and Peeta by scripting, rehearsing and then performing an intrapersonal role-play: one student performs the Katniss that loves Peeta, while the other student performs the Katniss that loves Gale. A student performing Katniss could sit between them, answering only very briefly to the arguments of the others (see also intrapersonal role-play in Chapter 8). Many, if not most, of the other characters have sufficient complexity to warrant detailed exploration too, for instance by setting an iceberg task (see Figure 9.1 for an iceberg task template). Students choose from the numerous different characters to complete this task. Figure 11.4 shows, for example, a student teacher's

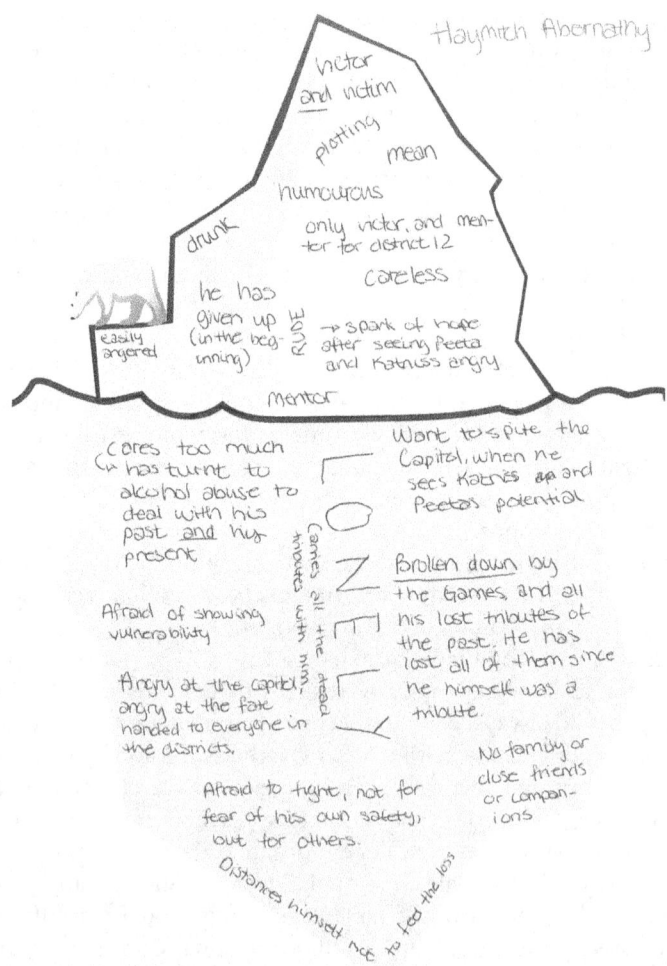

FIGURE 11.4 *Iceberg task – Haymitch Abernathy.*

iceberg task on Haymitch Abernathy (Norway 2021). After discussing what is in the text around a certain character and what is hidden between the lines, students make notes on the textual references on the iceberg above the waterline and add details on the larger subtext beneath the waterline.

Ecocriticism versus Conquer the Wilderness Script

The agenda of ecocriticism includes education towards global citizenship with an emphasis on critical thinking, in a world that is linked environmentally as well as socially, culturally, politically and economically. Ecocriticism is more than raising awareness about environmental issues – it rather takes an ethical stance by questioning the anthropocentric perspective that is the cause of the environmental crisis. Thus, ecocriticism is about broadening perspectives, highlighting anthropocentrism and developing empathy for human and nonhuman nature. Critical environmental humanities and ecocriticism therefore aim for social change, supported through a deeper understanding of literature.

In the first book of *The Hunger Games*, we learn that Panem 'rose up out of the ashes of a place that was once called North America', destroyed by 'the disasters, the droughts, the storms, the fires, the encroaching seas that swallowed up so much of the land' (Collins 2008: 21). The books offer the opportunity for perspective-taking – a move away from an anthropocentric, towards an ecocentric perspective. While exploring the sociopolitical context of the storyworld, there is ample opportunity to consider the harmful ideological constructs in the relationships between culture and nature in the series – as always, a reflection of the contemporary consumer-driven world.

The Capitol citizens are ignorant, self-absorbed and entirely indifferent to the exploitation of the districts: 'Panem is a microcosm of the system whereby developed nations exercise their economic power over poor populations in exchange for food or material goods' (Burke 2014: 562). The thoughts of the hedonistic Capitol seem only to revolve around luxury, food, fashions and grotesque surgical enhancements. This echoes the ever-growing aspiration for reinvention in the twenty-first century that Anthony Elliott (2021: 3) explores: 'In the name of a desire for total reinvention, the body is wrenched from nature.' Elliott discloses the disturbing topic of a makeover culture 'that is increasingly politically urgent in terms of its personal, social and environmental consequences' (2021: 5).

The compassionate and empathetic characters Katniss, Rue, Primrose (Prim) and Gale Hawthorne (who, however, increasingly loses compassion as the series progresses) are all named after plants. In her narration, Katniss personifies nature as a nurturing parent, as the woodlands yield the sustenance for her starving family: 'The woods became our saviour, and each day I went a bit further into its arms' (Collins 2008: 62). Mass industrial food production renders food processes invisible to the consumer; however Katniss, Gale and Peeta, in contrast to the citizens of the Capitol, are knowledgeable about how food resources reach their table and have great respect for the way the environment supports them. Peeta is a baker, seemingly an unusual choice of profession for the partner Katniss will eventually choose. However, Peeta cares, protects and provides fresh bread, the most basic food, exactly the security and support Katniss needs when she has been nearly destroyed.

Katniss learned hunting from her father and herbalism from her mother; she is skilled in trapping and hunting for food, which is how she manages to survive in the arena. She can melt into the wilderness, where she finds shelter, food and herbs that heal. This subverts the androcentric tradition of conquering the wilderness, a very familiar script in American culture as it was fundamental to the pioneer and colonial narratives of 'progress'. Katniss's connection to the wilderness aligns with the ecofeminist perspective, to 'immersion rather than confrontation, "recognition" rather than "challenge" ' (Garrard 2012: 84). The ecofeminist Val Plumwood, writing before the publication of *The Hunger Games* (2006: 123), considered we should distrust any model or tradition that does not integrate the human narrative with narratives of the land, illustrating 'rounded and embodied ways of knowing the land, for example, by walking over it, or by smelling and tasting its life, from the perspective of predator or prey'. This description describes Katniss perfectly.

Narrative versus Antinarrative – Closing Thoughts

The speculative nuances discussed in this chapter can be difficult for readers to discover alone. Shared booktalk will always reveal new perspectives and insights, even for the most experienced reader. As Aidan Chambers expresses it (2011: 107), 'talking about literature is a form of shared contemplation. Booktalk is a way of giving form to the thoughts and emotions stimulated by the book and by the meaning(s) we make together out of the text.' While the imaginative power of story in print media and as screen media are separately important for education in different ways, such as experiencing empathy and perspective-taking, I have found that together the media can be additionally harnessed for sharing critical perspectives and scrutinizing harmful ideological slants and scripts. The promise of education must surely be that critical literacy and a critique of the sociopolitical present can equip adolescents to evaluate their world and realistically help create a more auspicious politics for the future.

Thus, speculative fiction can contribute to engendering different options and to acting with foresight. Cook (2000: 58) suggests that a cognitive function of speculative story 'may be to create greater flexibility and adaptability in unforeseen circumstances. Imaginary worlds allow experimentation with possible eventualities which the mind, locked in its routines, might otherwise not have seen.' Boyd (2009: 124) maintains that story affords creativity and perspective-taking: 'By fostering our inclination to think about possible worlds, art allows us to see the actual world from new vantage points.' Cron (2012: 1) declares 'story is what enabled us to imagine what might happen in the future, and so prepare for it'. As a species 'we're wired to hunt for meaning in everything' (2012: 27), and our storytelling is a way of achieving this; in the past, as in the present, this may have been crucial for our survival, 'to explore our own mind and the minds of others, as a sort of dress rehearsal for the future' (2012: 9).

It is not the case that all narratives are valuable and support interculturality, theory of mind, empathy and perspective-taking, with opportunities for creativity and critical literacy. Napoleon in *Animal Farm* and President Snow in *The Hunger Games* propagate their own cult-of-personality stories – lies that deceive and mislead. Stories that propagandize, but also stories that that lack artistic integrity, genuine character development and carefully crafted story patterns, have been called *antinarratives*. Ellen Rose (2012: 98) argues that literary narrative formats 'demand certain cognitive propensities – attention, focus, discipline, and the willingness to defer gratification – that individuals who spend much of their time traveling the information slipstream tend increasingly not to possess'. The plethora of unreliable material that the internet offers, the ease with which snippets of information can be retrieved and the fabricated antinarratives created by the self-promotion of a celebrity culture and cult-of-personality stories among unscrupulous leaders may together be leading to an antinarrative energy that threatens to overpower literary narrative.

Boyd has developed the theory of 'art as cognitive play': art and literary narrative acting 'like a playground for the mind, a swing or slide or a merry-go-round of visual or aural or social pattern' (2009: 15). It seems to me that English language education must take advantage of such valuable and playful opportunities. Sustaining the reader's engagement with consistent character development is probably the strongest asset of literary narrative. Character-centred engagement in storytelling, or protagonism, leading to thoughtful feelings in the reader, has been a recurring topic in this book. The biographies of Louis Braille, Greta Thunberg, Ken Nedimyer and Frederick Douglass, as well as Malala's, Thanhha Lai's and Jacqueline Woodson's memoirs, tell compelling, moving and illuminating stories. The tale of Kwame and Ebo in *Illegal*, of Abia, Azzi, Kek, the sisters Jeannie and Sarah, and the many other refugee stories in this book are heart-rending. The troubled stories of Rosa and Hennie as apartheid painfully subsides, and Omar who suffers racism, the orphan Hugo, as well as Nicky and Kenny who suffer from poverty, all challenge the reader with new perceptions. Then, the speculative storyworlds of Katniss, Peeta, Gale and Finnick, as well as Albus and Scorpius, contribute intelligently as well as entertainingly to the development of thoughtful feelings. It is essential that education in general, as well as education for English language learners, does not relinquish the educational goals that literary narrative offers.

PART FIVE
Glossary of Key Terms

GLOSSARY OF KEY TERMS

This glossary places emphasis on terms that are used in international dialogues within English subject pedagogy and children's literature scholarship that are relevant for creativity in English teaching, interculturality, critical literacy and global issues. The terms included are from the areas of literary studies, cultural studies, education studies, teaching methodology and applied linguistics. Of course, terms do not have static meaning, and I focus in this glossary on how the included terms are being used in the present book, hopefully as a helpful guide, but not as absolute definitions for all possible contexts.

ableism Ableism refers to discrimination in favour of non-disabled people. Ableism stereotypes disabled people, characterizing them as defined by their disabilities. Labelling people in this way has disadvantageous effects as it limits agency, self-efficacy and options for action. See also *self-efficacy* and *stereotype*.

access Access to compelling texts is the single most important factor in providing efficacious language and literature learning (Krashen and Bland 2014). Access to a wide range of texts from different contexts and perspectives – through the internet, but also physical texts, for example through libraries – is essential for extensive reading, for compelling comprehensible input, inclusivity and avoiding the reading blip. Hence, it is extremely problematic that 'disadvantaged students from OECD countries are increasingly losing the cultural capital of having books in their home-learning environments' (OECD 2021: 140). Teachers also need access in order to be able to carefully select the most suitable age-appropriate texts for a literary apprenticeship and deep reading. See also *authenticity*, *compelling comprehensible input*, *extensive listening*, *extensive reading*, *inclusivity*, *learner autonomy*, *literary apprenticeship*, *out-of-school English*, *reading blip* and *usage-based approach*.

accommodation Accommodation is an aspect of communication that refers to adjusting one's speech to attune to a partner in order to communicate more effectively or to gain acceptance. Adults tend to adjust their speech when speaking to small children, and teachers often adjust their speech – such as speaking more slowly and clearly – to accommodate language learners. See also *child-directed speech*, *creative teacher talk*, *facial expression*, *prosodic features* and *scaffolding*.

aesthetic reading stance The aesthetic reading stance refers to experiencing the text by interacting with it, resulting in a lived-through transaction with the text (Rosenblatt 1982). This stance is contrasted with efferent reading. See also *deep reading* and *efferent reading stance*.

affective dimension of language learning Essential for sustaining motivation, the affective dimension of language learning includes pleasure in the language, in learning activities and in achievement. Students' feelings of well-being in the classroom and recognition by the teacher and peers are highly instrumental for their language learning. See also *affective filter*, *cognitive dimension of language learning*, *engagement with language*, *metacognition*, *motivation*, *physiological dimension of language learning*, *sociocultural dimension of language learning* and *willingness to communicate*.

affective filter The notion of the affective filter, introduced by Stephen Krashen, refers to how anxiety, stress, low self-confidence, boredom and lack of motivation experienced by language students will raise a filter or screen, and so hinder efficient second language acquisition. See also *think-pair-share*, *motivation* and *willingness to communicate*.

affinity spaces These are usually online spaces motivated by a common interest, such as fanfiction. The participants may join the space anonymously and can come from very diverse contexts. The content is fluid and created by interaction as the participants shape and reshape the site – in good affinity spaces, knowledge is shared, and informal learning happens. See also *knowledge equity*, *fanfiction* and *out-of-school English*.

agency Agency refers to the capacity of students, and any individuals, to act with self-determination. Limitations to agency and autonomy are often regulated by gatekeeping institutions, which can be influenced by gender, ethnicity, age, social class, religion and so forth. See also *diversity*, *ideology*, *knowledge equity* and *learner autonomy*.

allegory An allegory is a narrative in which certain characters or events seem to represent real-world issues and happenings, and therefore can be interpreted as a commentary on these issues. Allegorical themes are often a matter of interpretation and need not be understood as having sharply defined meanings. See also *fable*.

alliteration Alliteration is the repetition of initial consonant sounds in close succession. Poetic writers of children's literature use alliteration abundantly, as in this example from *Mouse Bird Snake Wolf* (Almond 2013), 'They stood up straight and they stared across the earth and they stared into their minds and they searched their thoughts and they searched their dreams and they wondered.' See also *anaphora*, *cacophony*, *onomatopoeia*, *polysyndeton*, *repetition*, *rule of three*, *stylistics*.

alterity See under *otherness*.

amplification through simplification This is a term used to explain how a cartoony, apparently simple style of portraying human characters in comics can lend focus and amplified universality to the meaning making (Scott McCloud 1993). The effect is widespread relatability to the character through a stripping down of specific details of appearance, leading to intensity of involvement.

anaphora Anaphora is a rhetorical device that creates rhythm and emphasis by repeating word sequences at the beginning of neighbouring sentences in prose, or the beginning of lines in poetry. Roger McGough uses anaphora to structure his poem, 'What I love about school', in which all stanzas begin with 'What I love about' and 'What I hate about' alternatively. See also *alliteration, cacophony, onomatopoeia, polysyndeton, repetition, rule of three, stylistics*.

androcentrism Androcentrism is the practice, which may or may not be conscious, of telling stories from a male point of view and under-representing women and girls in literature and the arts. Using male generic language leads to male-biased mental imagery and culturally minoritizes women. See also *marginalized* and *point of view*.

anthropocentrism Anthropocentrism, or humanocentrism, refers to how humans interpret the world in terms of human needs and values. It is argued that the human-centred perspective that regards humans as far more valuable than other species is the cause of the ecological crisis. See also *ecocentrism, environmentalism* and *speciesism*.

anthropomorphism Anthropomorphism is a literary device with an uninterrupted tradition from ancient times, referring to the attribution of human traits to non-human entities, particularly animals, often as a way to examine and interpret humanity and life experience from the human perspective. Anthropomorphic motifs are common in fairy tales, fables and throughout children's literature, particularly in picturebooks and animated films. See also *fable* and *protagonism*.

antinarrative A term that is increasingly used to refer to stories that lack integrity, character development and carefully crafted story patterns. Internet media (both mass communication and the interpersonal communication of social media) and print media are full of stories around individuals and celebrities, for example. Such antinarrative stories lack the veracity of carefully researched biography and carefully constructed plot, so are not narratives in the literary sense. See also *confirmation bias, echo chamber, information literacy* and *misinformation*.

artefact emotions Artefact emotions are an aesthetic response to a striking artistic creation, such as a literary text (Hogan 2014). Artefact emotion seems to be inspired by a combination of meticulous craft and cohesion with an inventive, deviating or unexpected schema-refreshing element. See also *literary apprenticeship, outcome emotions* and *schema refreshing*.

aural communication Aural communication refers to the transmission of audible information through the sense of hearing. While verbal communication can mean spoken or written and oral communication refers to the mouth and speaking, aural communication refers to the ear and hearing. See also *oracy* and *orality*.

authenticity Authenticity can refer to the nature of authentic texts and materials that feature authentic language use, which coursebooks usually do not, or do so only in excerpts. The vast world of cultural artefacts, although produced for a purpose other than teaching, may contribute to authentic second language acquisition. Authenticity can also refer to genuine, meaningful interactions in the classroom, around topics that are age-appropriate and matter to the school students. Equally, the tasks the teacher chooses to employ in the classroom can seem authentic to students' lives or may lack authenticity. See also *access, formulaic sequences, lexical chain, #ownvoices* and *task-based learning*.

back and forth With the back-and-forth technique student pairs act as teacher and learner in alternation. The 'teacher' first explains a concept or an idea to a partner. The partner listens to the explanation and takes notes. They then together check each other's interpretation. See also *teaching methodology* and *think-pair-share*.

BANA countries BANA refers to Britain, Australasia and North America. The term is often used as an adjective, such as BANA publishers of ELT coursebooks. BANA countries are those where there is much instrumental, commodified English language teaching in private language schools and in higher education for students from overseas (Holliday 1994). This is in contrast to English language teaching in state education globally, which tends to include wider educational and intercultural learning goals. See also *critical pedagogy, English subject pedagogy* and *native-speakerism*.

Bechdel test The Bechdel test, or Bechdel–Wallace test, calls attention to gender inequality in books and films. The test, first introduced by graphic artist and novelist Alison Bechdel, examines whether a film (or other narrative) has at least two female characters, whose names we get to know, and who talk to each other about something other than a man. The Bechdel test has drawn attention to the lack of breadth and depth of female characters in popular movies, and more recently also to gender one-sidedness in serious films and fiction. See also *gender* and *media literacy*.

biography Biography is the narrative presentation of the life story of a real person. Although a form of historical writing, in that the life story is normally told retrospectively, the presentation of the historical material may make use of different literary strategies to recreate the story. Biography is a nonfiction genre, focusing on factuality over fictionality, however the exact balance between factuality and fictionality will depend on how the text integrates the facts it relates. See also *genre* and *nonfiction*.

booktalk Booktalk centres around literature and refers to the exchange of feelings and thoughts stimulated by a text, and the consequent meaning making in a community as a form of shared contemplation (Chambers 2011). See also *literary apprenticeship*.

cacophony This term describes linguistic choices to evoke a discordant, confused or destructive situation by using jarring and grating words characterized by explosive sounds. This is shown in the following example from *The Iron Man* (Hughes 1968): 'All the separate pieces tumbled, scattered, crashing, bumping, clanging, down on to the rocky beach far below'. See also *alliteration, anaphora, onomatopoeia, polysyndeton, repetition, rhetorical device, rule of three, stylistics*.

canonical literature This refers to texts that have been culturally marked as classics of the literary canon. What is canonical is tentative and constantly subject to revision so that there is no absolute and fixed canon. Some scholars claim the selection of canonical literature is solely a matter of aesthetic values. However, this raises questions about who should have the power to determine these values – whether this is the preserve of privileged groups. Other scholars criticize canonical choices as prescriptivism and elitism: too aligned with dominant cultures and 'dead White men' and therefore discrimination. Yet some classics of literature aimed at adults are undisputed by literature scholars and known globally. Conversely, many traditionalist literature scholars are seriously ill-informed regarding canonical as well as noncanonical texts of children's literature. See also *knowledge equity*, *#ownvoices* and *We Need Diverse Books*.

caption A caption is a box within the panels of a graphic novel or comics containing some sentences. These usually represent the voice of a narrator. See also *gutter*, *panel*, *sound effects* and *speech balloon*.

chapter book The chapter book (or middle-grade fiction) is a format for children who can read independently, but still need short chapters, usually with some illustrations. The protagonists are often in the ten- to twelve-year-old age range. See also *typographic creativity*.

child-directed speech Child-directed speech (also caretaker speech, motherese or parentese) refers to the way caregivers speak to small children, often with an expressive sing-song voice, clear articulation, child-friendly word choices and repetition as well as supportive body language. See also *accommodation*, *creative teacher talk*, *prosodic features*, *recasting*, *scaffolding* and *zone of proximal development*.

children's literature Children's literature is an umbrella term that is usually considered by children's literature scholars to embrace many formats for young people, such as picturebooks, young adult fiction, oral literature, children's films, digital narratives, poetry and plays. Literature aimed at adolescents is included in the term because adolescents are legally still children until they reach the age of majority, which is 18 in many countries. See also *chapter book*, *graphic novel*, *picturebook*, *verse novel*, *young adult fiction*.

choral speaking Choral speaking is when an ensemble of speakers performs poetry or prose as a team, often speaking together with one voice, also using individual and other voice combinations. It differs from readers theatre in that the students learn their roles by heart in order to carefully arrange the performance. Choral speaking can use sound effects, body language, facial expressions and orchestrated prosodic features, but the speakers remain in the same space. See also *facial expression*, *prosodic features*, *sound effects* and *readers theatre*.

cinematic point of view Cinematic point of view, or point-of-view shot, is a device of multimodal texts like film, picturebooks and graphic novels. It refers to when we see what a character, usually the protagonist, is looking at, often seeing the back of their head in the panel or, in a film, following a shot of the character looking at something or someone. We then view the scene literally as if with the protagonist's eyes. See also

perspective-taking and *point of view*.
CLIL See *Content and Language Integrated Learning*.
cognitive dimension of language learning The cognitive dimension of language learning includes strategies such as repeating, translating, consolidating understanding by creating associations around language and mental images of language, guessing, and inferring as well as transferring new language to other contexts. See also *affective dimension of language learning, engagement with language, metacognition, physiological dimension of language learning* and *sociocultural dimension of language learning*.
cognitive styles Cognitive styles, or learning styles, refer to individual personality preferences in processing information. We have different ways of thinking, remembering and solving problems, which influence our attitudes, interactions and learning generally. The students who have different cognitive styles from their teacher are likely to be disadvantaged in language education, unless the teacher respects the different dimensions of language learning, differentiation in the classroom, different kinds of motivation and so forth. See also *affective dimension of language learning, cognitive dimension of language learning, deep attention, differentiation, holistic learning, hyper attention, metacognition, motivation, physiological dimension of language learning* and *sociocultural dimension of language learning*.
compelling comprehensible input The compelling comprehensible input hypothesis (Krashen and Bland 2014) is a further development of Krashen's work on comprehensible input (e.g. Krashen 2004). Optimal input should be so stimulating that students who are learning English are hardly aware that it is in a different language. It is argued that to a substantial extent language can be incidentally acquired through compelling reading or listening. See also *extensive listening, extensive reading, i + 1* and *literary apprenticeship*.
computer-mediated communication Computer-mediated communication (CMC) refers to exchanges using electronic devices, including emails, chatting, online forums, social media using network services and texting on mobile phones. Synchronous CMC refers to real-time, simultaneous communication. Asynchronous CMC refers to delayed communication without immediate response, such as emails. See also *holistic learning* and *physiological dimension of language learning*.
confirmation bias Confirmation bias refers to our inclination to search for information, interpret information, prioritize, and recall information in a way that affirms our already held beliefs. See also *antinarrative* and *echo chamber*.
Content and Language Integrated Learning (CLIL) This approach involves learning a subject such as art, history, geography or biology through the medium of a second language. CLIL usually takes place in the subject lesson, the focus is on the content via the new language, and assessment normally prioritizes the subject over language. See also *content-based language teaching* and *task-based learning*.

content-based language teaching Content-based language teaching refers to teaching that takes the subject matter of language education seriously as content, and not just as an illustration of new language exemplars. The justification for content-based language teaching includes the expectation that learners are more motivated through stimulating content, that language is more deeply contextualized through content, and that students' interests can be better involved. See also *Content and Language Integrated Learning* and *task-based learning*.

continuous partial attention Continuous partial attention (Rose 2010, Wolf 2018) is a form of (un)attentiveness that is contingent upon the internet and social media. Distracting activities, such as web surfing, social networking, and the need to connect and be connected, reduce deep attention and sustained concentration, for example in school and university students. See also *deep attention*, *digital natives*, *hyper attention* and *literary apprenticeship*.

coursebook A coursebook is a textbook for a specific subject like ELT and is usually published as a series of books to cover several levels and school grades. An ELT coursebook is designed to support teachers with preplanned lessons for the entire year, with many supplements that may be bought in addition to the student book; however, purchasing a complete set of supplements is invariably extremely expensive. The supplements may include a teacher's book, workbooks without an answer key for the individual students to write in, a workbook with a key for the teacher, audio CDs, DVDs, practice tests for the students at each level and a set for the teacher with an answer key. See also *textbook*.

creative teacher talk This is used in oral storytelling and picturebook read-alouds, particularly with elementary students for affective, aesthetic and cognitive engagement. Creative teacher talk (Bland 2015c) resembles repetitive child-directed speech. The teacher employs expressive prosodic features including a slower tempo, varying the volume, exuberant intonation and emphasizing rhythm. The teacher can highlight new language and new ideas using stress, dramatic pauses, gasps, and body language. Eye contact is important for rapport in creative teacher talk and sometimes exaggerated gesture and facial expressions. See also *accommodation*, *child-directed speech*, *facial expression*, *prosodic features* and *scaffolding*.

critical literacy Critical literacy is a process whereby students learn to analyse and evaluate texts with a critical stance. Critical literacy scrutinizes a text from different perspectives, both with and against the text (Janks 2019). The critical reader examines the text for the privileging of dominant voices and the consequent devaluation of outgroup sociocultural identities. Critical literacy encourages the reader to discover the ideology presented or hidden in a text and sensitizes the reader to issues of equity and social justice connected to texts. See also *deep reading*, *iceberg task*, *ideology*, *knowledge equity*, *outgroup*, *read against the text* and *sociocultural identities*.

critical pedagogy Critical pedagogy (Paulo Freire 2014, 30th edn) refers to an approach that explores the relationship between education and social change by challenging inequalities. In language education, these may be based on ethnicity, social class, gender, sexual orientation, religion, language and cultural identities, anthropocentrism and so forth. Reading against the text is an important strategy for uncovering implicit ideologies in coursebooks and children's literature. Critical pedagogy calls for agentic learning and activism, and rejects the cultural imperialism implied by certain traditional notions in language education, which might include English as a Foreign Language, native-speakerism, as well as English and American Literature Studies that ignore postcolonial and global literatures written in English. See also *agency*, *BANA countries*, *Bechdel test*, *English as a Foreign Language*, *fan activism*, *global education*, *in-depth learning*, *native-speakerism*, *read against the text*, *sociocultural identities* and *worldmindedness.*

critical thinking Critical thinking embraces many skills that should help to form unbiased judgements. These include the careful analysis and evaluation of evidence, inferencing from the evidence and interpretation, self-monitored open-mindedness and problem-solving. Critical thinking skills are crucial when navigating the information society and social media. See also *confirmation bias*, *critical literacy*, *critical pedagogy*, *disinformation*, *infodemic*, *information literacy* and *tolerance of ambiguity*.

cult of personality This refers to when an idealized and overblown image of a leader is created by constant propaganda, mass media and, in current times, the additional use of social media. The cult of personality targets the entire population, making use of extravagant praise and rallies, spectacle, the arts and an unquestioning emphasis on patriotism. Historically, the cult of personality phenomenon has referred to media-cultivated images of dictators such as Stalin, Hitler and Benito Mussolini. See *critical thinking*.

cultural identities See under *sociocultural identities*.

cultural studies The field of cultural studies is interdisciplinary, and investigates how cultural practices interact with systems of privilege and power connected to social phenomena. The field includes a focus on issues such as ideology, social class, ethnicity, sexual orientation and gender. In cultural studies, cultures are viewed as constantly shapeshifting, interacting sets of practices and processes. See also *culture*, *interculturality*, *intersectionality* and *sociocultural identities*.

culturally and linguistically diverse Culturally and linguistically diverse students are those with a different home or primary language from the language of schooling. This term is sometimes used for language learners in settings that recognize the strengths of cultural differences and that try to incorporate multilingualism in language education. See also *language of schooling* and *multilingualism*.

culture The concept of culture in language education no longer refers to sovereign states and is not a static, unidimensional concept. The notion of culture is plural, hybrid, complex and dynamic, and also refers to smaller sociocultural variables such as a school culture or neighbourhood culture. An aim of intercultural goals is to avoid the spreading and reinforcing of national stereotypes. See also *cultural studies*, *interculturality* and *sociocultural identities*.

danger of a single story The danger of a single story (Chimamanda Adichie 2009) refers to simplifying and unreflecting conception of and references to an Othered group that attributes limiting stereotypical characteristics to all in the group. See also *essentializing*, *principle of multivoicedness*, *#ownvoices* and *stereotype*.

deep attention Deep attention is important for mental focus, and for sustaining concentration over a prolonged period. While compelling texts are likely to support students in developing deep attention, overuse of social media is considered to result in greatly increased hyper attention and distractibility. See also *continuous partial attention*, *digital natives*, *hyper attention* and *literary apprenticeship*.

deep reading Deep reading means transacting with and participating actively in the literary text, building a mental representation of the storyworld and experiencing empathy and perspective-taking. Deep reading encompasses cognitively demanding contemplative processes and critical deliberation on word choices, talking around texts, inferencing from evidence, and filling gaps, negotiation of insights and sharing of understandings. Deep reading also entails reading critically and potentially against the text. See also *aesthetic reading stance*, *authenticity*, *critical literacy*, *embodied simulation hypothesis*, *empathy*, *extensive reading*, *iceberg task*, *intensive reading*, *mental representation*, *perspective-taking*, *read against the text*, *reciprocal teaching*, *schema refreshing* and *skimming*.

dialogic interaction Dialogic interaction does not intend to elicit correct interpretations and responses, but rather opens up the dialogue and encourages sustained interactive sequences that may involve different ideas and fresh perspectives: a dialogic space for new possibilities (Rupert Wegerif 2013). See also *danger of a single story*, *heteroglossia*, *#ownvoices*, *principle of multivoicedness* and *text ensemble*.

didactic and didactics The term 'didactic' is often used as a synonym for moralizing in English-speaking countries. This connotation means that the term 'didactics' is rather seldom used in international literature for the pedagogical aspects of teacher education (Hamilton 1999), although it is very commonly used in some European countries. See also *English subject pedagogy* and *teaching methodology*.

differentiation As students have different cognitive styles (or learning styles), different language-learning aptitudes, different out-of-school contexts and support, different needs for autonomy or structure, different linguistic repertoires as well as different physical and mental health situations, differentiation in the classroom is an important part of language education. Differentiation can refer to differences in challenge, different social interaction (group work or individual work), making use of different semiotic modes, holistic and multisensory learning.

See also *cognitive styles*, *holistic learning*, *multisensory learning*, *semiotic modes* and *special educational needs*.

digital literacy Digital literacy requires both cognitive and technical competences. It is an umbrella term that includes the ability to assess and create digital work, to navigate effectively in the non-linear medium of digital space, to critique digital content, to be alert to fraudulent digital activity, as well as to understand the social and emotional aspects of socializing and collaborating online. See also *digital natives*, *information literacy*, *media literacy* and *visual literacy*.

digital natives This refers to students who were born into the digital age and surrounded by the internet, video games, mobile phones and fast networking opportunities from the outset (Prensky 2001). In this way, digital natives are used to twenty-first-century technology and to multitasking and parallel processing of swift and continually accessible information. Digital natives are usually strong in the operational dimension of digital literacy but are often weak in information literacy, as the Pisa report (OECD 2021) has shown. See also *deep attention*, *digital literacy*, *hyper attention* and *information literacy*.

dimensions of language learning See under *affective dimension of language learning*, *cognitive dimension of language learning*, *metacognition*, *physiological dimension of language learning* and *sociocultural dimension of language learning*.

discourse genre Discourse genres (or textual genres) are communication situations that can be conversational and interactive, or non-interactive. Each type of text has its own specific characteristics or communication constraints, as certain language features that are more or less ritualized are likely to appear in specific oral or written communication events. For example, when writing a letter to a government office asking for information, formal language is typically used; when telling a joke, a punchline is expected; when writing a story in English, typically the past tense is used. See also *pragmatics* and *register*.

disinformation Disinformation is false information that is usually spread on the internet and via social media and is deliberately intended to deceive. It is often politically motivated and is a tactic akin to propaganda. See also *fake news*, *information literacy* and *misinformation*.

display question This refers to a question to which the teacher already knows the answer; therefore, a display question is not a genuine question. Teachers employ display questions to check knowledge or check for understanding. Display questions elicit a restricted response from the student and hardly any opportunity for reflection. See also *open question*.

diversity Diversity refers to unique differences which can be expressed in terms of ethnicity, linguistic and cultural background, gender, sexual orientation, social class, physical abilities, neurodiversity, religious beliefs and life experience. See also *agency*, *global issues*, *special educational needs* and *We Need Diverse Books*.

double-page spread Multimodal literary texts like picturebooks and graphic novels often have images that spread across two pages. This is called a double-page spread. Picturebooks are usually unpaginated, and there are up to fifteen double-page spreads, or openings, in a standard thirty-two-page picturebook. The first opening or double-page spread begins after the title page, which typically follows the endpapers and any frontmatter. See also *picturebook* and *recto and verso*.

drama conventions Drama conventions, also drama strategies, activities or techniques, are the building blocks of drama teaching methodology. Different conventions can be strategically combined to provide a structure when drama methods are employed for holistic, embodied learning. Drama conventions can be used without any script, or for comprehensive work with a stage play, a novel, or any kind of story. See also *gossip circle*, *holistic learning*, *hot-seating*, *intrapersonal role-play*, *mime*, *physiological dimension of language learning*, *role-on-the-wall*, *subtext strategy*, *teacher-in-role*, *total physical response* and *whoosh*.

dystopia A dystopia is a literary work, film or other fictional text, which depicts an unjust or undesirable imagined community that is often set in the future. The state is usually totalitarian or post-apocalyptic, and the storyworld is often characterized by the suffering and helplessness of individuals. Features that a dystopia may include are tyranny and oppression, poverty, environmental disaster, repression of individuality, with silencing and ignorance of the citizens due to the suppression of reading and books. See also *genre* and *storyworld*.

EAL See under *English as an additional language*.

echo chamber Despite widespread access to information through the internet, our exposure to certain ideologies may be very selective. A social media echo chamber is when like-minded people repeat claims they hear or read again and again within a partially closed loop, until many people believe that a particular version of the story is true. See also *antinarrative*, *confirmation bias*, *disinformation*, *fake news*, *infodemic*, *information literacy* and *misinformation*.

ecocentrism Ecocentrism (or biocentrism) denotes a system of values that is nature centred rather than human centred and therefore strongly supports environmental protection and biodiversity. See also *anthropocentricism*, *ecocriticism*, *environmentalism* and *speciesism*.

ecocriticism The approach of ecocriticism explores literary and cultural texts from an environmentalist perspective: are the texts more anthropocentric, or ecocentric with an environmental stance? Texts, including coursebooks, are evaluated in terms of whether they explicitly or implicitly support an environmental consciousness or implicitly support an environmentally harmful attitude. See also *anthropocentricism*, *ecocentrism*, *environmentalism* and *speciesism*.

edu-business This refers to multinational corporations as well as smaller national providers that offer educational publications, resources, and services such as online learning and teacher training. When national governments and school systems adopt their intensively marketed products and services widely, an edu-business becomes an extremely powerful influence on public education systems. See also *information literacy*, *knowledge equity* and *media literacy*.

educational learning goals of language teaching In school contexts, the language classroom is typically not limited to developing language – even when English is a new language for the students – but is also about using that language in meaningful and horizon-stretching ways. Thus, the English lesson has educational learning goals in addition to language learning goals. Educational goals that are referred to throughout this book include multiple literacy, interculturality and diversity competence, metacognition, learner autonomy, critical thinking and creative problem solving, empathy, creativity, as well as engaging in cross-curricular topics and global issues. This list is by no means exhaustive, but comprises educational goals particularly linked to using story in language education. See also *critical literacy*, *critical thinking*, *digital literacy*, *diversity*, *empathy*, *global issues*, *information literacy*, *interculturality*, *learner autonomy*, *literary literacy*, *metacognition*, *media literacy*, *multiple literacy* and *visual literacy*.

efferent reading stance When we read with the aim to extract information, for example instructions for the use of a gadget or medicine, we use the efferent reading stance (Rosenblatt 1982). This stance is contrasted with the *aesthetic reading stance*.

EFL See under *English as a foreign language*.

elementary school Elementary school, or primary school, is the first school that children attend, sometimes following preschool or kindergarten. The ages children start elementary school are usually between four and six. Children complete elementary school between the ages of ten and twelve, when, in many countries, lower secondary school/middle school follows.

ELL See under *English language learner*.

ELT and TESOL ELT (English language teaching) is an umbrella term for all diverse English learning and teaching settings, but it is not recognized as such worldwide. TESOL (teaching English to speakers of other languages) has a similar umbrella function in American English; however, TESOL refers only to adult language learning settings in British English.

embodied simulation hypothesis According to the embodied simulation hypothesis, we make meaning by recreating the experiences that the speaker or writer describes. The vision system in our brain activates to create a virtual visual experience and the auditory system activates to virtually hear in a dynamic and creative process. This suggests meaning is deeply personal, according to our different experiences (Bergen 2012). See also *empathy*, *neuroscience*, *semiotic modes* and *storyworld*.

empathy Empathy is the ability to understand the emotional state and feelings of another and experience corresponding feelings in ourselves. When reading fiction, we create a mental representation of a character's situation and feelings, and this enables us to feel in empathy with the character. See also *embodied simulation hypothesis*, *fan activism*, *mental representation*, *outcome emotions*, *perspective-taking* and *theory of mind*.

endmatter See under *paratext*.

engagement with language An engaged language learner is alert, pays focused attention to form and constructs their own knowledge as a learning strategy (cognitive dimension). An engaged student has a positive attitude to the language, is purposeful and autonomous (affective dimension). An engaged language learner works dialogically, takes initiative and is interactive (sociocultural dimension) (Svalberg 2009, 2012). See also *affective dimension of language learning*, *cognitive dimension of language learning*, *focus on form*, *metacognition*, *physiological dimension of language learning* and *sociocultural dimension of language learning*.

English as a foreign language (EFL) English as a foreign language (EFL) is a term often used in settings where English is not an official language, such as mainland Europe. EFL is slowly becoming less acceptable, however, as the notion of foreignness suggests that English is 'owned' by native speakers, whereas English – currently a global lingua franca – has long escaped any national ownership or dependence on national boundaries. See also *native-speakerism*.

English as an additional language (EAL) English as an additional language (EAL) refers to language learning in settings where English is the official language and usually the language of schooling. The English learners are students who speak other languages at home, for example, recent immigrants to English-speaking countries. See also *heritage language* and *mutilingualism*.

English as a second language (ESL) English as a second language (ESL) is often used interchangeably with EAL. However, countries where English is an official language but not the primary language of the majority (often former British colonies) are also considered ESL settings.

English language learner (ELL) In the United States, students who are culturally and linguistically diverse, with languages other than English as their primary or home language, are often called English language learners (ELLs), English learners (ELs) or emergent bilinguals. ELLs may receive separate instruction for a limited period of time but are also expected to have access to the regular curriculum. See also *content and language integrated learning*, *culturally and linguistically diverse*, *English as an additional language*.

ESL See under *English as a second language*.

English subject pedagogy English language and literature pedagogy is a research area that focuses on the theory, development, and evaluation of the effectiveness of evidence-based practices for English as a school subject in all school grades. It is an important focus of teacher education for future teachers of English. See *didactic and didactics* and *teaching methodology*.

environmentalism Environmentalism is concerned with the preservation and restoration of the natural environment. Environmental science studies areas such as pollution, climate change, plant and animal diversity. Environmentalism and environmental activism advocates for environmental justice. See also *anthropocentricism*, *ecocentrism* and *speciesism*.

epistemological racism Epistemological racism refers to when White people experience their advantageous position in the world as the norm. They fail to reflect and remain unaware, or deliberately ignore, that their authority position is due to White privilege, and in this way, they contribute to the continuation of that privilege. See also *ideology of inequality* and *marginalized*.

essentializing Essentialist thinking sees the essence or characteristics of a cultural group as common to all and fixed for all members of the group in all places and at all times. See also *danger of a single story*, *ethnocentrism* and *stereotyping*.

ethnocentrism Ethnocentrism means to apply one's own ethnicity or cultural context as a frame of reference, regarding one's own situation as a standard by which to judge different practices and customs in other cultural contexts. An ethnocentric identification with one's ingroup often leads to stereotyping members of the outgroup. See also *ideology of inequality*, *outgroup* and *stereotype*.

executive function Executive function refers to the control of cognitive processes such as energization, task-setting, consistent task monitoring and the ability to tune out distractions and pay deep attention. See also *deep attention* and *hyper attention*.

experiential approach to learning This approach emphasizes the role of students' experiences outside of school as well as in the classroom as important and relevant to their learning processes. Learning is about creativity and action as well as reflection, and this applies to learning language as much as to any other school subject. See also *critical pedagogy*, *fan activism*, *holistic learning* and *in-depth learning*.

extensive listening The widespread use of digital devices has meant that extensive listening has become an important contribution to out-of-school English learning. Online streaming services and audiobooks, for example, can provide motivating and exciting input. See also *compelling comprehensible input*, *extensive reading* and *out-of-school English*.

extensive reading Extensive reading, also free voluntary reading (Krashen 2004), is individual and silent reading for pleasure. The reading material should be easy, with the choice of a wide range of topics so that the learners are able to choose books they find compelling and can read extensively for effective language acquisition. Thus, extensive reading normally requires access to a well-stocked library. The teacher must be a role model by also reading extensively. See also *access*, *deep reading* and *intensive reading*.

fable Fables originally belonged to folk literature and were spread orally in many languages. In fables, animals or inanimate objects are anthropomorphized – they are able to speak and have human characteristics – as a way of revealing human foibles. There is often a concise maxim to end the fable. See also *allegory*, *anthropomorphism* and *protagonism*.

facial expression Facial expression, together with eye contact, is an important means of nonverbal communication, and plays a significant role in creative teacher talk as well as child-directed speech. See also *choral speaking*, *creative teacher talk*, *mime*, *prosodic features* and *scaffolding*.

fake news This refers to unethical ways of spreading false facts. Fake news can refer to propagandist journalism and the spreading of disinformation, sometimes as part of a synchronized influence operation designed to create social or political disruption. Fake news may also refer to poorly researched journalism and misinformation. Use of this term has also been criticized as it has sometimes been misused by high-profile politicians. See also *confirmation bias, disinformation, echo chamber* and *information literacy*.

fan activism Fan activism refers to associations that have been inspired by contemporary works of fiction to raise awareness of social concerns and challenge dominant power structures. The civic engagement of fan activists often includes supporting marginalized communities and drawing attention to climate change. The rise of fan activism, for example *Fandom Forward* (formerly The Harry Potter Alliance), illustrates the key role of fiction in building empathy: 'The stories we love bring us together, but the story of our world? That's up to us' (2021). See also *critical pedagogy, empathy, experiential approach to learning, global education, in-depth learning* and *outcome emotions*.

fanfiction Fanfiction, or fanfic, refers to stories or poetry written by fans of a book or movie and published online. Fanfiction is non-commercial and unauthorized and cannot be professionally published as it often infringes copyright laws. Published on the web, it recreates and often transforms the original text, potentially extending the lives of the original characters. See also *affinity spaces, reimagining* and *paratext*.

focus on form Focus on form (Michael Long 1991) refers to an approach that avoids teaching and testing grammar as isolated linguistic units or language building blocks, because learners do not develop language proficiency one grammar structure at a time however well these are taught. Focus on form means to overtly highlight a linguistic element as it arises incidentally in the classroom while the focus of teaching is on content, and language is the vehicle not the object of the lesson. See also *engagement with language, formulaic sequences, metalinguistic awareness* and *total physical response*.

format Literary formats can be multimodal, like the picturebook and graphic novel, hybrid like the verse novel or formats for fluent readers such as young adult novels. The format, or medium, refers to how the narrative is delivered, not the story content, which is the genre: dystopia, nonfiction, fable, fairy tale, fantasy and so forth. See also *genre*.

formulaic sequences Formulaic sequences are fixed or semi-fixed expressions or multi-word chunks or strings of language that facilitate fluency as they are acquired and used as a whole unit (Alison Wray 2002), such as 'It's your turn', 'Would you mind if...', 'Let's see'. Formulaic sequences constitute a substantial contribution to any authentic discourse (Norbert Schmitt 2004) and can convey information fast and express meaning quite succinctly. See also *access, authenticity, extensive reading, task-based learning* and *usage-based approach*.

functional literacy Functional literacy is the capacity to engage in those activities in which reading and writing are required for effective functioning in a community. A functionally literate person can continue to use reading, writing and calculation throughout their life for their professional and personal development. See also *information literacy* and *knowledge equity*.

future studies Future studies, or strategic foresight, is a relatively new academic field, taught at many tertiary institutions around the world. The study is interdisciplinary and includes a focus on envisaging plausible alternative and preferable future scenarios. The field of future studies draws insights from a range of disciplines, including social, technological, economic, environmental and political research. See also *speculative fiction*.

gallery walk This involves groupwork on a topic, each group creating a poster, which is hung on the classroom wall. The gallery walk takes place when the student groups rotate from poster to poster, discussing the ideas of the other groups and using sticky notes to add annotations with their own reflections, before moving to the next poster. See also *teaching methodology*.

gender While sex is a biological classification, gender is often understood as a social category. Gender roles are the result of socially constructed ideas about the behaviour of the different sexes and vary cross-culturally according to societal expectations of masculinity and femininity. See also *Bechdel test, gender identity, LGBTQ+* and *sexual orientation*.

gender identity Gender identity refers to each individual's deeply felt internal experience of gender, which usually but not always corresponds with the sex assigned at birth. See also *LGBTQ+* and *sexual orientation*.

genre Genre as a term has many meanings. With reference to literary texts, the term 'genre' most often characterizes the story content, such as horror, science fiction, dystopia, fairy tale, fantasy, speculative fiction, magic realism, postcolonial, historical fiction, alternate history, love story and nonfiction. See also *discourse genre* and *format*.

global education This is a global approach to mental development that seeks to expand limited subject knowledge promoted through school education. When classroom teaching is dependent on memorization and divorced from global culture, opportunities for critical pedagogy and activism – now vitally necessary due to issues such as the climate crisis – are lost. Children's literature can promote global education by helping young people think critically and constructively about themselves and their role in the global community. See also *critical pedagogy, experiential approach to learning, in-depth learning* and *worldmindedness*.

global issues Topics within global issues include racism, xenophobia, social class bias, sexism, homophobia, ableism, lookism, ageism, mental and physical health, and the environment. A new global issue that could belong to the discourse of language education with children and adolescents is the potentially dangerous effects of social media. See also *agency, diversity, group-focused enmity* and *worldmindedness*.

gossip circle Gossip circle is a drama convention that comments on the behaviour of characters in a story. The class stands in a large circle and students take turns to comment in a gossipy way on a character. A soft ball can be thrown to indicate who should speak next, adding the element of spontaneity. See also *drama conventions*.

graded reader These are books written for language learners at different levels. They are often simplified and abbreviated versions of older literary classics, which can be adapted cheaply when copyright has expired. They may also be especially written for language learners, particularly those following an extensive reading approach. Graded readers are usually aimed at adult or young adult target audiences and to ensure maximum sales follow requirements on sensitive topics for the different markets. See also *authenticity*, *canonical literature* and *PARSNIP*.

graphic novel Graphic novels are novel-length stories, usually bound like a book, told in words and images, and with carefully orchestrated artwork. Whereas comics are frequently ongoing series, graphic novels usually tell a stand-alone story, often dealing with complex fictional or nonfictional topics. See also *caption*, *gutter*, *panel*, *sound effects*, *speech balloon* and *typographic creativity*.

group hot-seating See under *hot-seating*.

group-focused enmity This refers to the hypothesis that different prejudices have a common generalized core that is based on an ideology of inequality of certain groups that are believed to be of lower status. The discrimination occurs solely on the basis of attributed group membership and is unconnected to the behaviour of individuals (Zick, Küpper and Hövermann 2011). See also *otherness and Other* and *outgroup*.

groupthink Groupthink characterizes how members of a cohesive group often avoid speaking up for fear of how their ingroup perceives them. Group interactions tend towards harmonious agreements, while new arguments or innovative outcomes are dismissed, thus creating one-dimensionality and ingroup bias. See also *ingroup*, *otherness and Other* and *outgroup*.

gutter The gutter is the space between panels in graphic novels and comics. The panels contain still images, and the story moves forward between these frozen moments. It is the gutter, though an empty space, that allows us to imagine that action is taking place (Scott McCloud 1993). See also *caption*, *panel*, *sound effects* and *speech balloon*.

heritage language A heritage language is a minority language usually acquired at home and different to the majority language. Heritage language speakers may belong to an immigrant, minoritized or indigenous community. The majority language is typically the language of schooling, and proficiency in the heritage language among heritage speakers may vary widely. See also *culturally and linguistically diverse*, *language of schooling* and *multilingualism*.

heteroglossia Heteroglossia (Mikhail Bakhtin) refers to how the many different voices in narrative, the characters and the narrator, have different idiosyncratic ways of using language to conceptualize the world in words, which for the reader is open to interpretation. See also the *principle of multivoicedness*.

holistic learning Often known as head, heart and hands learning (Gazibara 2013), holistic learning is multisensory, embodied learning. All dimensions of language learning are involved in holistic learning, and the whole (referring both to whole-person learning and whole language) is believed to be richer, more meaningful and dynamic than the sum of individual parts. See also *affective dimension of language learning*, *cognitive dimension of language learning*, *differentiation*, *embodied simulation hypothesis*, *metacognition*, *physiological dimension of language learning*, *sociocultural dimension of language learning* and *total physical response*.

homophobia Homophobia refers to an intolerant and negative attitude toward lesbian, gay, bisexual and transgender (LGBTQ+) communities. A lack of interaction with queer people is strongly associated with anti-queer prejudice, which is a difficult form of discrimination to combat. See also *group-focused enmity*, *ideology of inequality* and *LGBTQ+*.

hot-seating An extremely useful drama technique, hot-seating can easily be employed in order to delve more deeply into the motives, beliefs, actions and relationships of characters in any narrative. Group hot-seating – when several students sit at the front of the class as different characters – is fun and less stressful than individual hot-seating. The other students question them, and they must always answer in role. The hot-seated students can also turn to other characters for answers, always questioning and answering in role. See also *drama conventions*, *holistic learning* and *total physical response*.

hyper attention In the twenty-first century, it is observed that increasingly students demonstrate hyper attention more than deep attention in the way they process information. Students' reactions are fast, and they can switch rapidly between different tasks, but they need a high level of stimulation to avoid boredom. A goal of education is to encourage deep attention, the ability to focus deeply on a single object and for a longer period. See also *cognitive styles*, *deep attention* and *digital natives*.

i + 1 i + 1 refers to Stephen Krashen's comprehensible input hypothesis, which states that language learners progress when they receive language input that is slightly more advanced than their current level. The ideal level of input is known as i+1, whereby 'i' represents the learner's current interlanguage and knowledge of the context, and '+1' refers to the following stage of language acquisition. See also *scaffolding* and *zone of proximal development*.

iceberg task The iceberg task is a reflective, visual device to aid deep reading through group work. Students draw the outline of a large iceberg, with most of the mass below the waterline. They discuss what is in the text and what is hidden between the lines. They make notes on the text above the waterline of the iceberg and note down the larger subtext beneath the waterline. See also *critical literacy*, *deep reading* and *subtext strategy*.

identification fallacy The identification fallacy (Nikolajeva 2014) refers to when students are encouraged to identify with literary characters. This can lead to an uncritical alignment with a fictional character and delay the development of ToM, critical literacy and empathy. See also *critical literacy*, *empathy*, *intentional fallacy* and *theory of mind*.

ideology Ideology refers to belief systems and attitudes that underlie social practices and lived experience. Ideology implies habits of thought; these may be unexamined assumptions that are taken for granted and embedded in group interests. A text free of ideology is unthinkable (John Stephens 1992), therefore the need for questioning, critical, problematizing approaches to all texts. See also *canonical literature, critical literacy, critical pedagogy, fan activism, global education, group-focused enmity, ideology of inequality, information literacy, media literacy, native-speakerism, otherness and Other, #ownvoices, read against the text, schema refreshing, We Need Diverse Books, worldmindedness* and *xenophobia*.

ideology of inequality This is a common, sometimes subconscious, ideology that outgroups (social groups with which an individual does not identify) are of lower status. Group-focused enmity has been found to be based on an ideology of inequality. See also *groupthink, group-focused enmity, homophobia, ingroup, otherness and Other, outgroup* and *xenophobia*.

inclusivity Inclusivity refers to the practice of ensuring equal access to resources and opportunities for all students, but particularly those who are often excluded, minoritized or marginalized. This includes groups based on ethnicity or race, on gender or sexual orientation, on physical or mental (dis)abilities, on belief or absence of belief. See also *access, diversity* and *knowledge equity*.

in-depth learning In-depth learning (or deep learning) is an approach that aims to reconnect school and the world beyond, helping students to invest in their learning as they understand its relevance for life outside of school. In-depth learning involves the students as agentive and motivated participants, working collaboratively and with empathy while preparing for and confronting the challenges of today and of times ahead. See also *critical pedagogy, experiential approach to learning, global education* and *worldmindedness*.

indeterminacy Indeterminacy refers to the inevitable and often strategic gaps in literary texts that readers bridge –in different ways – through cultural knowledge, dialogue with peers and reading between the lines. In linguistics, indeterminacy refers to the ambiguity of language in use, or discourse, as well as language as a system, for example, when it is difficult to categorize what is grammatical and what is not. See also *postmodern literature* and *tolerance of ambiguity*.

infodemic A portmanteau word that combines the words 'information' and 'epidemic', infodemic refers to the wide-reaching spread of accurate as well as false information on important global topics, such as Covid-19. When an infodemic takes hold, it becomes difficult to disentangle essential and important information from rumour, fear and malicious disinformation. See also *confirmation bias, digital literacy, echo chamber, disinformation, fake news, information literacy* and *misinformation*.

information literacy An important research skill, information literacy (sometimes included under *digital literacy*) is the ability to recognize the need for information, the ability to track down the information, evaluate its reliability, and effectively make use of the information. Training information literacy has now become essential for everyone, as readers take much of their information from the internet, which, unlike serious journalism, has no gatekeeper function. See also *confirmation bias, digital literacy, disinformation, echo chamber, fake news, infodemic, knowledge equity* and *misinformation.*

informational literature See under *nonfiction.*

ingroup Ingroups are sociocultural groups that individuals identify with. They can be, for example, groups of friends, family, school community and professional associations. See also *groupthink, native-speakerism* and *outgroup.*

intensive reading This is a reading strategy that focuses on students deciphering the information in a text, such as a factual report or brief literary extract. Certain compartmentalized activities are associated with intensive reading, for example comprehension questions and answering true or false statements, and the main goal is usually instrumental – making use of the text for expanding vocabulary acquisition, exercising discrete grammar items and fostering communicative competence on a surface level. See also *authenticity, deep reading, efferent reading stance, extensive reading, formulaic sequences.*

intentional fallacy The intentional fallacy is the overestimation of the significance of an author's intention. The assertion is, on the contrary, that an author's intended meaning is not more valid or more important than readers' actual response to the work, particularly as authors generally create unintended meanings in addition to meanings they might have intended. See also *identification fallacy* and *read against the text.*

interculturality Interculturality relies on a fluid notion of culture and cultural diversity, and focuses on dialogue and mutual respect (UNESCO 2017a). It involves a shift in focus from an 'our culture versus their culture' narrative to engagement in processes of decentring – making the familiar strange – and perspective-taking. Interculturality is a transformative conceptualization that questions and discloses inequalities within and between social groups. See also *cultural studies, culture, intersectionality, knowledge equity* and *perspective-taking.*

interlocutor An interlocutor is a person involved in a conversation. There may be several interlocutors (conversation partners) in the dialogue. See also *accomodation* and *i + 1.*

intermediality In literature, this refers to the interconnection between different media. Increasingly, literary texts fall between different media, such as cinepoetic film, or a literary text mimics other storytelling media, such as *The Invention of Hugo Cabret* (Selznick 2007), a graphic novel which echoes the cinematography of silent movies. See also *intertextuality.*

intersectionality Intersectionality identifies interlocking factors of advantage or disadvantage and privilege or underprivilege, for example regarding gender, race, class, sexuality, religion and disability. See also *cultural studies, interculturality, knowledge equity* and *sociocultural identities.*

intertextuality Intertextuality is an expression that signifies the ways that a literary text playfully connects to other texts. The connections can be allusions to any feature of earlier texts, including language, style, characters, titles, settings, motifs and actions. A reimagining is a reworked text that intertextually rewrites and comments on an older text. See also *fanfiction*, *paratext*, *reimagining* and *postmodern literature*.

intrapersonal communication Intrapersonal communication refers to the process of unspoken internal dialogue, also called inner speech, often rehearsing perspective-taking and different attitudes, thoughts and feelings. While inner speech is typically silent, small children engage in imaginative interactions aloud, which is known as private speech. See also *perspective-taking* and *thoughtful feelings*.

intrapersonal role-play Intrapersonal role-play refers to the representation of an improvised argument of a character with him- or herself. Following a reflection and preparation phase, two students role-play the conflicting thoughts of the character, who can be represented by an empty chair or played by a third student who listens and responds briefly. Each student argues and tries to persuade the character they represent of the opposing position. See also *drama conventions*.

jigsaw activity This is a learning strategy that encourages students to teach each other. The class is divided into home groups with four or five students in each group. Each student is responsible for gaining understanding of one aspect of a subject the class is working on. The students regroup into teams that focus on the same aspect of the topic, and this becomes the expert group. After reflections and investigations, the students all return to their home groups and teach each other what they have learned. See also *learner autonomy*, *reciprocal teaching* and *teaching methodology*.

knowledge equity Knowledge equity is a concept that refers to the need to reconsider and expand what is valued as knowledge. This notion examines how different communities are obstructed from the opportunity to create and utilize knowledge through imbalanced configurations of power and privilege. See also *critical literacy*, *edu-business*, *functional literacy*, *information literacy* and *media literacy*.

language didactics See under *English subject pedagogy*, *didactic and didactics* and *teaching methodology*.

language of schooling The language of schooling, or common classroom language, is usually the majority or dominant language of a region. Typically, the language of schooling is also the teacher's primary language. This can disadvantage children who speak a heritage language at home, especially when their linguistic repertoire is not supported, valued, or even recognized. See also *culturally and linguistically diverse*, *heritage language* and *multilingualism*.

learner autonomy Learner autonomy means the focus is on learning rather than teaching. The teacher creates opportunity, space, and motivation for the students' development, using scaffolding and differentiation, and allowing the outside world into the classroom, helping the students become autonomous learners. See also *access*, *agency*, *jigsaw activity*, *reciprocal teaching* and *scaffolding*.

learning styles See under *cognitive styles*.

lexical chain The lexical chain is a feature of well-written authentic texts, when sequences of neighbouring words relate to the same topic, so creating a text that is rich in lexical density and cohesively interconnected. See also *authenticity* and *stylistics*.

LGBTQ+ This is an umbrella acronym used to refer to lesbian, gay, bisexual and transgender issues and communities. The Q+ refers to further groups of people who do not identify specifically with the LGBT categories. See also *gender identity* and *sexual orientation*.

literacy Basic literacy means the ability to read and write. The acquisition of basic literary is uneven globally; there is a disparity between male literacy and female literacy in countries where female education is not valued. The understanding of literacy has also changed due to digital technologies: 'Literacy in the 21st century is about constructing and validating knowledge. The more information there is, the more readers have to know how to navigate through ambiguity, and triangulate and validate viewpoints' (OECD 2021: 13). Consequently, the notion of literacy is now plural. See also *multiple literacy*, *critical literacy*, *digital literacy*, *functional literacy*, *information literacy*, *knowledge equity*, *literary literacy*, *media literacy* and *visual literacy*.

literary apprenticeship Through an age-appropriate apprenticeship into reading literary texts over several years, school students learn to take advantage of narrative in language education – affordances for motivation, perspective-taking, empathy, interculturality, ToM, creativity, critical literacy, literary literacy and learner autonomy. A literary apprenticeship supports deep reading rather than skimming, artefact emotions, engagement with language and with characters' perspectives. See also *access*, *artefact emotions*, *compelling comprehensible input*, *critical literacy*, *literary literacy*, *deep reading*, *empathy*, *learner autonomy*, *reading blip*, *reciprocal teaching* and *tolerance of ambiguity*.

literary literacy It is helpful for students to acquire some literary literacy. This means to be able to recognize the conventions and patterns of different genres, and to understand the significance of different semiotic modes in multimodal formats such as picturebooks and graphic novels. An interest in exploring rhetorical devices, characterization, settings and imagery – the tools of literary craftmanship – also belongs to literary literacy. See also *rhetorical device*, *semiotic modes* and *visual literacy*.

majority world This term was coined by Shahidul Alam in the 1990s as an alternative for expressions such as *third world* or *developing world* (Alam 2008). Many in Africa, Asia, Latin America and the Middle East prefer the term *majority world* as both more accurate and with fewer negative connotations. See also *BANA countries*.

marginalized This refers to an individual or community that is treated as peripheral or belonging to the margins of society. Marginalization makes involvement in mainstream political, cultural and social activities difficult and holds back civic engagement. See also *minoritized*.

media literacy Media literacy, or critical media literacy, means the ability to recognize that the world is represented in certain ways through the media, often

Western-centric and White-centric. Media literacy involves learning to understand the power structures of mass media and participatory media that shape representations and can therefore play a role in constructing views of reality. See also *critical literacy*, *edu-business*, *information literacy* and *knowledge equity*.

mental representation Mental representations or mental imagery enable us to create a mental model of our reading, and even of phenomena that do not exist. Mental imagery is often predominantly visual, but may involve representations of hearing, smell, touch or taste in addition, manifested in perceptions, emotions and thoughts. See also *deep reading* and *embodied simulation hypothesis*.

metacognition Metacognition refers to being mindful of one's own awareness, thinking and knowing. It includes the ability to monitor performance and strategies such as planning, checking, monitoring, selecting, revising, evaluating. See also *affective dimension of language learning*, *cognitive dimension of language learning*, *engagement with language*, *learner autonomy* and *sociocultural dimension of language learning*.

metalinguistic awareness Metalinguistic awareness refers to explicit and aware knowledge about language. This can be employed to reflect on linguistic choices for accuracy as well as for a specific context and specific purpose. Metalinguistic negotiation explores how linguistic choices are linked to rhetorical effects (Myhill 2020). See also *discourse genre*, *focus on form*, *pragmatics*, *rhetorical device*, *register* and *stylistics*.

methodology See under *teaching methodology*.

mime Mime refers to acting without using spoken language. Meanings are communicated silently through body language and facial expression. See also *drama conventions*, *facial expression*, *total physical response* and the *physiological dimension of language learning*.

minoritized This refers to a community that is treated as of lesser consequence. Their marginalized social status is unconnected to their numbers (therefore *minoritized* has replaced *minority*). Women may be slightly in the majority numerically but are minoritized in patriarchal societies. See also *marginalized*.

misinformation Misinformation is inaccurate information that is not reviewed or regulated in any way. It can consist of false rumours, online sites with careless factual errors or representing biased views. Readers' own bias can lead them to believe something is true and to trust information that supports their prior opinions. See also *antinarrative*, *echo chamber*, *disinformation* and *information literacy*.

motivation Motivation is key to success in language learning. Students may be *intrinsically motivated* to learn a new language; this is often the case with young, elementary-school students who are still very much engaged in acquiring L1(s). However, the English class must be age-appropriate if it is to take advantage of children's intrinsic motivation. Adolescent students and older are quite often *instrumentally motivated*, such as when they want to do well at school and in their professional life. Rod Ellis (1997) has identified motivation that depends on good results as *resultative motivation*, and this can have reciprocal effects by producing more success. Students who are fascinated by the alterity of a new language and associated new cultural environments are said to possess *integrative motivation*. Zoltán Dörnyei (2007) has demonstrated the importance of a *motivating classroom environment* that should include interaction, rewarding group activities, investing in the group, extracurricular activities and cooperation toward common goals. See also *affective filter, safe classroom climate, self-efficacy.*

multilingualism Most people worldwide are multilingual and speak at least two languages. Increasingly, children are involved in acquiring several languages, for example a heritage language, the language of schooling (which is usually also the teacher's primary language) as well as learning a new language or languages. A multilingual approach in education highlights the importance of maintaining a level playing field for children with a primary language different from the language of schooling, values their language repertoires and recognizes and supports their multilingual skills. See also *culturally and linguistically diverse, heritage language* and *language of schooling.*

multimodal text Multimodal texts communicate content through a combination of semiotic modes. Picturebooks, comics and graphic novels are multimodal texts in that they tell their stories through visual and linguistic modes: pictorial and verbal text on the page. Film and story apps are multimodal texts using moving image, speech and sound effects, gesture and action on the screen. See also *aural communication, multisensory learning, prosodic features, semiotic modes, sound effects* and *text.*

multisensory learning Multisensory learning refers to a learning situation that involves several senses. This is achieved by a combination of two or more of the different communicative modes: the visual (seeing), aural (hearing), kinaesthetic (movement) and tactile (touch). Thus, multimodal texts are always multisensory, as are drama and learning by doing. This is the most natural way of learning for children, and sensory anchoring is supported. Touch is vital for children, being able to touch and smell the books they read, balancing books on their laps and navigating through the pages with their fingers. This encourages curiosity about books and could help to avert the reading blip. Adolescents are also usually more engaged if their learning is multisensory. See also *differentiation, embodied simulation hypothesis, multimodal text, reading blip, semiotic modes.*

multiple literacy Multiple literacy, or multiliteracy, refers to a broader understanding of literacy in education. Communications around the globe increasingly express meanings multimodally, using combinations of linguistic, visual, audio, spatial and gestural modes. The educational approach of multiple literacy recognizes the importance of connecting students' own multimodal life experiences to their literacy practices in school. See also *critical literacy, digital literacy, functional literacy, information literacy, media literacy, visual literacy.*

multivoicedness See under *principle of multivoicedness.*

narrative Narrative, also called a story or a tale, is a ubiquitous feature of human meaning-making. Narrative is a structured account of experience and can be told as fictional story orally or in print-based media as well as screen-based media like film, documentaries and video games. See also *antinarrative*.

native-speakerism Native-speakerism refers to an ideology that teachers born into an English-speaking community – chiefly BANA countries – are more in command of up-to-date methodological approaches to language teaching and can offer a superior language model, principally in pronunciation (Holliday 2015). This leads to a native-speaker hegemony and privileged ingroup with vastly superior professional opportunities, while devaluing the cultural identity of English speakers from non-BANA countries. See also *BANA countries*, *English as a foreign language (EFL)* and *ingroup*.

neuroscience Neuroscience refers to how the integration of a number of sciences contribute to our understanding of the brain. This can be relevant for the study of literary response; for example, neuroscience can use brain imaging to examine a reader's response to variations in verse patterns. Other empirical research has shown how emotions are activated while reading literature by demonstrating physiological outcomes such as alterations in heart rate and respiration. See also *embodied simulation hypothesis*.

nonfiction Nonfiction, or informational literature, refers to an important body of literature that selects, organizes and interprets information, increasingly in a multimodal format with images that contribute to the factual account. Nonfiction is often presented in narrative form, for example in the genres of biography and autobiography, and can engage readers emotionally and intellectually. See also *genre* and *narrative*.

onomatopoeia Onomatopoeia refers to words that imitate the sound described, in the sense of auditory iconicity. It is often employed in children's literature, as in this example from *Mouse Bird Snake Wolf* (Almond 2013), 'And yes! The snake *hissed*. It lifted its head and it *hissed* again. It *slithered* towards them across the grass. Its scales glittered. Its eyes gleamed. It bared its sharp little teeth. It *flicked* its forked little tongue.' See also *alliteration*, *anaphora*, *cacophony*, *polysyndeton*, *repetition*, *rhetorical device*, *rule of three*, *stylistics*.

open question Open questions, or referential questions, promote creativity and motivate active participation as there is no specific correct answer, but many possible answers. Students are encouraged to think, and the reflective classroom discourse is an important learning process. See also *display question* and *tolerance of ambiguity*.

opening See under *double-page spread*.

oracy Oracy refers to the development of spoken language in educational settings. Oracy is an important skill to develop in the first language as well as in all additional languages. See also *orality*.

orality Orality is a mode rather than a skill. It refers to cultural uses of spoken language, with emphasis on techniques of remembering, for example by using repetitive, patterned, and additive language. Speeches, proverbs, and all kinds of oral storytelling make use of the rhetorical devices of orality. See also *oracy*.

orthographic decoding Fluent readers, and children who are more experienced readers, recognize orthographic word forms as wholes, as they have built up a sight vocabulary. Orthographic decoding is called the lexical route to reading, allowing more rapid and efficient word recognition than grapheme-to-phoneme translation alone – the phonological recoding of beginner readers. See also *phonological recoding*.

otherness and Other The condition of otherness, or alterity, is difference – being different from default, normative perceptions. Categorizing groups or individuals as the Other, also known as Othering, indicates our tendency to categorize difference and divergence from our cultural or societal expectations as *us* and *them*, as well as the tendency to treat the Other as a threat. See also *outgroup, group-focused enmity* and *xenophobia*.

outcome emotions These are emotions that tend to endure and continue to influence the reader or observer at the end of a moving narrative (Hogan 2014). The emotional response to story is empathetic, helps to build ToM and can be schema refreshing. See also *artefact emotions, empathy, schema refreshing* and *theory of mind*.

outgroup An outgroup is a sociocultural group with which an individual does not identify. Social groups and communities that are minoritized and marginalized as outgroups are not necessarily minorities. See also *ableism, groupthink, group-focused enmity, ideology of inequality, ingroup, otherness and Other* and *xenophobia*

out-of-school English In countries where English is not the majority language or an official language, the language used to be new to students when they commenced English lessons at school. In many contexts this is no longer the case, due to the accessibility of out-of-school English. Incidental exposure to English out-of-school may begin prior to classroom instruction and continues parallel to English language education in school. For example, the use of social media, gaming and online streaming services can be sources of extensive out-of-school English. While this contributes to authenticity and fluency in the language, it may contribute little to metalinguistic awareness or to educational learning goals of English language education. See also *access, affinity spaces, authenticity, educational learning goals of language teaching, extensive listening, knowledge equity* and *metalinguistic awareness*.

#ownvoices The #ownvoices hashtag was initiated by the author Corinne Duyvis (https://www.corinneduyvis.net/ownvoices/). It refers to accentuating the authentic voices of the minoritized, who write from their own perspective, as important for the empowerment and dignity of marginalized groups as well as accuracy of the storyworld. See also *authenticity*, White saviour narrative and We Need Diverse Books.

panel A graphic novel panel shows a moment in time. There may be many frozen moments enclosed in small panels on a page, or a single full-page panel. The shapes as well as size of the panels can vary. Frequently panels are rectangular with regular borders, or frames, and spaces in between known as gutters. But there may be no borders at all, or panels with unusual and irregular shapes. All panel features can affect the reading experience and meaning. See also *caption*, *gutter*, *sound effects* and *speech balloon*.

paratext The paratext refers to physical material and virtual elements surrounding a book. Components that frame the main text include the front and back covers, endpapers, and title page, as well as front- and endmatter such as foreword, glossaries, and maps, altogether this is also known as the peritext. In addition to the peritextual features that frame the physical book, reviews and online material on the book also belong to the paratext (Genette 1997). The paratext influences the interpretation by the reader and may never stop developing and contributing to the status of the work, although most paratextual elements are neither decided nor crafted by the actual author of the text. See also *canonical literature*, *fanfiction* and *intertextuality*.

PARSNIP principle PARSNIP is the acronym standing for politics, alcohol, religion, sex, narcotics, -isms and pork. These topics are considered sensitive or taboo in certain markets and are therefore mostly excluded by graded reader and coursebook publishers that aim to cater for an international market, in order to avoid impacting sales. See also *graded readers*.

partly determining context The best context to support students in predicting and acquiring new expressions that they read or hear is partly determining (Krashen 1999). Context can refer to language, pictures, world knowledge of certain situations, and expectations. Too little context is insufficient to support the guessing of words and meanings from context, and overdetermining context reduces the need to pay attention and invest mental effort, which is important for second language acquisition. See also *i + 1*, *scaffolding* and *zone of proximal development (ZPD)*.

peritext See under *paratext*.

persona In poetry and verse novels, the person who speaks is known as the persona. When we read a verse novel, we seem to hear the persona speaking their thoughts directly to us. Sometimes the persona quotes other characters' direct speech, but, unlike a narrator, seldom delivers extended narrative description. See also *verse novel*.

persons of colour Persons of colour is an umbrella term in the United States and elsewhere to refer to vastly disparate ethnic groups who do not self-identify as White. Persons of colour is often considered preferable to other terms for peoples of non-European origin because it is associated with the social justice movement. See also *epistemological racism*.

perspective-taking There are two dimensions of perspective-taking. Conceptual perspective-taking is the ability to comprehend another's thoughts, feelings and attitudes. Perceptual perspective-taking is the ability to understand another's sensory experience, seeing as if through their eyes, and hearing as if through their ears (or imagining not being able to hear in the case of a deaf person). See also *cinematic point of view*, *empathy*, *interculturality*, *intrapersonal communication*, *point of view*, *theory of mind* and *thoughtful feelings*.

phonological recoding Phonological recoding is the process that supports young children's transformation of written words into their phonological representations – the mental representations of the sounds of words in spoken language. Most beginner readers initially use grapheme-phoneme correspondences to recode new and unknown words they encounter in their reading via a non-lexical route. See also *orthographic decoding*.

physiological dimension of language learning This important dimension of language education is often neglected beyond the elementary school and is almost entirely excluded from computer-mediated communication. However, holistic language learning embraces the physiological dimension, the multisensory, and all modes of communication including gesture, body language, facial expression, and movement. Thus, drama activities, playing games, choral speaking, acting out poems and story, crafting, mime, and total physical response should belong to language learning in all school settings. See also *affective dimension of language learning, cognitive dimension of language learning, drama conventions, embodied simulation hypothesis, holistic learning, mime, semiotic modes, sociocultural dimension of language learning* and *total physical response*.

picturebook The picturebook, or picture book, is a multimodal literary format. It can be an object of art, for the interanimation between the verbal text and the images and carefully orchestrated layout together create the potential literariness and aesthetic nature of the picturebook format. To emphasize its compound nature, the format is now frequently spelled as a compound noun: picturebook. There are picturebooks in many genres, including toy stories, animal stories, adventure stories, refugee stories and biography. Challenging wordless picturebooks for adolescents and adult readers as well as for children have recently become popular. See also *double-page spread, paratext, recto and verso* and *wordless picturebook*.

plurilingualism See under *multilingualism*.

point of view Literary point of view refers to when we understand a narrative through the perspective and interpretation of events of a certain character. In the case of first-person narration, the narrator shares their point of view with the reader. See also *cinematic point of view* and *perspective-taking*.

polysyndeton Polysyndeton is a rhetorical device with an additive effect that is often used in children's literature and oral literature. The conjunction *and* (sometimes also the conjunctions *but, or, nor*) is repeatedly used in close succession to create a majestic, intense or urgent tone. This is shown in the following example from *The Firework-Maker's Daughter* (Pullman 1995), '*And* her throat was parched *and* her lungs were panting in the hot thin air, *and* she fell to her knees *and* clung with trembling fingers as the stones began to roll under her again.' See also *orality* and *rhetorical device*.

polyvocality See under *principle of multivoicedness*.

postmodern literature Postmodern literature refers to playful, usually recent texts that disrupt expectations. Features of postmodern literature may include irony, intertextuality, magic realism, alternate history, and indeterminacy. See also *indeterminacy*, *intertextuality* and *reimagining*.

pragmatics Pragmatic skills are social language skills and refer to an understanding of how context affects how we speak and write. We need to adjust our language use based on the discourse genre, the situation, and our interlocutors, for example informal social proficiency in oral and written language is different from the requirements for academic writing. See also *discourse genre*, *interlocuter*, *metalinguistic awareness* and *register*.

principle of multivoicedness The principle of multivoicedness, or polyvocality, refers to the proposition that in order to avoid a dominance of an already over-represented perspective (usually male, White and from the West), texts from different origins should be studied in an ensemble. New voices may challenge traditional positions and invite critical thinking. See also *danger of a single story*, *dialogic interaction*, *heteroglossia*, *#ownvoices* and *text ensemble*.

productive skills Productive skills mean the ability to produce language through speaking and writing. Productive skills need to be supported by receiving and understanding language through listening and reading. See also *receptive skills*.

prosodic features Prosodic features of speech are important in expressing emotions and attitudes, and include intonation, tone, stress, pause, tempo, volume and rhythm. Sometimes child-directed speech and scaffolded teaching make use of exaggerated prosodic features. See also *child-directed speech*, *creative teacher talk* and *scaffolding*.

protagonism Protagonism (Steven Brown et al. 2019) refers to the phenomenon that narrative seems to be typically character driven and not primarily plot driven. Thus, character interaction and psychological dynamics are central to contemporary story. This is not the case with the traditional fairy tale, nor with earlier narrative fiction, which tends to be plot driven. See also *fable* and *anthropomorphism*.

read against the text Reading against the text (also reading against the grain or resistant reading) is a technique to disclose stereotypes in a text as well as absences. These are often absences that the author was not aware of, for example when agentic female characters or persons of colour are completely absent, are represented merely by a token character, or are represented by far fewer characters than would typically be the case in the society the storyworld reflects. See also *critical literacy*, *critical pedagogy*, *essentializing*, *ethnocentrism*, *intentional fallacy*, *stereotype* and *persons of colour*.

readers theatre Readers theatre in the classroom is a dramatic interpretative reading of drama or narrative, with a script in hand. The students do not use costumes and generally no physical action is involved. Instead, they use orchestrated vocal expression to animate and interpret the story sequence. See also *choral speaking*, *facial expression*, *prosodic features* and *sound effects*.

reading blip The reading blip (German: *Leseknick*) refers to the age when many children lose interest in reading, typically around the age of twelve. The reading blip may be temporary – just a blip – but if adolescents are not given access to age-appropriate and compelling books that are well suited to their interests and reading level, the reading blip is likely to become a serious disruption for lifelong learning. See also *access* and *literary apprenticeship*.

realia Realia refers to authentic objects a teacher brings into the classroom to elicit language, scaffold new language and aid understanding or often to focus attention during storytelling. See also *multisensory learning* and *scaffolding*.

recasting Recasting is a technique used to support language learners by correcting errors without disturbing the communication flow. The teacher recasts the learner's utterance in a corrected form and often with more detail, much as a parent adds detail to a child's early attempts at talk. See *child-directed speech*.

receptive skills The term 'receptive skills' refers to listening and reading with understanding. Receptive skills support productive skills; for example, building reading skills can contribute to the development of writing. Receptive narrative ability refers to the development of understanding in very young children that narrative refers to others' experiences, which helps them become conscious of their own experiences. See also *productive skills*.

reciprocal teaching Reciprocal teaching is a dialogic, cooperative process of learning from literary text. Groups of four students discuss a section of text – this works particularly well around a full-page graphic novel panel or picturebook spread – and each student takes on a role (these are not absolutely fixed): oral summarizing, clarifying, predicting, and questioning or connecting. Gradually the students acquire strategies for how to learn from story. See also *deep reading*, *literary apprenticeship* and *teaching methodology*.

recto and verso In left-to-right reading, including English language books, the recto is the page on the right, and the verso is the page on the left. Title pages and chapter headings are nearly always placed on a recto page. See also *double-page spread* and *picturebook*.

register Register is a term that labels characteristics of language in particular communicative situations, for a particular purpose or in a specific social setting. Teachers talking to students in the classroom will typically use a different register from when they talk to their own children at home. See also *discourse genre* and *pragmatics*.

reimagining A reimagining is a retelling of a traditional story such as a fairy tale, but with a twist or new perspective. A reimagining can also be a transmedia story, that is, the transformation from one format or medium into another. Reimaginings are frequently from a monomodal text to a multimodal text, such as a graphic novel, a film, a television adaptation, a stage play or the artwork and retellings of fanfiction. See also *fanfiction*, *intertextuality* and *postmodern literature*.

repetition Repetition is the basis of all language and literature, just as it is the basis of music and all arts that rely on pattern. Repetition is also essential for first and second language acquisition. Repeated language patterns can add meaning, when each new iteration of a repeated element provides a new nuance, more depth, accumulated layers and shades of significance, reinforcing meaningful language acquisition. Language learning without meaningful repetition is unthinkable. See also *orality, rhetorical device, salience* and *stylistics*.

rhetorical device Rhetorical devices, or stylistic devices, are techniques that writers (and speakers) employ to convey meanings persuasively. Rhetorical devices can render an argument or perspective more compelling and can engage the reader by evoking an emotional response. See also *alliteration, anaphora, cacophony, metalinguistic awareness, onomatopoeia, orality, polysyndeton, repetition, rule of three, stylistics*.

role-on-the-wall Role-on-the-wall is a visual presentation best used to record the perspectives of different characters towards each other. Groups of two to three students choose a character then select a colour to represent their character. They draw the character's outline on a large poster, and fill it with information, such as thoughts, feelings, and key lines of their character, using pens of the same colour as the outline. When the outlines fully represent their character, the students swap posters and annotate the other role posters – using the colour of their own figure and writing from their figure's perspective – but on the outside of the other character outlines. Finally, the role posters are attached to the wall, for the annotations on the various characters may be further edited as more insights arise. See also *drama conventions*.

rule of three The rhetorical rule of three, or tricolon, is an inviting and catchy pattern that is ubiquitous in children's literature, poetry and oral literature as well as in advertising, political slogans and speeches. In creative writing, three words or phrases typically build to a crescendo, as in this example from *The Firework-Maker's Daughter* (Pullman 1995), 'She dragged herself on bleeding knees up and up, *until* every muscle hurt, *until* she had no breath left in her lungs, *until* she thought she was going to die; and still she went on.' See also *orality, rhetorical devices* and *stylistics*.

safe classroom climate Establishing a safe classroom climate means seeking to provide an environment where all learners feel safe and empowered to share their thoughts and feelings. Such a classroom is characterized by respect for diversity, for others' voices and an inclusive atmosphere for all. See also *differentiation, diversity, inclusivity, motivation* and *special educational needs*.

salience Salient language refers to language that is made noticeable in some way, for example through repetition, emphasis, or surprise, and therefore more readily acquired. Salience can also refer to prominence in multimodal texts – how a pictorial feature is made more striking in a graphic novel or picturebook, for example, affecting the response and interpretation. See also *repetition* and *rhetorical device*.

scaffolding Scaffolding refers to support for learners – often language learners – in the same way that builders need the support of a scaffold or platform when working on the facade of a house. The learning scaffold must be flexible and gradually dismantled when no longer needed, handing responsibility over to the learner.

Scaffolded learning is often a site for learning opportunities in everyday classroom discourse, typical of many classroom routines, but also used when sharing a literary text and students need comprehension support. See also *accommodation*, *child-directed speech*, *creative teacher talk*, *prosodic features*, *teachable moment* and *zone of proximal development*.

schema refreshing A schema refers to a mental structure or bundle of knowledge in memory which helps us recognize a situation we have met before by filling in default values. New experiences are assimilated to these mental representations or schemata, reinforcing our understandings. Literary texts are sometimes able to help the reader or beholder see a phenomenon from a completely fresh angle, defamiliarizing and opening the reader's eyes to new perspectives. This is known as schema refreshing. See also *artefact emotions*, *outcome emotions* and *perspective-taking*.

self-efficacy High self-efficacy supports the student in making the effort to complete a task, and the belief that persistence will lead to success. When students are given the confidence that they have the ability to succeed, their self-efficacy is reinforced, leading to continued exertion in the face of challenge. Achieving challenging goals will further build confidence and determination. See also *motivation* and *willingness to communicate*.

semiotic modes Semiotic modes of communication are meaning-making sign systems. A multimodal text makes use of two or more modes: the linguistic (written and spoken words), visual (moving and still images), auditory (prosodic features in spoken language, sound effects, silence and music), gestural (gestures, body language, facial expressions and movement) and spatial (physical spacing, position and proximity). See also *aural communication*, *differentiation*, *facial expression*, *multimodal text*, *multisensory learning*, *prosodic features* and *sound effects*.

sexual orientation This refers to an individual's enduring capacity for romantic, emotional, and physical attraction to a person or persons of a particular sex or gender identity. See also *LGBTQ+*.

single story See under *danger of a single story*.

skimming Skimming refers to brisk browsing through screen-based or print-based text. Used ever more frequently, skimming means rapid reading for gist or scanning of a page to spot key words or information. This custom does not lead to deep reading, grasping complexity, reflection and developing insight. See also *deep reading* and *literary apprenticeship*.

sociocultural dimension of language learning The sociocultural dimension of language learning includes interacting in the target language with others, listening to and responding to partners, taking turns, rehearsing in teams, researching and pooling information, collaborative writing and perspective-taking. See also *affective dimension of language learning*, *cognitive dimension of language learning*, *engagement with language*, *metacognition*, *perspective-taking* and *physiological dimension of language learning*.

sociocultural identities Our sociocultural identities, or cultural identities, are overlapping and complex. An individual's ethnicity group membership intersects with other sociocultural identities, for example gender, age, socio-economic class, religion, sexual orientation and mental/physical ability. See also *culture*, *cultural studies*, *intersectionality* and *interculturality*.

sound effects Sound effects are generated, often heightened sound used to emphasize and enhance the content of a performance in the classroom, in the theatre, in film, or in any media. Graphic novels silently recreate sound effects through onomatopoeia and sound lines that visually symbolize certain sounds. See also *choral speaking*, *graphic novels*, *panel*, *readers theatre* and *speech balloon*.

special educational needs Students have special educational needs (SEN) if they have a learning difficulty or disability that calls for special educational provision. A student with SEN or a disability may have difficulties with speaking, listening, reading and/or writing. They may also be challenged in their behaviour, concentration, or physical ability. See also *safe classroom climate*, *differentiation* and *diversity*.

speciesism Speciesism is an anthropocentric bias that values certain species over others, often according to whether animals are useful to humans or not. Speciesism allows for the exploitation of animal species by human beings by means of assuming superiority of the human species over nonhuman species. See also *anthropocentricism*, *critical pedagogy*, *ecocentrism* and *environmentalism*.

speculative fiction Speculative fiction is about seeing the world from new directions, with imaginative speculation on how things could have been in the past or may become in the future. It is an umbrella term that includes alternate history, utopia, dystopia, science fiction and fantasy. See also *dystopia* and *future studies*.

speech balloon The speech balloon, or speech bubble, is an important device for displaying the speech of characters in a graphic novel, or comics. The balloon has a tail, which points to a certain character, indicating that they are speaking. Speech balloons are often cloud shaped, but there are many variations on this. The convention for representing thought is a balloon with a tail of little bubbles leading to the character. See also *caption*, *gutter*, *panel* and *sound effects*.

stereotype Stereotypes are socially and culturally constructed. They represent unreflective attributing of certain characteristics to a whole group of people. As these characteristics are usually negative, the stereotyping can lead to serious discrimination against minoritized groups, including verbal and physical abuse, and even genocide. See also *danger of a single story*, *essentializing* and *ethnocentrism*.

storyworld Storyworld is a term in narratology that refers to a created fictional world. When the reader enters the world of the book both cognitively and imaginatively the response is dynamic and embodied. See also *deep reading*, *embodied simulation hypothesis* and *mental representation*.

stylistics A wide definition of style and stylistics embraces the study of linguistic expression and the description of its effect on the reader as well as the study of distinctive stylistic features of literary texts, including pictoral narrative and films (Michael Burke 2014). Stylistics explores how the discourse of a narrative presents the events and situations of a storyworld. See also *alliteration, anaphora, cacophony, onomatopoeia, orality, polysyndeton, repetition, rhetorical device* and *rule of three*.

subtext strategy This is a convention in drama teaching that encourages students to voice the thoughts of characters by freezing the action at pivotal moments. The subtext strategy can be profitably prepared using the iceberg task, with students writing down characters' key lines above the water line and thoughts below on an iceberg poster. When the scene is acted out, students freeze the action at critical moments and another student voices the thoughts of the character who was speaking. See also *drama conventions* and *iceberg task*.

task-based learning Task-based learning is similar to project learning in that the students must complete an authentic, real-world task, typically in small groups, and use the target language while fulfilling the task. The students focus on the task, not primarily on language learning. Moreover, assessment is based on successful completion of the task and not on language acquisition. See also *authenticity, content-based language teaching, motivation, teaching methodology* and *willingness to communicate*.

teachable moment This refers to seizing opportunities in classroom discourse to develop language or knowledge when relevant to a situation that arises spontaneously. In order to exploit teachable moments (Peterson and Eeds 2007), teachers need to be able to respond flexibly and creatively, but within students' zone of proximal development. See also *scaffolding* and *zone of proximal development*.

teacher-in-role Teacher-in-role is a drama convention that is used when the class is working on a scenario – a public meeting or a demonstration, for example – and the teacher takes on a role within the story. In this position, the teacher-in-role is able to steer the role-play in a fresh direction without interrupting, the teacher can supply new information to take the students further, can model language and extend the students' ideas, can pretend to need help to elicit more participation from the students and create renewed tension and dramatic energy. See also *drama conventions, holistic learning, scaffolding* and *zone of proximal development*.

teacher education Unlike teacher training, teacher education does not assume predictability in language learning, but rather prepares student teachers for the need to readjust and modify practices according to each unique classroom context. The operationalization of theory and its realization in terms of practical craft, dependent on reflective enquiry and each concrete learning environment, become the goal, not the pedagogical techniques themselves. See also *English subject pedagogy, teacher training* and *teaching methodology*.

teacher training Teacher training may refer to the school-based mentoring of student teachers in their teaching practice, or the in-service further development of teachers. The term 'teacher training', however, suggests the training of certain unchanging techniques or craft for language teachers. Thus, teacher training, as opposed to teacher education, may indicate that there are solutions for predictable, unchanging problems (Widdowson 1990). This is distinct from research-based teacher education and reflective inquiry for language teachers. See also *teacher education* and *teaching methodology*.

teaching methodology The methodology of teaching English to language learners is one aspect of language teacher education. Teaching methodology refers to the evidence-informed practical craft and pedagogical techniques for the execution of activities in language teaching, including areas such as interculturality and pragmatics. Teaching methodology is not fixed and unchanging but is dependent on the needs of the target learners and each concrete learning environment. See also *teacher education* and *teacher training*.

TESOL See under *ELT and TESOL*.

text A text is an artefact that is used for communication and carries meaning that is often open to interpretation. A wide definition of text includes all literary texts, but also maps, charts, pictures, plays, movies, advertisements, documentaries and so forth. See also *discourse genre*, *multimodal text* and *semiotic modes*.

textbook A textbook refers to a book gathering together comprehensive content with the intention of explaining and illustrating a certain branch of study. Textbooks are used extensively in education in print and digital format, both at school and for academic studies. See also *coursebook*.

text ensemble A text ensemble is a pedagogically designed collection of texts. In order to be true to the principle of multivoicedness, the text ensemble must include different epistemological positions, question often unquestioned perspectives, invite critical thinking and in this way resist closure. See also *#ownvoices* and *principle of multivoicedness*.

textual genre See under *discourse genre*.

theory of mind Theory of mind (ToM) refers to the understanding that others have beliefs, thoughts and feelings that are different from one's own. This does not mean an ability to read minds, but insight into other minds, and the ability to develop a *theory* of another person's mental state. See also *empathy* and *perspective-taking*.

think-pair-share The teacher initiates this strategy by asking a question and inviting the students to consider individually what they know or what their thoughts are on a topic. Next each student pairs with a partner to hear and share ideas. The students have time to think through their ideas and formulate their language before further sharing in a whole-class discussion. See also *affective filter*, *teaching methodology* and *willingness to communicate*.

thoughtful feelings Thoughtful feelings (Ratner 2000) are feelings that co-exist with thoughts and involve cognition. Emotions are modelled in well-crafted stories, which are then in the position to generate thoughtful feelings in the reader, listener and beholder. See also *embodied simulation hypothesis*, *empathy*, *interculturality*, *intrapersonal communication*, *perspective-taking*, *point of view* and *theory of mind*.

tolerance of ambiguity Tolerance of ambiguity in a language learner is a helpful characteristic for dealing constructively with difference, unfamiliarity and lack of certainty. Tolerance of ambiguity can allow the reader of a literary text to cope with uncertainty and different possible interpretations. Thus, it is critical to cultivate tolerance of ambiguity both for successful second language acquisition and for a successful literary apprenticeship. See also *critical thinking*, *indeterminacy* and *literary apprenticeship*.

ToM See under *theory of mind*.

total physical response (TPR) Total physical response (TPR) is the term used in language teaching that refers to situations when teachers provide language input, and the students respond with whole-body actions (Asher 1969). While the emphasis is on listening comprehension and meaning, for example when students respond to commands, or act out a story with body language, facial expression and movement, the input can also provide a focus on form. See also *drama conventions*, *focus on form*, *mime*, *physiological dimension of language learning* and *whoosh*.

transmedia stories See under *reimaginings*.

tricolon See under *rule of three*.

typographic creativity This refers to the playful use of typography, often used in picturebooks and increasingly in chapter books, which may intensify or add to the meaning of the printed words. Size variations and thickness of type can be used to signify importance, emotion or tone of voice. Alternating distinctive fonts may distinguish the words or thoughts of different characters, the words may dance off the horizontal lines and there may be a creative use of marks such as dots and asterisks. See also *chapter book*, *graphic novel* and *picturebook*.

verse novel Contemporary verse novels are narratives written mostly in free verse, that is without rhyme or regular metre. The rhythm and the arrangement on the page, frequently with short, titled poems, are important organizing principles. Evocative verses and semi-blank pages appeal to the reader's imagination. The verse novel is often a first-person narrative, with only one voice or persona, but the story may also be told through several voices. See also *format* and *persona*.

verso See under *recto and verso*.

visual literacy Visual literacy is the ability to derive meaning from, interpret and learn from information presented in images. A shift in emphasis from verbal text towards multimodal representation with a strong visual meaning-making component has led to an educational focus on visual literacy. The creation of multimodal presentations and the evaluation of presentations – such as recognizing a preoccupation with format instead of content in slideshows – are also concerns of visual literacy. See also *multiple literacy*, *critical literacy*, *digital literacy*, *functional literacy*, *information literacy*, *literacy*, *literary literacy* and *media literacy*.

We Need Diverse Books This is a nonprofit organization that was created in 2014 to promote diversity in children's literature and publishing. To reach this goal, the nonprofit We Need Diverse Books (https://diversebooks.org/about-wndb/) has created programmes to support and celebrate diversity in children's literature and to mentor authors and illustrators from diverse backgrounds, promoting the use of diverse books in schools. See also *#ownvoices*.

White saviour narrative The White saviour narrative, or script, was an extremely common trope in movies throughout the twentieth century and is still ongoing in the twenty-first century (Hughey 2014). This includes White protagonists having helpers who are persons of colour, and a White protagonist rescuing Black characters from difficulties or danger. See also *danger of a single story* and *#ownvoices*.

whoosh This drama convention can be used to familiarize students with the plot and characters of a story they are going to read. A whoosh (Joe Winston 2022) is both fun and very effective, as it introduces the main characters in a multisensory way. The students stand in a circle; the teacher invites individual learners into the circle, to improvise the characters she describes. The students use mime or improvise dialogue, depending on their age and self-confidence. Whenever certain characters should leave the scene, the teacher waves her arms and calls out 'whoosh' to that character. This stratagem can also send the entire class back to their places, for example, if chaos threatens to take over. See also *drama conventions, holistic learning* and *total physical response*.

willingness to communicate Willingness to communicate (WTC) is a concept that is connected to students' motivation, self-confidence and learning anxiety. Lowering the affective filter is key in attaining students' WTC. Strategies to achieve this include using differentiation and varying the activities, employing task-based learning, building on students' knowledge and out-of-school relevance. Using authentic materials and initiating pair work before large-group activities are important in supporting WTC. See also *affective filter, differentiation, experiential approach to learning, motivation, self-efficacy, task-based learning* and *think-pair-share*.

wordless picturebook A wordless picturebook (or picture book) is a book that is entirely created through pictures, or pictures and minimal text in the case of an almost wordless picturebook. The text can be on a complex topic, which readers infer and interpret through the illustrations. In the language learning class, amongst other activities, the reader may be asked to recreate the narrative or dialogue orally as well as in writing. See also *picturebook* and *visual literacy*.

worldmindedness Worldmindedness refers to global openness and the disposition to reflect on how our actions and decisions concern us not only locally but also affect all peoples around the world. See also *critical pedagogy, fan activism, global education, ideology* and *in-depth learning*.

xenophobia Xenophobia refers to fear of difference or otherness. The fear manifests as dislike or hatred of strangers, foreigners, persons from different cultural contexts and different ethnic backgrounds. See also *groupthink, group-focused enmity, ideology of inequality, ingroup, otherness and Other* and *outgroup*.

young adult fiction This refers to fiction that resonates particularly with readers from twelve to eighteen years of age, and the protagonists are usually in this age group. However, young adult fiction is often popular with older readers too. The themes are sometimes humorous and frequently thought-provoking, troubled and dark. Young adult fiction in language education contexts is often more suitable for high school/higher grades in secondary school. See also *fanfiction*.

young learners The expression 'young learners' usually refers to language learners up to the age of twelve, so not including adolescents (Bland 2015d). However, applied linguists working with adults in tertiary contexts sometimes use the term 'young learners' as applying to students in all school grades in compulsory education.

zone of proximal development (ZPD) The zone of proximal development (Vygotsky 1978) refers to the distance between a student's independent developmental level and the student's potential development with the support of an adult or interacting with more capable peers. In order to make use of learners' ZPD, the cognitive challenge and risk-taking supported by collaboration must remain in balance with the student's current level of skill. See also *partly determining context, reciprocal teaching, scaffolding, teachable moment* and *i + 1*.

zoomorphism In literature and art, zoomorphism refers to when humans are represented with animal-like features and the behaviour of humans is portrayed with the characteristics of non-human animals. See also *anthropomorphism*.

BIBLIOGRAPHY

12 Years a Slave (2013), [Film] Dir. Steve McQueen, USA: Fox Searchlight Pictures.
13th (2016), [Documentary] Dir. by Ava DuVernay, USA: Netflix. https://www.youtube.com/watch?v=krfcq5pF8u8 (accessed 20 June 2021).
Alexander, Kwame (2014), *The Crossover*, New York: Houghton Mifflin Harcourt.
Almond, David, illus. Dave McKean (2013), *Mouse Bird Snake Wolf*, Somerville, MA: Candlewick Press.
Almond, David (2014), *Klaus Vogel and the Bad Lads*, Edinburgh: Barrington Stoke.
Angelou, Maya (1993), On the Pulse of Morning. https://www.youtube.com/watch?v=59xGmHzxtZ4 (accessed 23 June 2021).
Applegate, Katherine (2007), *Home of the Brave*, New York: Square Fish.
Atypicle (2017), [Online streaming TV series] Created by Robia Rashid, USA: Netflix.
Baldacchino, Christine, illus. Isabelle Malenfant (2014), *Morris Micklewhite and the Tangerine Dress*, Toronto: Groundwood Books.
Barroux (2015), *Where's the Elephant?* London: Egmont.
Belle (2014), [Film] Dir. Amma Asante, UK: Fox Searchlight Pictures.
Bilston, Brian (2016), *You Took the Last Bus Home*, London: Unbound.
Bilston, Brian, illus. José Sanabria (2019), *Refugees*, London: Palazzo.
BlacKkKlansman (2018), [Film] Dir. Spike Lee, USA: Focus Features.
Bradbury, Ray (1952/1997), A Sound of Thunder, in R. Bradbury (ed.), *Golden Apples of the Sun and Other Stories*, 203–15, New York: HarperCollins.
Browne, Anthony (1992), *Zoo*, London: Random House.
Browne, Anthony (1998), *Voices in the Park*, London: Random House.
Bryant, Jen, illus. Boris Kulikov (2016), *Six Dots: A Story of Young Louis Braille*, NewYork: Alfred A. Knopf.
The Butler (2013), [Film] Dir. Lee Daniels, USA: The Weinstein Company.
A Call to Learning for Climate Education (2020), [Short film], Prod. Project Everyone. https://worldslargestlesson.globalgoals.org/resource/call-to-learning/ (accessed 7 June 2021).
Carle, Eric (2002), *'Slowly, Slowly, Slowly,' said the Sloth*, New York: Penguin Random House.
Clements, Andrew (1996), *Frindle*, New York: Atheneum Books for Young Readers.
Colfer, Eoin and Donkin, Andrew, illus. Giovanni Rigano (2017), *Illegal*, London: Hodder Children's Books.
Collins, Suzanne (2008), *The Hunger Games*, London: Scholastic.
Collins, Suzanne (2009), *Catching Fire*, London: Scholastic.
Collins, Suzanne (2010), *Mockingjay*, London: Scholastic.

Copp, Mary Wagley, illus. Munir D. Mohammed (2019), *Wherever I Go*, New York: Atheneum Books for Young Readers.
Davies, Nicola, illus. Rebecca Cobb (2018), *The Day War Came*, London: Walker Books.
Daywalt, Drew, illus. Oliver Jeffers (2013), *The Day the Crayons Quit*, London: HarperCollins.
DeRolf, Shane, illus. Michael Letzig (1997), *The Crayon Box That Talked*, New York: Random House.
Dieckmann, Sandra (2017), *Leaf*, London: Flying Eye Books.
Dragon Prince (2018), [Animated streaming TV series] Created by Aaron Ehasz and Justin Richmond, USA: Netflix.
Fandom Forward (2021), [Website] https://fandomforward.org/ (accessed 18 September 2021).
Frost, Helen (2006), *The Braid*, New York: Frances Foster.
Frost, Helen (2011), *Hidden*, New York: Square Fish.
Gaiman, Neil, illus. Chris Riddell (2014), *The Sleeper and the Spindle*, London: Bloomsbury.
Garland, Sarah (2012), *Azzi In Between*, London: Frances Lincoln.
George the Poet (2015), My Mandela, in *Search Party, The First Collection of Poetry*, 78–80, London: Virgin Books. https://www.youtube.com/watch?v=IHZ2L7um_9E (accessed 3 July 2021).
Greder, Armin (2007), *The Island*, Sydney: Allen & Unwin.
Greder, Armin (2020), *Diamonds*, Sydney: Allen & Unwin.
Green Book (2018), [Film] Dir. Peter Farrelly, USA: Universal Pictures.
Hate Crime (2017), [Short film] Performed by author George the Poet, created by Matthew Huntley, *Equality and Human Rights Commission*. https://www.youtube.com/watch?v=Y8ijWc8T0-4 (accessed 3 July 2021).
The Hate U Give (2018), [Film] Dir. George Tillman Jr., USA: 20th Century Fox.
The Help (2011), [Film] Dir. Tate Taylor, USA: Walt Disney Studios.
Heartstopper (2022), [Online streaming TV series] Dir. Euros Lyn, UK: See-Saw Films.
Hesse, Karen (2003), *Aleutian Sparrow*, New York: Aladdin Paperbacks.
The Hidden Impact of The Smartphone Industry (2021), [Short film] Created by Fairphone https://www.youtube.com/watch?v=QRi4srOjtSM (accessed 9 October 2021).
Home (2017), [Short film] Performed by author Warsan Shire, created by Garrett Mogge, Halle Voos, Haley Parsley and Abigail Pelton. https://www.youtube.com/watch?v=nI9D92Xiygo (accessed 13 July 2021).
Hughes, Ted (1968), *The Iron Man*, London: Faber and Faber.
Hugo (2011), [Film] Dir. Martin Scorsese, USA: Paramount Pictures.
The Hunger Games (2012), [Film] Dir. Gary Ross, USA: Lionsgate.
The Hunger Games: Catching Fire (2013), [Film] Dir. Francis Lawrence, USA: Lionsgate.
The Hunger Games: Mockingjay – Part 1 (2014), [Film] Dir. Francis Lawrence, USA: Lionsgate.
The Hunger Games: Mockingjay – Part 2 (2015), [Film] Dir. Francis Lawrence, USA: Lionsgate.
Khan, Rukhsana, illus. Christiane Krömer (2014), *King for a Day*, New York: Lee & Low Books.
Lai, Thanhha (2011), *Inside Out & Back Again*, New York: HarperCollins.

Lerwill, Ben, illus. Masha Ukhova, Stephanie Son, Chellie Carroll, Hannah Peck and Iratxe López de Munáin (2020), *Climate Rebels*, London: Puffin Books.
Lewis, Gill, illus. Jo Weaver (2017), *A Story Like the Wind*, Oxford: Oxford University Press.
The Life Cycle of A T-shirt (2017), [Animated short film] Written by Angel Chang, created by TED-Ed https://www.youtube.com/watch?v=BiSYoeqb_VY (accessed 9 October 2021).
Lindstrom, Carole, illus. Michaela Goade (2020), *We Are Water Protectors*, New York: Roaring Brook Press.
McGough, Roger, illus. Monks, Lydia (2004), *All the Best. The Selected Poems of Roger McGough*, London: Penguin Books.
McGowan, Anthony (2019), *Lark*, Edinburgh: Barrington Stoke.
Mangrove (2020), [Film] Dir. Steve McQueen, UK: BBC Studios.
Marley, Bob (2020), [Animated short film] *Redemption Song*. https://75.bobmarley.com/ (accessed 23 June 2021).
MC Grammar (2021), Song *Save the Planet*, created by Wonder Raps. https://www.youtube.com/watch?v=FreR7ZhqRQQ (accessed 30 October 2021).
Messner, Kate, illus. Matthew Forsythe (2018), *The Brilliant Deep*, San Francisco: Chronicle Books.
Mian, Zanib, illus. Nasaya Mafaridik (2019), *Planet Omar. Accidental Trouble Magnet*, London: Hodder Children's Books.
Milner, Kate (2017), *My Name Is Not Refugee*, Edinburgh: The Bucket List.
Morris, Jackie, illus. James Mayhew (2017), *Mrs Noah's Pockets*, Burley Gate: Otter-Barry Books.
Naidoo, Beverley (2001), The Playground, in B. Naidoo (ed.), *Out of Bounds. Stories of Conflict and Hope*, 120–44, London: Puffin.
Naidoo, Beverley (2006), The Playground, in C. J. Fourie (ed.), *New South African Plays*, 34–87, London: Aurora Metro Press.
Naylor-Ballesteros, Chris (2019), *The Suitcase*, London: Nosy Crow.
Orwell, George (1949), *Nineteen Eighty-Four*, Harmondsworth: Penguin Books.
Orwell, George, adapted and illus. Odyr (2019), *Animal Farm. The Graphic Novel*, London: Penguin Classics.
Oseman, Alice (2018–2021), *Heartstopper*, Vol. 1–4, UK: Hodder Children's Books.
Ouimet, David (2019), *I Go Quiet*, Edinburgh: Canongate Books.
Pattison, Darcy, illus. Joe Cepeda (2003), *The Journey of Oliver K. Woodman*, San Diego: Harcourt.
Porter, Pamela (2005), *The Crazy Man*, Toronto: Groundwood Books.
Prince Ea (2015), *Man vs Earth*. https://genius.com/Prince-ea-man-vs-earth-annotated (accessed 26 April 2021).
Pullman, Philip (1995), *The Firework-Maker's Daughter*, London: Corgi Yearling Books.
Pullman, Philip, illus. Peter Bailey (1996), *Clockwork*, London: Doubleday.
Pullman, Philip (2012), *Grimm Tales*, London: Penguin Books.
Rang-tan: The Story of Dirty Palm Oil (2018), [Animated short film] Dir. Salon Alpin, Greenpeace International. https://www.youtube.com/watch?v=TQQXstNh45g (accessed 19 May 2021).
Rowling, J. K. (2017), *Fantastic Beasts and Where to Find Them, Newt Scamander* (2nd edn), London: Bloomsbury.
Selma (2015), [Film] Dir. Ava DuVernay, USA: Paramount Pictures.
Selznick, Brian (2007), *The Invention of Hugo Cabret*, New York: Scholastic.

She-Ra and the Princesses of Power (2018), [Animated streaming TV series] Created by Noelle Stevenson, USA: Netflix.

Shire, Warsan (2015), [Poem] *Home*. https://www.facinghistory.org/standing-up-hatred-intolerance/warsan-shire-home (accessed 7 June 2021).

Sleeping Beauty (1959), [Animated film] Dir. Clyde Geronimi, USA: Walt Disney Productions.

The Social Dilemma (2020), [Documentary] Dir. Jeff Orlowski, USA: Netflix.

Taylor, James (2020), [Song] You've Got to Be Carefully Taught, in *American Standard*. https://www.youtube.com/watch?v=ehNu_rzzsRw (accessed 31 July 2021).

There's A Monster in My Kitchen (2020), [Animated short film] Dir. Fabian Erlinghauser and Tomm Moore, Greenpeace International. https://www.youtube.com/watch?v=8rIjVDo_u8c (accessed 19 May 2021).

Thorne, Jack (script), story by J. K. Rowling and John Tiffany (2016), *Harry Potter and the Cursed Child*, London: Little, Brown Book Group.

Three Seconds (2016), [Short film] Dir. Spencer Sharp, with Prince Ea and 'Man vs Earth', USA. https://www.youtube.com/watch?v=sacc_x-XB1Y (accessed 4 April 2021).

Thurber, James (1939), The Rabbits Who Caused All the Trouble, *The New Yorker*, 26 August.

Tucker, Zoë, illus. Zoe Pesico (2019), *Greta and the Giants*, London: Frances Lincoln.

Ululate:) (2012), [Short film] Created by Wambura Mitaru. https://www.youtube.com/watch?v=1fPGqEpLYuQ (accessed 20 October 2021).

Walker, David, illus. Damon Smyth and Marissa Louise (2018), *The Life of Frederick Douglass: A Graphic Narrative of a Slave's Journey from Bondage to Freedom*, California: Ten Speed Press.

What They Took with Them (2016), [Short film] Created by The UN Refugee Agency. https://www.youtube.com/watch?v=xS-Q2sgNjl8 (accessed 1 August 2021).

When They See Us (2019), [Online streaming TV miniseries] Created by Ava DuVernay, USA: Netflix.

Woodson, Jacqueline (2014), *Brown Girl Dreaming*, New York: Nancy Paulsen.

The World's Largest Lesson Animation (2020), [Animated short film] Written by Ken Robinson, created by Sarah Cox. https://worldslargestlesson.globalgoals.org/resource/malala-introducing-the-the-worlds-largest-lesson/ (accessed 7 June 2021).

Yousafzai, Malala, illus. Kerascoët (2017), *Malala's Magic Pencil*, London: Puffin Books.

REFERENCES

Aase, L., Fleming, M., Pieper, I. and Sâmihăian, F. (2007), Text, literature and *Bildung* – comparative perspectives, in I. Pieper (ed.), *Text, literature and Bildung*, 6–30, Strasbourg: Council of Europe.

Abednia, A. (2015), Practicing critical literacy in second language reading, *International Journal of Critical Pedagogy*, 6 (2): 77–94.

Adichie, C. N. (2009), The danger of a single story, *TED Talk*, 7 October. https://www.ted.com/talks/chimamanda_ngozi_adichie_the_danger_of_a_single_story?language=en (accessed 2 March 2021).

Agnew, K. (2001), Chapter books, in V. Watson (ed.), *The Cambridge Guide to Children's Books in English*, 139, Cambridge: Cambridge University Press.

Aitchison, J. (1994), 'Say, say it again Sam': The treatment of repetition in linguistics, in A. Fischer (ed.), *Repetition*, 15–34, Tübingen: Narr.

Alam, S. (2008), Majority world: Challenging the west's rhetoric of democracy, *Amerasia Journal*, 34 (1): 88–98.

Alasmari, N. and Alshae'el, A. (2020), The effect of using drama in English language learning among young learners: A case study of 6th grade female pupils in Sakaka City, *International Journal of Education and Literacy Studies*, 8 (1): 61–73.

Aleixo, P. and Norris, C. (2010), The comic book textbook, *Education and Health*, 28 (4): 72–4.

Alexander, J. (2005), The verse-novel: A new genre, *Children's Literature in Education*, 36 (3): 269–83.

Alexander, J. (2010), The affordances of orality for young people's experience of poetry, in M. Styles, L. Joyl and D. Whitley (eds), *Poetry and Childhood*, 211–18, Stoke on Trent: Trentham Books.

Alfes, L., Guttke, J., Lipari, A. C. and Wilden, E. (2021), 'Who controls the past controls the future': Benefits and challenges of teaching young adult dystopian fiction, *Children's Literature in English Language Education*, 9 (1): 12–31.

Almond, D. (2010), Acceptance speech by David Almond: 2010 Hans Christian Andersen Author Award winner, *IBBY*. https://www.ibby.org/subnavigation/archives/ibby-congresses/congress-2010/detailed-programme-and-speeches/david-almond (accessed 19 September 2021).

Arizpe, E., Farrar, J. and McAdam, J. (2017), Picturebooks and literacy studies, in B. Kümmerling-Meibauer (ed.), *The Routledge Companion to Picturebooks*, 371–80, Abingdon: Routledge.

Arizpe, E. and Ryan, S. (2018), The wordless picturebook: Literacy in multilingual contexts and David Wiesner's worlds, in J. Bland (ed.), *Using Literature in English Language Education*, 63–81, London: Bloomsbury Academic.

Asher, J. (1969), The total physical response approach to second language learning, *The Modern Language Journal*, 53 (1): 3–17.

Attridge, D. (1995), *Poetic Rhythm: An Introduction*, Cambridge: Cambridge University Press.

Bakhtin, M. M. (1990), *Art and answerability. Early philosophical essays*, M. Holquist and V. Liapunov (eds), Austin: University of Texas Press.

Ball, P. (2011), *The Music Instinct: How Music Works and Why We Can't Do without It*, London: Vintage.

Baron, N. S. (2015), *Words Onscreen: The Fate of Reading in a Digital World*, Oxford: Oxford University Press.

Barthes, R. (1989), The death of the author, in P. Waugh and P. Rice (eds), *Modern Literary Theory, A Reader*, 114–18, New York: Bloomsbury.

Bassnett, S. and Grundy, P. (1993), *Language through Literature*, London: Longman.

Bear, A. and Agner, R. (2021), Why more countries need female leaders, *U.S.News*, 8 March. https://www.usnews.com/news/best-countries/articles/2021-03-08/why-countries-with-female-leaders-have-responded-well-to-the-pandemic (accessed 23 March 2021).

Bergen, B. (2012), *Louder Than Words: The New Science of How the Mind Makes Meaning*, New York: Basic Books.

Bernstein, R. (2009), Dances with things: Material culture and the performance of race, *Social Text*, 27 (4): 67–94.

Bertoldi, E. and Bortoluzzi, M. (2019), *Let's Tell a Tale: Storytelling with Children in English L2*, Udine: Forum, Università degli Studi di Udine.

Betancourt, D. (2019), The voice behind some of the top black superheroes in comics is now writing about Frederick Douglass, *The Washington Post*, 15 January. https://www.washingtonpost.com/arts-entertainment/2019/01/15/voice-behind-some-top-black-superheroes-comics-is-now-writing-about-frederick-douglass/ (accessed 11 February 2021).

Bhroin, C. N. and Kennon, P., eds (2012), *What Do We Tell the Children? Critical Essays on Children's Literature*, Newcastle upon Tyne: Cambridge Scholars.

Bigelow, M. (2019) (Re)considering the role of emotion in language teaching and learning, *Modern Language Journal*, 103 (2): 515–16.

Bishop, R. S. (1990), Mirrors, windows, and sliding glass doors, *Perspectives: Choosing and Using Books for the Classroom*, 6 (3): ix–xi.

Bland, J. (2013), *Children's Literature and Learner Empowerment. Children and Teenagers in English Language Education*, London: Bloomsbury Academic.

Bland, J. (2014), Interactive theatre with student teachers and young learners: Enhancing EFL learning across institutional divisions in Germany, in S. Rich (ed.), *International Perspectives on Teaching English to Young Learners*, 156–74, Basingstoke: Palgrave Macmillan.

Bland, J. (2015a), Drama with young learners, in J. Bland (ed.), *Teaching English to Young Learners. Critical Issues in Language Teaching with 3–12 Year Olds*, 219–38, London: Bloomsbury Academic.

Bland, J. (2015b), Grammar templates for the future with poetry for children, in J. Bland (ed.), *Teaching English to Young Learners*, 147–66, London: Bloomsbury Academic.

Bland, J. (2015c), Oral storytelling in the primary English classroom, in J. Bland (ed.), *Teaching English to Young Learners*, 183–98, London: Bloomsbury Academic.

Bland, J. (ed.) (2015d), *Teaching English to Young Learners. Critical Issues in Language Teaching with 3–12 Year Olds*, London: Bloomsbury Academic.

Bland, J. (2016), English language education and ideological issues: Picturebooks and diversity, *Children's Literature in English Language Education*, 4 (2): 41–64.

Bland, J. (2018a), Annotated bibliography: Literary texts recommended for children and young adults in ELT, in J. Bland (ed.), *Using Literature in English Language Education: Challenging Reading for 8–18 Year Olds*, 277–300, London: Bloomsbury Academic.

Bland, J. (2018b), Introduction: The challenge of literature, in J. Bland (ed.), *Using Literature in English Language Education: Challenging Reading for 8–18 Year Olds*, 1–22, London: Bloomsbury Academic.

Bland, J. (2019), Teaching English to young learners: More teacher education and more children's literature!, *Children's Literature in English Language Education*, 7 (2): 79–103. https://clelejournal.org/article-4-teaching-english-young-learners/ (accessed 31 January 2021).

Bland, J. (2022), Picturebooks that challenge the young English language learner, in Å. M. Ommundsen, G. Haaland and B. Kümmerling-meibauer (eds), *Exploring Challenging Picturebooks in Education: International Perspectives on Language and Literature Learning*, 122–42, London: Routledge.

Bland, J. and Strotmann, A. (2014), The Hunger Games trilogy: An ecocritical reading, *Children's Literature in English Language Education*, 2 (1): 22–43.

Bobkina, J. and Stefanova, S. (2016), Literature and critical literacy pedagogy in the EFL classroom, *Studies in Second Language Learning and Teaching*, 6 (4): 677–96.

Bomer, R. (2010), Orality, literacy, and culture: Talk, text, and tools in ideological contexts, in D. Wyse, R. Andrews and J. Hoffman (eds), *The Routledge International Handbook of English, Language and Literacy Teaching*, 205–15, Abingdon: Routledge.

Bordwell, D. and Thompson, K. (2001), *Film Art: An Introduction*, 6th edn, New York: McGraw-Hill.

Botelho, M. J. (2021), Reframing mirrors, windows, and doors: A critical analysis of the metaphors for multicultural children's literature, *Journal of Children's Literature*, 47 (1): 119–26.

Boyd, B. (2009), *On the Origin of Stories: Evolution, Cognition, and Fiction*, Harvard: Harvard University Press.

Boyd, B. (2018), The evolution of stories: From mimesis to language, from fact to fiction, *WIREs Cognitive Science*, 9 (1): 1–16.

Bradford, C. (2010), Whiteness, in D. Rudd (ed.), *The Routledge Companion to Children's Literature*, 254–5, Abingdon: Routledge.

Bransford, J. D., Brown, A. and Cocking, R., eds (1999), *How People Learn: Brain, Mind, Experience, and School*, Washington, DC: National Academy Press.

Bredella, L. (2013), Literary texts, in M. Byram and A. Hu (eds), *Routledge Encyclopedia of Language Teaching and Learning*, 2nd edn, 431–7, London: Routledge.

Breunig, M. (2005), Turning experiential education and critical pedagogy theory into praxis, *Journal of Experiential Education*, 28 (2): 106–22.

Brevik, L. (2016), The gaming outliers. Does out-of-school gaming improve boys' reading skills in English as a second language? in E. Elstad (ed.), *Educational Technology and Polycontextual Bridging*, 39–61, Rotterdam: Sense Publishers.

Brevik, L. and Rindal, U. (2020), Language use in the classroom: Balancing target language exposure with the need for other languages, *Tesol Quarterly*, 54 (4): 925–53.

Brown, C. W. and Habegger-Conti, J. (2017), Visual representations of indigenous cultures in Norwegian EFL textbooks, *Nordic Journal of Modern Language Methodology*, 5 (1): 16–34.

Brown, S., Berry, M., Dawes, E., Hughes, A. and Tu, C. (2019), Character mediation of story generation via protagonist insertion, *Journal of Cognitive Psychology*, 31 (1): 326–42

Buell, L. (1995), *The Environmental Imagination*, Cambridge, MA: Harvard University Press.

Burke, B. (2014), 'Reaping' environmental justice through compassion in The Hunger Games. *ISLE: Interdisciplinary Studies in Literature and Environment*, 22 (3): 544–67.

Burke, M. (ed.) (2014), *The Routledge Handbook of Stylistics*, Abingdon: Routledge.

Burmark, L. (2008), Visual literacy: What you get is what you see, in N. Frey and D. Fisher (eds), *Teaching Visual Literacy Using Comic Books, Graphic Novels, Anime, Cartoons, and More to Develop Comprehension and Thinking Skills*, 5–25, Thousand Oaks, CA: Corwin Press.

Byatt, A. S. (2004), Happy ever after, *The Guardian*, 3 January. http://www.theguardian.com/books/2004/jan/03/sciencefictionfantasyandhorror.fiction (accessed 9 March 2021).

Byram, M. (2020), Assessment of intercultural competence and intercultural communicative competence, in M. Dypedahl and R. Lund (eds), *Teaching and Learning English Interculturally*, 164–85, Oslo: Cappelen Damm Akademisk.

Byram, M., Gribkova B. and Starkey, H. (2002), *Developing the Intercultural Dimension in Language Teaching*, Strasbourg: Council of Europe.

Cadden, M. (2011), The verse novel and the question of genre, *The ALAN Review*, 21–7. https://scholar.lib.vt.edu/ejournals/ALAN/v39n1/pdf/cadden.pdf (accessed 19 July 2021).

Cameron, L. (2003), Challenges for ELT from the expansion in teaching children, *ELT Journal*, 57 (2): 105–12.

Canagarajah, S. (1999), *Resisting Linguistic Imperialism in English Teaching*, Oxford: Oxford University Press.

Candlin, C. (2014), General editor's preface, in V. Kohonen, R. Jaatinen, P. Kaikkonen and J. Lehtovaara (eds), *Experiential Learning in Foreign Language Education*, xi–xvii, London: Routledge.

Carr, N. (2020), The Shallows: What the Internet Is Doing to Our Brains, updated edn, New York: Norton.

Carroll, J. (2017), Literary meaning: An evolutionary perspective, in *Literary Universals Project*, University of Connecticut. https://literary-universals.uconn.edu/2017/02/09/literary-meaning-and-universals/ (accessed 4 March 2021).

Carroll, J. (2018), Evolutionary literary theory, in D. H. Richter (ed.), *A Companion to Literary Theory*, 423–38, Hoboken, NJ: Wiley.

Carter, R. (2015), Epilogue: Literature and language learning in the EFL classroom, in M. Teranishi, Y. Saito and K. Wales (eds), *Literature and Language Learning in the EFL Classroom*, 316–20, Basingstoke: Palgrave Macmillan.

Cates, K. (2013), Global education, in M. Byram and A. Hu (eds), *Routledge Encyclopedia of Language Teaching and Learning*, 2nd edn, 277–80, London: Routledge.

Celik, B. (2019), The role of drama in foreign language teaching, *International Journal of Social Sciences & Educational Studies*, 5 (4): 112–25.

Chambers, A. (2011), *Tell Me, with the Reading Environment*, Stroud: The Thimble Press.

Chang, A. and Millett, S. (2017), Narrow reading: Effects on EFL learners' reading speed, comprehension, and perceptions, *Reading in a Foreign Language*, 29 (1): 1–19. https://eric.ed.gov/?id=EJ1137890 (accessed 9 March 2021).

Chang, S. L.-Y. (2009), *Acting It Out: Children Learning English through Story-based Drama*, PhD thesis, University of Warwick. http://wrap.warwick.ac.uk/3128/ (accessed 22 October 2021).

Chomsky, N. (1988), The view beyond: Prospects for the study of mind, in N. Chomsky (ed.), *Language and Problems of Knowledge. The Managua Lectures*, 133–70, Cambridge, MA: MIT Press.

Christensen, L. (2009), *Teaching for Joy and Justice: Re-imagining the Language Arts in the Classroom*, Milwaukee, WI: Rethinking Schools.

Chute, H. (2019), The graphic novel versions of literary classics used to seem lowbrow. No more, *The New York Times*, 12 November. https://www.nytimes.com/2019/11/12/books/review/the-iliad-a-graphic-novel-adaptation-gareth-hinds.html?searchResultPosition=1 (accessed 11 February 2021).

Clement, J. and Long, C. (2012), *Hugo, Remediation, and the Cinema of Attractions, or, the Adaptation of Hugo Cabret, Senses of Cinema*, 63. https://www.sensesofcinema.com/2012/feature-articles/hugo-remediation-and-the-cinema-of-attractions-or-the-adaptation-of-hugo-cabret/ (accessed 1 July 2021).

Coltheart, M. (2005), Modeling reading: The dual route approach, in M. J. Snowling and C. Hulme (eds), *The Science of Reading: A Handbook*, 6–23, Oxford: Blackwell.

Cook, G. (2000), *Language Play, Language Learning*, Oxford: Oxford University Press.

Cook, V. and D. Singleton, eds (2014), *Key Topics in Second Language Acquisition*, Clevedon: Multilingual Matters.

Connors, S. (2014), 'I try to remember who I am and who I am not': The subjugation of nature and women in *The Hunger Games*, in S. Connors (ed.), *The Politics of Panem: Challenging Genres*, 137–56, Rotterdam: Sense.

Council of Europe (2018a), *Reference Framework of Competences for Democratic Culture: Competences for Democratic Culture and the Importance of Language*. 1680a217cc (coe.int) (accessed 15 February 2022).

Council of Europe (2018b), *Reference Framework of Competences for Democratic Culture: Volume 1 Context, Concepts and Model*. https://www.coe.int/en/web/reference-framework-of-competences-for-democratic-culture/rfcdc#Volume1 (accessed 21 February 2021).

Coutts-Smith, K. (1991), Some general observations on the problem of cultural colonialism, in S. Hiller (ed.), *The Myth of Primitivism*, 5–18, London: Routledge.

Crawford, L. and McLaren, P. (2003), A critical perspective on culture in the second language classroom, in D. Lange and M. Paige (eds), *Culture as the Core: Perspectives on Culture in Second Language Learning*, 127–57, Greenwich, CT: Information Age Publishing.

Cron, L. (2012), *Wired for Story*, Berkeley: Ten Speed Press.

Crookes, G. and Schmidt, R. (1991), Motivation: Reopening the research agenda, *Language Learning*, 41 (4): 469–512.

Crystal, D. (1998), *Language Play*, London: Penguin Books.

Cummins, J. (2014), Foreword, in C. Hélot, R. Sneddon and N. Daly (eds), *Children's Literature in Multilingual Classrooms*, 1–7, London: Institute of Education Press.

Currie, M. (2011), *Postmodern Narrative Theory*, 2nd edn, London: Macmillan.

Damasio, A. (1999), *The Feeling of What Happens: Body and Emotion in the Making of Consciousness*, New York: Harcourt.

Davies, N. (2016), The day the war came – A poem about unaccompanied child refugees, *The Guardian*, 28 April. https://www.theguardian.com/childrens-books-site/2016/apr/28/the-day-the-war-came-poem-about-unaccompanied-child-refugees (accessed 8 July 2021).

Day, R. and Bamford, J. (2002), Top ten principles for teaching extensive reading, *Reading in a Foreign Language*, 14 (2): 136–41. http://www.nflrc.hawaii.edu/rfl/October2002/day/day.html (accessed 23 January 2021).

Deacon, S. H., Mimeau, C., Chung, S. C. and Chen, X. (2019), Young readers' skill in learning spellings and meanings of words during independent reading, *Journal of Experimental Child Psychology*, 181: 56–74.

Deardorff, D. K. (2006), Identification and assessment of intercultural competence as a student outcome of internationalization, *Journal of Studies in International Education*, 10 (3): 241–66.

Decke-Cornill, H. (2007), Literaturdidaktik in einer 'Pädagogik der Anerkennung': Gender and other suspects, in W. Hallet and A. Nünning (eds), *Neue Ansätze und Konzepte der Literatur- und Kulturdidaktik*, 239–58, Trier: WVT Wissenschaftlicher Verlag Trier.

Delanoy, W. (2018), Literature in language education: Challenges for theory building, in J. Bland (ed.), *Using Literature in English Language Education: Challenging Reading for 8–18 Year Olds*, 141–57, London: Bloomsbury Academic.

Dervin, F. (2010), Assessing intercultural competence in language learning and teaching: A critical review of current efforts, in F. Dervin and E. Suomela-Salmi (eds), *New Approaches to Assessing Language and (Inter-)Cultural Competences in Higher Education*, 157–74, Frankfurt am Main: Peter Lang.

Dervin, F. (2017a), *Critical Interculturality*, Newcastle upon Tyne: Cambridge Scholars Publishing.

Dervin, F. (2017b), Critical turns in language and intercultural communication pedagogy: The simple-complex continuum (*simplexity*) as a new perspective, in M. Dasli and A. R. Diaz (eds), *The Critical Turn in Language and Intercultural Communication Pedagogy: Theory, Research and Practice*, 58–72, New York: Routledge.

Dervin, F. (2017c), Human rights education and intercultural education, in J. Zajda and S. Ozdowski (eds), *Globalisation, Human Rights Education and Reforms*, 239–49, Dordrecht: Springer.

Deszcz-Tryhubczak, J. and Jaques, Z. (2021), Towards intergenerational solidarity in children's literature and film, in J. Deszcz-Tryhubczak and Z. Jaques (eds), *Intergenerational Solidarity in Children's Literature and Film*, xi–xxvii, Jackson: University Press of Mississippi.

Dietz, G. (2018), Interculturality, in H. Callan (ed.), *The International Encyclopedia of Anthropology*, 1–9, Hoboken, NJ: Wiley.

Dolan, J. (2013), *The Feminist Spectator in Action: Feminist Criticism for the Stage and Screen*, Basingstoke: Palgrave Macmillan.

Dörnyei, Z. (2007), Creating a motivating classroom environment, in J. Cummins and C. Davidson (eds), *International Handbook of English Language Teaching* (Vol. 2), 719–31, New York: Springer.

Dubrofsky, R. and Ryalls, E. (2014), *The Hunger Games*: Performing not-performing to authenticate femininity and whiteness, *Critical Studies in Media Communication*, 31 (5): 395–409.

Duncan, S. and Paran, A. (2018), Negotiating the challenges of reading literature: Teachers reporting on their practice, in J. Bland (ed.), *Using Literature in English Language Education*, 243–59, London: Bloomsbury Academic.

Dylman, A. S. and Bjärtå, A. (2018), When your heart is in your mouth: The effect of second language use on negative emotions, *Cognition and Emotion*, 33 (6): 1284–90. https://www.tandfonline.com/doi/full/10.1080/02699931.2018.1540403 (accessed 5 July 2021).

Egan, K. (1986), *Teaching as Story Telling: An Alternative Approach to Teaching and Curriculum in the Elementary School*, Chicago: University of Chicago Press.

EHRC (2017), George the Poet and the commission team upon hate crime film, *Equality and Human Rights Commission*, 16 June. https://www.equalityhumanrights.com/en/our-work/news/george-poet-and-commission-team-hate-crime-film (accessed 3 July 2021).

Eitel, A. and Scheiter, K. (2015), Picture or text first? Explaining sequence effects when learning with pictures and text, *Educational Psychology Review*, 27 (1): 153–80.

Elliott, A. (2021), *Reinvention*, 2nd edn, London: Routledge.

Ellis, G. (2018), The picturebook in elementary ELT: Multiple literacies with Bob Staake's Bluebird, in J. Bland (ed.), *Using Literature in English Language Education*, 83–104, London: Bloomsbury Academic.

Ellis, G. and Ibrahim, N. (2015), *Teaching Children How to Learn*, Peaslake: Delta Publishing.

Ellis, N. (2012), Formulaic language and second language acquisition: Zipf and the phrasal teddy bear, *Annual Review of Applied Linguistics*, 32: 17–44.

Ellis, N. (2017), Usage-based approaches to language, language acquisition, and language processing. Plenary, 12 July at *The 14th International Cognitive Linguistics Conference: Linguistic Diversity and Cognitive Linguistics*, Estonia. [Video]. UTTV. https://www.uttv.ee/naita?id=25911&keel=eng

Ellis, N. and Larsen-Freeman, D. (2009), Constructing a second language: Analyses and computational simulations of the emergence of linguistic constructions from usage, in N. Ellis and D. Larsen-Freeman (eds), *Language as a Complex Adaptive System*, Special issue of *Language Learning*: 59.

Ellis, N., O'Donnell, M. and Römer, U. (2013), Usage-based language: Investigating the latent structures that underpin acquisition, *Language Learning*, 63 (Supp. 1): 25–51.

Ellis, R. (1997), *Second Language Acquisition*, Oxford: Oxford University Press.
ELT Footprint (2019), [Website] https://eltfootprint.org/ (accessed 9 October 2021).
Enever, J. (2015), The advantages and disadvantages of English as a foreign language with young learners, in J. Bland (ed.), *Teaching English to Young Learners: Critical Issues in Language Teaching with 3–12 Year Olds*, 13–29, London: Bloomsbury Academic.
Fenner, A.-B. (2012), Promoting intercultural competence and *Bildung* through foreign language textbooks, in M. Eisenmann and T. Summer (eds), *Basic Issues in EFL Teaching and Learning*, 371–84, Heidelberg: Winter Verlag.
Fleming, M. (2001), *Teaching Drama in Primary and Secondary Schools*, London: David Fulton Publishers.
Fleming, M. (2007), The literary canon: Implications for the teaching of language as subject, in I. Pieper (ed.), *Text, Literature and Bildung*, 31–8, Strasbourg: Council of Europe.
Fleming, M. (2013), Drama, in M. Byram and A. Hu (eds), *Routledge Encyclopedia of Language Teaching and Learning*, 2nd edn, 209–11, London: Routledge.
Fleming, M. and Schofer, P. (2013), Literary theory and literature teaching, in M. Byram and A. Hu (eds), *Routledge Encyclopedia of Language Teaching and Learning*, 2nd edn, 443–9, London: Routledge.
Foster, J. (2010), From Mickey Mouse to Maus: The comic book is dead; Long live the graphic novel! *IBBY*. https://www.ibby.org/index.php?id=1045 (accessed 11 May 2021).
Freebody, K. and Finneran, M. (2013), Drama and social justice: Power, participation and possibility, in M. Anderson and J. Dunn (eds), *How Drama Activates Learning*, 47–63, London: Bloomsbury.
Freire, P. (1985), Reading the world and reading the word: An interview with Paulo Freire, *Language Arts*, 62 (1): 15–21.
Freire, P. (2014), *Pedagogy of the Oppressed*, 30th anniversary edn, New York: Bloomsbury.
Fullan, M., Gardner, M. and Drummy, M. (2019), Going deeper, *Educational Leadership*, 76 (8): 65–9.
Gaiman, N. (2013), Neil Gaiman: Why our future depends on libraries, reading and daydreaming, *The Guardian*, 15 October. https://www.theguardian.com/books/2013/oct/15/neil-gaiman-future-libraries-reading-daydreaming (accessed 9 May 2021).
García-González, M., Véliz, S. and Matus, C. (2020), Think difference differently? Knowing/becoming/doing with picturebooks, *Pedagogy, Culture & Society*, 28 (4): 543–62.
Gardner, H. (2006), *Five Minds for the Future*, Boston, MA: Harvard Business School.
Garibay, J. C. (2015), *Creating a Positive Classroom Climate for Diversity*, Los Angeles: UCLA. https://equity.ucla.edu/know/inclusion-strategies/ (accessed 6 March 2021).
Garrard, G. (2012), *Ecocriticism*, London: Routledge.
Gay, G. (2010), *Culturally Responsive Teaching: Theory, Practice, & Research*, 2nd edn, New York: Teachers College Press.
Gazibara, S. (2013), 'Head, heart and hands learning' – A challenge for contemporary education, *Journal of Education Culture and Society*, 1: 71–82.

Gee, J. P. (2001), Reading as situated language: A sociocognitive perspective, *Journal of Adolescent & Adult Literacy*, 44 (8): 714–25.

Gee, J. P. (2018), Affinity spaces: How young people live and learn online and out of school, *Phi Delta Kappan*, 99 (6): 8–13. https://kappanonline.org/gee-affinity-spaces-young-people-live-learn-online-school/ (accessed 23 January 2021).

Genette, G. (1997), *Paratexts: Thresholds of Interpretation*, translated J. E. Lewin, Cambridge: The University of Cambridge.

Global Witness (2006), *The Truth about Diamonds*, London: Global Witness Publishing https://www.globalwitness.org/en/archive/truth-about-diamonds/ (accessed 1 August 2021).

Goatly, A. (2004), Corpus linguistics, systemic functional grammar and literary meaning: A critical analysis of *Harry Potter and the Philosopher's Stone*, *A Journal of English Language, Literature in English and Cultural Studies*, 46: 115–54.

Gordon, J. (2019), In review – I go quiet, *downthetubes.net*, 24 October. https://downthetubes.net/?p=111910 (accessed 29 July 2021).

Gottschall, J. (2012), *The Storytelling Animal. How Stories Make Us Human*, New York: Houghton Mifflin Harcourt.

Grabe, W. (2009), *Reading in a Second Language. Moving from Theory to Practice*, Cambridge: Cambridge University Press.

Graham, J. (2005), Reading contemporary picturebooks, in K. Reynolds (ed.), *Modern Children's Literature*, 209–26, Basingstoke: Palgrave Macmillan.

Gray, J. (2002), The global coursebook in English language teaching, in D. Block and D. Cameron (eds), *Globalization and Language Teaching*, 151–68, London: Routledge.

Gray, J. (2016), ELT materials: Claims, critiques and controversies, in G. Hall (ed.), *The Routledge Handbook of English Language Teaching*, 95–108, Abingdon: Routledge.

Guilherme, M. (2019), The critical and decolonial quest for intercultural epistemologies and discourses, *Journal of Multicultural Discourses*, 14 (1): 1–13. https://www.tandfonline.com/doi/full/10.1080/17447143.2019.1617294 (accessed 5 March 2021).

Habegger-Conti, J. (2021), 'Where am I in the text?' Standing with refugees in graphic narratives, *Children's Literature in English Language Education*, 9 (2): 52–66.

Hall, G. (2015), Recent developments in uses of literature in language teaching, in M. Teranishi, Y. Saito and K. Wales (eds), *Literature and Language Learning in the EFL Classroom*, 13–25, Basingstoke: Palgrave Macmillan.

Hall, G. (2016), Using literature in ELT, in G. Hall (ed.), *The Routledge Handbook of English Language Teaching*, 456–69, Abingdon: Routledge.

Hall, G. (2018), Literature and the English language, in P. Seargeant, A. Hewings and S. Pihlaja (eds), *The Routledge Handbook of English Language Studies*, 265–79, Abingdon: Routledge.

Hamilton, D. (1999), The pedagogic paradox (or why no didactics in England?), *Pedagogy, Culture and Society*, 7 (1): 135–52.

Harmgarth, F. (1999), *Das Lesebarometer – Lesen und Umgang mit Büchern in Deutschland*, Gütersloh: Bertelsmann Stiftung.

Hayles, K. (2007), Hyper and deep attention: The generational divide in cognitive modes, *Profession 2007*: 187–99.

Heathfield, D. (2014), *Storytelling with Our Students*, Bournemouth: Delta Publishing.

Heggernes, S. L. (2019), Opening a dialogic space: Intercultural learning through picturebooks, *Children's Literature in English Language Education*, 7 (2): 37–60.
Heggernes, S. L. (2022), Intercultural learning through Peter Sís' The Wall: Teenagers reading a challenging picturebook, in Å. M. Ommundsen, G. Haaland and B. Kümmerling-meibauer (eds), *Exploring Challenging Picturebooks in Education: International Perspectives on Language and Literature Learning*, 163–82, London: Routledge.
Heider, F. and Simmel, M. (1944), An experimental study of apparent behavior, *The American Journal of Psychology*, 57 (2): 243–59.
Herman, D. (2005), Storyworld, in D. Herman, M. Jahn and M.-L. Ryan (eds), *Routledge Encyclopedia of Narrative Theory*, 569–70, Oxford: Routledge.
Hogan, P. C. (2014), Stylistics, emotion and neuroscience, in M. Burke (ed.), *The Routledge Handbook of Stylistics*, 516–30, Abingdon: Routledge.
Holley, L. and Steiner, S. (2005), Safe space: Student perspectives on classroom environment, *Journal of Social Work Education*, 41 (1): 49–64.
Holliday, A. (1994), The house of TESEP and the communicative approach: The special needs of state English language education, *ELT Journal*, 48 (1): 3–11.
Holliday, A. (2015), Native-speakerism: Taking the concept forward and achieving cultural belief, in A. Swan, P. Aboshiha and A. Holliday (eds), *(En)Countering Native-speakerism: Global Perspectives*, 11–25, Basingstoke: Palgrave Macmillan.
Hollindale, P. (1988), Ideology and the children's book, *Signal*, 55 (1): 3–22.
Hughey, M. (2014), *The White Savior Film: Content, Critics, and Consumption*, Philadelphia: Temple University Press.
Hunt, P. (2001), *Children's Literature*, Oxford: Blackwell.
Hunt, P. (2014), The classic and the Canon in children's literature, in C. Butler and K. Reynolds (eds), *Modern Children's Literature*, 2nd edn, 9–23, London: Palgrave Macmillan.
Hunt, P. (2018), Foreword, in J. Bland (ed.), *Using Literature in English Language Education: Challenging Reading for 8–18 Year Olds*, xi–xiv, London: Bloomsbury Academic.
Hutcheon, L. A (2012), *Theory of Adaptation*, 2nd edn, New York: Taylor & Francis.
Iacoboni, M. (2009), *Mirroring People: The Science of Empathy and How We Connect with Others*, New York: Farrar, Straus and Giroux.
Iacozza, S., Costa, A. and Duñabeitia, J. A. (2017), What do your eyes reveal about your foreign language? Reading emotional sentences in a native and foreign language, *PLoS ONE*, 12 (10): 1–10. https://journals.plos.org/plosone/article?id=10.1371/journal.pone.0186027 (accessed 5 July 2021).
IRSCL (2022), IRSCL Statements. http://www.irscl.com/statements.html (accessed 22 April 2022).
Isozaki, A. H. (2014), Flowing toward solutions: Literature listening and L2 literacy, *The Journal of Literature Teaching*, 3 (2): 6–20.
Isozaki, A. H. (2018), Strategically building reading fluency: Three strands of new listening-reading research, *Extensive Reading World Congress Proceedings*, 4: 189–97. https://pdfs.semanticscholar.org/e625/091d8f45d7d9c71148a70d8686da9ada4377.pdf (accessed 9 March 2021).

Jacobs, G. and Goatly, A. (2000), The treatment of ecological issues in ELT coursebooks, *ELT Journal*, 54 (3): 256–64.

Jahoda, G. (2012), Critical reflections on some recent definitions of 'culture', *Culture & Psychology*, 18 (3): 289–303.

Janks, H. (2019), Critical literacy and the importance of reading with and against a text, *Journal of Adolescent & Adult Literacy*, 62 (5): 561–4.

Janks, H. (2020), Critical literacy in action: Difference as a force for positive change, *Journal of Adolescent & Adult Literacy*, 63 (5): 569–72.

Jerrim, J., Lopez-Agudo, L. and Marcenaro-Gutierrez, O. (2020), Does it matter whatchildren read? New evidence using longitudinal census data from Spain, *Oxford Review of Education*, 46 (5): 515–33.

Jowett, G. and O'Donnell, V. (2006), *Propaganda and Persuasion*, 4th edn, California: Sage.

Kaminski, A. (2016), *The Use of Singing, Storytelling and Chanting in the Primary EFL Classroom: Aesthetic Experience and Participation in FL Learning*, PhD thesis, Swansea University. https://cronfa.swan.ac.uk/Record/cronfa54359 (accessed 22 June 2021).

Kaminski, A. (2019), Young learners' engagement with multimodal texts, *ELT Journal*, 73 (2): 175–85.

Kearney, C. (2003), *The Monkey's Mask. Identity, Memory, Narrative and Voice*, Stoke on Trent: Trentham Books.

Keating, P. (2005), Point of view (cinematic), in D. Herman, M. Jahn and M.-L. Ryan (eds), *Routledge Encyclopedia of Narrative Theory*, 440–2, Abingdon: Routledge.

Kerridge, R. (2006), Environmentalism and ecocriticism, in P. Waugh (ed.), *Literary Theory and Criticism*, 530–43, Oxford: Oxford University Press.

Kersten, S. (2015), Language development in young learners: The role of formulaic language, in J. Bland (ed.), *Teaching English to Young Learners. Critical Issues in Language Teaching with 3–12 Year Olds*, 129–45, London: Bloomsbury Academic.

Kessler, G., Rizzo, S. and Kelly, M. (2020), President Trump made 18,000 false or misleading claims in 1,170 days, *The Washington Post*, 14 April. https://www.washingtonpost.com/politics/2020/04/14/president-trump-made-18000-false-or-misleading-claims-1170-days/ (accessed 23 March 2021).

Kessler, R. C., Amminger, G. P., Aguilar-Gaxiola, S., Alonso, J., Lee, S. and Ustun, T. B. (2007), Age of onset of mental disorders: A review of recent literature, *Current Opinion in Psychiatry*, 20 (4): 359–64.

Kidd, D. and Castano, E. (2013), Reading literary fiction improves theory of mind, *Science* 342 (6156): 377–80.

Kidd, D., Ongis, M. and Castano, E. (2016), On literary fiction and its effects on theory of mind, *Scientific Study of Literature*, 6 (1): 42–58.

Kiefer, B. and Wilson, M. (2011), Nonfiction literature for children, in S. Wolf, K. Coats, P. Enciso and C. Jenkins (eds), *Handbook of Research on Children's and Young Adult Literature*, 290–9, New York: Routledge.

Kim, K. H. (2016), *The Creativity Challenge: How We Can Recapture American Innovation*, New York: Prometheus Books.

Klippel, F. (2006), Literacy through picture books, in J. Enever and G. Schmid-Schönbein (eds), *Picture Books and Young Learners of English*, 81–90, Berlin: Langenscheidt.

Knoepke, J., Richter, T., Isberner, M.-B., Naumann, J. and Neeb, Y. (2014), Phonological recoding, orthographic decoding, and comprehension skills during reading acquisition, *Zeitschrift für Erziehungswissenschaft*, 17: 447–71.
Kramsch, C. (1993), *Context and Culture in Language Teaching*, Oxford: Oxford University Press.
Kramsch, C. (2009), *The Multilingual Subject*, Oxford: Oxford University Press.
Kramsch, C. and Zhu, H. (2016), Language and culture in ELT, in G. Hall (ed.), *The Routledge Handbook of English Language Teaching*, 38–50, Abingdon: Routledge.
Krashen, S. (1999), *The Arguments Against Whole Language & Why They Are Wrong*, Portsmouth: Heinemann.
Krashen, S. (2004), *The Power of Reading: Insights from the Research*, 2nd edn, Portsmouth, NH: Heinemann.
Krashen, S. (2013), Free reading: Still a great idea, in J. Bland and C. Lütge (eds), *Children's Literature in Second Language Education*, 15–24, London: Bloomsbury Academic.
Krashen, S. and Bland, J. (2014), Compelling comprehensible input, academic language and school libraries, *Children's Literature in English Language Education*, 2 (2): 1–12. https://clelejournal.org/compelling-comprehensible-input/ (accessed 23 January 2021).
Kreft, A. and Viebrock, B. (2014), To read or not to read: Does a suitcase full of books do the trick in the English language classroom? *Children's Literature in English Language Education*, 2 (1): 72–92. https://clelejournal.org/to-read-or-not-to-read/ (accessed 31 January 2021).
Kress, G. and van Leeuwen, T. (2021), *Reading Images: The Grammar of Visual Design*, 3rd edn, Abingdon, Oxon: Routledge.
Krömer, C. (2014), [website] Artist Statement, *Christiane Krömer Illustration*. http://www.christianekromer.com/artist-statement.html (accessed 17 April 2021).
Kubota, R. (2020), Confronting epistemological racism, decolonizing scholarly knowledge: Race and gender in applied linguistics, *Applied Linguistics*, 41 (5): 712–32.
Kutcher, S. (2017), [YouTube video blog] *The Inter-Relationship of Mental Health States: Language Matters*. https://www.youtube.com/watch?v=LsowyMnqCRs&t=1s (accessed 29 July 2021).
Langer, J. (1997), Literacy acquisition through literature, *Journal of Adolescent & Adult Literacy*, 40: 602–14.
Larsen-Freeman, D. (2011), A complexity theory approach to second language development/acquisition, in D. Atkinson (ed.), *Alternative Approaches to Second Language Acquisition*, 48–72, Abingdon: Routledge.
Lazere, D. (1987), Critical thinking in college English studies, *Eric Digest*. https://files.eric.ed.gov/fulltext/ED284275.pdf (accessed 5 July 2021).
Le Guin, U. (1985), *Language of the Night. Essays on Fantasy and Science Fiction*, New York: Berkley Books.
Le Hunte, B. and Golembiewski, J. (2014), Stories have the power to save us: A neurological framework for the imperative to tell stories, *Arts and Social Sciences Journal*, 5 (2): 73–6.
Lee, L. (2012), Bridal Hunger Games, *The New York Times*, 13 April 2012. https://www.nytimes.com/2012/04/15/fashion/weddings/Losing-Weight-in-Time-for-the-Wedding.html (accessed 20 February 2021).

Leland, C., Lewison, M. and Harste, J. (2013), *Teaching Children's Literature: It's Critical!* New York: Routledge.

Lenz, C. and Nustad, P. (2019), *Dembra – Theoretical and Scientific Framework*. https://dembra.no/en/om-dembra/ (accessed 21 February 2021).

Liu, S. (2014), L2 reading comprehension: Exclusively L2 competence or different competences? *Journal of Language Teaching and Research*, 5 (5): 1085–91.

Long, M. (1991), Focus on form: A design feature in language teaching methodology, in K. De Bot, R. Ginsberg and C. Kramsch (eds), *Foreign Language Research in Cross-Cultural Perspective*, 39–52, Amsterdam: John Benjamins.

Lugossy, R. (2012), Constructing meaning in interaction through picture books, *C.E.P.S Journal*, 2 (3): 97–117.

Lupton, M. J. (1998), *Maya Angelou: A Critical Companion*, Westport, CT: Greenwood Press.

McAuliffe, M. and Khadria, B. (2019), *World Migration Report 2020*, Geneva: International Organization for Migration (IOM). https://publications.iom.int/books/world-migration-report-2020 (accessed 6 July 2021).

McCallum, R. and Stephens, J. (2011), Ideology and children's books, in S. Wolf, K. Coats, P. Enciso and C. Jenkins (eds), *Handbook of Research on Children's and Young Adult Literature*, 359–71, New York: Routledge.

McCloud, S. (1993), *Understanding Comics. The Invisible Art*, New York: HarperCollins.

Macedonia, M. (2019), Embodied learning: Why at school the mind needs the body, *Frontiers in Psychology*, 10 (2098): 1–8.

McGillis, R. (2011), Literary studies, cultural studies, children's literature, and the case of Jeff Smith, in S. Wolf, K. Coats, P. Enciso and C. Jenkins (eds), *Handbook of Research on Children's and Young Adult Literature*, 345–55, New York: Routledge.

McTaggart, J. (2008), Graphic novels. The good, the bad and the ugly, in N. Frey and D. Fisher (eds), *Teaching Visual Literacy Using Comic Books, Graphic Novels, Anime, Cartoons, and More to Develop Comprehension and Thinking Skills*, 27–46, Thousand Oaks, CA: Corwin Press.

Maley, A. (2004), Foreword, in J. Spiro (eds), *Creative Poetry Writing*, 3, Oxford: Oxford University Press.

Maley, A. (2013), *Creative Writing for L2 Students and Teachers*, in J. Bland and C. Lütge (eds), *Children's Literature in Second Language Education*, 161–72, London: Bloomsbury Academic.

Margaryan, S., Paul, A. and Siedler, T. (2018), Does education affect attitudes towards immigration? Evidence from Germany. IZA Discussion Paper No. 11980. https://ssrn.com/abstract=3301739 (accessed 28 February 2021).

Meek, M. (1993), What will literacy be like? *Cambridge Journal of Education*, 23 (1): 89–99.

Meßmer, A.-K., Sängerlaub, A. and Schulz, L. (2021), *'Quelle: Internet'? Digitale Nachrichten- und Informationskompetenzen der deutschen Bevölkerung im Test*, Berlin: Stiftung Neue Verantwortung. https://www.stiftung-nv.de/de/publikation/quelle-internet-digitale-nachrichten-und-informationskompetenzen-der-deutschen (accessed 23 March 2021).

Miller, L. (2018), Teens already know how to overthrow the government, *The Cut*, 16 March. https://www.thecut.com/2018/03/parkland-students-emma-gonzalez-david-hogg.html (accessed 18 January 2021).

Mirhosseini, S. A. (2018), Issues of ideology in English language education worldwide: An overview, *Pedagogy, Culture & Society*, 26 (1): 19–33.

Morris, P. (2022), *Creative Writers in a Digital Age. Swedish Teenagers' Insights into Their Extramural English Writing and the School Subject of English*, Licentiate Thesis, Mälardalen University. http://mdh.diva-portal.org/smash/record.jsf?pid=diva2%3A1611856&dswid=-2391 (accessed 14 February 2022).

Moses, L. (2014), What do you do with hands like these? Close reading facilitates exploration and text creation, *Children's Literature in English Language Education*, 2 (1): 44–56.

Mourão, S. (2015), The potential of picturebooks with young learners, in J. Bland (ed.), *Teaching English to Young Learners. Critical Issues in Language Teaching with 3–12 Year Olds*, 199–217, London: Bloomsbury Academic.

Mourão, S. (2016), Picturebooks in the primary EFL classroom: Authentic literature for authentic responses, *Children's Literature in English Language Education*, 4 (1): 25–43. https://clelejournal.org/sh-html/ (accessed 27 March 2021).

Mpike, M. (2019), Diversity and positive representation in Nordic children's literature, in J. Ninos (ed.), *Actualise Utopia: From Dreams to Reality*, 53–69, Oslo: Kulturrådet.

Muller, V. (2012), Virtually real: Suzanne Collins's The Hunger Games trilogy, *International Research in Children's Literature*, 5 (1): 51–63.

Muñoz, C. and Spada, N. (2019), Foreign language learning from early childhood to young adulthood, in A. De Houwer and L. Ortega (eds), *The Cambridge Handbook of Bilingualism*, 233–49, Cambridge: Cambridge University Press.

Murphy, V. (2014), *Second Language Learning in the Early School Years: Trends and Contexts*, Oxford: Oxford University Press.

Myhill, D. (2010), Rhythm and blues: Making textual music with grammar and punctuation, in D. Wyse, R. Andrews and J. Hoffman (eds), *The Routledge International Handbook of English, Language and Literacy Teaching*, 170–81, Abingdon: Routledge.

Myhill, D. (2020), Wordsmiths and sentence-shapers. Linguistic and metalinguistic development in secondary writers, in H. Chen, D. Myhill and H. Lewis (eds), *Developing Writers across the Primary and Secondary Years: Growing into Writing*, 194–211, Abingdon: Routledge.

Myhill, D. A., Lines, H. and Jones, S. M. (2018), Texts that teach: Examining the efficacy of using texts as models, *L1-Educational Studies in Language and Literature*, 18: 1–24.

Narančić Kovač, S. (2016), Picturebooks in educating teachers of English to young learners, *Children's Literature in English Language Education*, 4 (2): 6–26.

Naylor-Ballesteros, C. (2019), [Website] The Suitcase is a book about being more trusting and open – As well as migration, *BookTrust*. https://www.booktrust.org.uk/news-and-features/features/2019/june/the-suitcase-is-a-book-about-being-more-trusting-and-open--as-well-as-migration/ (accessed 7 July 2021).

Neelands, J. (2004), *Beginning Drama 11–14*, 2nd edn, London: David Fulton.

Niemi, H. (2016), Academic and practical: Research-based teacher education in Finland, in B. Moon (ed.), *Do Universities Have a Role in the Education and Training of Teachers?* 19–33, Cambridge: Cambridge University Press.

Nicholas, H. and Lightbown, P. (2008), Defining child second language acquisition, defining roles for L2 instruction, in J. Philp, R. Oliver and A. Mackey (eds),

Second Language Acquisition and the Younger Learner. Child's Play? 27–51, Amsterdam: John Benjamin.
Nikolajeva, M. (2014), *Reading for Learning: Cognitive Approaches to Children's Literature*, Amsterdam: John Benjamins.
Nikolajeva, M. (2018), Emotions in picturebooks, in B. Kümmerling-meibauer (ed.), *The Routledge Companion to Picturebooks*, 110–18, Abingdon, Oxon: Routledge.
Nikolajeva, M. (2021), Afterword. The case of the evil (step)mother, or the impossibility of intergenerational solidarity, in J. Deszcz-Tryhubczak and Z. Jaques (eds), *Intergenerational Solidarity in Children's Literature and Film*, 231–45, Jackson: University Press of Mississippi.
Nodelman, P. (1992), The Other: Orientalism, colonialism, and children's literature, *Children's Literature Association Quarterly*, 17 (1): 29–35.
Nodelman, P. (2010), Picturebook narratives and the project of children's literature, in T. Colomer, B. Kümmerling-meibauer and C. Silva-Díaz (eds), *New Directions in Picturebook Research*, 11–26, London: Routledge.
Nodelman, P. and Reimer, M. (2003), *The Pleasures of Children's Literature*, 3rd edn, Boston: Allyn and Bacon.
Nussbaum, M. (1998), *Cultivating Humanity: A Classical Defence of Reform in Liberal Education*, Cambridge, MA: Harvard University Press.
Nussbaum, M. (2004), Women's education: A global challenge, *Signs*, 29 (2): 325–55.
Oatley, K. (2017), On truth and fiction, in M. Burke and E. Troscianko (eds), *Cognitive Literary Science. Dialogues between Literature and Cognition*, 259–78, New York: Oxford University Press.
Oatley, K. and Djikic, M. (2014), How reading transforms us, *The New York Times Sunday Review*, 19 December. https://www.nytimes.com/2014/12/21/opinion/sunday/how-writing-transforms-us.html?searchResultPosition=1 (accessed 30 March 2021).
OECD (2021), *21st-Century Readers: Developing Literacy Skills in a Digital World*, PISA, Paris: OECD Publishing. https://www.oecd.org/publications/21st-century-readers-a83d84cb-en.htm (accessed 22 May 2021).
Olstrom, C. (2011), *Undaunted by Blindness: Concise Biographies of 400 People Who Refused to Let Visual Impairment Define Them*, 2nd edn, Watertown, MA: Perkins School for the Blind.
Ommundsen, Å. M., Haaland, G. and Kümmerling-meibauer, B. (2022), *Exploring Challenging Picturebooks in Education: International Perspectives on Language and Literature Learning*, London: Routledge.
O'Neill, C. (2013), Foreword, in M. Anderson and J. Dunn (eds), *How Drama Activates Learning*, xix–xxi, London: Bloomsbury Academic.
Ong, W. (2002), *Orality and Literacy*, 2nd edn, London: Routledge.
Orwell, G. (1945), You and the Atom Bomb, *Tribune*, 19 October. https://www.orwellfoundation.com/the-orwell-foundation/orwell/essays-and-other-works/you-and-the-atom-bomb/ (accessed 21 March 2021).
Oxfam (2015), *Education for Global Citizenship. A Guide for Schools*, Oxford: Oxfam.
Oziewicz, M. (2015), *Justice in Young Adult Speculative Fiction: A Cognitive Reading*, Abingdon: Routledge.

Oziewicz, M. (2018), Exploring challenges of the graphic novel format: Brian Selznick's *The Invention of Hugo Cabret, Wonderstruck* and *The Marvels*, in J. Bland (ed.), *Using Literature in English Language Education: Challenging Reading for 8–18 Year Olds*, 25–40, London: Bloomsbury Academic.

Padberg-Schmitt, B. (2020), Increasing reading fluency in young adult readers using audiobooks, *Children's Literature in English Language Education*, 7 (1): 31–51. https://clelejournal.org/article-2-increasing-reading-fluency/ (accessed 31 January 2021).

Pantaleo, S. (2008), *Exploring Student Response to Contemporary Picturebooks*, Toronto: University of Toronto Press.

Paran, A. and Wallace, C. (2016), Teaching literacy, in G. Hall (ed.), *The Routledge Handbook of English Language Teaching*, 441–55, Abingdon: Routledge.

Parsons, L. (2004), Ella evolving: Cinderella stories and the construction of gender-appropriate behavior, *Children's Literature in Education*, 35 (2): 135–54.

Pennycook, A. (1999), Introduction: Critical approaches to TESOL, *TESOL Quarterly*, 33 (3): 329–48.

Pennycook, A. (2016), Politics, power relationships and ELT, in G. Hall (ed.), *The Routledge Handbook of English Language Teaching*, 26–37, Abingdon, Oxon: Routledge.

Peters, S., Golden, S., Eloul, L. and Higson-Smith, C. (2021), Thousands of Eritreans fled repression at home. Many got caught up in Ethiopia's fighting. Past trauma and new threats are taking a toll on refugees' mental health, *The Washington Post*, 4 November. https://www.washingtonpost.com/politics/2021/11/04/thousands-eritreans-fled-repression-home-many-got-caught-up-ethiopias-fighting/ (accessed 2 January 2022).

Peterson, R. and Eeds, M. (2007), *Grand Conversations: Literature Groups in Action*, updated edn, New York: Scholastic.

Plumwood, V. (2006), The concept of a cultural landscape. Nature, culture and agency in the land, *Ethics and the Environment*, 11 (2): 115–50.

Perkins, D. (1994), *The Intelligent Eye: Learning to Think by Looking at Art*, Los Angeles: Getty Publications.

Porto, M. and Zembylas, M. (2020), Pedagogies of discomfort in foreign language education: Cultivating empathy and solidarity using art and literature, *Language and Intercultural Communication*, 20 (4): 356–74.

Prensky, M. (2001), Digital natives, digital immigrants, *On the Horizon*, 9 (5): 1–6.

Prior, M. (2019), Elephants in the room: An 'affective turn,' or just feeling our way? *The Modern Language Journal*, 103 (2): 516–27.

Provost, G. (2019), *100 Ways to Improve Your Writing*, updated edn, New York: Berkley.

Rasheed, Z. (2020), Why are Thai students protesting against King Vajiralongkorn? *Aljazeera*, 26 August. https://www.aljazeera.com/news/2020/8/26/why-are-thai-students-protesting-against-king-vajiralongkorn (accessed 18 January 2021).

Ratner, C. (2000), A cultural-psychological analysis of emotions, *Culture & Psychology*, 6 (1): 5–39.

Read, C. (2008), Scaffolding children's learning through story and drama, *Children & Teenagers: Young Learners and Teenagers SIG Publication*, IATEFL, 08 (2): 6–9.

Reese, D. (2000), Contesting ideology in children's book reviewing, *Studies in American Indian Literatures*, 12 (1): 37–55.

Renandya, W. A., Krashen, S. and Jacobs. G. M. (2018), The potential of series books: How narrow reading leads to advanced L2 proficiency, *LEARN Journal: Language Education and Acquisition Research Network*, 11 (2): 148–54.

Reynolds, K. (2007), *Radical Children's Literature*, Basingstoke: Palgrave Macmillan.

Risager, K. (2021), Language textbooks: Windows to the world, *Language, Culture and Curriculum*, 2 (34): 119–32.

Rixon, S. (2013), *British Council Survey of Policy and Practice in Primary English Language Teaching Worldwide*, London: British Council. https://www.teachingenglish.org.uk/sites/teacheng/files/D120%20Survey%20of%20Teachers%20to%20YLs_FINAL_Med_res_online.pdf (accessed 24 November 2021).

Robinson, D. (1973), *The History of World Cinema*, London: Methuen.

Robinson, D. (2015), Marie-Georges-Jean Méliès. French Magician, Filmmaker. *Who's Who of Victorian Cinema*. https://www.victorian-cinema.net/melies.php (accessed 24 June 2021).

Rose, E. (2010), Continuous partial attention: Reconsidering the role of online learning in the age of interruption, *Educational Technology*, 50 (4): 41–6.

Rose, E. (2012), Hyper attention and the rise of the antinarrative: Reconsidering the future of narrativity, *Narrative Works. Issues, Investigations, & Inventions*, 2 (2): 92–102. https://journals.lib.unb.ca/index.php/NW/article/view/20173 (accessed 25 January 2021).

Rosenblatt, L. (1982), The literary transaction: Evocation and response, *Theory into Practice*, 21 (4): 268–77.

Roth, M. S. (2019), *Safe Enough Spaces: A Pragmatist's Approach to Inclusion, Free Speech, and Political Correctness on College Campuses*, New Haven: Yale University Press.

Rudd, D. (ed.) (2010), *The Routledge Companion to Children's Literature*, Abingdon, Oxon: Routledge.

Rushdie, S. (2021), *Languages of Truth*, London: Jonathan Cape.

Salomon, G. (2016), It's not just the tool but the educational rationale that counts, in E. Elstad (ed.), *Educational Technology and Polycontextual Bridging*, 149–61, Rotterdam: Sense Publishers.

Sands-O'Connor, K. (2019), British children's books are still too white – Responsibility to change them is on all involved, *The Conversation*, 14 November. https://theconversation.com/british-childrens-books-are-still-too-white-responsibility-to-change-them-is-on-all-involved-126853 (accessed 7 June 2021).

Saville-Troike, M. and Barto, K. (2017), *Introducing Second Language Acquisition*, 3rd edn, Cambridge: Cambridge University Press.

Schleicher, A. (2021), Editorial. 21st century readers, in C. Young (ed.), *21st-Century Readers: Developing Literacy Skills in a Digital World, PISA*, 3–4, Paris: OECD Publishing.

Schmitt, N. (ed.) (2004), *Formulaic Sequences. Acquisition, Processing and Use*, Amsterdam: John Benjamins.

Schmitt, N., Jiang, X. and Grabe, W. (2011), The percentage of words known in a text and reading comprehension, *The Modern Language Journal*, 95 (1): 26–43.

Selby, D. and Pike, G. (2000), Civil global education: Relevant learning for the twenty-first century, *Convergence: An International Journal of Adult Education*, 33 (1–2): 138–49.

Selivan, L. (2018), *Lexical Grammar: Activities for Teaching Chunks and Exploring Patterns*, Cambridge: Cambridge University Press.

Serafini, F. (2005), Voices in the park, voices in the classroom: Readers responding to postmodern picture books, *Reading, Research and Instruction*, 44 (3): 47–65.

Serafini, F. (2008), Approaching, navigating, and comprehending picturebooks, *WSRA Journal*, 47 (2): 5–9.

Serratrice, L. (2019), Becoming bilingual in early childhood, in A. De Houwer and L. Ortega (eds), *The Cambridge Handbook of Bilingualism*, 15–35, Cambridge: Cambridge University Press.

Short, K. (2009), Critically reading the word and the world: Building intercultural understanding through literature, *Bookbird: A Journal of International Children's Literature*, 47 (2): 1–10.

Short, K. (2011), Reading literature in elementary classrooms, in S. Wolf, K. Coats, P. Enciso and C. Jenkins (eds), *Handbook of Research on Children's and Young Adult Literature*, 48–62, New York: Routledge.

Simonton, D. K. (2006), Creativity around the world in 80 ways... but with one destination, in J. Kaufman and R. Sternberg (eds), *The International Handbook of Creativity*, 490–6, New York: Cambridge University Press.

Simpson, J. (2016), English for speakers of other languages: Language education and migration, in G. Hall (ed.), *The Routledge Handbook of English Language Teaching*, 177–90, Abingdon: Routledge.

Sipe, L. (2008a), Learning from illustrations in picturebooks, in N. Frey and D. Fisher (eds), *Teaching Visual Literacy Using Comic Books, Graphic Novels, Anime, Cartoons, and More to Develop Comprehension and Thinking Skills*, 131–48, Thousand Oaks, CA: Corwin Press.

Sipe, L. (2008b), *Storytime. Young Children's Literary Understanding in the Classroom*, New York: Teachers College Press.

Skela, J. (2014), The quest for literature in EFL textbooks – A quest for Camelot? *English Language and Literature Teaching*, 11 (1): 113–36.

Slaughter, V. (2015), Theory of mind in infants and young children: A review, *Australian Psychologist*, 50 (3): 169–72.

Smith, F. (2012), *Understanding Reading, a Psycholinguistic Analysis of Reading and Learning to Read*, 6th edn, New York: Routledge.

Smith, F. (2015), *Landmarks in Literacy: The Selected Works of Frank Smith*, New York: Routledge.

Smith, M. and Wilhelm, J. (2002), *Reading Don't Fix No Chevys: Literacy in the Lives of Young Men*, Portsmouth: Heinemann.

Spiro, J. (2004), *Creative Poetry Writing*, Oxford: Oxford University Press.

Stephens, J. (1992), *Language and Ideology in Children's Fiction*, Harlow: Longman.

Stephens, J. (2010a), Ecocriticism, in D. Rudd (ed.), *The Routledge Companion to Children's Literature*, 168–9, Abingdon, Oxon: Routledge.

Stephens, J. (2010b), Ideology, in D. Rudd (ed.), *The Routledge Companion to Children's Literature*, 192–3, Abingdon, Oxon: Routledge.

Stephens, J., Belmiro, C. A., Curry, A., Lifang. L. and Motawy, Y. S., eds (2018), *The Routledge Companion to International Children's Literature*, Abingdon: Routledge.

Sternberg, R. (2006), Introduction, in J. Kaufman and R. Sternberg (eds), *The International Handbook of Creativity*, 1–9, New York: Cambridge University Press.

Stevick, E. (1980), *Teaching Languages: A Way and Ways*, Rowley: Newbury House.

Støle H., Mangen A. and Schwippert K. (2020), Assessing children's reading comprehension on paper and screen: A mode-effect study, *Computers & Education*, 151: 1–13.

Sun, C.-H. (2017), The value of picture-book reading-based collaborative output activities for vocabulary retention, *Language Teaching Research*, 21 (1): 96–117.

Sundqvist, P. and Sylvén, L. K. (2014), Language-related computer use: Focus on young L2 English learners in Sweden, *ReCALL*, 26 (1): 3–20.

Svalberg, A. M.-L. (2009), Engagement with language: Interrogating a construct, *Language Awareness*, 18 (3–4): 242–58.

Svalberg, A. M.-L. (2012), Language awareness in language learning and teaching: A research agenda, *Language Teaching*, 45 (3): 376–88.

Taxel, J. (2003), Multicultural literature and the politics of reaction, in D. Fox and K. Short (eds), *Stories Matter. The Complexity of Cultural Authenticity in Children's Literature*, 143–64, Urbana: National Council of Teachers of English.

Thein, A. H., Beach, R. and Parks, D. (2007), Perspective-taking as transformative practice in teaching multicultural literature to white students, *English Journal*, 97 (2): 54–60.

Thompson, M. (2016), From Trump to Brexit rhetoric: How today's politicians have got away with words, *The Guardian*, 27 August. https://www.theguardian.com/books/2016/aug/27/from-trump-to-brexit-rhetoric-how-todays-politicians-have-got-away-with-words (accessed 2 March 2021).

Thompson, R. and McIlnay, M. (2019), Nobody wants to read anymore! Using a multimodal approach to make literature engaging, *Children's Literature in English Language Education*, 7 (1): 61–80. https://clelejournal.org/article-4-nobody-wants-read-anymore/ (accessed 31 January 2021).

Thomson, D. (2015), *How to Watch a Movie*, London: Profile Books.

Thornbury, S. (2002), *How to Teach Vocabulary*, Harlow: Pearson Longman.

Thornbury, S. (2017), L is for language arts, *An A-Z of ELT. Scott Thornbury's blog*. 13 August. https://scottthornbury.wordpress.com/2017/08/13/l-is-for-language-arts/ (accessed 18 January 2021).

Tomlinson, B. (2011), Seeing what they mean: Helping L2 readers to visualize, in B. Tomlinson (ed.), *Materials Development in Language Teaching*, 2nd edn, 357–78, Cambridge: Cambridge University Press.

Toolan, M. (2008), Verbal art: Through repetition to immersion, *Shanghai International Studies University: Second International Stylistics Conference*. artsweb.bham.ac.uk/mtoolan/ (accessed 31 October 2021).

Toolan, M. (2012), Poems: Wonderfully repetitive, in R. Jones (ed.), *Discourse and Creativity*, 17–34, London: Pearson.

Tschida, C., Ryan, C. and Ticknor, A. (2014), Building on windows and mirrors: Encouraging the disruption of 'Single Stories' through children's literature, *Journal of Children's Literature*, 40 (1): 28–39.

UNESCO (2013), *Culture and Nature: The Two Sides of the Coin*. http://www.unesco.org/new/en/culture/themes/culture-and-development/the-future-we-want-the-role-of-culture/the-two-sides-of-the-coin/ (accessed 28 February 2021).
UNESCO (2017a), *Basic Texts of the 2005 Convention on the Protection and Promotion of the Diversity of Cultural Expressions*, 2017 edn, Paris: United Nations Educational, Scientific and Cultural Organization.
UNESCO (2017b), *Reading the Past, Writing the Future. Fifty Years of Promoting Literacy*, Paris: United Nations Educational, Scientific and Cultural Organization.
UNHCR (2018), *Report of the United Nations High Commissioner for Refugees Part II – Global Compact on Refugees*. https://www.unhcr.org/search?comid=3b4f07fd4&cid=49aea93a20&scid=49aea93a16&tags=UNHCR%20Annual%20Reports%20General%20Assembly (accessed 11 July 2021).
United Nations Development Programme (2020), *COVID-19 Pandemic. Humanity Needs Leadership and Solidarity to Defeat the Coronavirus*. https://www.undp.org/content/undp/en/home/coronavirus.html (accessed 20 February 2021).
Ur, P. (2020), Review of S. Walsh and S. Mann (eds) The Routledge handbook of English language teacher education, *ELT Journal*, 74 (4): 517–20.
Utdanningsdirektoratet (2019), *Core Curriculum – Values and Principles for Primary and Secondary Education*, Oslo: Norwegian Government. https://www.udir.no/lk20/overordnet-del/?lang=eng (accessed 22 January 2021).
Utdanningsdirektoratet (2020), *Læreplan i engelsk. ENG01-04*. https://www.udir.no/lk20/eng01-04
Valente, D. and Mourão, S. (forthcoming 2022), Picturebooks as vehicles: Creating materials for pedagogical action, *Children's Literature in English Language Education*, 10 (2).
van Dijk, T. (1998), *Ideology: A Multidisciplinary Approach*, London: Sage.
van Lier, L. (1994), Forks and hope: Pursuing understanding in different ways, *Applied Linguistics*, 15 (3): 328–46.
Vanderbeke, D. (2006), Comics and graphic novels in the classroom, in W. Delanoy and L. Volkmann (eds), *Cultural Studies in the EFL Classroom*, 365–75, Heidelberg: Winter.
Vasquez, V. M., Janks, H. and Comber, B. (2019), Critical literacy as a way of being and doing, *Language Arts*, 96 (5): 300–11.
Vezzali, L., Stathi, S., Giovannini, D., Capozza, D. and Trifiletti, E. (2015), The greatest magic of Harry Potter: Reducing prejudice, *Journal of Applied Social Psychology*, 45: 105–21.
Volkmann, L. (2011), On the nature and function of stereotypes in intercultural learning, in G. Linke (ed.), *Teaching Cultural Studies. Methods – Matters – Models*, 15–38, Heidelberg: Universitätsverlag Winter.
von Merveldt, N. (2018), Informational picturebooks, in B. Kümmerling-Meibauer (ed.), *The Routledge Companion to Picturebooks*, 231–45, Abingdon, Oxon: Routledge.
Vygotsky, L. (1978), *Mind in Society*, Cambridge, MA: Harvard University Press.
Walker, P. (2013), Research in relationship with humans, the spirit world, and the natural world, in D. M. Mertens, F. Cram and B. Chilisa (eds), *Indigenous Pathways into Social Research: Voices of a New Generation*, 299–316, Walnut Creek, CA: Left Coast Press.
Waterston, M. L. (2011), The techno-brain, *Generations – Journal of the American Societyon Aging*, 35 (2): 77–82.

Wegerif, R. (2013), *Dialogic: Education for the Internet Age*, London: Routledge.
Wehrmann, J. (2019), Beyond the Garrison: Global education and teaching (Canadian) literature in the EFL classroom, in A. Kostoulas (ed.), *Challenging Boundaries in Language Education*, 107–20, Cham: Springer.
Whitelaw, J. (2017), Arts-based literacy learning like 'new school': (Re)framing the arts in and of students' lives as story, *English Education*, 50 (1): 42–71.
Widdowson, H. (1990), *Aspects of Language Teaching*, Oxford: Oxford University Press.
Winston, J. (2022), *Performative Language Teaching in Early Education: Language Learning through Drama and the Arts for Children 3–7*, London: Bloomsbury Academic.
Wolf, M. (2018), *Reader, Come Home: The Reading Brain in a Digital World*, New York: HarperCollins.
Wolf, M. and Barzillai, M. (2009), The importance of deep reading. What will it take for the next generation to read thoughtfully – Both in print and online? *Educational Leadership*, 66 (6): 32–7.
World Health Organization (2020), *Adolescent Mental Health*, 28 September https://www.who.int/news-room/fact-sheets/detail/adolescent-mental-health (accessed 28 July 2021).
Wray, A. (2002), *Formulaic Language and the Lexicon*, Cambridge: Cambridge University Press.
Wyse, D. and Ferrari, A. (2015), Creativity and education: Comparing the national curricula of the states of the European Union and the United Kingdom, *British Educational Research Journal*, 41 (1): 30–47.
Yousafzai, Z. (2014), My daughter, Malala, *TED Talk*, 24 March. https://www.ted.com/talks/ziauddin_yousafzai_my_daughter_malala?language=en (accessed 4 April 2021).
Zapf, H. (2008), Literary ecology and the ethics of texts, *New Literary History*, 39 (4): 847–68.
Zhu, H. (2010), Language socialization and interculturality: Address terms in intergenerational talk in Chinese diasporic families, *Language and Intercultural Communication*, 10 (3): 189–205.
Zick, A., Küpper, B. and Hövermann, A. (2011), *Intolerance, Prejudice and Discrimination. A European Report*, Berlin: Friedrich-Ebert-Stiftung. https://pub.uni-bielefeld.de/record/2018626 (accessed 21 February 2021).
Zipes, J. (2007), *When Dreams Came True. Classical Fairy Tales and Their Tradition*, 2nd edn, New York: Routledge.

INDEX

ableism 22, 49, 85, 282
A Call to Learning for Climate Education (Project Everyone) (short film) 93
access 55, 63, 75, 82, 85, 90, 185–6, 233, 263
  definition 282
  library 12
  literary texts 47
  technology 12, 27
accommodation 49, 63, 282
activate and investigate 263–5
  Animal Farm 263–5
  Braid, The 203–4
  I Go Quiet 231–2
  Life of Frederick Douglass 132–4
  Malala's Magic Pencil 81–2
  Playground, The 184–5
  Wherever I Go 107–8
aesthetic response 19, 23, 34, 47, 58, 78, 142–5, 148, 152, 155, 158, 163, 189, 244
  reading stance 11, 18, 38, 283
affective dimension of language learning 180, 202, 283
affective filter 160, 283, 318
affinity spaces 12, 283
agency 22, 24–5, 37, 44, 84, 102, 119, 133, 136, 151, 172–3, 185
  critical literacy 22, 24, 197–200
  definition 283
  ideological and canonical issues 66–71
Alexander, Kwame, *Crossover, The* 209–10
allegory 119, 267, 283
alliteration 53, 60, 62, 116, 153, 156, 158, 235, 283
Almond, David
  Klaus Vogel and the Bad Lads 247–9
  Mouse Bird Snake Wolf 176–8
Alpin, Salon, *Rang-tan: the story of dirty palm oil* (short film) 88
alterity. *See* otherness
amplification through simplification 112–13, 129, 170, 283
anaphora 53, 158, 284
An A-Z of ELT (blog) 8
androcentrism 21–2, 284
Angelou, Maya, *On the Pulse of Morning* 138
anthropocentrism 22, 271, 277, 284
anthropomorphism 94, 284
antinarratives 278–80, 284
Applegate, Katherine, *Home of the Brave* 207, 211–13
artefact emotions 53, 142–5, 148, 163, 284, 303
Asante, Amma, *Belle* (film) 138
aural communication 10, 284
authenticity 32, 38, 47, 58–9, 156, 182, 199, 213, 218, 284–5. *See also* inclusivity

back and forth 122, 190, 245, 285
Baldacchino, Christine, *Morris Micklewhite and the Tangerine Dress* 235–7
BANA countries 7, 35, 285
Baron, Naomi 14, 17, 152
Barroux, *Where's the Elephant?* 89–90
Bechdel test 198–9, 241, 285
Bergen, Benjamin 13–14, 52, 293
Bildung 37–8
Bilston, Brian
  Refugees 116, 120–1
  You Took the Last Bus Home 121

biography 1, 17, 49, 78–9, 85–6, 130, 135, 255, 284, 285, 306, 309
  autobiography 17, 78–9, 86, 306
booktalk 51, 56, 76, 130, 230, 243, 246, 278, 285
Boyd, Brian 13, 15, 23, 145, 257, 279
Bradbury, Ray, *A Sound of Thunder* 197
Brevik, Lisbeth 2, 12
Brown, Anthony
  Voices in the Park 243–4
  Zoo 93–9
Bryant, Jen, *Six Dots: A Story of Young Louis Braille* 85
buzz words 275
Byram, Michael 35–6, 43

cacophony 53, 285
Candlin, Christopher 29, 31–2, 37, 41, 49
canonical literature 10, 17, 38, 50, 68–9, 130, 140, 188, 190–1, 258–9, 270, 285–6
caption 107, 114, 120, 128, 132, 136, 140, 262, 269, 286
Carle, Eric, '*Slowly, Slowly, Slowly,*' *said the Sloth* 156
Carr, Nicholas 16, 18, 75
Carroll, Joseph 13, 42, 48, 252
celebrity culture 271, 274–7, 279, 284
Cepeda, Joe 168–9
Chambers, Aidan 22, 51, 130, 278, 285
chapter books 15, 17, 19, 57, 59, 157, 161–3, 235, 244, 247, 286
characterization 20, 23, 44–8, 62, 128, 134, 161–3, 170, 190–1, 205, 214, 231, 241, 275, 303
characterless stories 45–6
child-directed speech 63, 286, 288, 295, 310
children's literature 48, 58
  aesthetic nature 19
  definition 286
  extensive reading 12
  as high-quality input 58–61
  ideology issues 32–4, 66–71
  inventive repetition 158
  prestigious awards 202, 244
  range of formats 19–20, 48
  social issues 243
  visual narratives 101, 116
  worldwide interest 25–7
choral speaking 62, 210, 286
Cinderella script 274–7
cinematic point of view 128, 132, 286–7
Clements, Andrew, *Frindle* 157
CLIL. *See* content and language integrated learning
Cobb, Rebecca 105, 112
cognition 51–2, 56, 104, 126
  emotion 104, 142–4, 148, 163
cognitive dimension of language learning 180, 223, 287
cognitive literary criticism 227–8
cognitive styles 16–17, 60, 287
Colfer, Eoin and Donkin, Andrew, *Illegal* 116, 121–6, 279
Collins, Suzanne
  Catching Fire 155, 271, 273
  Hunger Game 13, 21, 140, 157, 194, 217, 252, 258, 270–4, 277–9
  Mockingjay 271–3
comics 13, 44–5
compelling comprehensible input 11, 47, 287
computer-mediated communication (CMC) 56, 287
confirmation bias 275, 287
Content and Language Integrated Learning (CLIL) 133, 246, 287
content-based language teaching 2, 8, 288
continuous partial attention 17, 288
Cook, Guy 160, 279
Copp, Mary, *Wherever I Go* 105–6, 108, 110–11, 113
Council of Europe 36, 38–9, 52, 64, 71
coursebook 10–11, 21, 24, 29–32, 34–6, 38, 53, 60, 67, 69, 78, 87–8, 104, 115, 186, 201
  definition 288
  for English language learners 11
  information literacy 21
  language teaching 10, 24, 29–30
  limitations 30–2

Covid-19 20, 26, 35, 157, 245, 264
creative response 25, 34, 58, 86, 113–14, 136–8, 166, 186–7, 205–7, 233–5, 258, 269
creative teacher talk 63–4, 66, 77, 95, 288, 295
creative writing
  cohesion and lexical chains 155–6
  idea of fantastic beasts 173–5
  inventive repetition 158–9
  letters, emails, blogs 168
  mentor texts 158
  playful use of language 64, 154, 157, 173, 181, 210, 279, 301, 309, 317
  process 151–2
  semantic and phonological patterns 152–3
  sensory imagery 154–5
  setting and characterization 161–2
  students success tips 152
  variation 156–8
critical literacy 4, 21–2, 68–70, 189, 191–2, 194, 197, 228, 274, 278–9, 288. *See also* literary apprenticeship; verse novels
  definition 21–2
  literary apprenticeship 7
  media 19
critically engage
  Animal Farm 265–9
  Braid, The 204–5
  I Go Quiet 232–3
  Life of Frederick Douglass 135–6
  Malala's Magic Pencil 82
  Playground, The 185–6
  Wherever I Go 110–11
critical pedagogy 25, 68, 288–9
critical thinking 9, 22–3, 26, 39, 41, 44, 177, 179–80, 258, 265, 267, 277, 310, 316
  challenges 41, 44
  cult of personality 263–4, 279
  definition 21–2, 289
  educational goals 10, 293
  information literacy 21
  language teaching 39
Cron, Lisa 141, 143, 279
cult of personality 263–4, 279, 289

cultural identities. *See* sociocultural identities
culturally and linguistically diverse students 12, 53, 91, 96, 102, 289
cultural reference 34–6
cultural studies 2, 87, 228, 252, 289
culture 21, 30–2, 37–9, 41–2, 52, 61, 78
  celebrity 274–9
  definition 289–90
  democratic 38–9, 50, 64, 71
  elementary school 128
  evolving nature 228–9
  meaning 29
  national 48–9, 254, 269
  orality 153
  as plural and fluid 34–7, 49–50
  teaching 31
Cummins, Jim 151, 160, 177

danger of a single story 43, 84, 290
Daniels, Lee, *Butler, The* (film) 139
Davies, Nicola, *Day War Came, The* 105, 112–13
Daywalt, Drew, *Day the Crayons Quit, The* 170–3
Decke-Cornill, Helene, *principle of multivoicedness* 43
deep attention 16–17, 288, 290, 295, 299
deep reading 11, 27, 63, 69, 78–9, 104–5, 128–30, 140–2, 182, 199, 202–4, 217, 221, 227, 229, 263, 265, 271
  critical perspectives 23–7
  deep reading framework 23–6, 34, 78–9, 105, 113, 130, 182, 203, 229, 261, 265
  definition 290
  different text formats and genres 10
  goals 11, 27
  literary apprenticeship 7, 13–16
  narrative *versus* anti-narrative 278–80
  of stories 34, 42, 49
Delanoy, Werner 43, 272
Dervin, Fred 36–7, 48–50
dialogic interaction 1
  definition 290
  in language education 10, 24

dialogic learning 1, 31, 34, 41–4, 44, 261
didactic and didactics 2, 30, 290
Dieckmann, Sandra, *Leaf* 108–10
differentiation 25, 60, 290–1
digital literacy 70, 291
digital natives 129, 147, 291
dimensions of language learning 52, 78. *See also* affective dimension of language learning; cognitive dimension of language learning; metacognition; physiological dimension of language learning; sociocultural dimension
discourse genre 156, 168, 173, 291
disinformation 20, 26, 127, 157, 172, 260, 264, 272, 275, 291
display question 76, 291
diversity 21–2, 42
  competence 24–5, 37–9
  definition 291
  global education 27, 29, 41–2
  interculturality and 33–4, 48–9
  literary text affordances 41
  positive attitude 3
  twenty-first-century movements 33
Dörnyei, Zoltán 180, 305
double-page spread 82–3, 89–90, 92, 105, 111, 140, 147, 172, 230, 234, 239, 291–2
drama conventions 190–2, 198, 292
DuVernay, Ava
  Selma (film) 139
  When They See Us (TV miniseries) 139
dystopia 1, 257–8, 266, 271, 292

EAL. *See* English as an additional language (EAL)
echo chamber 20, 26, 275, 292
ecocentrism 42, 93, 252, 267, 292
ecocriticism 87, 94–5, 252, 267–9, 277–8
  definition 292
  global citizenship agenda 277
edu-business 275, 292–3
educational learning goals of language teaching 1, 3, 7–11, 21, 23–5, 41, 43, 112, 173, 179, 207, 265, 280, 293, 307

efferent reading stance 11, 18, 293
Ehasz, Aaron and Richmond, Justin, *Dragon Prince* (TV series) 38
elementary school 44, 230, 243
  children's literature 19, 57
  definition 293
  drama teaching 181, 188
  epistolary writing 168
  graphic novels 128
  literary apprenticeship 54
  picturebooks 41, 88
  starting with stories 14
  visual narrative 104, 108, 112, 114, 122
Ellis, Gail 70, 96, 98
Ellis, Nick 27, 51, 55, 57
Ellis, Rod 304–5
embodied simulation hypothesis 14, 52, 154, 293
empathy 9–10, 23–4, 29, 35, 39, 64, 70–1, 78, 96, 101–3, 118, 139, 142, 202, 204, 214, 223, 227, 265, 277–9, 293
endmatter. *See paratext*
English as a foreign language (EFL) 2, 30, 294
English as an additional language (EAL) 2, 294
English as a second language (ESL) 2, 243, 294
English language education 1, 3, 10, 34–7
  canonical issues 66–71
  concept of foreignness 2
  engagement with language 52, 293–4
  international outlook 34–5
  materials 29–30
  subject-specific goals 7–10
  teaching goals 7–10
English language learner (ELL) 7–8, 11, 19, 31, 280, 294
English language teaching (ELT) 50, 67
  course book, limitation 30–2
  design and content 12
  educational goals 3, 7
  state-funded schools 10
English subject pedagogy 2–4, 42, 294
environmentalism 27, 42, 75, 86–93, 99, 110, 227, 234, 252–5, 271, 277–8, 292, 294, 297

epistemological racism 135, 273, 294–5
epistolary writing 168
Erlinghauser, Fabian and Moore, Tomm, *There's A Monster in My Kitchen* (short film) 88
essentializing 36, 39, 47–8, 295
ethnocentrism 21–2, 48, 214, 227, 247–9, 273, 295
evidence-informed practice 4, 316
executive function 20, 295
experiential approach to learning 25, 31, 295
experiment with creative response
  Animal Farm 269
  Braid, The 205–7
  I Go Quiet 233–5
  Life of Frederick Douglass 136–8
  Malala's Magic Pencil 86
  Playground, The 186–7
  Wherever I Go 113–14
extensive listening 11–12, 295
extensive reading 10–12, 43, 62, 69, 295

fable 108, 116, 118, 257, 261–2, 264–5, 295
facial expression 63, 77, 96, 112, 122, 125, 128, 170, 186, 194, 210, 295
fairy-tale script 274–7
fake news 20, 127, 275, 295–6
fan activism 15, 30, 296
Fandom Forward (The Harry Potter Alliance) (website) 15, 296
fanfiction 24, 30, 58, 173, 296
fantasy writing 173–8
Farrelly, Peter, *Green Book* (film) 139
Fleming, Mike 68–9, 154, 194, 199, 259
focus on form 30, 55, 62, 81, 116, 296
format 20, 75–6, 79, 96, 126, 128, 130, 140, 148, 156, 160–1, 176, 190–1, 200–3, 205, 216, 218, 258, 261–2, 297
formulaic sequences 53, 57–60, 151, 156, 235, 296
Forsythe, Matthew 91–2
Freire, Paulo 25, 67–8, 288
Frost, Helen
  Braid, The 203–5, 208
  Hidden 207–9
functional literacy 18–19, 70, 82–3, 152, 266, 296–7
future studies 263, 297

Gaiman, Neil 20, 117, 144, 237–42
  Sleeper and the Spindle 237–42
gallery walk 83, 125, 297
Gardner, Howard 25, 43, 178, 199–200
Garland, Sarah, *Azzi In Between* 114–15
Garrard, Greg 86, 94, 278
Gee, James Paul 12, 14–15
gender 36–7, 42, 68, 81, 112, 227–8, 269
  definition 297
  expression 235–42
  gender identity 37, 297
genre 1, 10, 20, 62, 70, 79, 89, 130, 156, 163, 168, 173, 203, 262, 264, 271
George the Poet
  Hate Crime 250–2
  Search Party, The First Collection 252
Geronimi, Clyde *Sleeping Beauty* (animated film) 237, 239, 241–2
global education 27, 38, 41–2, 229, 297
global issues 9–10, 21, 25, 49–50, 67–8, 81–2, 87, 203, 227–65, 270, 297
  cognitive literary criticism 227–8
  cultural identities 228–9
  environmentalism 252–5
  ethnocentrism and prejudice 247–9
  gender expression 235–7
  poverty and inequality 243–7
  racism 39–40, 48–9, 133, 135, 138–9, 185, 227, 273, 280, 294
Goade, Michaela 90
gossip circle 192–3, 297–8
Grabe, William 12, 190
graded reader 11–13, 31, 298
graphic novels 1, 12, 15, 17, 19, 24, 47–8, 298
  graphic novel conventions 128–9
Gray, John 13, 31

Greder, Armin
  Diamonds 245–7
  Island, The 247
group-focused enmity 39–41, 135, 298
group hot-seating. *See* hot-seating
groupthink 39, 298
gutter 129, 132, 298

Habegger-Conti, Jena 31, 149
Hall, Geoff 56, 156, 199
Hayles, Katherine 16–17
Heggernes, Sissil 9, 82
Heider, Fritz and Simmel, Marianne, *An experimental study of apparent behavior* (short film) 46
heritage language 170, 298
Hesse, Karen 216
  Aleutian Sparrow 207, 214–18
heteroglossia 43, 243, 298
Hidden Impact of The Smartphone Industry, The (short film) 254
Hogan, Patrick 53, 115, 126, 139, 143, 148, 163, 284, 307
holistic learning 56, 180, 298–9
Holliday, Adrian 2, 34, 185, 285, 306
homophobia 22, 39–40, 49, 234, 299
hot-seating 136, 192, 209, 299
Hughes, Ted, *The Iron Man* 285
human rights 27, 39, 81–2, 101, 105, 185, 246, 250, 271–2
Hunt, Peter 11, 33, 60, 95, 258
hyper attention 17, 299

iceberg task 194, 217, 276–7, 299
identification fallacy 299
ideology 1, 15, 21–2, 25, 40, 47, 135, 191, 227, 237
  children's literature 32–4
  definition 299–300
  language education 66–71
ideology of inequality 40, 47, 298, 300
inclusivity 4, 38, 227–9, 300
in-depth learning 1, 7, 16, 30, 38, 42, 49, 75, 87, 93, 99, 101, 104. *See also* global issues; speculative fiction
  citizenship education 101
  classroom text 25–7, 87

  definition 300
  picturebook 93, 99
  refugee stories 104
indeterminacy 58, 76, 141, 244, 300
infodemic 20, 157, 275, 300
informational literature. *See* nonfiction
information literacy 20–1, 24, 44, 70, 134, 185, 259, 263, 265, 275, 300–1
ingroup 39, 47, 102, 301
intensive reading 10–11, 301
intentional fallacy 22, 301
intercultural competence 9, 32, 35–8, 43, 50, 232
intercultural dialogue
  definition 36–7
  democratic culture 38–9
interculturality 1–2, 4, 7, 9, 19, 24–5, 27, 29, 48–50
  critical 48–50
  definition 301
  diversity competence 37–8, 42
  verse novels 207–23
interlocutor 49, 62, 301
intermediality 146, 301
intersectionality 42, 301
intertextuality 58, 146, 238–9, 243–4, 301–2
intrapersonal communication 51, 60, 302
intrapersonal role-play 192–4, 198, 276, 302
i+1 58, 299

Janks, Hilary 89, 192
Jeffers, Oliver 170–1
jigsaw activity 203–4, 302

Kaminski, Annett 57, 64, 152
Kerascoët 78–80
Khan, Rukhsana, *King for a Day* 78, 84–5
Kidd, David 23, 47, 115, 126
knowledge equity 185–6, 228, 275, 302
Kramsch, Claire 15, 26, 62
Krashen, Stephen 11–12, 43, 47, 58, 62, 141, 189, 282, 287, 295, 308
Krömer, Christiane 78, 84
Kulikov, Boris 85

Lai, Thanhha, *Inside Out & Back Again* 207, 218–21
language didactics. *See* English subject pedagogy; didactic and didactics; teaching methodology
language learning
  context-bound phenomenon 54–5
  dynamic ways of engagement 51–2
  embodied phenomenon 56
  high-quality and challenging input 52–3
  intercultural education and culture of democracy 50–1
  orthographic decoding 53–4
  pattern recognition 56–8
  phonological recoding 53–4
language of schooling 2, 53, 64, 86, 101, 302
language teaching 10, 24, 29–30
  coursebook, limitations 30–2
  design and content 12
  educational goals 1, 3, 7–11, 23–5, 41–3, 179, 265, 280, 293
  L1 and L2 speakers 8
  state-funded schools 10
Larsen-Freeman, Diane 51, 57
Lawrence, Francis, *The Hunger Games: Catching Fire and Mockingjay – Part 1 and Part 2*, (films) 273
learner autonomy 4, 9–10, 21, 24, 39, 63, 179, 185, 259, 265, 293, 302–3
learning styles. *See* cognitive styles
Lee, Spike, *BlacKkKlansman* (film) 139
Lerwill, Ben, *Climate Rebels* 252–3
lesbian, gay, bisexual and transgender (LGBT) 31
Lewis, Gill, *A Story Like the Wind* 116–19
lexical chain 53, 60, 116, 302–3
  cohesion and 155–6
LGBTQ+ 33, 70, 199, 303
Life Cycle of A T-shirt, The (animated film) 254
Lindstrom, Carole, *We Are Water Protectors* 90
literacy
  critical 1, 4, 7, 19, 21–2, 68–70, 189, 191–2, 197–200, 207, 215, 217, 228, 278–9, 288, 299, 303
  definition 303
  engagement 177–8
  functional 18–19, 70, 82–3, 152, 266, 296
  information 20–1, 44, 70, 134, 185, 259, 263, 265, 275, 291, 300
  literary 19–20, 70, 203, 244, 303
  media 19, 21, 70, 136, 265, 303–4
  visual 19, 32, 70, 76, 244, 317
literary apprenticeship
  creative writing 158
  definition 303
  in elementary school 54
  features 18, 21, 27
  for all students 16
  lower-secondary or middle school 15
  oral storytelling 64
  picturebooks 17, 76, 99
  purpose of 7
  second language acquisition and 58, 71
  starting with stories 14
  story characters 38
  young English language learners 19
literary literacy 19–20, 70, 203, 244, 303
literary texts 1, 22, 38
  character representations 22–4, 47
  compelling story 2–3
  coursebooks 10
  deep reading 16
  diversity engagement 27, 29–30, 41
  educational goals 9, 25
  multimodal 17–19, 48, 54, 57–60, 70, 75, 78, 103, 115, 120, 128–30, 140–2, 147–8, 168, 203, 286, 291, 296, 303, 305–6, 309, 311–13, 317
  polyvocal or multivoice 47
  repetition and iteration 61–3
  usage-based practices 56–8
L1 education 1, 8–9, 15, 54, 57–8, 160
Louise, Marissa 130
L2 acquisition 1, 8–9, 11, 14, 35, 43, 51, 54, 57–9, 62–4, 89, 104, 160, 173, 177, 179, 190, 259–61
  need for children's literature 51–61

Mafaridik, Nasaya 249, 251
majority world 35, 213, 303
Maley, Alan 152, 158
marginalized 30, 33–4, 37, 50, 87, 104, 133, 135, 202, 213, 303
Marley, Bob, *Redemption Song* 138
Mayhew, James 91
McGough, Roger, *Sound Collector, The* 159–60
McGowan, Anthony, *Lark* 162, 244–5, 247
MC Grammar, *Save the Planet* (song) 160–1
McKean, Dave 176–7
McQueen, Steve, *12 Years a Slave* and *Mangrove* (films) 139
media literacy 19, 21, 70, 136, 303–4
media multitasking 16–18
mental representation 14, 24, 47, 52–3, 58, 78, 128, 141, 245, 304
Messner, Kate, *Brilliant Deep* 91–3
metacognition 9, 23–4, 265, 304
metalinguistic awareness 151, 158, 304, 307
methodology. *See* teaching methodology
Mian, Zanib, *Planet Omar. Accidental Trouble Magnet* 249–50
Milner, Kate, *My Name is Not Refugee* 105, 108–9
mime 81, 113, 135, 182–3, 304. *See also* drama conventions; facial expression; physiological dimension of language learning; total physical response
minoritized 30, 32–4, 70, 135, 139, 185, 202, 304
misinformation 20, 304
Mitaru, Wambura, *Ululate* (short film) 184
Morris, Jackie, *Mrs Noah's Pockets* 91
motivation 12, 23, 27, 47, 60, 151–2, 177, 180, 187–9, 259, 304–5
Mourão, Sandie 50, 57, 76, 243–4
multilingualism 1, 70, 151, 184, 305
multimodal text 12, 17, 57–8, 70, 103, 115, 120, 128–30, 140, 305
multiple literacy 2, 9–10, 18, 24, 41–2, 70, 76, 265, 305

multisensory learning 14, 24, 27, 128, 147, 154, 160, 180, 203, 290, 298, 305, 309, 318
multivoicedness 29, 42–4, 50, 305. *See also* principle of multivoicedness
Myhill, Debra 115, 151–2, 158, 162, 304

Naidoo, Beverley, *Playground, The* 182, 184–5, 187
narrative
  anti 278–80
  character driven 44, 48
  creative writing 161
  definition 306
  English language education 10–16
  on global issues 68, 228, 242, 246, 250
  graphic novels 129–32, 135, 139–43, 145
  heteroglossia 43
  imagination 50
  picturebook 75–6, 78, 85
  pleasures of 54
  reader perception 52–3, 70
  single 17
  speculative fiction 257–8, 260, 269–71, 273–4, 278–80
  types 20
  verse novels 201–3, 205, 209, 214
  visual-verbal 115, 119, 125
native-speakerism 185, 289, 306
Naylor-Ballesteros, Chris, *Suitcase, The* 105, 111–12
Neelands, Jonothan 181, 192, 209
neuroscience 56, 142, 147, 227–8, 306
Nikolajeva, Maria 14–15, 25, 50, 70, 95, 115, 142, 170, 227–8, 299
Nodelman, Perry 22, 33, 75, 141
nonfiction 17, 21, 47, 58, 76, 85, 89, 93, 99, 126, 128, 131–2, 135–6, 252, 306
Nussbaum, Martha 50, 82–3

Oatley, Keith 13, 22–3, 30, 126
Odyr 129, 258–61, 263–4, 266–8
OECD 9, 20, 26, 127, 130, 282, 291, 303
Ong, Walter 153, 156, 201

onomatopoeia 53, 58, 60, 158, 167, 235, 306, 314
opening (picturebook) 25, 44, 46, 105, 107, 109, 125, 209, 306. *See also* double-page spread
open question 76–7, 306
oracy 57, 153, 306
orality 64, 115
    creative writing 152–3
    definition 306–7
    features 203
    stage 211
    verse novels 223
oral storytelling 64–6. *See also* creative teacher talk
Orlowski, Jeff, *Social Dilemma, The* (documentary) 17
orthographic decoding 53–4, 307
Orwell, George
    Animal Farm, The Graphic Novel 129, 258–70, 279
    Nineteen Eighty-Four 266–7
Other, the 32, 307
otherness 2, 29, 39, 64, 71, 113, 120, 307
Ouimet, David, *I Go Quiet* 229–31
outcome emotions 53, 126, 139, 307
outgroup 47, 249, 307
out-of-school English 12–13, 307
#ownvoices movement 33–4, 38, 43, 90, 135, 138–40, 307
Oziewicz, Marek 20, 23, 70, 140

panel
    of animalism 261–2, 269
    in comics 44–5, 167
    definition 307–8
    in graphic novel 114, 122, 129–30, 132–3, 140
    reciprocal teaching 124
Paran, Amos 10, 15, 69, 120, 191, 271
paratext 30, 58, 60, 308
PARSNIP principle (avoiding Politics, Alcohol, Religion, Sex, Narcotics, -isms and Pork) 13, 31, 308
partly determining context 141, 308
Pattison, Darcy, *Journey of Oliver K. Woodman, The* 168–70

Pennycook, Alastair 3, 67
peritext. *See* paratext
persona 202, 209, 216, 218, 308
persons of colour 33, 308
perspective-taking 15, 23, 37, 41, 43–4, 49, 51, 53, 60, 139, 208, 277–9, 308
Pesico, Zoe 88–9
phonological recoding 53–5, 309
physiological dimension of language learning 180, 309
picturebooks 1, 12, 14, 16–17, 19, 21, 41–2
    characters and book friends 78
    creative teacher talk 63–4, 76–7, 95, 288
    deep reading framework 78–85
    definition 309
    development and potentials 75–6
    drama 187
    environmental 88–99
    examples 79–99, 105, 108, 111–14, 116, 120, 168, 170, 172, 176, 243–5
    fairy tales 188
    lexical chain 156
    potentiality 76
    QR code 105
    shared reading 237
    significance 230, 235
    teacher's role 76–7
    young audience 14
plays and drama
    balance achievement 181–2
    conventions 191–7
    creativity 180–1
    critical literacy 197–200
    deep reading framework 182–7
    key aspects 181–2
    teaching and learning approach without walls 187–8
Plumwood, Val 94, 278
plural identities 35, 49
plurilingualism. *See* multilingualism
poetics of literature 53, 62, 90, 112, 115–21, 151–61, 201–2, 230, 237, 283, 301
poetry 1, 11, 19, 48, 62, 90, 93, 112–13, 116–21, 138, 153–6,

159–64, 168, 191, 201–5, 209–11, 215–17, 221–3, 228, 235, 250–2, 284, 286, 296, 308, 309, 312, 317
point of view 128, 132, 136, 171, 309
polysyndeton 53, 153, 163, 309
polyvocality. *See* principle of multivoicedness
Porter, Pamela, *Crazy Man, The* 207, 213–14
postmodern literature 239, 241, 309–10
pragmatics 10, 12, 310, 316
Prince Ea, *Man vs Earth* 93
principle of multivoicedness 42–4, 84, 139, 260, 310
print-based and screen-based story 17–18, 145–8, 306, 313
productive skills 55, 57, 64, 69, 116, 310, 311
prosodic features 63, 77, 186, 210, 310
protagonism 23, 46, 78, 87, 128, 165, 241, 279, 310
Pullman, Philip
  Clockwork 163, 165–8
  Firework-Maker's Daughter 153, 162–3

Rashid, Robia, *Atypical* (TV series) 38
Ratner, Carl 53, 104, 126, 228, 316
read against the text 22, 140, 189–91, 197–200, 289, 310
readers theatre 62, 112, 186, 221, 269, 310
reading blip 78, 127, 310–11
realia 63, 77, 311
recasting 63–4, 70, 77, 311
receptive skills 55, 116, 311
reciprocal teaching 55, 124, 133, 238–9, 311
recto and verso 81, 94–5, 105, 170, 311
Reference Framework of Competences for Democratic Culture, Council of Europe publication 36, 38–9, 52, 64, 71
register 63, 128, 168, 312
reimagining 24, 30, 58, 91, 235, 237–9, 241, 312
repetition 43, 53, 55, 60–3, 65, 115–17, 153, 156, 158–60, 163, 176, 201, 205, 235, 312–13
rhetorical device 20, 53, 116, 151, 154, 163, 284, 303, 307, 309, 312
Riddell, Chris 237–42
Rigano, Giovanni 111, 121–5
Risager, Karen 87, 101, 228
Robinson, Ken, *World's Largest Lesson Animation, The* (short film) 93
role-on-the-wall 157, 192, 194–8, 313
Rose, Ellen 16–17, 199, 279, 288
Rosenblatt, Louise 11, 38, 283, 293
Ross, Gary, *The Hunger Games* (film) 273
Rowling, J. K.
  Fantastic Beats and Where to Find Them, Newt Scamander 173
  Harry Potter and the Cursed Child 21, 188–94, 197, 199–200, 237
rule of three 53, 60, 154, 163, 312
Rushdie, Salman 135, 189

safe classroom climate 102–5, 135, 185, 312
salience 57, 59, 312
Saville-Troike, Muriel 51, 57, 60, 64
scaffolding 63, 77, 87, 152, 158, 160, 243, 262, 312–13
schema refreshing 53, 58, 163, 208, 274, 313
Scorsese, Martin, *Hugo* (film) 147
self-efficacy 33, 39, 103, 135, 152, 177, 180, 313
Selznick, Brian, *Invention of Hugo Cabret, The* 128, 130, 140–8
semiotic modes 18, 186, 290, 303, 305, 313
Serafini, Frank 19, 64, 99
sexual orientation 37–8, 313
Shire, Warsan, *Home* 116, 119–20
Short, Kathy 21, 41, 223
single stories, danger of 43–4, 84, 290, 313
Sipe, Lawrence 76–7, 94
skimming 9, 16, 313
Smith, Frank 18, 172, 271
Smyth, Damon 129, 131–5, 137
social injustice 271–2

social justice 1, 4, 25, 37, 68, 70, 82, 102, 227, 265, 271
social media
  adverse effects 16–17, 20, 103, 264, 271, 274
  elementary students 75
  important topic 242
  language learning through 12
  media literacy 21, 35
  neologisms and portmanteau 157
  social interactions 26–7, 43
sociocultural dimension of language learning 52, 78, 180, 313
sociocultural identities 33, 67, 140, 313–14
sound effects 21, 107, 129, 186, 269, 314
special educational needs 245, 314
speciesism 22, 267, 314
speculative fiction 157, 257–8, 260, 269–71, 273–4, 278–80, 314. *See also* deep reading
speech balloon 94, 111, 128–9, 132, 136, 140, 237, 262, 269, 314
Spiro, Jane 152, 154
Stephens, John 33, 67, 70, 86–7, 300
stereotype 29, 31–2, 36, 38, 47, 115, 131, 199, 208, 232, 237, 248–9, 273, 314
Stevenson, Noelle, *She-Ra and the Princesses of Power* (TV series) 38
storytellers 46, 95
storytelling
  characterization, significance 44–6, 279
  inventing and reinventing 145
  for language education 50
  oral 1, 48, 63–6, 154, 238
  pictorial 18
  power of 118
storyworld 15, 24, 27, 33, 37, 41, 47–50, 52, 57–8, 60, 128, 141, 188–90, 202–3, 243, 247, 257, 270, 277, 280, 314
stylistics 53, 60, 116, 246, 314–15
subtext strategy 192, 194–6, 198, 315
syndrome of group-focused enmity 39–41

task-based learning 172, 178, 315
Taxel, Joel 33–4, 42
Taylor, James, *You've Got to Be Carefully Taught* (song) 251–2
Taylor, Tate, *Help, The* (film) 139
teachable moment 77, 315
teacher education 1–2, 4, 7, 13, 31, 34–5, 37, 59, 63–4, 69–71, 155, 160, 163, 179, 181, 187, 189, 241, 258, 271, 273–4, 315
teacher-in-role 186, 192, 209, 315
teacher training 292, 315–16
teaching methodology 2, 181, 316
technology 12, 27, 61, 127, 186, 257
TESOL 293, 316
text
  comprehension and recreating 30
  definition 316
  formats and genre 10
  literary 10–11, 19, 24, 29, 49–50, 52, 58, 130, 136, 151, 259, 273
  multimodal text 12, 58, 128–9
  verbal 12
textbook 11, 29, 32, 35, 173, 316
text ensemble 43, 84–6, 105, 108, 112, 213, 273, 316
textual genre. *See discourse* genre
theory of mind (ToM) 22–3, 46, 53, 279, 316
think-pair-share 80–1, 112, 117, 316
Thornbury, Scott 8, 151
Thorne, Jack 188–9
  Harry Potter and the Cursed Child 188–94, 197, 199–200, 237
thoughtful feelings 53, 98, 104, 126, 132, 151, 180, 192, 212, 223, 276, 279–80, 316
Thurber, James, *Rabbits Who Caused All the Trouble* 264–5
Tiffany, John 189
tolerance of ambiguity 39, 64, 71, 77, 232, 316–17
Toolan, Michael 62, 156
total physical response (TPR) 98, 113, 192, 317
transmedia stories. *See* reimagining
tricolon. *See* rule of three

Tucker, Zoe, *Greta and the Giants* 88–9
typographic creativity 76, 119, 129, 210, 249, 317

UNESCO 18, 30, 41, 301
UNHCR 110, 116–17, 221
unpuzzle and explore
   Animal Farm 261–3
   Braid, The 203
   I Go Quiet 230–1
   Life of Frederick Douglass 130–2
   Malala's Magic Pencil 79–81
   Playground, The 182–4
   Wherever I Go 105–7
verse novels 1, 19, 59, 191
   absence of wordiness 220
   characterization and plot 205, 211
   creativity 207, 210
   critical literacy 207, 215, 217
   definition 317
   diversity of voices 213
   emotional and cognitive affect 204, 209, 214
   format 201–3, 218
   for higher grades in secondary school 203
   historical narrative 214–15, 221
   iceberg task template 217
   interculturality 207, 212, 223
   language education through 223
   love story 216
   pivotal moment group poster 212
visual literacy 19, 32, 70
   definition 317
   of teacher and young learners 76
   through intertextuality 244
von Merveldt, Nikola 17, 21, 85, 132, 135

Walker, David, *Life of Frederick Douglass: A Graphic Narrative of a Slave's Journey from Bondage to Freedom* 85, 129–32, 134–8
Weaver, Jo 116–18
Wegerif, Rupert 44, 257, 290
We Need Diverse Books (nonprofit organization) 33, 317–18
What They Took with Them (short film) 116–17
White saviour narrative 139–40, 273–4, 318
whoosh 182–4, 192, 318
wilderness script 277–8
willingness to communicate 33, 318
Winston, Joe 62, 180, 182, 188, 318
Woodson, Jacqueline, *Brown Girl Dreaming* 207, 221–3
wordless picturebook 76, 89, 245, 318
worldmindedness 229, 318

xenophobia 49, 113, 234, 247, 250

young adult fiction 57, 270, 286, 318–19
young learners 55, 57, 63, 76, 78, 93–4, 115, 182, 319
   environmental awareness 86–8
Yousafzai, Malala, *Malala's Magic Pencil* 78–81, 83–4, 86

Zapf, Hubert 87–8
zone of proximal development (ZPD) 87, 319
zoomorphism 94, 243, 319

www.ingramcontent.com/pod-product-compliance
Lightning Source LLC
Chambersburg PA
CBHW072119290426
44111CB00012B/1708